Destruction by Deceit

A Chronicle of President Obama's 2nd Term

2013 – 2016

Jay Ewert

Chapter 1

Judicial Legacy

One of the most impactful actions any U.S. President engages in is the appointment of Supreme Court Justices and Federal Judges. President Obama made 2 Supreme Court appointments during his 1st term. President Obama appointee's, Justice Sonia Sotomayor and Justice Elena Kagan join Justice Ruth Bader Ginsburg and Justice Stephen Breyer to form the liberal wing of the Supreme Court. The conservative wing consists of Justice Clarence Thomas and Justice Samuel Alito who serve to provide reliable conservative jurisprudence. The late Justice Antonin Scalia was the 3rd member of the conservative wing of the Supreme Court whose untimely death in February 2016 left a vacant seat that is yet to be filled to this day. President Obama appointed Judge Merrick Garland to replace Justice Scalia but the Senate chose to pass on his confirmation, delaying it for the next President to fill. Justice Anthony Kennedy and Chief Justice John Roberts complete the court and are widely considered to be the centrist members of the Supreme Court but they lined up with liberals on same sex marriage and The Affordable Care Act aka Obama Care decisions so their centrist status is questionable.

If our next President appoints another liberal to the Supreme Court, the deck will be stacked to render nothing but politically correct liberal progressive 5-4 rulings that could remove many of the freedoms that Americans have enjoyed for over 2 centuries. This is the reason Senate Republicans refused to even consider Judge Merrick Garland who may not be as liberal as Sotomayor and Kagan but as an Obama appointee he represents a risk too high to take. Today's politically charged Supreme Court has been legislating from the bench as opposed to deciding cases based on a fair and balanced rendering of justice. America's judicial system should represent a blind justice system that treats all equally so there's no place for political bias in our judicial system but it does exist and in fact it appears to be the driving force behind recent

Supreme Court decisions on controversial social issues like same sex marriage and socialistic health care.

Creative Destruction

Political Correctness is tearing this nation down so I refuse to participate in this highly destructive agenda designed to manipulate the populous. This book describes the political landscape and the political facts throughout President Obama's 2nd term in a fashion that throws political correctness out the window. I call it the way I see it, so please understand nothing in this book is sugar coated! Truth can't be bent or twisted, it must be laid out raw and bare. President Obama's legacy to the American people represents the most significant advances ever made in the politically correct liberal progressive movement in our countries history, creating a great divide in America that erased decades of advances in race relations while political and religious divisions also grew to a very great extent. President Obama set out to take apart everything our founding fathers established. The Constitution is nothing more than a major inconvenience to this President as is the case with most liberals. They believe it's so outdated that we should just throw it out and start over which is a very scary notion. The most significant promise he kept before being elected to his first term was his promise of "fundamental change." Sadly, more than half of the population, the uninformed, didn't consider the fact that change can be either good or bad. To assume he was talking about the good kind of change was naive on the part of those who voted for him. He would become known as the "my way or the highway" President. The President's plan to create dependence on big government and the loss of basic freedoms for all Americans was destructive from the outset. He considers the ACA aka Obama Care and the Iran nuclear deal to be the crown jewels of his Presidency when in fact Obama Care alone brought about catastrophic destruction and the Iran nuclear deal represents the greatest national security threat we face today.

He set the stage to destroy America during his first term and then rapidly went in for the kill during his second term. At the beginning of his second term he appointed 2 highly incompetent people to high level positions in his cabinet. Secretary of State John Kerry is the best example which became most apparent during negotiations of the Iran nuke deal but HHS Secretary Kathleen Sebelius runs a close second with implementation of the ACA to begin on her watch which did not go well to put it mildly. President Obama's intentional refusal to address the $16.5 trillion budget deficit at the beginning of his second term made it clear that he didn't care about the fiscal stability of our nation. He systematically raised taxes, increased government spending, weakened the military, performed several unconstitutional acts, supported illegal aliens, ignored Israel, and allowed Muslim terrorists around the globe to strengthen their ability to destroy America. His foreign policy consisted of giving billions to terrorist regimes in Islamic Middle East countries with Iran at the top of the list, allowing Bashar al-Assad in Syria to use chemical weapons on the Syrian people, allowing Iran to enrich uranium for nuclear bombs and expand their influence over Syria and Iraq, snubbing our most important ally in the Middle East which of course is Israel, doing as little as possible while ISIS terrorists established the Caliphate in Syria and Iraq and allowing Russia to take over the once sovereign nation of Crimea while propping up Bashar al-Assad in Syria and selling ICBM's to Iran. President Obama has become nothing short of a joke on the World stage. His weak foreign affairs policy was disastrous because strength and only strength commands respect but the President's weak policies made him the least respected President on the world stage in decades and the United States by extension became highly disrespected on the global stage. Not good!

President Obama's support for Islam that was born out of his Muslim roots and progressive ideology was made known his first week in office (1st term) when he authorized $20 million in aid to the Palestinian Authority, which was founded by Yasser Arafat, the father of modern terrorism, and funds Hamas terrorists in the Gaza strip. Shortly after his first month in office he pledged more than $900 million to rebuild Gaza and to shore up the Palestinian Authority. The President also made it clear very early on that he wanted to see Israel withdraw from most of the West Bank which Israel has a legal right to under international law because they prevailed after Jordon attacked them in the 6-day war of 1967. President Obama not only condemned Israeli settlements in the West Bank, but he said if Israel wanted to defuse the Iranian threat to wipe Israel off the map they better start evacuating settlements in the West Bank. The President then called for Israel to withdraw from Eastern Jerusalem, the entire West Bank, and the Golan Heights. He demanded that they accept the influx of millions of foreign Arabs as Israeli citizens. President Obama's extreme disrespectful treatment of Israeli Prime Minister Benjamin Netanyahu and expression of resentment and hostility toward Israel confirms his anti-American commitment to do everything in his power to support Muslim terrorists.

One of the most surprising revelations about this President is his lack of patriotism. He rejects the notion that America is exceptional; a nation above all other nations; the world's great superpower. He sees America as nothing more than a nation among other nations; not necessarily any better and quite possibly not as good as some in his mind. His apology tour at the start of his 1st term was our first detailed look at this aspect of his perverted geopolitical views that place a heavy emphasis on globalization. Michelle Obama addressed the nation after her husband's victory speech when elected the first time and said it was the first time in her life she felt proud to be an American. This went over most people's heads at the time but in hind sight it was a clear signal of what was to come. This President had a definite agenda to lower the bar for America in relation to the rest of the world and I'm saddened to say that he was successful.

Imperial Presidency

President Obama became proficient at doing the DC shuffle to sidestep any attempt by Republicans to expose his destructive agenda. His overall intent was to change America and make it a Social Democracy which translates to a strong dose of socialism in America. While he was intent upon the redistribution of wealth, he had no problem being on the receiving end of the most lavish lifestyle ever to be paid for by the American people. He had 5 chefs for Air Force 1 and vacations for the first family were outrageously extravagant. His reign at the top has become widely known as the "Imperial Presidency." President Obama is an egotistical, ideological, narcissistic, demagogue. His ideology leaves no room for reality. His ego leaves no room for humility. The truth is nothing more than an inconvenience to this President. His narcissism is extreme enough to be characterized as a form of mental illness. He is deeply racial, aggressively partisan, grossly incompetent, an inflexible liberal ideologue, secretive, dishonest, dogmatic, and dictatorial.

Unsustainable Debt

The National Debt will be in focus throughout the entirety of this book. When Ronald Reagan was president he managed to balance the budget without raising taxes and when he left office there was very little debt. At the beginning of Bill Clinton's 1st term he inherited $300 billion in debt and when he left office 8 years later there was a substantial surplus. At the beginning of Barak Obama's 1st term he inherited $6 trillion in debt that George W. Bush ran up mainly due to the Iraq war. During the President's 1st term he allowed the debt to grow to $16.5 trillion. The fed is printing about $2 trillion a year in new currency. Some of this new money replaces old money that's worn out but it's nowhere near a wash so the U.S. Treasury is reducing the value of the dollar worldwide by issuing so much new currency. We will be looking at the cause of the huge increase to our debt under President Obama and how it ballooned to almost $20 trillion during his 2nd term.

Blissful Ignorance

The focus of this book is on President Obama's second term because he was then in a better position to avoid accountability for the destruction he would inflict upon the American people. Most Americans who voted for President Obama in 2012 were uninformed. Well over half the electorate believed President Obama's lies because he sounded good and he was popular with celebrities. He also promised on numerous occasions that anyone earning less than $250,000 a year would not be hit with any kind of new taxes. That promise didn't even have time to soak in before it was broken! Most Americans didn't understand the seriousness of $16.5 trillion in National debt at the end of 2012. When they got their first "wake up call" in the form of less take home pay in January 2013 due to the payroll tax increase, the realization that President Obama's promises may not come to pass brought about the beginning of an awakening that came too late as many people were still oblivious and this not because they weren't intelligent. So many folks are so wrapped up in advancing their careers, raising families and attempting to maintain some semblance of a social life that all their time is used up with none left to carefully examine the political landscape. As we got deeper into the President's 2nd term, this segment of the population would further realize that President Obama lied to them on several levels. President Obama is a demagogue with a very destructive liberal progressive agenda. The culmination of President Obama's actions and the failure of Congress to stand up to him would be disastrous. Senator Harry Reid (Senate majority leader until Jan. 2015) was a powerful co-conspirator with the President. Senator Reid reminds me of a Will Rogers quote when he once famously said, "Our government keeps sending Congressmen on extravagant trips overseas, the problem is they keep coming home."

This book will document the events in chronological order that brought our nation to the brink of disaster. The book was written in real time, so as the narrative unfolds you'll notice that the language is present tense. As you are reading you may of course already have knowledge of the outcomes of various events but I believe that this format will give the reader more complete insight into the incremental process that led to the various outcomes. I do hope our elected officials in Washington will learn from the misguided agenda of the Obama administration and that the compilation of events in this book, viewed as they were unfolding, will also provide insight into ways our government may better serve the American people. I'm a firm believer in the notion that historical analysis is the most effective means of learning what not to do in the future. Also, that learning from things that worked well could provide insight into how they could work again, provided previous successes are viewed through the lens of current events. I pray this book will provide a significant part of the historical record to insure this chapter in American history does not repeat itself!

Chapter 2

Israel's Precarious Position

January 2013

On 1/30/2013 Israeli war planes bombed a convoy of trucks in Syria headed for Lebanon and dropped bombs on a chemical weapons plant in Syria near Damascus, the capital city of Syria. The Syrian convoy of trucks headed for Lebanon was carrying Russian SA17 Anti-Aircraft missiles with the intent to deliver these missiles to Hezbollah terrorists in Lebanon. The strike on the chemical weapons plant near Damascus speaks for itself. The development and possession of chemical weapons by the Syrian military with the intent to use them not only on Israel but also on their own people cannot be allowed. Leaders in Iran recently stated that they would consider an attack on Syria to be an attack on Iran. Earlier this morning leaders in Iran and Syria have already begun to threaten a retaliatory attack on Israel. Iran has also made it clear that they will continue to pursue the development of nuclear capabilities which further heightens the threat they pose.

At this point I believe it is important to look at the big picture in the Middle East, particularly when it comes to threats Israel has been preparing for over decades. Let's first look at the geopolitical element which poses an ominous threat to Israel. Egypt borders Israel to the south, Jordon borders Israel to the southeast, Syria borders Israel to the east, Lebanon borders Israel to the north, and the Gaza Strip borders Israel to the west. The Gaza strip and the countries that border Israel, with the partial exception of Jordon, have high numbers of Islamist Jihadists who pose a serious threat to Israel. Hezbollah has a strong presence in Lebanon and Hamas controls the Gaza strip. The Muslim Brotherhood has a strong presence in Egypt and they maintain a strong relationship with Hamas in Gaza. Syria has a variety of Sunni and Shia sects that form a conglomerate of terrorist networks but it becomes even more complex when we consider Bashar al-Assad in Damascus who happens to be a very bad actor with ties to both Iran and Russia. We must of course also consider countries like Iran, Pakistan, Afghanistan, Iraq and Turkey that are rife with terrorist activity of several varieties with al-Qaeda and the Taliban being the most prevalent at this point. Saudi Arabia, Yemen, the United Arab Emirates, Kuwait, Bahrain, Qatar and Oman have a little less terrorist activity within their borders but nevertheless do have several bad actors. Saudi Arabia is a country that the United States maintains very strong ties with due to the extreme amount of oil we buy from them and they are also a major buyer of U.S. debt. The complexities within Saudi Arabia alone are extensive and shrouded in mystery. One very troublesome sect within Saudi Arabia that no one wants to lift the veil on is Wahhabism, the most extreme sect of Jihadists within Islam. Most Wahhabi activity takes place outside of Saudi Arabia but it is an export of Saudi Arabia. Suffice it to say that the Middle East is an extremely large and complex group of Muslim countries that requires constant vigilance.

Israel is the most important ally of the United States anywhere in the Middle East. You need look no further than your Bible to gain a full understanding of the importance of our support for Israel. God has already supernaturally protected Israel during 3 wars that took place since the re-acquisition of this God given land by the people of Israel. The Israeli war of independence (Nov. 1947 – July 1949), the 6-day war (June 1967) and the Yom Kippur war (Oct. 1973). Israel was incredibly outnumbered and had inferior armaments during these attacks designed to extricate the people of Israel from the land. Israel prevailed in all 3 wars and has gone on to become one of the most powerful military forces in the world. Israel possesses the most sophisticated missile defense system (Iron Dome) in the world. More importantly, God will supernaturally protect Israel as he did in the 3 wars described above.

The United States of America was founded by devout Christian men. Our great nation was founded upon Christian principles and we should remain true to the God given wisdom our founding fathers relied upon. Our complete support of Israel should be our highest priority. President Obama has snubbed Israel at every turn. During his 1st term in office President Obama logged more miles on Air Force One than any previous President. Given such extensive travel around the world, why did the President overlook a single trip to Israel? He has not set foot on Israeli soil since he was elected President in 2008. There is no excuse for this. He claims to be supportive of Israel but I believe actions are stronger than words.

Mounting Problems

February 2013

Iran is dangerously close to reaching their goal of becoming a nuclear power as Iran will have enough nuclear material to make an atomic bomb by this summer. Their plutonium heavy water reactor will be operational by early next year. Al Qaeda affiliates are rapidly forming throughout the Middle East and northern Africa. Terrorists throughout the Middle East know full well that President Obama's rhetoric threatening a military response on terrorists is nothing more than an idle threat. Terrorists also know that substantial reductions to the U.S military will take place if sequestration goes into effect in March. The Budget Control Act, Sequestration, was proposed and signed into law by President Obama in 2011. Sequestration budget cuts were designed to be extreme to motivate Congress to avoid it at all costs. President Obama missed his Feb.1st deadline to submit his budget proposal. The President must be flexible enough to work with Congress so that a budget plan that doesn't include more taxes and calls for cuts that make sense can be instituted to prevent the automatic "across the board" cuts that sequestration would bring about but it's more likely that pigs will fly first.

When hard working Americans received their first paycheck in 2013 their hard work was rewarded with a decrease in take home pay due to payroll tax increases. President Obama promised this would not happen prior to his re-election and as of 2/3/13 he is on record that further tax increases are forthcoming. As take home pay is going down, gas and food prices are going up. It doesn't take a genius to determine that our economy is doomed to a continued decline due to out of control government spending and tax increases that inhibit economic growth.

As our country's real problems are mounting at an alarming rate, President Obama has clearly demonstrated that all he cares about is raising taxes, appointing incompetent people to the highest positions in our government, making sure homosexuals are allowed to be Boy Scout's and Boy Scout troop leaders among other initiatives to support transgender rights, forcing unaffordable and ineffective health care insurance upon Americans, providing amnesty for illegal aliens, and keeping guns out of the hands of law abiding citizens! What's wrong with this picture? This Presidents liberal agenda doesn't address any of the real problems our country is facing and the policies he does support are extremely destructive.

Intelligent Americans know and understand that the only way to stimulate the economy is to lower taxes on the people in America who create jobs whether it be small businesses or larger corporate businesses and to remove many of the debilitating federal government imposed regulations on business. This frees businesses up to invest more money to grow their business therefore creating new jobs in the process. Lower income people rely on more affluent people to hire them so they can bring a paycheck home instead of an unemployment check from the government. Basically, what I'm proposing here is known to liberals like President Obama as trickle-down economics and they absolutely insist it does not work but President Reagan proved that it does because this is the method he employed and it was very successful back in the 1980's. President Obama attempts to make Americans believe that the government can create jobs, but his failed $868 billion stimulus plan during his 1st term is proof that the government is worthless when it comes to job creation. There's little to no evidence that the Presidents nearly $1 billion so-called stimulus did much of anything for the American people. The President had described it as an initiative that would dramatically improve our overall infrastructure and that in the process many jobs would be created to accomplish this. By now we should have seen a great deal of noticeable improvement to our infrastructure but there's no evidence of this and all that taxpayer money didn't even move the needle on unemployment. Big government became much larger so bureaucrats who run big government bureaucracies were the beneficiaries while the American people who paid for it suffered!

Socialistic Health Care

As if the decrease in take home pay due to increased payroll taxes in 2013 isn't enough, Americans can also look forward to another decrease in their take home pay or even the loss of their job due to the Affordable Care Act. Let's take a painful look at some of the details. $716 billion will be taken out of Medicare and put into Obama Care. Obama Care makes massive changes to Medicare. Obama Care, with more than 160 provisions affecting Medicare, overhauls traditional Medicare. These provisions affecting Medicare increases the governments control over the delivery of care, hits Doctors with unsustainable payment cuts, and leaves taxpayers with higher deficits. Medicare will be completely unrecognizable from its original structure. The ACA mandates that any company employing 50 employees or more must provide ACA coverage for those employees who work 30 or more hours a week. Companies will let employees go to stay under the 50-employee threshold and they will limit many employees to less than 30 hours weekly to avoid offering Obama Care as a group plan to that group of employees creating way too much part time employment. Companies will be forced to raise retail prices to cover the increased cost for Obama Care so all consumers will be paying more for virtually every kind of product or service. Obama Care will result in 17 new taxes or penalties which will burden Americans. Individuals who don't sign up for Obama Care will get hit with a tax penalty of 1% of their gross income for 2014 and then it continues to increase each successive year. The GAO, government accountability office, advised taxes will increase by $2.8 trillion over 10 years to fund Obama Care. This is nearly double original estimates and implementation hasn't even begun yet! The GAO also projects that Obama Care will increase the budget deficit by $6.2 trillion over 10 years.

ACA enrollment is set to begin Oct. 1st, 2013 and the effective date is set for January 1st 2014, but most employers are already limiting hours for many employees and they're not hiring any new full time employees. The rules and regulations for Obama Care are so lengthy and complicated that virtually no American knows what to expect. Congress doesn't even know what to expect. The bill itself is 2700 pages. No wonder they passed it without knowing what was in it. The regulations are printed on **20,000 pages!** The application to apply for Obama Care is 61 pages. It is so long and confusing that people will need to hire a specialist to fill out the form. The IRS will process the applications and will serve as the enforcement agency of the law which will force an expansion of the IRS. The President is building a huge bureaucracy to handle this socialistic program. As more specific information is revealed throughout 2013, Americans will begin to see that Obama Care is far from what we were led to believe initially. Obama Care awards monetary incentive points to Hospitals who keep care costs for Senior's to a minimum. Private practice physicians will be bailing out in droves due to prohibitive operational costs. Obama Care won't even be fully implemented until 3 years from now. It was set up this way so Americans don't get all the bad news up front. The only people who benefit are very poor people who are on Medicaid, but try to find a **good** Doctor who will accept Medicaid for treatment and you'll find there aren't any. It's tough enough with Medicare. Everyone else will pay significantly more for all health care costs (premiums, co-pays, and deductibles) plus increased costs for retail products and services. President Obama promised in 3 televised speeches that if you like your existing health care plan you will be able to keep it under Obama Care. As it turns out, 98% of existing health care plans don't meet the legal requirements so all Americans will be forced to find a new Obama Care approved health care plan or pay the tax penalty.

We were told that the "Affordable Healthcare Act" will be affordable. **Not true!** President Obama promised in 2010 that health care premiums would drop by $2500. a year for a family of 4. **Not true!** The least expensive family plan for a family of 4 will cost over $20,000. annually by 2016, up from $12,000. in 2010. The GAO projects that claim costs will rise by 32% on average in America by 2016 due to pre-existing condition coverage mandated under the law. Younger Americans will be hit hard. Their health care costs will double under Obama Care. Over 30 million people will still be left uninsured! Obama Care is totally unsustainable and unconstitutional even though the Supreme Court upheld the law because they defined it as a tax. Implementation of Obama Care will be disastrous! Before Obama Care passed, then Speaker of the House Nancy Pelosi (D-CA) incredibly declared "we have to pass it to see what's in it." I guess no one in Congress wanted to read the 2700-page bill to find out. Obama Care is an elaborate socialistic "wealth re-distribution scheme" because younger healthier people and even the entire middle class are penalized as they're forced to pay more to cover older less healthy people, people with pre-existing conditions and lower income people. Congressman Paul Ryan (R-WI.) included the repeal of Obama Care in the proposed House budget. All Americans would benefit if Obama Care is repealed but the likelihood of this happening at this point is slim to none. When was the last time a major government program was done away with? Never! Ronald Reagan once famously said, "No government ever voluntarily reduces itself in size. Government programs, once launched, never disappear. Actually, a government program is the nearest thing to eternal life we'll ever see on this earth!" The Democrat majority in the Senate and the President will make sure Obama Care remains the law of the land, albeit the worst law ever passed in American history.

Cry Uncle

President Obama cares more about people who entered the United States illegally than he does for existing citizens who were born here. Existing U.S. citizens are out of work to the tune of 8% of the population but this government issued percentage doesn't include those who have quit looking for work altogether so the actual percentage of unemployed is more like 15%. The workforce participation rate has been hovering at around 62% for some time now which is dismal. Our government needs to focus on getting our existing citizens back to work before they do anything for people who entered our country illegally! The Presidents uncle, Onyango Obama from Kenya has been living in the United States illegally for over 40 years. He was arrested on a "DUI" charge recently. His attorney negotiated a plea bargain and Onyango is now out on probation. He has a deportation hearing coming up in December. I doubt that he is concerned because his nephew the President will surely handle things for him.

Gun Control

Keeping guns out of the hands of law abiding citizens is not the answer to solving the murders of innocent Americans at the hands of mentally ill people. Civil confinement of those who are determined to be dangerous mentally ill people would be an important step in the right direction. Mental Health records should be computerized so that law enforcement agencies would have access to a person's mental health history in real time. People with a history of mental illness should be required to register a detailed accounting of their mental illness. This detailed accounting could prevent unwarranted accusations of an innocent mentally ill person as well as revealing possible dangers that law enforcement agents should be aware of regarding others. These steps may have prevented the tragic murder of Chris Kyle (Navy Seal hero) by Eddie Ray Routh in Texas. At this point, President Obama's gun control proposal includes universal background checks on American's who want to purchase a gun. This would only create a universal registry of law abiding citizens. Criminals have access to a network of other criminals that give them the ability to buy any sort of weapon on the black market. I challenge anyone to go to any prison and ask any criminal how they would go about buying a firearm and I assure you that the criminal would immediately reply "the streets." Criminals don't want a record of their firearm purchase. Mentally ill people aren't necessarily stupid when it comes to obtaining a firearm or committing a murder. Their mental illness has more to do with their senseless motive to commit murder and then go on to commit suicide in most cases.

Actual enforcement of existing gun control laws would be a good starting place. American citizens must fight to protect the Constitution because President Obama clearly won't, even though he swore under oath that he would. 911 emergency response times are inadequate to protect people who are under attack by home intruders. The assumption that attacks upon our private property is generally committed by a single perpetrator is wrong. If a woman is at home with her children while her husband is at work and finds her home under attack by 4 or 5 intruders, she would need a weapon that fires more than 2 to 6 bullets. 6 bullets might take out one intruder but what about the other 3 or 4. She should have the right to adequately protect herself and her children with a sufficient supply of bullets to take out multiple intruders. If a ban on semi-automatic rifles such as AR14's should to go into effect, Americans ability to protect themselves would be greatly reduced. Personal protection is an individual responsibility which should not be limited by government intervention. Our government suggests that women should utilize rape whistles, call boxes, and ball point pens or even urinate and vomit on the attacker. These are actual government recommendations!

The tragic murder of innocent kids at Sandy Hook elementary school in New Town, Connecticut in 2012 and the senseless murder of people at a movie theater in Aurora, Colorado also in 2012 would not have been prevented by a ban on any sort of firearm. The crazy people who commit these senseless murders either already possess firearms or could easily obtain any sort of firearm on the black market. So-called "gun control laws" only keep guns out of the hands of law abiding citizens who should be allowed to possess firearms for their own protection. Criminals, whether they are mentally ill or not, will always find a way to obtain any sort of weapon they desire. Chicago has some of the strictest gun control laws in the country but gun violence there is about as bad as it gets. Gun violence in Chicago increased when gun control was tightened. Early this year Sheriff's in 39 States have already declared that they will not enforce laws that ban possession of firearms by law abiding citizens.

Breakfast of Champions

February 7th, 2013

Dr. Benjamin Carson, author of "Saving America" and "America the Beautiful" was the keynote speaker at the **National Prayer Breakfast** today. Dr. Carson is a Pediatric Neurosurgeon at Johns Hopkins in Maryland. He had the courage to throw "Political Correctness" out the window as he spoke from the heart not only about the problems we face in America today, but he also offered detailed solutions which were articulated in such a way that his speech made perfect sense to most Americans, both Democrat and Republican. Dr. Carson was warned by the Presidents staff members before taking the podium that he shouldn't say anything that would offend the President. President Obama was sitting very close to the podium during Dr. Carson's speech. Apparently, the content of Dr. Carson's speech came as a surprise to President Obama. The Presidents expression became increasingly grim during Dr. Carson's speech. The Obama staff member who booked Dr. Carson for this speaking engagement was probably looking for a new job before the speech was even over.

Dr. Carson reminded everyone that America belongs to the people, not the government. He emphasized the need to educate the populous because people need to think for themselves. Entrepreneurial thinking should be encouraged. Today's government is oppressive. Americans need to exercise their freedom to be entrepreneurs. "Special Interest Groups" discourage people from thinking for themselves. Special interest groups have essentially become the 4th branch of the government. Americans need to go back to our roots and focus on principles as set forth by our founding fathers.

Dr. Carson advocates a "flat tax" as opposed to the complicated and convoluted tax system in place today. A "flat tax" system would make the government equally accountable to everyone and would provide the people with a fair and equitable share in the cost of government as opposed to the tax burden falling on the shoulders of the middle class and above with absolutely no skin in the game for lower wage earners along with less incentive to advance in their careers. Our economy would grow and thrive under a "flat tax" system because it would encourage entrepreneurs to expand their businesses which would create more jobs which in turn creates a much larger tax base.

Dr. Carson spoke at length about our $16.5 trillion budget deficit. Responsible spending cuts must take place to reduce this huge debt. He pointed out that it is immoral to pass this debt on to future generations. Dr. Carson advocates the "Penny Plan" introduced in 2011 by Rep. Connie Mack (R-FL.). Mack's "Penny Plan" would cut one penny out of every dollar **spent** by the federal government from year to year for the next 6 years. This plan would balance the budget by FY 2019 assuming revenues don't exceed 18% of GDP by 2019. It would cut the accumulated budget deficits by an estimated $7.5 trillion over 10 years. It would in fact be 8 years before the budget is in balance and the National debt starts getting paid down.

He spoke about a complete restructuring of our health care system based on "Health Savings Accounts." Everyone would be accountable for the allocation of funds for their health care. It would force people to be more responsible because the incentive would be there to make sure money is not wasted for procedures that may not be necessary. This more active role by all Americans would insure the most useful application of their existing funds. Everyone would have control of their own destiny. Dr. Carson also pointed out that we need health insurance reform. We need to make it possible for insurance companies to make money without denying coverage.

It's time for people to take a stand to prevent big government from dictating to us. We need to exercise our freedom of speech to bring about extensive change before it is too late. Dr. Carson is the best example of this because he is making a difference and he doesn't even hold a public office. The response to his speech has been overwhelmingly supportive. We need to build on his proposals so the people of America will have the opportunity to regain possession of our country.

State of the Union

February 12, 2013

President Obama made his "State of the Union" address on Wednesday 2/12/13. As expected he called for a higher level of government spending and higher taxes. He used the terminology "investing in America's future" to make big government spending sound more appealing. Anytime you hear a politician talk about investing in America, it's important to understand that's code for a higher level of big government spending and higher taxes. He said further tax increases would be necessary for wealthy Americans and that tax deductions that benefit wealthy Americans must be removed but when the dust settles, it's always the middle class who carry too much of the tax burden based on the percentage they pay compared to income level. He failed to mention that the wealthy Americans he spoke of represent 20% of our population and already pay 72% of total federal income tax. The top 1% pays about 32% of all federal taxes. He also failed to mention that the possible removal of tax deductions such as interest paid on home mortgages and charitable deductions will have a huge effect on the middle class as well as wealthy people but of course he's not going to bring that up especially in a State of the Union address.

He went on to outline numerous ways to justify big government spending as he said we need a government that invests in broad based growth such as research and development to improve our energy sources. He spoke of a reduction in pollution and a transition to more sustainable sources of energy while he spoke of climate change (formerly Global Warming) and the need to control it and went as far as to say that he would drive this initiative on his own by exercising executive orders if Congress doesn't support his actions. He spoke about climate change as if it were a proven theory. He talked about government "fix it first" programs to repair bridges and roads at a cost of $50 billion which would be above and beyond what we're already spending on this type of infrastructure. Roads and bridges were supposed to be taken care of during his $868 billion 1st term stimulus program but all that money was spent to make big government bigger instead of improving infrastructure. He went on with government spending to help people re-finance their homes and spoke of government funded education programs designed to improve the quality of schools for early childhood education. He spoke of federal aid for colleges that provide affordable tuition and went on to outline his policies on immigration reform as he asked for a comprehensive immigration reform bill that would create reduced waiting periods for immigrants to become U.S. citizens. He said he advocates a paycheck fairness act to help women in the workplace and he wants to raise the minimum wage to $9.00 per hour from $7.25 with no regard for the negative impact on small businesses who operate on very slim profit margins. He advocates big government spending to create jobs even after his first term stimulus plan fell flat when $868 billion failed to produce the desired results. Unemployment grew to 10% after wasting almost $1 trillion taxpayer dollars to increase the size of government. Big government is incapable of job creation. He wants a government funded campaign to improve the voting experience which is code for the support of voter fraud which Democrats always benefit from.

President Obama believes we can spend our way to prosperity. He believes anything and everything can be fixed by spending taxpayer dollars. 47 million Americans are on food stamps thanks to big government which is the equivalent of 1 in 7 Americans. This represents a 65% increase of Americans on food stamps since 2008. President Obama will go back to the well again and again to increase taxes so the government can continue its spending spree while the budget deficit keeps growing. The Presidents endless spending proposals here are representative of a giant socialistic initiative that amounts to full blown socialism which has never worked. He's living in a completely unrealistic ideological fantasyland completely void of reality.

The President went on to promise that America will maintain the best military the world has ever known. He also promised that America will do anything necessary to prevent Iran from becoming a nuclear power. He said America must help Yemen, Mali, and Libya to develop military strength so they can police terrorist threats without American intervention. The absurdity of this proposal is so over the top it's just plain stupid! The President must want to prevent American intervention so any money given to Yemen, Mali, or Libya will go directly to the terrorists because President Obama apparently has no problem with the Jihadists. He talks about expanding our military strength but he came up with sequestration in 2011 which will bring about a reduction of $500 billion over 10 years to our military if it goes into effect on 3/1/13. This after the President had already cut the defense budget by $550 billion. A $1 trillion cut to the defense budget over 10 years is way too much. There are many other programs that should be cut before any military cuts take place. He is not willing to work with Congress to pass a budget which would responsibly cut government spending without raising taxes again. President Obama obviously wants the destructive cuts to go into effect so he can blame Republicans. Everything is political with this President.

The President spoke of numerous lofty goals with no detailed explanation as to how they could be accomplished. The economic implications of President Obama's proposals should raise red flags of concern within the Obama administration but they always throw caution to the wind and plow ahead because they're addicted to spending. He attempted to portray himself as the protector of the middle class while his agenda would only destroy the middle class through higher taxes and unsustainable debt. He didn't even mention our unsustainable $16.5 trillion national debt in his speech.

Senator Marco Rubio(R-FL) delivered a brilliant Republican rebuttal after the President's speech. Rubio, along with most Republicans, believes opportunity comes from a vibrant free enterprise economy, not big government. Big government will limit opportunity and hold people back. He made the point that Obama Care will cause companies to lay employees off and refrain from hiring new employees because of higher health care costs. In answer to

President Obama's assertion that government must combat climate change, Senator Rubio pointed out that the government can't control the weather. He supports the Republican philosophy that economic growth through free enterprise will help the middle class while the President's proposed tax increases will prevent job growth in the private sector. Senator Rubio pointed out that we should focus on growth of our energy infrastructure by utilizing our reserves of Coal, Natural Gas, and Oil before we go to foreign countries to supply our energy needs. He pointed out that a balanced budget amendment with spending reforms can solve our financial problems. Our strength has always come from our people, not our government. Government can't fix the moral breakdown in our country. America must preserve economic liberty and reduce wasteful government spending. The liberal left didn't know how to respond to a working class Hispanic Republican who supports conservative values and they clearly didn't like it. There's nothing in their playbook that addresses this; yet. All they could find to criticize was Senator Rubio's need to take a drink of water during his speech.

President Obama has lied to America on a continual basis. He lied in the 3rd debate on 10/22/12 when he said that sequestration was proposed by Congress when it was he and Treasury Secretary Jack Lew who conjured it up but miscalculated because they thought Congress would reject it on its face. He lied last year when he claimed that he would work toward a reduction of the budget deficit through his support for spending cuts. He stood by and allowed Senator Harry Reid (D-NV), Senate majority leader, and the rest of the Senate to avoid passing a budget for 4 years. As of today, we are 2 weeks away from the $85 billion automatic "across the board" spending cuts that sequestration calls for and Congress still hasn't passed a budget that calls for intelligent spending cuts because the President won't work with them to reach a bipartisan solution. President Obama has no respect for the Constitution. It has been 23 days since President Obama was recently inaugurated President for his 2nd term and he has already laid the groundwork to cause irreparable damage. The time is long overdue for conservative Republicans to stand up to President Obama the Demagogue and fight to save our great nation. Congressman Paul Ryan(R-WI), Senator Ted Cruz (R-TX), Senator Tim Scott (R-SC), Senator Marco Rubio (R-FL), Senator Rand Paul (R-KY), Senator Tom Coburn (R-OK), and Senator Jim Inhofe (R-OK) are among the Republicans who have begun to speak out and stand up to the President. They represent some of the conservatives who are working to pass a budget with intelligent spending cuts before sequestration goes into effect and they are working to block Chuck Hagel from becoming Secretary of Defense, John Brennan from becoming CIA director, and Jack Lew from becoming U.S. Treasury Secretary. These men will likely be confirmed but such questionable appointments should be subjected to intense scrutiny before their eventual confirmation and any chance of passing a budget with a Democrat majority in the Senate is quite unrealistic. The Republican Senators I've listed here in addition to Congressman Ryan are not without fault so I don't want to leave the impression that they are political saints because they too are frequently part of the problem. They do serve as a buffer to prevent the liberal Democrats from spending us into oblivion!

Bad Example

February 15, 2013

President Obama is on his way to West Palm Beach, FL. today for a long weekend vacation to play golf with Tiger Woods. The first lady Michelle is on her way to Aspen, CO. with both daughters for their long weekend vacation. The first family just spent 17 days in Hawaii for Christmas and the New Year. The cost of these vacations which U.S taxpayers pay for is staggering. The cost of security alone is huge. It costs $180,000. per hour to fly Air Force One. Fiscally responsible Americans should wonder why the President and First Lady would take such extravagant and expensive vacations when the budget deficit is over $16 trillion, 8% of the population is out of work, and those who are fortunate enough to have a job must worry about how they will live within their budgets with less take home pay due to tax increases and the higher cost of food and gas. Those fiscally responsible middle class Americans should wonder why they must live within the confines of their budget when the Federal government continues to spend with reckless abandon. The President's plan to build the financial stability of the middle class isn't off to a very good start. President Obama should set a fiscally responsible example as our leader but instead he consistently sets a **bad example**. I'm sure he could suffer through a vacation at Camp David which would be affordable, but he obviously isn't the least bit concerned with setting a good example by taking more affordable vacations.

Decrease to the Increase

February 19, 2013

President Obama addressed the nation today with a message that sequestration would be disastrous and placed all blame on Republicans in Congress. This is just another scare tactic like the fiscal cliff scare. He failed to mention that sequestration was his proposal and he signed it into law in 2011. He lied and said that Republicans were unwilling to work with him to pass a budget that would prevent sequestration from going into effect. Obama failed to mention that his budget reduction proposal included more tax increases that Republicans could not begin to agree to after they had already increased taxes 2 months earlier to postpone sequestration until 3/1/13. If President Obama would just agree to smart spending cuts and no more tax increases, a deal could be reached to pass a budget and avoid the automatic "across the board" spending reductions that sequestration would bring about. Intelligent spending reductions create economic stability. The President has rejected 2 recent budget proposals submitted by Republicans that could have prevented sequestration. Sequestration calls for $85 billion in automatic "across the board" spending reductions. $44 billion of that amount will be cut in fiscal 2013 and the balance is prorated to future years. The amount is not the problem. The problem is that sequestration spending reductions will reduce our military strength to a harmful extent when the cuts could be taken in other areas that would not be harmful. One example of wasteful spending is the 2.2 billion spent every year giving away free cell phones to low income people. We could also do without expensive "out of town" government conferences and extremely expensive vacations taken by the President and his family. Foreign Aid could be reduced. There are numerous examples of wasteful spending that could be cut. Sequestration is more of a structural problem than a financial problem. Sequestration includes $1.2 trillion in automatic spending reductions spread over 10 years. In 2013, sequestration will reduce the projected $3.8 trillion (3,800 billion) budget by $44 billion in automatic spending reductions (1.2% of the $3.8 trillion budget). The $85 billion represents $29 billion in domestic spending cuts and $56 billion in defense spending cuts. It should be noted that the President and Secretary of Defense can move money around after sequestration to appropriate spending where it is needed most such as the military. Also, the Secretary of Defense has the power to prioritize the areas of defense to be cut. $85 billion isn't even a sufficient reduction in spending but these cuts should be applied intelligently instead of setting up arbitrary across the board cuts. Obviously, it would be better to cut wasteful spending first. If our government can't cut 1.2% of the projected $3.8 trillion budget for 2013, we will never come close to reducing our huge budget deficit. We will still spend more in 2013 than we did in 2012 even with the $44 billion in spending reductions, so the $44 billion represents a **decrease to the increase**. Technically there is no cut. The projected federal budget for 2013 was increased by 17% over 2012. Given this fact why would anyone lose their federally funded job (unless they are a new hire) when we are still going to spend more money this year than last year.

We will never see progress towards reducing the budget deficit unless reductions are made to entitlements such as Social Security, Medicare, Medicaid, and Welfare. So far President Obama has adamantly refused reductions to entitlement spending and if he ever agrees to reductions to entitlements he will insist on large tax increases to go along with it. The Republican majority in the House will be a major frustration for the President throughout his 2nd term.

Cyber Espionage

February 23, 2013

China owns $1.2 trillion in U.S. debt. America borrowed this money from China to partially fund our out of control government spending. Now we've learned that China is hacking into government and private business computer systems. They are acquiring an enormous amount of sensitive information on our infrastructure that could give them the edge when it comes to international competition in business. More importantly they are acquiring information on our defense capabilities that could give them a major advantage militarily. This information could also be sold to the highest bidder. China has hacked into New York Times and Washington Post systems along with extensive hacking into Pentagon systems. President Obama has failed to take the lead to prevent this infringement on our trade and economic secrets mainly because we owe China so much money. The President's failure to act against this international property theft leaves us in a vulnerable situation. This **cyber espionage** is led by a secret Chinese military unit. The information they obtain is generally used for military planning. The proprietary data China is accumulating could enable them to sabotage critical infrastructure such as our aging electrical grid. It's doubtful that China would attack us any time soon because their economy is so dependent on excessive American exports from China. We need to set up sophisticated cyber security to prevent any sort of attack on our infrastructure. President Obama needs to inform China that there is a consequence to this kind of espionage. This is a critical issue that requires a leadership role from the President. He has failed to be a leader on everything else so it's a bit of a stretch to expect that he would lead on this issue. The only thing he knows how to do is to act in a political role. His political strength gives him an edge during a campaign to get elected but it's worthless once he's in office. In office, the only way to be effective is to take on a leadership role. President Obama continually takes trips on Air Force One around the country making speeches to rally his political base when he should be spending time in Washington DC leading the nation by working with Congress. He needs to be reminded that he has already won the election so there is no need to continue campaigning. I understand that he leads the Democrat party and that he's campaigning for Democrats in Congress and for the overall good of the party along with promoting his political agenda but he has a big job to attend to so less campaigning and more governance would be highly advisable. The President's greatest weakness is his inability to work with others. He prefers the dictator role which has no place in America's government. President Obama doesn't like the fact that the President works for the people. As stated in the Gettysburg Address by Abraham Lincoln, we're reminded of government by the people, for the people and of the people.

February 27 2013

Today President Obama spoke at the unveiling of the Rosa Parks statue in Washington DC. Michelle Obama couldn't find time in her busy schedule to show up for this occasion. You would think that when the most courageous African American woman in U.S. history is being honored that the African American First Lady could show some respect and be present when this incredible woman is being honored. Her husband gave a nice speech and why Michelle couldn't be there to support her husband and to honor another African American woman who is incredibly deserving of honor is beyond my comprehension. Michelle finds time to announce the winner of the Oscar for best picture at the Academy Awards, she appears on late night talk shows and afternoon talk shows, but she can't find time to honor the memory of Rosa Parks.

My Way or the Highway

February 28 2013

The Republican "sequester replacement proposal" which would have offered President Obama more authority to allocate the spending cuts, was killed by the Democrat controlled Senate today with a vote of 62 to 38. President Obama had threatened to veto that bill in the unlikely event that it passed. This bill would have made it possible for division heads to pick and choose where the spending cuts would be made. They could have cut wasteful spending as opposed to across the board cuts. This is blatant irresponsibility on the part of the President and the Senate. 5 weeks ago, Republicans in the House approached several key division heads and asked if they would prefer to choose where the cuts would be made instead of the across the board cuts. They overwhelmingly expressed positive support for this course of action. President Obama and the Senate chose the political approach instead of true leadership. A leader would work with everyone involved to reach a consensus based on the opinions of all parties. The Presidents strategy is to blame House Republicans for any fallout that takes place due to Sequestration.

President Obama has always taken the approach of **"my way or the highway."** He insists on being the "Imperial President." Even though the President and the Senate made a boneheaded decision today based on the President's huge ego, the across the board spending cuts that will go into effect tomorrow won't even be noticeable by most Americans because the decrease to the increase in spending is very small. The $3.6 trillion projected budget for fiscal 2013 represents a 17% increase over last year, so the $44 billion in cuts for fiscal 2013 called for by the sequester is far less than the increase to the 2013 budget, hence it's a decrease to the increase as opposed to straight cuts.

When Senate Chaplain Rev. Barry Black delivered the invocation today he prayed **"Rise up Oh God and save us from ourselves"**.

Veteran Washington journalist Bob Woodward of the Washington Post recently wrote an article which offered proof that the Sequester originated in the White House and was the brainchild of Jack Lew who was recently appointed Secretary of the Treasury by the President. President Obama went on to propose the Sequester to Congress and then reluctantly signed it into law. Yesterday Bob Woodward received an e-mail from White House economic advisor Gene Sperling that stated "you will regret staking out that claim" referring to Woodward's statement of the fact that the Sequester was originally proposed by President Obama. Numerous reporters have received similar threats from the White House. The President has also made veiled threats directed at Republicans in the House and Conservatives on the Supreme Court. This proves that the President Obama is in over his head as President because a competent President would never find it necessary to threaten Legislative and Judicial branches of government along with highly respected journalists. Our government is structured to separate power between the Executive, Legislative and Judicial branches as set forth by the Constitution. No single branch possesses ultimate power but President Obama would be very happy if the Executive branch had more power than the other two. He believes he knows better than our founding fathers, hence his continued unconstitutional actions.

Education Secretary Arnie Duncan made the statement that Teachers throughout the country would receive pink slips advising them that they will not be needed next fall as the result of sequestration. Republican members of the House launched an investigation of this claim and found that it wasn't even close. When questioned about it today, Duncan had to concede that not a single teacher would lose their job as the result of sequestration. As it turns out the total extent of the situation was that one teacher in West Virginia received a notice of transfer to a different school. This is the kind of misdirection that can be expected out of the corrupt culture that exists within the Obama administration.

Chapter 3

Foreign Aid Accountability

Pakistani Dr. Shakil Afridi risked his life to provide the U.S. with the information that directly helped Seal Team 6 find and kill Osama bin Laden in Pakistan. Dr. Afridi has been imprisoned, brutally tortured, and sentenced to life in prison for treason by Pakistan's intelligence agency. It's a travesty that this hero is being tortured and his family threatened for the crime of helping America. It's an outrage that the United States continues to send $2 billion a year in foreign aid to Pakistan while Dr. Afridi is suffering in a Pakistan prison.

Egyptian President Mohamed Morse recently attempted to seize absolute power and impose Islamic Sharia Law on the Egyptian people and massive protests and violence have erupted throughout Egypt. The Obama Administration responded by agreeing to send 20 F-16 fighter jets and 200 Abrams Tanks to Egypt as part of the $2 billion in U.S. taxpayer dollars that are sent to Egypt each year for so-called "foreign aid". The fact that the Pentagon has handed over $213 million worth of top notch F-16 fighter jets to a Muslim-Brotherhood led government that is attempting to impose Islamic Sharia Law in Egypt is so very wrong. On 3/4/13 the U.S. Government pledged to give Egypt another $250 million to bolster their failing economy. President Obama is allowing this madness of supporting Anti-American regimes overseas while he is intentionally weakening our military.

This policy of sending billions in taxpayer dollars overseas for so-called "foreign aid" to countries that hate America and Israel could end up becoming an international disaster. It should also be noted that foreign aid should only be given if the U.S. gets a benefit from it. There is no benefit from giving money to terrorist regimes. The concept is that by giving money to terrorist regimes we are basically buying protection for America. A better use of U.S. taxpayer dollars would be to use it to strengthen our military which is the best investment in our security. We shouldn't necessarily cut off all foreign aid to Muslim Countries but a significant reduction would send the message that there is a price to be paid for anti-American actions and that U.S. foreign aid recipients will be held accountable for their use of aid provided by the United States.

March Madness

March 1, 2013

President Obama made a televised appearance in front of the White House Press Corps today. He continued to place all blame for the across the board spending cuts called for by the Sequester on those pesky Republicans in Congress. After he finished speaking he opened it up for questions from the White House Press Corp. aka "The Lapdog Media." The questions were softballs as would be expected from this group. The first question was from a reporter named Julie. She asked the President if he was in any way responsible for sequestration going into effect today. After President Obama spoke for about 15 minutes without even answering the question, he asked Julie for an example of what he should have done. Julie apparently was caught off guard and she froze, either not knowing what to say or fearful of speaking her mind for obvious reasons. I'm sure numerous House Republicans and many Fox News correspondents who were viewing this exchange were wishing they had the opportunity to answer that question in that setting. I know I was. The President could have worked with Congress to cut spending intelligently instead of arbitrary across the board cuts that the Sequester calls for. There's an incredible amount of wasteful spending that could be cut instead of arbitrarily taking cuts where they aren't needed.

It's ironic that all Americans had 2% of their personal budgets reduced this year due to the payroll tax hike and they're making due, but Democrats are complaining about the necessity to cut government spending due to the Sequester that Congress passed with a Democrat majority in the Senate. The government's budget was increased by 17% for fiscal 2013. I'm sure the American people would be very happy if their personal budgets could be increased by 17% but of course that didn't happen for them. Democrats in Congress and the President are crying over a 1.2% cut in spending due to the Sequester for fiscal 2013 when their total budget was increased by 17% so they're complaining about a decrease to the substantial increase. President Obama doesn't care that the American people are dealing with a government imposed decrease to their take home pay, increasing gas prices, increasing food prices and increasing health care costs. All he cares about is flying around the country in Air Force One to the tune of $180,000. per hour, making ideological speeches when he should be in Washington DC leading the nation by working with Congress instead of dictating to them.

Republicans in the House reluctantly agreed to a substantial tax increase in early January and now the President and Democrats in the Senate want another tax increase. The government doesn't have a revenue problem. The government has a spending problem. The government will be out of money on March 27, 2013 because the continuing resolution to fund the government will expire. These economic deadlines will never end if our government can't make progress to reduce the $16.6 trillion in debt. America will be bankrupt soon if government spending isn't dramatically reduced. America needs leadership from the President but he apparently doesn't know how to lead because we haven't seen any leadership out of him yet.

In the days leading up to March 1st 2013, the President made some televised speech's and said that if the Sequester goes into effect thousands of teachers will lose their jobs, children won't receive necessary vaccinations, border security will be seriously compromised (as if he cares), head start programs for 3 and 4 year-olds will end, airport security will be seriously compromised, military readiness will be drastically reduced (again as if he cares) and basically life as we know it in America will end. At least half of the population believes this stuff. The Sequester doesn't cut anything because it's just a decrease to the increase. When the President spoke today he was backing up big time and now it turns out we really aren't in such bad shape after all. He had to change his rhetoric because 3 weeks from now everybody will be looking around and notice that none of those dire predictions occurred. President Obama has no credibility but over half the population still approves of his performance as President. I think the old saying "ignorance is bliss" is sadly a big part of the equation.

March 2, 2013

Now that we are at the front end of the minimal sequester spending cuts going into effect, Wall Street is still showing up with record highs. Part of the reason for this, in addition to favorable treatment by the Federal Reserve, is that the spending reductions are the first move in a long time to reduce the size of our government. If this becomes an ongoing trend it would create the possibility for further growth in the private sector and House Republicans have made it clear they will stand their ground on no more tax increases. The Federal Reserve makes a huge contribution to market growth through their bond buying program and by keeping interest rates low. Another significant reason for this upward trend in the stock market is the fact that most companies have significant International interests. Profits from International investments are driving the growth of most companies. Growth is flat here at home but trade with other countries and production in foreign countries is showing dramatic growth. This certainly doesn't help the picture here at home particularly as it relates to job creation in the U.S., but many corporations are taking advantage of opportunities beyond our borders. It has become a fact of life that we now live in an era of global economics and big business favors free trade instead of fair trade because they fear higher consumer prices due to the higher cost of labor in the U.S., so they go along to get along with the global business community for fear of rocking the boat. Another reason corporate profits are up would be that they are operating with fewer employees due to government imposed regulations and higher taxes. Smaller payrolls translate to increased profits but growth is hindered with fewer employees. Any corporation would prefer to grow their business to create more profit through a higher volume of business which creates more jobs but big government is holding them back in addition to their own fears over fair trade with much smaller trade deficits if any deficit at all.

Dumb and Dumber

The United States government should be run more like "a company" intent on showing a profit or at the very least breaking even. Any company run similarly to the U.S. government would be out of business very quickly. No company would direct their investment dollars in a wasteful manner. CEO's and division heads would be out of a job if they were involved in wasteful spending. Of course, American businesses can't print more money and they have a set timeline they must adhere to regarding their debt. If our government were held to the same standard it would successfully put an end to big government bureaucratic incompetence not to mention endless spending with no accountability.

Speaking of wasteful spending, let's look at where a lot of your hard-earned taxpayer dollars are going. This kind of spending is so senseless that the executive branch could easily be characterized as **dumb and** the legislative branch that works as a co-conspirator rates the label **dumber**! Of course, I think we all know the actual reason for wasteful government spending. It's called pork! This is the stuff that's slipped into legislation as an accommodation to politicians for support of the bill in question to satisfy the special interests they're beholden to. This is an endless cycle that over the years has just become business as usual with no regard for the American people hence the need for term limits to at least reduce this corrupt practice.

- $2.2 billion annually for free cell phones to low income Americans, many of whom don't qualify and some are dead.
- $316 million for NASA to send Astronauts to Mars. Let's wait to do this once our debt is gone. It shouldn't be a priority when we're almost $17 trillion in debt.
- $51 million to maintain empty Federal Courthouses
- $15.3 million for one of the infamous Bridges to nowhere in Alaska
- $10 million for a remake of "Sesame Street" for Pakistan
- $3.8 million to study human / elephant conflict
- $35 million allocated annually for political party conventions
- $35.3 million for politicians partying from the Presidential Election Campaign Fund
- $14 million for Air Force green energy effort (Dept. of Defense)
- $120 million for dead federal employee's benefits (U.S. office of personnel management
- $27 million to Morocco to stimulate their economy by teaching them how to make pottery
- $1.5 million for a study at a Boston Hospital to prevent obesity in Lesbians!
- $3 million for a study on the effect of crystal meth on monkeys!
- $3.9 billion in fraudulent tax refunds
- $1 billion annually to advertise and promote the federal government
- $5.2 million to study goldfish social interaction!
- $480 million annually to planned parenthood – radical pro-abortion group

The list goes on as $2 trillion was added to the nation's debt by the "Budget Control Act" in 2011. President Obama's debt commission issued recommendations to reduce the debt by more than $3.5 trillion over the next decade. The government accountability office issued a report identifying over $200 billion in unnecessary, duplicative programs. Sadly, these suggestions and others were ignored by both chambers of Congress and the President. In 2011 the House and Senate appropriations committees agreed to slash the budget of the "Government Accountability Office", the only government agency that distinguished itself by identifying hundreds of billions of dollars in budget savings. The "Super Committee" was created in 2012 to address the debt crisis. When the "Super Committee" turned out to be a super failure, President Obama came up with sequestration. The President is moving forward with his typical partisan political focus and is intent upon teaching Republicans a lesson.

President Obama was given the option to apply sequestration cuts intelligently to cut wasteful spending but he refused because he didn't get his tax increase, at least that was his excuse because he wouldn't have favored spending cuts under any circumstances anyway. Defense cuts due to sequestration will do the most damage. These defense cuts were the primary reason why the Sequester was never supposed to occur. The defense budget had already been cut by $550 billion before the Sequester. Defense will be cut by another $500 billion over 10 years due to sequestration. These extreme cuts will hurt our military preparedness. It's not fair to our military or the American people. It's not too late to do something about it because President Obama could work with Congress to cut wasteful spending instead of cuts that will hurt our military. The President must put politics aside and lead by working with Congress but this won't happen because President Obama is prepared to let people suffer to make Republicans look bad and to maintain out of control spending. White House tours were cancelled and the reason given was due to sequestration cuts. Closing the people's house is going too far and it wasn't at all necessary. The Sequester was not the cause of this and it is apparent because the U.S. Capital tours went on as usual. Numerous White House expenses could have been cut before tours were cancelled. Household expenses for the White House cost $1.4 billion annually. Vacations for the President and family cost $20 million annually. White House tours cost $3.8 million annually. Surely the cost for household expenses and vacations could be cut by $3.8 million to keep the people's house open. Eric Boling and Sean Hannity (Fox News correspondents) offered to personally pay for the White House tours and never received a reply from the White House. It's just another example of the President wanting to make the American people suffer to place blame on Republicans. This course of action is backfiring on the President. Thank goodness there are enough American's out there who recognize a scare tactic for what it is. President Obama is dealing with the politics of the problem and not the problem itself. To say he is acting irresponsibly is an extreme understatement.

President Obama's primary motivation to make Republicans look bad, even when he will harm the American people in the process, is because looking forward to the 2014 election he wants a Democrat majority in the House and a continuation of the Democrat majority in the Senate. He would then be able to raise taxes, redistribute income, and spend with reckless abandon. If this were to occur, our nation would be bankrupt by the time President Obama leaves office in 2016 if not before.

Spending Madness

March 5, 2013

This week the House will pass a bill to fund the government through the balance of fiscal 2013 and give the DOD flexibility to intelligently appropriate sequestration spending cuts. Unfortunately, the Senate will never agree to intelligent spending reductions because that would be too intelligent. Revenues will be at an all-time high of $2.7 trillion for fiscal 2013. With a 2013 budget of $3.6 trillion we will have a budget deficit of about $1 trillion for 2013. We've run trillion dollar deficits for 4 consecutive years. Obviously, the need for significant spending cuts is critical. Unfortunately, President Obama doesn't care. It's inexcusable and irresponsible that the Senate has failed to pass a budget for over 4 years now. The government is funded by back to back "continuing resolutions." This continual practice of operating without an actual budget is by design and predominately carried out by Senate majority leader, Senator Harry Reid, with the blessing of the President.

Filibuster

March 6, 2013

President Obama's approval rating has dropped to 49% from 56% in a very short timeframe. At least the light turned on for 7% of the population. The Presidents scare tactics prior to sequestration going into effect are coming back to haunt him now that none of those dire predictions have come to pass. At this point the only thing President Obama has going for his agenda is the fact that close to half of America doesn't care. This segment of the population doesn't even know we are close to $17 trillion in debt or they don't understand the ramifications of that kind of debt. They are only thinking about the things that revolve around their little world such as their job, interaction on social media, material stuff, music, movies, sports and the celebrities who make up the entertainment industry. All they know about President Obama is that they consider him to be one of those celebrities because he hangs out with many of them and he works at projecting that image so they think he's cool. This mentality exists on a much grander scale than ever before.

Individual liberty is in jeopardy now more than ever before. The Constitution exists to protect these liberties but when government commits unconstitutional acts our liberties are under attack. The Supreme Court should protect us from these attacks on our individual liberties but they don't always do so. On June 28th,2012 the Supreme Court incorrectly ruled that Obama Care would stand as law of the land. Chief Justice John Roberts explained that Obama Care is essentially a tax that can legally be placed upon the American people. The way Obama Care is structured it is essentially a federal tax but Obama Care (the tax) invades the reserved rights of the States. Obama Care (the tax) is a statutory plan to regulate and control. Obama Care (the tax) is a means to an unconstitutional end. Obama Care is a socialistic scheme to establish a precursor to single payer, basically Medicare for all Americans which would be a socialistic disaster. Once it fails, and it will fail, politicians in Washington DC will say the only way to fix it is to advance to single payer. What a scam!!!

As I am writing this today, Senator Rand Paul has been speaking for over 10 hours on the Senate floor. This old-fashioned **filibuster** is in protest of John Brennan's appointment as director of the CIA. One of the biggest issues is the possibility of Drone attacks directed at American citizens on American soil. This requires further definition in terms of the differentiation between a terrorist actively involved in a terrorist attack or a person thought to allegedly be involved in terrorist activities who is just sitting in a cafe. John Brennan and President Obama support the latter and Attorney General Eric Holder has not absolutely ruled out his support of this. American citizens have a right to due process in the form of a trial in court and must be found guilty before a penalty is imposed. Placing this kind of power in the hands of a single person in the absence of a legal ruling is another direct violation of our individual liberty and is unconstitutional. Those of us who are paying attention need to actively support our leaders in Congress who are fighting to uphold the Constitution. Certain types of Drone activity over American soil is unconstitutional. President Obama's continual disrespect for constitutional law must not be allowed.

Terrorist Controversy

March 7, 2013

John Brennan was confirmed by the Senate today as director of the CIA. After Senator Rand Paul spoke on the Senate floor for over 13 hours yesterday, we all finally received an answer to his question asking if the President would order a drone attack on a U.S. citizen on U.S. soil who is not engaged in combat against America. After attempting to get a straight unambiguous answer to this question for over 6 weeks which should have been an easy direct answer, Attorney General Eric Holder replied today with the answer **NO**. This paved the way for John Brennan's confirmation as CIA director. The premise here is that an American citizen on United

States soil who might be involved in planning terrorist activity could be apprehended by law enforcement and given a trial. Due process would take its course and justice would be rendered. In America, citizens have a constitutional right to a trial. On the other hand, if a terrorist is in an airplane and is clearly in the process of flying into a building in America, he absolutely should be shot out the sky by a drone. The U.S. now has over 7000 drones. The use of drones on American citizens in foreign countries is an on-going debate, but their use over American soil is a settled debate and should be subject to rules of engagement that give American citizens their constitutional right to a trial provided they are not actively engaged in a terrorist attack.

Sulaiman Abu Ghaith, Osama Bin Laden's son in law, was apprehended in Jordan last week, transported to New York City, and charged with conspiracy to kill Americans. Abu Ghaith was Al-Qaida's spokesman in 2001 and 2002. On the morning of 9/12/2001 he appeared in a video alongside Bin Laden, and spoke on behalf of al-Qaida, warning the United States and their allies that "a great storm is gathering against you" and called upon "the nation of Islam" to do battle against "the Jews, the Christians, and the Americans." He later delivered a speech and warned that "the storms shall not stop, especially the airplanes storm" and advised Muslims and opponents of the United States "not to board any aircraft and not to live in high rises." The President's decision to bring Abu Ghaith to New York was made without informing Congress. This stirred controversy because many legislators felt that it is a bad precedent to be set when the President acts on something of this magnitude without informing Congress in advance. A press conference was held with Senator Lindsey Graham (R-SC) and Senator Kelly Ayotte (R-NH). Ayotte commented "And when we find someone like this, this close to Bin Laden and senior al-Qaida leadership, the last thing in the world we want to do, in my opinion, is put them in civilian court. This man should be in Guantanamo." Graham said "so we are putting the administration on notice. We think that sneaking this guy into the country, clearly going around the intent of Congress when it comes to enemy combatants, will be challenged." House Intelligence Chair Mike Rogers (R-MI) said, "al-Qaida leaders captured on the battlefield should not be brought to the United States to stand trial. We should treat enemy combatants like the enemy. The U.S. court system is not the appropriate venue." This civil case that is being tried in New York will cost the taxpayers a lot of money. Classified information must be submitted by the prosecution in discovery in a civil court. Abu Ghaith could gain access to that classified information through his attorney and get it to an al-Qaida operative. This would never happen in a military tribunal where this should be tried.

Benghazi

6 Months of Deceit

6 months after the al-Qaida attack on the U.S. Diplomatic Mission in Benghazi, Libya, the Obama administration is still lying and covering up on the "before, during, and after" of this attack that cost the lives of 4 Americans including Ambassador Christopher Stevens and Communications Specialist Sean Smith who perished at the diplomatic mission compound in Benghazi. The U.S. Diplomatic Mission in Benghazi had already been attacked twice prior to the 9/11 attack and Ambassador Stevens had made numerous strong requests for additional security weeks ahead of the 9/11 attack. Libyan authorities had also warned of an eminent attack. Just the fact that the anniversary of 9/11 was coming up soon should have raised red flags big time. President Obama and Secretary of State Hillary Clinton not only refused additional security, they reduced security at the U.S. Diplomatic Mission in Benghazi prior to the attack. The attack on the diplomatic mission occurred at 4:00PM EST and lasted for about one hour then a second wave attack on the CIA annex located several blocks from the diplomatic mission occurred several hours later. After the attack was underway at the diplomatic mission, a CIA rescue team including Navy Seals who were 400 miles away in Tripoli, Libya came to defend the CIA annex. Once the severe attack began on the CIA annex, our defenders fought bravely and many lives were saved but Navy Seals Tyrone Woods and Glenn Doherty perished in a mortar attack while they were firing on the terrorists from the roof of the CIA annex. President Obama and Secretary of State Hillary Clinton were advised immediately once the attack was in progress. Nothing was heard from either of them until the next morning at about 10:00AM EST when they claimed the attack was in response to a youtube.com video. No mention of al-Qaida was made. It is incredible that the President and the Secretary of State would just go to sleep that night without making a single phone call to anyone in Libya or anyone else for that matter to stay abreast of events as they were unfolding. Ambassador Stevens and Sean Smith died at about 9:00PM EST that night while the President and Secretary of State did nothing but get ready for bed.

A C.I.A. gun running operation had been underway in Libya for weeks prior to the 9/11 attack. The Commander in Chief and Secretary of State had been fully aware of this operation that may have played a role in the 9/11 attack. After the attack, President Obama wanted to keep it quiet because of the looming Presidential election and the mainstream media was very cooperative in this effort. The President wanted to maintain his false campaign narrative that al-Qaida is on the run. Secretary of State Hillary Clinton promised the Gold Star families of the victims over the coffins of their loved ones that everything possible would be done to find and kill the perpetrators of the attack and to find and prosecute the producer of the fictional youtube.com video. 6 months later President Obama and Secretary Clinton were fully aware of the location of al-Qaida training camps in eastern Libya and the hotel in Benghazi where the al-Qaida leader who planned the attack was staying because he'd been interviewed by the press at the hotel. Obviously, the President had no intention of going after these terrorists. Little has been done to seek accountability for the lack of security that made this tragic attack on the United States possible. Actually, our people should have been pulled out at least a month earlier just as the British did with their people there and even the Red Cross who pulled their people out so we should have followed their lead or better yet, should have done it first. Republicans in Congress have promised they will not let up until the truth behind this entire incident is exposed. Nothing is being done by the President because he was only concerned with his campaign for a 2nd term as President.

In the aftermath of the terrorist attack on the U.S. in Benghazi, President Obama plans to finally travel to Israel for the 1st time as President. His primary intent for making this trip is to bolster U.S. relations with the Arabs of the PLO, a terrorist organization founded by Yasser Arafat, the father of modern terrorism. This will not only be a slap in the face to the Israeli's, but it makes a statement that he is only concerned with Islam and it also makes a statement to Israel that America will not be there to sufficiently support them as Hamas in Gaza, Hezbollah in Lebanon and others supported by the PLO set the stage to attack Israel. This will be disastrous for U.S. relations with our most important ally in the Middle East and clearly President Obama doesn't care.

Dog and Pony Show

March 12, 2013

Now that President Obama's approval rating has dropped by about 7 points he has begun to reach out to Republican's with the main stream media close at hand to maximize photo ops. Last week he took 12 Republican Senators out to dinner and then had lunch with Congressman Paul Ryan (R-WI) the following day to discuss Ryan's budget proposal. This week he has 4 meetings set up with Republicans to have budget talks, again with the main stream media on his heels with camera's in hand. This insincere political maneuvering is just a waste of time. It may temporarily fool some people into thinking progress is being made but once it becomes apparent that nothing has been accomplished, mudslinging will resume.

March 13, 2013

As the Obama **"dog and pony show"** with Republicans continues today, Paul Ryan submitted the House budget proposal but the President has not submitted his proposal yet. President Obama is the first president in 92 years to submit his budget after both chambers of Congress have revealed theirs. The President's budget was due on February 4th but he now says he will submit his budget on April 8th. Given the fact that the Democrat controlled Senate hasn't passed a budget for over 4 years, the President and Democrats in the Senate prefer not to have one. Paul Ryan's budget will allow spending to increase by 3.4% a year which will match what we bring in annually in revenue and his plan will balance the budget in 10 years but to do so the Affordable Care Act must be repealed. Democrats unveiled their budget today. Senator Patty Murray's budget projects $1.7 trillion in additional revenue and a spending increase of 5% a year. Republicans have already agreed to $1 trillion in Obama Care taxes and another $600 billion in additional taxes due to the fiscal cliff crisis so there is no possibility that they would agree to the Democrats budget proposal. President Obama said today that "We don't have an immediate crisis over the debt." He also said "we don't need to balance the budget just for the sake of balancing the budget." These insane bold statements reveal the fact that the President clearly plans on running the debt up to over $20 trillion by 2016. It's time for Republicans to become more aggressive. Surely Republican's know that Paul Ryan's budget won't get past the Senate or the President because it calls for the repeal of the ACA. Democrats and Republicans will be so far apart on a budget deal that the only effective course of action Republicans could take would be to force a government shut down by taking a strong stand against the continuing resolution to fund the government coming up on March 27th. If this were to occur President Obama would just blame Republicans for a government shut down just like he blamed them for sequestration.

President Obama appointed Illegal alien advocate Thomas E. Perez, current asst. Attorney General for the civil rights division of the DOJ, as Secretary of Labor today. As AAG, he has already expanded illegal alien benefits by arranging for discounted college tuition and driver's licenses. He has advocated racially selective enforcement of the law. He will face a difficult approval process by Republicans in the Senate but just like Chuck Hagel, Jack Lew, and John Brennan he will ultimately be approved.

Green Waste

March 15, 2013

President Obama's attempts at economic stimulus and green energy programs have failed miserably. $868 billion was spent wastefully on the American Recovery and Reinvestment Act of 2009. The President claimed that this would be a big job creator. To the contrary, unemployment made it all the way to 10% in 2010. His next bright idea was to give $535 million to Solyndra, a California based solar company. Solyndra filed for bankruptcy on September 8th, 2011. President Obama made sure they received another $67 million before they went bankrupt. In May of 2010 the President visited their plant in California and was so impressed that he tried to get them another $467 million to make the taxpayer investment almost a billion dollars. It's bad enough that the government wasted $602 million on a company doomed to failure, but an even billion would have added insult to injury. As President Obama continues an attempt to advance his green energy initiative, Congress is focused on the Keystone XL pipeline. TransCanada Corp's Keystone XL pipeline would facilitate access to Canada's substantial oil reserves in northern Alberta. The pipeline would move oil from Alberta, Canada to Port Arthur, Texas refineries. It would not only create jobs but it would provide affordable oil for America and reduce the amount of oil we obtain from the Middle East and South America. Many Democrats in the Senate are in favor of the Keystone pipeline so it does have bi-partisan support.

Budget Battle

President Obama is 3 months into his 2nd term and all signs point to miserable failure. Our government has been operating without a budget throughout his entire Presidency. His 2013 budget was due the 4th of February and he still hasn't presented it. The House and Senate have budget proposals but it's not a priority for the President. He doesn't even think $17 trillion in debt is a problem. The only hope of funding the government is a continuation of continuing resolutions (kicking the can further down the road). The House budget calls for the repeal of Obama Care so there's no hope that it will get past the Senate or the President. The Senate budget significantly increases taxes ($1 trillion increase) and increases the already huge debt so there is no hope that the House would approve it. Whatever President Obama comes up with will be moot because it will be just as ridiculous as the Senate budget proposal. The President has never even received one vote, not even a Democrat vote, for any Presidential budget proposal since he's been in office so one can only conclude this is by design because he doesn't want a budget. An actual budget would spell too many constraints for the President. He prefers more of a free flowing non-plan. Once again gridlock reigns. Politics on both sides are so extremely partisan that our government will continue going downhill with no meaningful accomplishments for the American people. We are over 2 weeks into sequestration and nothing has been done to appropriate the Sequester spending cuts intelligently. The damage being done to our military and the American people is inexcusable. Republicans in the House have passed 2 bills to date that would execute the sequestration spending cuts intelligently but Democrats in the Senate and the President won't go along with intelligent cuts therefore responsibility for any damage created by arbitrary across the board cuts belongs to the President and Democrats in the Senate.

Botched Trip to Israel

March 21, 2013

President Obama is in Israel for the first time since he became POTUS. He has held meetings with Israeli President Shimon Peres and Prime Minister Benjamin Netanyahu. The President has ignored Prime Minister Netanyahu since he became President. When Prime Minister Netanyahu came to the White House President Obama treated him with disrespect. He told the Prime Minister that the Israelis should treat the so-called Palestinians, Arabs of the Palestinian Liberation Organization, as their moral equivalent. A statement like that is a strong testimony to his ignorance. President Obama has been asleep at the wheel regarding his foreign policy with Israel because he doesn't care. If he thinks this single trip to Israel will serve to patch up his relationship with them he is sadly mistaken as his agenda for Israel and the rest of the Middle East isn't even close to that of Prime Minister Netanyahu. He knows that Israel is highly dependent on the United States because of their tenuous geopolitical situation in the Middle East so he takes advantage of that dependence which is counterproductive.

Unrest in Syria escalated yesterday when fighting between Sunni Syrian terrorists (Free Syrian Army) and the Shiite Syrian regime led by President Bashar al-Assad included a possible chemical attack. The United Nations will initiate an investigation to determine if in fact chemical weapons were used by either the Syrian leadership or their Sunni enemies. It would represent a very serious violation of International law if chemical weapons were used even if it was to a limited extent to test the waters so to speak because innocent Syrian citizens are placed in harms-way not to mention its heinous nature. Syria represents a serious "powder keg" that demands the attention of the entire peace loving International community. The instability in Syria could cause their stockpile of weapons to fall into the hands of more aggressive terrorists. This could be disastrous, but even their possible use of these weapons calls for scrutiny. Hamas terrorists in the Gaza strip fired 4 rockets at Southern Israel today. Hamas terrorists obtain their weapons from Muslim Brotherhood terrorists in Egypt who President Obama is very friendly with. Hamas was formed by the Muslim Brotherhood.

Iran's supreme leader, Ayatollah Khomeini, announced yesterday that if Israel attacks Iran they will annihilate Tel Aviv and Haifa Israel. President Obama would like Israeli President Shimon Peres and Prime Minister Benjamin Netanyahu to think they are all in agreement that they cannot allow Iran to become a nuclear power. President Obama has no credibility when it comes to threats directed at Iran. Iranian leadership doesn't believe he has the courage to order a military strike on them. America should be taking a very careful look at the possibility of an air strike on Iran's nuclear facilities. Iran's response to such an attack could be severe but a nuclear armed Iran would be disastrous. Aside from a military strike, America should resist buying any oil from Iran. America must become energy independent.

Israel never should have given up the Gaza strip to the Palestinian Authority terrorist regime. Israel lost the Gaza strip by pulling their settlements in Gaza with the hope that this concession would create a peaceful outcome. I assure you that today Israel would love to have a do over on that terrible decision. The Palestinian Authority allowed Hamas terrorists to take control of Gaza. If Israel pulls their settlements in Judea and Samaria (aka the West Bank), history could repeat itself with the loss of Judea and Samaria by Israel. President Obama is attempting to convince Israel to give up their settlements in Judea and Samaria as a bargaining chip for peace with the Palestinian Authority. It is important to note that there is no such thing as a Palestinian in modern times. These people are Arab refugees from Jordon and other parts of the Middle East. Yasser Arafat merely picked the name Palestinians as a ploy to give themselves false legitimacy. The God ordained land of Israel was provided to the Jewish people when Moses led the Jewish people out of slavery in Egypt and into the promised land. Roman Emperor Hadrian applied the name Palestine to the land in 135 A.D. after Rome crushed the 2nd Jewish revolt. Emperor Hadrian took the name of the ancient enemies of Israel, the Philistines and Latinized it to Palestine. The Philistines were not Middle Eastern people. They were European people from the Adriatic Sea region next to Greece. The Arab refugees from Jordon and elsewhere are descendants of Ishmael, Hagar's son by Abraham. Ishmael's descendants make up the Arab nation. Israelis are descendants of Isaac, Sarah's son by Abraham. Sarah was Abraham's wife and Hagar was Sarah's maid servant. God made his covenant with Isaac. Peace between Israel and the Arabs residing in the land is a pipe dream. This peace will never come to pass any more than peace will ever exist between Israel and Hamas terrorists in the Gaza strip or any other radical Islamist terrorists in the Middle East. To allow the formation of a Palestinian State in Judea and Samaria would be a huge mistake by Israel. Israel is at the center of a hotbed of radical Islamist terrorists who exist all around them. As our most important ally in the Middle East, Israel should have the full support of the United States but President Obama flatly refuses to fully support Israel.

President Obama's teleprompters were working overtime while in Israel. He addressed a large group of Israeli people today (comprised mainly of College students) and was met with a very warm response. I'm sure most of them are too young to realize the need for skepticism regarding anything President Obama says. The President did not meet with Israel's Knesset, the legislative branch of Israel's government, but he did meet with Palestinian Authority President Mahmoud Abbas in Ramallah. President Obama praised the Palestinian Authority led by Abbas. When President Obama appeared with Abbas today there was a huge banner that pictured Yasser Arafat, the father of modern Islamist terrorism, above him. There's your first clue that you're appearing with an Islamist terrorist. This revealed extreme ignorance, or unbelievable contempt toward Israel on President Obama's part. I'd like to hear what President Peres and Prime Minister Netanyahu are saying behind the Presidents back. To make matters worse, President Obama agreed to give the Palestinian Authority $500 million. To give this to terrorists who have overrun Judea and Samaria by their sheer numbers alone is a crime. President Obama's entire trip to Israel elevates "talking out of both sides of your mouth" to a whole new level. The Palestinian Authority presides over the Gaza strip, controlled by Hamas terrorists, as well as the Arabs in Judea and Samaria. One of the biggest issues for the Arabs residing in Israel is the development of Israeli settlements in Judea and Samaria. President Obama supports these Arabs ruled by the Palestinian Authority on this issue but could not and will never convince Israeli Prime Minister Benjamin Netanyahu to back off developing Israeli settlements in Judea and Samaria or to agree to the formation of a Palestinian State. The biggest obstacle is the Arab demand for a return to 1967 borders and a Palestinian capital in Jerusalem. President Obama is making the same mistake that Bill Clinton made. Clinton believed that he could be the catalyst in the formation of peace between Israelis and Arabs. In Clinton's mind this would be his predominate legacy as President. He came no closer than President Obama will. Both Clinton and President Obama refused to acknowledge the religious implications that exist. The Jewish religion leaves no room for further compromise on the God given land provided to the nation of Israel based on the borders as defined by God Almighty. Israeli leaders now acknowledge the huge mistake they made by giving up the Gaza strip and allowing Arabs to settle in Judea and Samaria. The formation of a Palestinian State with their capital in Jerusalem would compound the problem. The tenets of Islam will never allow peace with Israel. It's true that many Arabs residing in the land and Israelis desire peace but observance of their respective religions by the Islamists and deeply religious Jews prohibit peace. Many American politicians, including President Obama, have no understanding or respect for Israel's right to the entirety of their God given land. President Obama botched his entire trip to Israel. He didn't even take it seriously. To even talk about a peace process is ludicrous. Israel is surrounded by factions who hate them and would like nothing more than to blast them off the face of the earth. President Peres and Prime Minister Netanyahu are fully aware of President Obama's extreme support for Islam which was fostered out of his Muslim upbringing. They were cordial to him during his stay there strictly because Israel's alliance with America is very important regardless of President Obama's inept abilities. America's military support for Israel is critical given Iran's nuclear aspirations. Aside from critical discussions that took place regarding Iran, President Obama would have done better to have stayed home. All in all, President Obama's trip to Israel was an embarrassment.

President Obama's foreign policy or lack of one throughout the entirety of the Middle East has failed miserably. Under the Obama administration, America has been absent from productive interaction with all Middle East countries. The Arab countries have no respect for President Obama. He has shown himself to be weak. They only have respect for strength. When they perceive weakness they typically strike. With instability in Syria due to civil war and the use of chemical weapons, America needs to be prepared for possible military action there in addition to a possible military strike on Iran. Both must be done in concert with Israel. Given President Obama's nonexistent relationship with Israel combined with Secretary of Defense Chuck Hagel's disrespect for Israel, this becomes a complicated proposition. President Obama made some very strong statements condemning chemical weapon use in Syria and nuclear development in Iran while he was in Israel. Neither President Obama nor Secretary Hagel have any experience with large and complicated military strikes that we could soon be faced with. President Obama is in so far over his head in the Middle East that failure is inevitable which will leave the world in great danger.

Fiscal Fight

Congress passed a bill today to avert a government shut down on March 27th. Once again, we have another continuing resolution to fund the government in place of an actual budget. This CR will fund the government thru September 2013. The House passed Paul Ryan's budget plan today with 0 votes from Democrats. The House budget calls for the repeal of Obama Care not only because it's bad for all Americans but because the House budget includes many important new health care provisions that support balancing the budget and is beneficial for all Americans. The health care provisions in the House budget would enhance Medicare as opposed to Obama Care which completely changes Medicare with 160 provisions that make it unrecognizable and less desirable. President Obama has rendered himself irrelevant in the budget process because his last budget received 0 votes from anyone, Democrats or Republicans, and he hasn't even presented a budget this time around even though it was legally due by Feb. 4th. With Medicare and Social Security on an unsustainable path, a reasonable budget is needed more than ever. It's inconceivable that our government has not had a budget during the entire time President Obama has been in office.

The cost of one night in London and one night in Paris for Vice-President Joe Biden and his cronies came to $1,044,388. The limo bill was $321,000. The 36 suites in each hotel were occupied partially by secret service agents but most were for lobbyists. I find this difficult to comprehend. It reflects an extreme lack of respect and caring for our country. Americans visiting Washington DC still won't be able to tour the White House, but they can take the "Elvis music cruise", the "Salem Witch-Hunt" tour, or the "wine tasting express" which costs the government over $1.2 million. $1.2 million would cover the cost of White House tours for 16 weeks. Looks like the governments priorities for Americans visiting Washington DC need to be examined.

March 22, 2013

The Senate voted against the House budget today. No surprise there. The Senate did pass their budget today by a vote of 50 – 49 with no Republican votes in favor. The Senate budget calls for $1 trillion in new taxes predominately targeting wealthy Americans. 0 Democrat votes in the House for the House budget and 0 Republican votes in the Senate for the Senate budget is hardly a reflection of bi-partisan legislation. The House and Senate are so far apart on a budget deal, that it doesn't look as though there's any possibility of reaching an agreement. If the President comes up with his budget by April 8th that will further complicate the situation.

Gun Fight

March 29, 2013

It has become apparent that Senate majority leader Harry Reid intends to introduce a new gun control bill that will include mandatory universal background checks and a limit to the number of rounds that a gun magazine can hold. He hopes to get the bill passed with a simple majority vote by Democrats in the Senate. Senators Rand Paul (R-KY), Ted Cruz (R-TX), Marco Rubio (R-FL), Jim Inhofe (R-OK), and Mike Lee (R-UT) announced today that they have submitted a letter to Harry Reid informing him that they will filibuster his bill to force a 60-vote majority to get the bill passed. These Republican Senators have grave concerns regarding the unconstitutional, fear mongering based attempt to gradually disarm American citizens. Even more disconcerting is the fact that the President and his administration believe they can exert dictatorial power, circumventing Congress to attack our second amendment rights. We cannot allow the government to disarm us. Our second amendment rights are our last protection against a tyrannical government. A free people are not told what guns they can or cannot own. A free people are not made to feel guilty to convince them to give up their guns. A free people are not made to feel like criminals for simply standing up for their second amendment right to bear arms. These Republican Senators believe that we must continue to send a message to our government that they cannot pick and choose which parts of the Constitution they will adhere to. Disarming the populace is a step towards taking greater and greater control of our lives. Democrats in the Senate and the President must be held to their oath to defend all parts of the Constitution.

Chapter 4

Easter Miracle

April 2, 2013

President Obama's dire predictions (scare tactic) regarding sequestration spending cuts designed to blame Republicans has backfired once again. Recent polls reveal a backlash directed at the White House. Now that the President finds himself deflecting criticism for sequester spending cuts, several "pots of gold" have suddenly been found. DHS, DOD and TSA have suddenly found money to prevent furloughs that were said to be necessary due to sequester spending cuts. Hundreds of border security agents who had been notified of pending furloughs are now on the job with no furloughs in sight. As North Korea intensifies threats of war with South Korea and possible attacks on the U.S., the Pentagon has found money to prevent furloughs of military personnel stationed in South Korea. With no change in the length of time it takes to clear security at major airports, it has become apparent that TSA has also found money that wasn't supposed to be available. This miraculous appearance of found money is a typical MO for the Obama administration when the perceived outcome isn't part of the original plan. Apparently, this is the kind of change President Obama was talking about when he promised "hope and change."

Mounting Failures

April 3, 2013

President Obama is presently plagued by an inability to advance his agenda on immigration reform and gun control. The President and Democrats in the Senate were attempting to establish guest worker programs and several other immigration reforms that would basically provide amnesty for the 12 million illegal aliens who are presently in America. Since Republicans are insisting on securing the borders first, it will be extremely difficult for Democrats to advance their immigration reform agenda which does not include securing our borders. Thankfully, President Obama has made no progress in his unconstitutional attempt at gun control. He continues to exploit the victims of tragedies like the Sandy Hook elementary school massacre in New Town, Connecticut. Several Democrats are even supporting Republicans to avoid unconstitutional restrictions on gun owners because their constituents are demanding it. Our government needs to deter and punish violent criminals based on laws that already exist, but the Democrat and Presidential focus is on punishing law abiding citizens for purely political reasons which is an attack on our Constitution.

President Obama's promise to small business employees that affordable health care insurance will be available through their employers under Obama Care has now entered the "never mind" category. This provision under Obama Care has now been delayed by one year and will likely never come to fruition. At this point it is projected that 1/3 of employers will cancel Obama Care coverage for their employees and just pay the $2000. fine for not making it available. It's sad when so-called affordable health care insurance is so expensive that companies will save money by paying the fine as opposed to providing the coverage.

It was just announced that tens of thousands of health care professionals, union workers, and community activists will be hired as "navigators" to help Americans choose Obama Care options starting Oct. 1st, 2013. I love President Obama's misleading titles like "navigators" instead of "bureaucrats" and "invest" instead of "spend." These so-called navigators could earn $20. to $48. an hour. Over 140,000 people will be hired for these jobs. This will cost the American taxpayer over $10 billion annually. It could take these government workers hours to help people fill out the 61-page application which will then go to the enlarged IRS to be processed. Americans utilize private sector accountants for tax preparation but President Obama couldn't pass up the opportunity to waste more taxpayer money for another forced Obama Care inconvenience. The "train wreck" that is Obama Care will just get bigger and bigger until it implodes after billions will have been wasted. After $800 billion was wasted for President Obama's failed economic stimulus package, unemployment grew to 10% and 284,000 college graduates are now working for minimum wage. After $602 million was wasted on the hope of developing solar energy by Solyndra who went bankrupt in the process, American taxpayers will now pay for the billions in waste chewed up by Obama Care. As I am writing this on 4/4/13, I pray that Obama Care will be repealed before 1/1/14 when implementation begins but this appears to be wishful thinking on my part.

Medicare cancer patients are now being turned away from cancer clinics due to sequester spending cuts. This could easily be avoided by excluding Sequester spending cuts on cancer drugs for Medicare patients. The President is in California and Congress is not in session. It's a crime that a political agenda is the cause of suffering for large numbers of cancer patients who depend on Medicare. Cancer patients will encounter another obstacle when their health care benefits drop off dramatically after the age of 65 due to an Obama Care regulation. This is basically a death sentence for Cancer patients who paid into Medicare their entire life to insure adequate "health care" in their old age.

$1.9 billion in government loans was originally projected as the set-up cost for independently run health insurance exchanges to provide Obama Care health insurance. The original projected cost has now ballooned up to $5.7 billion that taxpayers must pay for exchanges in just 17 states. There is also another $3 billion in block grants that will go to the 26 states that have chosen not to set up the exchanges to do something similar on their own. 7 states are still undecided so the cost will go up once these States decide which way to go. People who will receive loans to run the exchanges are un-vetted regarding their competence or political affiliations. It has already become apparent that loans in most cases are based on political favors and not competence. This will be a failed proposition before it ever gets off the ground. The only thing that can be assured is that a large amount of taxpayer dollars will be wasted once again. Most Americans don't even know yet that their privacy goes out the window with Obama Care. Doctors who accept Obama Care will be required to maintain their patient's medical records on a National data base. Under Obama Care the government will now have complete access to everyone's medical records. This makes the **HIPAA** law "privacy rule" obsolete. HIPAA still protects an individual's privacy with respect to other people but not the government. This government imposed invasion of citizen's privacy is outrageous. This entire health care insurance fiasco has been forced upon the American taxpayer. We were deceived from the beginning. Every initial projected cost for all facets of Obama Care has increased dramatically (most by 4 to 10 times higher) and we are still 3 and ½ years away from full implementation. Actual implementation won't even officially begin until 1/1/14 and we have already received more bad news than most people can even process. Most Americans don't know what's in the 20,000 pages of regulations yet much less the 2700 pages of the bill itself because few have the time or patience to wade through all the bureaucratic details, so it's difficult to imagine how much more bad news is yet to come over the next 3 and ½ years.

April 4, 2013

While North Korea's leader, Kim Jong Un, is making the strongest threats against the United States in recent years, President Obama is in San Francisco actively involved in fund raising efforts for Democrats in Congress. The President has a history of weakness militarily. He hasn't addressed North Korea's threats at all and hasn't ordered any military positioning in response to their threats. Secretary of Defense Chuck Hagel ordered one navy vessel with missile defense capabilities to the area and ordered a fly over of two B-2 bombers but nothing more. A Carnival cruise ship would be more of a threat! This kind of weak response will only embolden North Korea. President Obama's relaxed demeanor in the face of serious threats is anti-American. The Presidents obvious priority of Democrat fund raising in California as opposed to addressing a serious threat of attack by North Korea on the U.S. territory of Guam or South Korea is beyond irresponsible. A strong show of American force would end the threat but President Obama doesn't care. The President supports pulling naval ships out of the Persian Gulf when Iran is on the verge of completing their nuclear program. Just as seen in the North Korea threat, Iran will also be emboldened to complete development of a nuclear weapon which they plan to fire on Israel. It's a known fact that when radical Islamic terrorists sense weakness they are then highly motivated to go on the offensive.

April 5, 2013

Next in line on President Obama's list of priorities is "strong arming" banks to extend home loans to people with bad credit. He wants the federal housing authority to guarantee the loans with taxpayer money. Bill Clinton already made this mistake which led to the housing bubble and subsequent real estate bust. Easy money invites stupidity and bad behavior. Taxpayers will pay for the defaults down the road when we haven't even finished cleaning up the mess that the Clinton and Bush administrations made. Once again this is yet another move to make big government bigger. It makes no difference to the President if any of his programs fail provided he creates more big bureaucracies to increase the size of already big government. He'll do anything to increase spending so he can further increase taxes and create as much dependence as possible on big government.

These failures along with all the rest documented so far in this book should reinforce the need for limited government and flourishing free enterprise as established by our founding fathers as opposed to socialistic big government. The latter will fail every time as we have seen, but ideological liberals insist on beating a dead horse.

Game the System

April 6, 2013

People have figured out how to work the system that President Obama and his Democrat partners in crime have created. This is a real-life example:

A realtor with 28 years of experience in Pontiac, MI. made a startling discovery recently that's worth sharing. Here it is in his words.

I was showing homes in Pontiac, MI. one afternoon recently and showed up at a home at the 4:00PM time my appointment was scheduled for. After I woke up the homeowner, she let us in and then proceeded to tell my buyers and me that she has already executed a contract to sell the home on a short sale. A short sale is a sale where the bank accepts less money than what is owed on the home. After some chit-chat, she proceeded to tell us that she and her sister, who also lived in the area, were buying each other's homes via the short sale process. I mentioned to her that I thought relatives could not be involved in those transactions. She smiled and said, "We have two different last names so no one knows the difference." She went on to tell us that each owed over 100K on their homes and were in the process of buying each other's homes for about 10 – 15K cash. To top it off, they were each receiving $3000. in government provided relocation assistance at closing. My buyers and I were amazed that she was outright admitting to fraud and yet, she continued. She began to tell us that the best part of their scheme was that because they currently were not working, they are now receiving Section 8 vouchers. I said I thought those were for renters and she said, "That's the best part; me and my sister are going to be renting our homes to each other so we don't even have to move, and President Obama is going to give each of us $800. a month to pay the rent!" She then picked up a picture she had framed of the President and did a little happy dance around her living room and while she kissed the picture she was singing, "Thank you Obama, Thank you Obama." So, here's the bottom line. Both scammers got $80,000 in debt forgiven, $3000. in cash for relocation when in fact they did not relocate and, to boot, you and I will be paying through our taxes $1600. in rent for them, each month...... perhaps for the rest of their lives!

Is it any wonder why so many people have decided that all they must do is vote for the Democrats and they will be taken care of for life at the expense of the taxpayers? I wouldn't be at all surprised if they are receiving food stamps, free cell phones, and whatever other programs are available for anyone who is willing to lie to get assistance. These women went from working and paying about $900. each in mortgage payments, to staying home and getting paid $800. each per month to live in the same home they had been living in and all they had to do was lie on a few papers. This craziness must stop! I'm sure this kind of fraud is going on every day all across the country and no one wants to touch the subject of big government welfare programs because they might offend someone or lose some votes. By the way...she had an almost new SUV in the driveway, 3 flat screen TV's, and a very nice computer.

It's the new American way...for all those who voted to help the less fortunate...Cheers! ...they are now living high as they **game the system** of big government bureaucratic incompetence.

This realtor, who shall remain nameless for being so forthcoming, has shared something that should outrage hard working tax paying citizens across the land. Of course, in their corrupt practice these sisters are sacrificing their dignity and must live with their illegal scam but the current system is set up in such a way as to make it easy to avoid accountability so willing recipients who even go as far as to work the system must live with their corrupt laziness that is enabled by our government. Our welfare system which should be nothing more than a temporary safety net, has evolved into a system designed to create dependence on big government. It's all about control my friends! When large portions of the populous are dependent on their government hand-outs they can easily be controlled and held back from making productive contributions to society which would reduce the need for excessive government assistance. The beast of big government is not your friend.

Smoke and Mirrors

April 10, 2013

President Obama finally presented his budget for 2014. He was over 2 months late and 3 weeks behind the House and Senate. The Presidents late timing alone makes his budget irrelevant. The House, Senate, and the President are so far apart on their budgets that there is no hope for a bi-partisan compromise. President Obama missed his calling. He should become a comedian when he leaves office because his budget is laughable. He does possess great comedic timing and he uses it to his advantage regarding his likeability. He said there are no "smoke and mirrors" in his budget. Anytime we're told we aren't going to be lied to, you can most assuredly expect a lie. When President Obama insists' there are no "smoke and mirrors" in his budget, you can take it to the bank that his budget consists of nothing but "smoke and mirrors." Let's look at some "smoke and mirrors" as well as some exaggerations.

President Obama said the government has created 6.5 million jobs since he became President (not true). He said his budget will grow the economy (not true). His failed $868 billion stimulus initiative from his first term proves that big government can't create growth in the economy. He said his budget invests in new manufacturing hubs. We know anytime President Obama uses the word "invest" he is talking about excessive government spending. In this case, he is referencing more spending on his already failed green energy initiative. He said he wants to re-build roads, bridges, and schools. I thought that's what he was doing with the almost $1 trillion stimulus. Our infrastructure is indeed in need of a great deal of rebuilding but where are the results from his 1st term stimulus package? The States have a responsibility to build infrastructure too. It should be a joint venture but this President never even mentions participation by the States. President Obama continues to promote high quality pre-schools paid for by the federal government. A school voucher program which has been proven to work could accomplish this for a whole lot less money. He said he wants to help the middle class send their children to college. I think he's talking about much more than just help. 54% of young Americans coming out of college don't even have a job yet. 284,000 college graduates are working for minimum wage. The ability for these young Americans to re-pay their student loans is so unrealistic that their credit will be ruined before they ever apply for their first home loan not to mention that our federal government is the creditor who is getting burned on these loans. President Obama's budget specifies a raise in the minimum wage. This will only force small business to reduce the number of people they employ and it opens the door for automation in fast food restaurants. Small business profit margins won't allow for an increase in the minimum wage so it's a job killer. Any astute business person understands this. The only solution to this mountain of problems is a vastly improved economy and the only way to accomplish this is to reduce the burdensome regulations and taxes that are stifling businesses in America. We need to unleash our free enterprise system to allow it to grow the economy. The resulting increase in revenue without the need to raise taxes will sufficiently fuel our governments actual needs.

President Obama said his budget will replace sequester spending cuts, which were his idea in the first place, with smarter cuts (not true). He failed to mention that his so-called smarter cuts aren't even planned to begin until 2017 and beyond thru 2023 when he is out of office. The fact is those proposed cuts will never see the light of day, but of course his budget calls for canceling the sequester cuts early in 2014. He said his budget suggests new ways to reduce the cost of health care. His budget calls for price controls on Medicare providers which will cause Medicare providers to refuse care for Medicare beneficiaries. The "Affordable Health Care Act" aka Obama Care is already so unaffordable for private insurance consumers and employers that it's on the verge of falling apart (we should be so lucky). He said his budget meets Republicans more than half way (not true). President Obama's budget never balances the budget. The President's budget creates $8.2 trillion in new debt over 10 years but the Republican budget balances the budget over 10 years. President Obama's budget calls for $3.8 trillion in spending for 2014 which represents a 6% increase over 2013. The President's budget raises taxes by $1.1 trillion for 2014 and calls for $964 billion in **new** spending for 2014. President Obama's budget reduces spending by a paltry $119 billion over 10 years which becomes null and void when you factor in the new spending that is 9 times more than the $119 billion to be cut for just one year. Also it would be a miracle if his proposed cuts ever occur.

The Good, the Bad, and the Ugly

The House Republican budget is **good**, the Senate Democrat budget is **bad**, and the President's budget is just plain **ugly**. President Obama's budget isn't even serious. It is consistent in that not one Republican or Democrat has ever voted for an Obama budget and the likelihood of his new budget receiving a single vote is slim to none. The Presidents claim that his budget will shrink the deficit, grow the economy, and create jobs is ridiculous. Once again President Obama has failed to do his job. His total lack of leadership is appalling. It becomes increasingly obvious that he is out to destroy America. His agenda is more destructive than any single terrorist attack ever leveled on America. If he did possess any leadership ability he would be able to work with Congress to accomplish productive governance for America. His agenda of higher taxes to enable increased spending which makes already big government even bigger will kill the economy and devastate the lives of all Americans. His plan is to position himself to realize his greatest ambition which is **Socialism** in America.

Memphis Soul Concert

The White House spent $430,000. to throw a party called the "**Memphis Soul Concert**" this evening. They will spend another $1.3 million to broadcast the concert on PBS. The cost of is outrageous while the White House is closed to the public. Justin Timberlake, Queen Latifa, and Cindy Lauper were among the performers at the concert. The President was cracking jokes and rocking out with Michelle. It's true that previous Presidents have also had concerts at the White House but never while the White House is closed to the public which no previous President has ever considered doing. Congress made sure that our Nation's Capital, which also requires Secret Service security, remained open to the public while the President uses the lame excuse that the secret service made the decision to close the White House to the public. Does he really think we believe that the Secret Service has decision making power greater than the President of the United States?

In the Blink of an Eye

April 15, 2013

2:56PM EST, it was a beautiful day in Boston. Large crowds were gathered downtown at the finish line of the Boston Marathon cheering for family members and friends as they finished the 26-mile marathon. **In the blink of an eye** this grand tradition turned to disaster. At 2:57PM EST two bombs, approximately 100 yards apart, exploded, one right after the other, at the finish line of the Boston Marathon on Boylston St. As I am writing this, 4 and ½ hours after the start of the Boston Marathon, there are reports of 3 deaths, Lu Lingzi, Kristie Campbell, and 8-year old Martin Richard. There are also 26 severe injuries at this point. It has been reported that many of the injuries are classified as catastrophic. 14 of the injuries involve the loss of limbs. In addition, by the end of the day, about 150 more injuries were reported with varying degrees of severity. At 4:23PM it was reported that 2 more bombs had been found and were presently being dismantled. Bomb detecting dogs are still checking for additional explosive devices. Major security precautions are presently under way in New York City and Washington DC. ATF, FBI, and National Guard troops are being mobilized in downtown Boston in addition to City and State police. Massachusetts Governor Deval Patrick and Police Commissioner Ed Davis just completed a televised briefing. It is believed that the bombs were IED's (Improvised Explosive Device) because ball bearing shrapnel was found. Doctors treating injured victims had to remove nails and other metallic fragments from their patients. Pieces of a pressure cooker were found. Authorities said analysis of recovered bomb materials revealed content very much like IED's found in Afghanistan and Pakistan. At 6:10PM President Obama made a televised statement. His demeanor was very calm and he refrained from calling this a **terror** attack. He called it a tragedy which doesn't begin to adequately describe this heinous act of terrorism. This terrorist attack was pure **evil**. It was pre-meditated multiple murder and torture of the worst kind! In failing to call this a terrorist attack and simply referring to it as a tragedy is an insult to the victims, their families, and the American people. Calling this terror attack a tragedy leaves the door open for people to be sympathetic toward the perpetrators. President Obama's casual politically correct description of this act of terror is disgusting. He condemned this attack and promised that the perpetrators will be found and will bear the full weight of justice in the same way he condemned the Benghazi attack. After doing nothing about the Benghazi attack, why should anyone believe he would support doing anything about this act of terror. The terrorist attack on the U.S. consulate in Benghazi, Libya was also an act of pure evil as was the Boston attack. One is not worse than the other. They are both equally horrendous terrorist attacks upon America. In truth, both are known as Islamic Jihad but this President, who understands this, will never tell us the truth on this front.

Shot Down

April 17, 2013

It took over 3 hours for the President to make a **weak** televised address after the Boston terrorist attack. Today, 45 minutes after the Senate voted down unconstitutional gun control legislation, President Obama was on TV ranting and raving against those in the Senate who voted no. The bill, which would have expanded background checks for gun purchases at gun shows and on the internet, received a vote of "54 for and 46 against." 60 votes in favor were needed to pass due to the Senate filibuster rule. President Obama said it is a "shameful day" in Washington DC. He went on to politicize his statement by saying "it wasn't worth it" for Congress to protect the nation's children. The Presidents continual exploitation of the victims of the New Town, Connecticut shooting is disgraceful. 46 Senators are upholding their oath to protect the Constitution while President Obama does everything possible to relegate the Constitution as being "out of date." It was indeed a "shameful day" in Washington DC today, but not because of the Senate's action. The President's actions are the shameful ones.

Boston Strong

April 19, 2013

The identity of the Boston Marathon terrorists became known today. 26-year old Tamerlan Tsarnaev was shot and killed early this morning by authorities in Watertown, Massachusetts. His younger brother, 19-year old Dzhokhar Tsarnaev evaded authorities during the "shoot out" and is still at large. Over 200 rounds were exchanged and Dzhokhar, who was wounded during the firefight, left 7 homemade explosives behind. Prior to the Watertown "shoot out" the brothers shot and killed a college security officer, 26-year old Sean Collier, carjacked an SUV, and hurled explosives at Police in Watertown. Both brothers are of Chechen ethnicity. Tamerlan was born in Dagestan, a Russian region, which is near Chechnya. Dzhokhar was born in Kyrgyzstan. Both immigrated to America in 2003. Tamerlan flew to Moscow in Jan. 2012 and remained in Russia for 6 months from Jan. 12th until July 17th 2012. While there he spent time in Dagestan which is one of the world's most notorious hotbeds of radical Islamist terrorists. Ironically, Dzhokhar became a U.S. citizen on 9/11/12, the date of the terrorist attack on the U.S. Diplomatic Mission in Benghazi. Tamerlan was married to a U.S. citizen and had a 3-year old daughter. Tamerlan had a You Tube page featuring videos about Islamic Jihad. He became a legal permanent resident of the U.S. in 2007 and studied engineering at Bunker Hill Community College in Boston. Dzhokhar was enrolled at the University of Massachusetts Dartmouth and lived in Cambridge. Tamerlan and Dzhokhar were classified as refugees when they came to America in 2003 so they immediately became eligible to receive welfare which they did in fact obtain. There is something very wrong about two immigrants who arrive in the U.S. from an area of the world known for radical Muslim terrorists and we welcome them with open arms and money as well!

8:45PM   Authorities captured Dzhokhar Tsarnaev Friday night in Watertown, Massachusetts. A Watertown resident discovered blood on the canvas cover on his boat. He then looked under the cover and discovered more blood and a crumpled body. He called the Watertown Police and they arrived on the scene along with many other law enforcement authorities. An exchange of gunfire took place and then Dzhokhar was finally apprehended at 8:45PM. He was immediately transported to a Boston hospital to receive medical treatment for his wounds.

Enemy Combatanttede

April, 20 2013

Attorney General Eric Holder has refrained from classifying Dzhokhar Tsarnaev as an enemy combatant. It makes no difference that Dzhokhar was an American citizen. Once you engage in a premeditated attack on America, you forfeit your status as a citizen. The FBI, CIA, DOJ, and DHS need as much time as is necessary to obtain information from Dzhokhar regarding his knowledge of other radical Islamic jihadist's in America or other countries. He will undoubtedly be found guilty and will receive the death penalty. That leaves what we don't know which is what knowledge he has of future threats and who he and his brother worked with in planning the Boston Marathon bombing. If he prematurely lawyers up, it would be a crime against American citizens. This guy is not deserving of any favorable treatment whatsoever. He should be treated as the **enemy combatant** that he is!

April 22, 2013

Federal charges were formally brought today against Dzhokhar Tsarnaev for conspiring to use a WMD to kill Americans. He was given his Miranda rights. The Obama administration, which won't even refer to this as an "act of terror", now refuse to classify this terrorist as an "enemy combatant" because he is a U.S. citizen. He will be tried in civilian court which would also have been the case even if he was classified as an enemy combatant. U.S. citizens have been tried as enemy combatants for decades. The mainstream media has already begun their sympathetic campaign to portray this terrorist as a victim. This is beyond idiotic and it's anti-American. The number of people injured has now been updated to 282 as the result of the bombing.

In August 2009, John Brennan then Secretary of DHS, released a statement that the war on terror is over. The Obama administration has actively attempted to sell this ridiculous assertion to the American people ever since Osama bin Laden was captured and killed. The Obama administration obviously doesn't care about an effort to interrogate Dzhokhar Tsarnaev. Based on the public safety exception, the FBI began interrogating Dzhokhar but after only 16 hours of interrogation a federal magistrate judge showed up at the hospital room and read Dzhokhar his Miranda rights effectively shutting down the interrogation. This came as a total surprise to the FBI agents. They were making progress but had a long way to go. The public safety exception could have allowed for more time before the suspect was read his Miranda rights. When significant progress is being made and critical information is being obtained, interrogators are allowed under the public safety exception to continue the interrogation while they are still receiving important information. The length of time allowed under the public safety exception is ambiguous but under these circumstances leniency could surely have been observed by the court. This early termination of the interrogation had to have originated with Attorney General Eric Holder. Once again, the Obama administration endangers the American people to protect a Muslim terrorist. Now that he has been Mirandized, 3 public defenders were provided so we won't learn anything about other Muslims they were affiliated with in Dagestan, Russia, Chechnya, or the United States. We won't learn of existing plots to murder more Americans on U.S. soil. We won't learn about other existing terror cells in America. We won't learn who was financing these brothers and who taught them how to make these very sophisticated pressure cooker bombs. It is incredibly obvious that these brothers did not act alone although the Obama Administration is already attempting to definitively state they did in fact act alone as they attempt to sweep this horrendous terrorist attack under the rug. Intelligence gathering to learn about plans for future terrorist attacks should have been our highest priority. We never would have found Osama bin Laden if it wasn't for "water boarding" of enemy combatants at Gitmo. Obama did away with "enhanced interrogation" which has limited our ability to acquire intelligence and now he prematurely ends the interrogation of Dzhokhar Tsarnaev before the FBI could finish their effort to obtain critical intelligence to protect Americans. This was either a colossal mistake or an intentional act to harm America.

Conservative Islam?

One of the most recent politically correct identities is "Conservative Islam." I suppose this is an invention from the main stream media to assign a non-offensive identity for so-called "peaceful Muslims." The belief that we must distinguish between "peaceful Muslims" and "non-peaceful Muslims" is ludicrous. All Muslims believe Mohammed is the messenger of God (from the 1st pillar of faith). All Muslims must pay the Zagat tax (from the 4th pillar of faith). Mohammed wrote the Quran. All Muslims believe the Quran to be the word of Allah, their God. Make no mistake; Allah and the one true God (the God of Abraham, Isaac and Jacob, the God of the Bible) are **not** one in the same! Allah was a figment of Mohammed's vivid imagination but millions of Muslims believe this lie. The Quran states that Muslims must "kill the infidel" (Surah 2:191, 193; Surah 5:33; Surah 8:12,60,65; Surah 9:2-3, 5, 29,73,123; Surah 22:19; Surah 33:60; Surah 47:4 and Surah 66:9). The Sahih "Hadith" is also considered to be the word of Allah, their God, and was also written by Mohammed. The Hadith also commands Muslims to engage in Jihad to kill the infidel. Anyone who claims that Islam is a peaceful religion after reading these passages from the Quran is mentally challenged. A significant percentage of the Zagat tax goes toward Islamist Jihad (holy war). Given the fact that all Muslims believe they are called to "kill the infidel" and all Muslims know a percentage of the Zagat (Muslim tax) goes toward Jihad, how could any Muslim possibly claim they are peaceful and don't believe the most basic tenets of Islam? Sharia law is another evil tenet of Islam that is embedded in their religion which more closely resembles a political system. Muslims are widely known for their use of **deception!** The only difference between radical Islamist Muslims and other Muslims is that the radicals are more vocal and more actively engaged in Islamist Jihad. This doesn't let the other Muslims off the hook. Very few Muslim leaders (Clerics and Imams) anywhere in the world have ever spoken out against acts of terrorism around the world. For that matter, when was the last time you heard any Muslim condemn any terrorist act anywhere in the world? The obvious answer is almost never. It is no secret that many Muslims consider America to be "The Great Satan." Many Muslims who live in America are hypocrites! They enjoy the very way of life they are so critical of and it's true that many do live peaceful lives and even serve in our military, our government and are even police officers on occasion. These peaceful Muslims are the apostates and thankfully they appear to be the majority but many Muslims are attempting to force Americans to assimilate to their societal customs in America as opposed to Muslims assimilating to our society. Jihad has already wreaked havoc in America leaving death and destruction in its wake and if Sharia law is established in pockets of isolated Muslim communities we would experience further destructive effects perpetrated by Islamists in America. The "politically correct" polices of the Obama administration are to blame for this outrageous infringement upon our way of life, our rights and the loss of our security. President Obama actively promotes the "politically correct" movement which is tearing America down.

24-year old Katherine Russell, Tamerlan Tsarnaev's wife and mother of their 3-year old daughter, has already "lawyered up." Her attorney won't allow her to be questioned. No charges have been brought against her yet. She did make a statement that she believes in the Koran and in the tenets of Islam. She converted to Islam from Christianity in 2010 when she married Tamerlan. She also claims she had no knowledge of Tamerlan's bombing plans. She works as a home health care aid and claims she works about 70 to 80 hours a week while Tamerlan would stay home to care for their 3-year old daughter and make bombs. Tamerlan's controlling chauvinistic persona and his domineering Muslim tendencies would surely motivate him to tell his wife about his plans for Jihad to establish his male dominance and to feed his huge ego. It would be extremely naïve to think otherwise. Katherine Russell should be under extreme scrutiny to determine what she knew. She is the most likely person in the U.S. to conspire with her husband to advance their Jihadist plans.

Treason

April 23, 2013

A new GOP report detailing the terrorist attack on the U.S. diplomatic mission in Benghazi was released today. This new report confirms that a reduction in the security force took place shortly before the attack on 9/11/2012. It is now a proven fact that the reduction in security was approved by the highest levels in the State Department including then Secretary of State Hillary Clinton. Senator Lindsey Graham's staff found a document at the State Department which authorized the reduction in security at the U.S. diplomatic mission in Benghazi with Hillary Clinton's signature on it. In Jan. 2013, then Secretary of State Hillary Clinton lied under oath during a Senate hearing and said she had no knowledge of the over 600 requests by Ambassador Christopher Stevens for heightened security or of the actual reduction in security at the diplomatic mission in Benghazi. The only possible explanation for this terribly irresponsible action is that the Obama administration knew the attack was forthcoming and made a choice to sit on their hands to prop up the new fledgling Muslim government in Libya that this administration worked to place in power after they ousted Gaddafi.

Barak Hussein Obama and others alleged complicit were formally charged with high treason in a March 2009 federal criminal complaint filed by retired Navy LCDR Walter Francis Fitzpatrick III and filed with James R. Dedrick U.S. Attorney, Eastern District Tennessee, and Edgar Schmutzer, Dedrick's Assistant U.S. Attorney. From the official complaint – "Your criminal ascension manifests a clear and present danger. You fundamentally changed our form of government. Confident of holding your silent agreement and admission, I identify you as a foreign born domestic enemy. My sworn duty, Mr. Obama, is to stand against what you stand for. You are not my President. You are not my Commander in Chief." There is nothing at all ambiguous about this statement. The basis upon which Commander Fitzpatrick makes his charge is equally straight forward.

If Commander Fitzpatrick's charge of treason is found to be false, it would constitute an act of mutiny on behalf of Commander Fitzpatrick. Mutiny is a crime which requires Court Martial and carries the penalty of death, therefore Commander Fitzpatrick has risked his very life to expose Barak Obama's crimes against America. The complaint goes on to say, "You, Mr. Obama, have broken in and have entered the White House by force of contrivance, concealment, conceit, dissembling, and deceit. Posing as an imposter President and Commander in Chief, you have stripped civilian command and control over the military establishment. Known military criminal actors – command racketeers – are now free in the exercise of military government intent upon destruction of America's constitutional government."

Commander Fitzpatrick is a career Naval officer who graduated the Annapolis Naval Academy in 1975 and spent a lifetime serving his country with honor and distinction. He is not known as any form of conspiracy crackpot or extreme right-wing trouble maker. Based on the Manual of Courts-Martial, Commander Fitzpatrick **must** be charged with mutiny if his treason charges against Barak Obama are in any way false. Such charges have **not** been filed against Commander Fitzpatrick. Not doing so constitutes an admission of guilt on President Obama's part.

As of this writing Commander Fitzpatrick has not been charged with Mutiny. For Commander Fitzpatrick to be charged with mutiny, the Commander's charge of high treason filed against Barak Obama would need to be proved false. To be proven false, President Obama's secret files would have to be revealed for discovery, which explains why the President has not charged the Commander with mutiny. Commander Fitzpatrick has been jailed numerous times in Monroe, Tennessee for various felony charges which he has never been convicted of. He has been persecuted non- stop by the U.S. government ever since he filed charges against President Obama in March 2009.

Proof that President Obama is a pro-jihadist and Islamist continues to mount. After the Boston terrorist massacre, the President said "we need to take care not to rush to judgment. Not about motivation and not about groups of people." I'm not sure where to even begin with a statement like that. Radical Islamist Muslims are motivated by their mandate to "kill the infidel." During a speech in India, President Obama said that Islam is one of the world's great religions. He said Islam is a religion of peace, justice, fairness, and tolerance. When asked about what he thought of Jihad, he replied that Jihad has many meanings and is subject to interpretation. Barak Hussein Obama was raised as a Muslim in Indonesia so it should come as no surprise that he is at the very least sympathetic to Islam. It's time for liberals to give up their protective posture for their fearless leader. They look foolish when they attempt to defend President Obama.

Fort Hood Terrorist Attack

President Obama refuses to call the terrorist murders at Fort Hood Islamic Jihad. This is just one more insult directed at all Americans. Nidal Malik Hasan, a U.S. Army Major serving as a psychiatrist, murdered 13 people and injured 30 more on November 5th 2009 at Fort Hood near Killeen, Texas. It was the worst shooting ever to take place on an American military base. The DOD and Federal law enforcement agencies along with President Obama have called it **workplace violence**. Hasan was yelling "Allahu Akbar" while he was murdering people! The DOD is refusing to award purple hearts and financial benefits for families of those killed and for wounded victims! A joint terrorism task force was aware of e-mail communications between Hasan and Yemen-based cleric Anwar al-Awlaki, and that Hasan's colleagues had been aware of his increasing radicalization for several years. Fort Hood Police SWAT shot Hasan while he was engaged in his shooting spree and his wounds caused him to be paralyzed from the waist down. Hasan was charged with 13 counts of pre-meditated murder and 32 counts of attempted murder. He is facing the death penalty upon conviction. Since the Obama administration insists upon defining this act of Islamic Jihad as "workplace violence," Major Hasan is on leave **with pay** until he is convicted! This is incredible. This guy murders 13 people and injures 30 more while yelling "Allahu Akbar" and he is rewarded with a paid vacation! Once again, the fact that President Obama refuses to call this an act of Islamic Jihad is a crime against the victims and the families of the victims in addition to the American people. Let's be clear, we're talking about 13 Gold Star families that President Obama is persecuting as he subtly defends Islamic Jihad by omission of the truth!

Cover Up #2

As if the Benghazi cover up wasn't enough, the Obama administration has now begun their cover up on what they knew before the Boston terror attack. The FBI and CIA had intelligence from Russian intelligence agencies in 2011 that Tamerlan Tsarnaev is a radical Islamist who should be under strict surveillance. When information like this comes from a Russian intelligence agency, red flags should have gone up all over the place. This was before Tamerlan even traveled to Moscow and spent 6 months in Dagestan, Russia and Chechnya from Jan. till July 2012. DHS knew about his trip to Russia and should have had this guy under a microscope upon his return but because of the Obama administrations lax policies on terrorism, which they don't even call terrorism, Tamerlan was free to make bombs and prepare for the attack that occurred on April 15th, 2013 because he wasn't under any kind of surveillance. The lame attempts to cover up this huge oversight began when the FBI said Tamerlan's trip to Russia went unnoticed due to the misspelling of his name. Then a different story surfaced when DHS director Janet Napolitano said there was a "ping" (alert) when he left the country but that the investigation on him was suspended by the time he returned to the United States. James Clapper, Director of National Intelligence, should have been coordinating with the FBI, DHS, and CIA in efforts to be sure each agency had access to the same intelligence and were working together to prevent a terrorist attack like the Boston Marathon bombings. This outrageous oversight caused the death of 4 people and the injury of 282 people. How could James Clapper fail to do his job in this situation? His job was recently created for this exact inevitability. Secretary of State John Kerry made a statement today about Tamerlan Tsarnaev's trip to Russia and said he returned with knowledge of how to execute a bombing. Occasionally, Secretary Kerry and even Vice President Biden provide us with spontaneous moments of truth that must result in rebuke by the administration but it's great for the people when it happens. The Obama administration immediately went on the defensive and had a State department spokesman make a statement which contradicted Secretary Kerry's statement. The Obama administrations intentional appeasement of terrorism makes us look weak. President Obama should know that when radical Islamic jihadists perceive weakness they go on the offensive. His politically correct appeasement policies will continue to result in the deaths and injury of American citizens.

April 24, 2013

Today we learned that Tamerlan Tsarnaev purchased some very powerful fireworks at "Phantom Fireworks," a New Hampshire fireworks store. It has also been revealed that the brothers used a detonating device made from toy remote control cars. The bombs made with pressure cookers, metallic shrapnel, gun powder from the fireworks, and remote control devices were very sophisticated. They were much too sophisticated to learn how to make from a magazine as has been reported or from an internet web site. Tamerlan must have received training while in Russia to have acquired the ability to make such sophisticated bombs. We also learned that once the brothers carjacked a Mercedes SUV after the Boston bombings, their plan was to drive straight to New York with 6 more bombs they already had in their possession and detonate them in Times Square. If the vehicle hadn't been low on gas they would already have been well on their way to New York. Thank God when they stopped for gas in Watertown, MA. everything went south for the terrorists. This was when the owner of the Mercedes made his escape and dialed 911 from the convenience store across the street. Shortly thereafter, the firefight ensued and after 200 rounds had been fired Tamerlan lay mortally wounded on the ground and Dzhokhar got away in the stolen Mercedes after running over his brother effectively finishing him off, only to be found and apprehended a few hours later. Once Dzhokhar was in custody, overwhelming praise was heaped upon the Boston Police, Massachusetts State Police, FBI, DHS, and CIA when in fact all they did was follow up on leads provided from the public at large. A "Lord and Taylor" security camera provided the footage of

Tamerlan and Dzhokhar on Boylston St., backpacks in hand, prior to the bombing. The owner of the carjacked Mercedes called 911 after making a daring escape. If this brave citizen hadn't done this the brothers would have been free to travel to New York City to bomb Times Square. A homeowner in Watertown, Mass. found Dzhokhar hiding in his boat and called authorities who then identified the suspect and successfully apprehended him. Basically, authorities didn't accomplish anything without help from outside sources. Their follow up was indeed swift and effective but very little credit was attributed to the people who made it all possible.

Chapter 5

Obama Care Explained

April 25, 2013

Donald Trump recently offered this very informative explanation of Obama Care. The following is an exact quote from Donald Trump. "Let me get this straight…. We're going to be gifted with a health care plan we are forced to purchase and fined if we don't, which purportedly covers at least ten million more people, without adding a single new Doctor, but provides for 16,000 new IRS agents, written by a committee whose chairman says he doesn't understand it, passed by a Congress that didn't read it but exempted themselves from it, and signed by a President who smokes, with funding administered by a Treasury Chief who didn't pay his taxes, for which we'll be taxed for four years before any benefits take place, by a government which has already bankrupted Social Security and Medicare, all to be overseen by a surgeon general who is obese, and financed by a country that's broke!!! **What the hell could possibly go wrong?"**

Student Loan Crisis

Student loan debt in America has grown to a total of $1 trillion. Student loan debt is the largest form of debt in the U.S. aside from home mortgages. The negative affect this has on the economy is staggering. When students graduate from college they are deep in debt before they can find a job, **if** they can find a job. If they can't find a job they just borrow more money and stay in school. They wind up digging a hole so deep its mind boggling to think about how to dig out. Home ownership is so far out of reach it's just a distant pipedream. The default rate on these loans is already very high. Since the government funds most of these loans, guess who winds up holding the bag. It's difficult to comprehend that over 1/16th of our $16.7 trillion national debt is tied up in student loans. A ceiling for these loans with attached controls and regulations should have been established long ago. Presently the biggest problem is that nobody is even talking about this. It's being treated as if it doesn't exist. Since it can't remain ignored much longer, I'm sure the Obama administration will present a plan to forgive a huge chunk of this debt as uncollectable and just allow it to be absorbed into our increasing national debt or just do nothing while the default rate continues to rise!

Evasive Answers

April 30, 2013

The President made a televised appearance before the White House Press Corp. today and when he opened the floor for questions, Ed Henry, Fox News White House correspondent, was called upon for the 1st question. Ed initially asked about the "red line" that had been crossed with the use of chemical weapons on Syrian insurgents in Syria. The President responded with an ambiguous and rambling dissertation that didn't adequately answer the question. Ed followed up and asked about alleged threats upon survivors of the Benghazi attack on 9/11/12 to discourage them from coming forward to testify about the State Department's failure to respond to the attack. State Department survivors were threatened with the end of their careers and possibly even death. The President said he was not familiar with the notion that anyone was being blocked from testifying and that he would investigate. Another member of the Press Corp. asked a twofold question about inadequate surveillance of the Tsarnaev brothers prior to the Boston Marathon bombing and the State Department's failure to respond to the Benghazi attack. The President gave a long rambling response to part 1 of her question and completely ignored the Benghazi element of her question.

Overall the Press conference was a complete waste of time. The President spent 50 minutes answering questions from the press corp. and didn't really say anything. When the President decided, enough of this, he quickly made his way for the door but then heard a question about Jason Collins (NBA center) and immediately returned to the podium. Do you suppose he would have returned to answer another Benghazi question? Apparently gay basketball players trump Benghazi. The President spoke for about 5 minutes praising Jason for his courage to come out of the closet as he segued into a dissertation about how wonderful gay people are and that they should be afforded every opportunity that any other person may have. Once again, the President needs to examine his priorities. We should although be somewhat forgiving because fielding questions without a teleprompter can be quite a challenge for the President.

Stalled Agenda

At this point in President Obama's 2nd term it has become apparent that his liberal agenda is stalled. Thankfully, he has failed to advance any key objective in his 2nd term agenda so far. His gun control initiative is dead in the water (The President and Harry Reid are beyond angry over that one). He's failed to do anything about so-called global warming and his green energy initiative has also failed to produce any of his desired results. After the costly failure of taxpayer money invested in bankrupt Solyndra ($602 billion down the drain), even Democrats won't touch anything green other than money for the time being. Immigration reform is still on the table at this point but Democrats and Republicans in Congress are so far apart on this issue that there is no hope of any productive legislation getting through either chamber. Obama Care is headed for implosion and any federal legislation to advance the nationwide legalization of same sex marriage has about as much of a chance of passing as federal legalization of marijuana at this point. The Supreme Court is the Presidents only hope on the fronts of Obama Care and same sex marriage. President Obama has been determined to shut down our Naval base at

Guantanamo Bay but hasn't offered a single viable solution as to where the enemy combatants housed there would go. The President has exercised stiff resistance to the classification of anyone as an enemy combatant. Of course, this is the President who insists the war on terror is over. President Obama's only hope to do away with Gitmo would be to declare it a small business and tax it out of existence. The President's budget proposal (which was presented over 2 months late) is laughable. This budget has as much chance of receiving a single vote on either side of the aisle as any of his previous budgets. President Obama couldn't even succeed at blaming the GOP for the alleged disaster that Sequester spending reductions would bring about. After squashing the Sequester replacement bill passed by the House, the Presidents blame game backfired and came back on him. Obviously, it would be unrealistic to hope that any positive development might occur regarding reducing the increasing National debt, not that the President cares, and an upswing in the economy would be way out of the realm of possibilities.

The only thing that can be expected is the continuation of the never-ending campaign. The President is learning that his dictatorial style is highly ineffective due to the separation of powers in the structure of our government. He's attempted to utilize the main stream media as the 4th branch of the government. He refers to Capitol Hill as if they are an enemy combatant. President Obama's only hope at this point would be to see a Democrat majority in both chambers of Congress after the 2014 Congressional election. As we've seen, a Democrat majority in the Senate isn't sufficient to help the President. No worries Mr. President, you can always fall back on your career as a standup comedian. If that doesn't work out you could join the politically correct police; or a career in real estate might be just the thing, but remember not to refer to the master bedroom as such because it's now known as the owner's suite. We wouldn't want to offend anyone now would we. As enticing as those prospects may sound, I'm sure you've already considered joining Bill and Hillary Clinton on the highly lucrative speaking circuit; just don't forget your teleprompter!

Partners in Crime

May 1, 2013

3 University of Massachusetts Dartmouth students were arrested in Boston today. These students were actively engaged in covering up the aftermath of the Boston Marathon bombing. All 3 are close friends of Dzhokhar Tsarnaev. Dias Kadyrbayev and Azamat Tazhayakov are charged with conspiracy to obstruct justice. Both are in the U.S. on student visas. Robel Phillipos is charged with lying to investigators. Robel is a U.S. citizen. All 3 of these young men are from Kazakhstan. They were texting back and forth with Dzhokhar while he was still on the run. They went to Dzhokhar's apartment and picked up a backpack with empty firecracker

shells and his laptop computer. They took these items and threw them in a nearby dumpster. The question that begs to be answered is why throw away a perfectly good laptop computer unless you knew key evidence would be found on it. Large firecracker shells should have aroused suspicion if you didn't already know that they were used to make bombs as these young men did.

At this point all 3 have attorneys and are being held because they chose not to post bail. One can only hope that the court will make an example of these young men and pronounce a very strong sentence upon them. A message should be sent that the U.S. will not tolerate any level of participation in a terrorist attack on Americans. Dzhokhar now has 4 attorneys to handle his defense. Given the existing evidence he'll need all the help he can get. I must wonder if a life sentence for a 19-year old may be worse than the death penalty. Obviously, his marijuana smoking and social media days are already behind him.

Cover Up 101

May 3, 2013

The Obama administrations **cover up** of the terrorist attack on the U.S. Diplomatic Mission in Benghazi, Libya has been textbook, from the lame attempt to blame it on a spontaneous demonstration in response to a "you tube" video, to the Presidents denial of threats made against State Department and CIA officials to thwart their testimony. Hillary Clinton (then Secretary of State) appeared before a Senate hearing and lied throughout the hearing about the State Department's role in the cover up. She went as far as to say "What difference, at this point, does it make." It is of course important to note that the President was actively involved in his re-election campaign at the time. The truth about the Benghazi terrorist attack just didn't fit with the Presidents campaign narrative that was attempting to say the war on terror is over and Al Qaeda has become a diminished force now that Osama bin Laden is dead. The State Department Accountability Review Board not only intentionally failed to reveal the truth but they went as far as blocking members of Congress from viewing unclassified State Department documents which to this day have not been provided.

Three State Department officials, who are survivors of the Benghazi attack, have now decided to come forward regardless of the threats and will initially testify before a House hearing on Wednesday 5/8/13. Two of the three witnesses have obtained legal counsel. Victoria Toensing will represent **Gregory Hicks**, Deputy Chief of Mission in Libya and her husband Joe DiGenova will represent **Mark I. Thompson**, Deputy Coordinator for Operations in the State Departments Counterterrorism Bureau. **Eric Nordstrom**, Diplomatic Security Officer who was the regional security officer in Libya, will also testify. Incredibly, the State Department has denied clearance for Victoria Toensing and Joe DiGenova to interview their clients in person prior to the hearing.

State Department spokesman Patrick Ventrell called both attorneys liars in a televised statement today. I sense a bit of fear coming out of the State Department which is understandable under the circumstances. Gregory Hicks was the number two man after Ambassador Christopher Stevens in Libya. Gregory, in addition to Ambassador Stevens, had made numerous requests for additional security at the Diplomatic Mission in Benghazi in the months leading up to the 9/11 attack. Staffers working for Senator Lindsey Graham were finally allowed to review State Department documents on the attack. It took months to obtain authorization and when they went to the State Department to review the documents, they weren't allowed to remove any and they were carefully watched while they searched for relevant information. After hours of searching, they found the document that ordered a reduction to the security detail for the embassy just prior to the attack. This order was authorized and signed by then Secretary of State, Hillary Clinton. The reduction in the security detail was not due to the cost. Deputy Assistant Secretary of the State Department, Charlene Lamb, testified during the October Senate hearing that financial resources were not an issue. Any attempt to blame insufficient security on a lack of money is invalid not only because of Charlene Lamb's sworn testimony but also because common sense tells us that the Commander in Chief surely has the authority to order additional security in a situation like Benghazi.

Benghazi Whistleblowers

May 8, 2013

Gregory Hicks, Mark Thompson, and Eric Nordstrom appeared before the House Oversight Committee on Capitol Hill today. These 3 men have no political agenda. They are diplomats whose only concern is getting the truth out there for many reasons but predominately because they were very close to Ambassador Stevens and Sean Smith. They feel, as many do, that the cover up to advance a political agenda (get Obama re-elected as President) is an insult to the families and friends of the 4 victims. These people along with the American people deserve the truth. The State Department Accountability Review Board never interviewed then Secretary of State Hillary Clinton, Gregory Hicks, Deputy Chief of Missions for Libya, or Mark Thompson, Deputy Coordinator of Operations for the State Departments Counterterrorism Bureau. It's incredible that the 3 highest ranking people in the State Department, as relating to Libya, who should have been the first to be interviewed; never were. Today, Gregory Hicks testified, "I was stunned, my jaw dropped, and I was embarrassed" when he heard about Ambassador Susan Rice making the claim, on 5 televised Sunday news programs, that the assault was the result of a demonstration gone violent over a "You Tube" anti-Islamist video. Today's hearing proved beyond the shadow of any doubt that this "smoke screen" was a lie. David Petraeus, then CIA director, said he knew immediately that it was a terrorist attack. The CIA had submitted a draft of "talking points" to the State Department detailing all the facts surrounding the attack which included references to the Ansar al-Sharia militia group which is an affiliate of Al Qaeda. The State Department revised these talking points **11** times. They were so watered down that it was easy for the President and the State Department to spin the attack any way they desired. Victoria Nuland, State Department Spokesperson, was at the center of these revisions but the direction to revise the talking points had to come from the top. Cheryl Mills, State Department Chief of Staff, instructed Gregory Hicks not to have any conversations with Congressman Jason Chaffetz, Head of the House Oversight Committee, or any other Congressman unless the attorney she appointed was present. There is no precedent for this! Why would it be necessary for a State Department attorney to be present unless his role was to protect the cover up? Why try to impede and obstruct a conversation between Gregory Hicks and Congressman Jason Chaffetz. Gregory Hicks testified today that he was demoted from Deputy Chief of Missions for Libya to Desk Officer after he began to speak out exposing the cover up. Gregory Hicks is a career diplomat with 22 years of service in the State Department. This radical form of retaliation to punish Gregory for coming forward with the truth is un-American.

Mark Thompson testified that he requested deployment of the "Foreign Emergency Support Team" from Aviano, Italy but was told that FEST had been "taken off the menu of options." F16's could easily have taken off from Aviano, Italy, then refueled in Sicily, and flown to Benghazi in about 3 hours. It is widely believed that mere fly over's by F16's would have been sufficient to scare off the terrorists. Navy Seal teams were also available in Stuttgart, Germany and Croatia (Charlie-1-10) which is close to Aviano, so they could also have been in Benghazi in 3 to 4 hours. Any or all these teams would have been in Benghazi well before the attack began on the CIA annex where Navy Seals Ty Woods and Glen Doherty lost their lives. They were all told to **stand down**. A Special Forces team in Tripoli (1 hour and 15-minute flight time to Benghazi) was told to **stand down** right before they took off for Benghazi to help fight off the terrorists. Gregory Hicks spoke directly with Hillary Clinton at 2:00AM (Benghazi time) to fill her in on the terrorist attack and she made no mention of a demonstration resulting from a "You Tube" video that of course never took place. Pentagon officials informed Secretary of Defense Leon Panetta at 10:30PM (Benghazi time) and Panetta was coordinating with Hillary Clinton at 11:40PM (Benghazi time). The **stand down** order for the team in Tripoli was given after the phone conversation between Hillary Clinton and Gregory Hicks at 2:00AM Benghazi time. The biggest unanswered question of the day is; **who gave the stand down order?** Just the fact that the identity of this person is being hidden should raise red flags all over the place. The Special Forces team, Delta Force, in Tripoli and the Navy Seals, Seal Team 6, in Italy, Germany, and Croatia were extremely frustrated over the stand down orders. They were fully prepared to take off and could have made a huge difference. Gregory Hicks testified that the team in Tripoli (where he was) was furious when the stand down order was given. The refusal to provide adequate security before the attack, the failure to act during the attack, and the subsequent **cover up** is an outrage.

Admiral Michael Mullen, former Joint Chiefs Chair (retired) and Ambassador Thomas Pickering, former U.S Ambassador to El Salvador, were the co-chairmen of the State Department Accountability Review Board which handled the investigation of the Benghazi attack. Both declined to testify at the hearing today. Both are close friends of Bill Clinton. Right before the hearing, the State Department issued a statement saying that they did agree to appear but Congressman Darrell Issa, House Oversight and Reform Committee Chairman said the State Department statement is 100% **not** true. Neither made an appearance at the hearing. There is not one fact to support a single statement made by the State Department regarding Benghazi. At the end of the day, several questions remained unanswered. Congressman Elijah Cummings, ranking Democrat on the House Oversight Committee, said he felt there is a definite need to hold additional hearings. Obviously, Congressman Darrell Issa agreed. It should come as no surprise that the main stream media (ABC, NBC, CBS, CNN, CNBC, MSNBC, NYT and WAPO) devoted very little time to report on today's hearing. It's disgraceful that they even consider themselves to be journalists. They are more aptly described as "public relations" representatives for the liberal left.

700 retired "special forces" individuals have signed a letter asking Congress to form a special committee with subpoena power to further investigate to get answers to the unanswered questions.

IRS – **I**ntensive **R**elentless **S**crutiny

May 10, 2013

The IRS admitted today to targeting conservative groups with extra scrutiny by ordering audits to question their non-profit tax exempt status. They targeted over 170 conservative groups and 0 liberal groups. The IRS has already issued an apology for this practice. While giving liberal groups a complete pass, conservative groups such as the Tea Party, Romney campaign contributors, "Z Street" a pro-Israel group, and even Dr. James Dobson who heads up a Christian Ministry called "Focus on the Family" were targeted for **unfair audits**. This is a perfect example of big government tyranny. The intimidation factor alone is very effective to tyrannize conservatives. The Obama administration is using the IRS as a political weapon. True to Obama's Chicago style aggression, anyone who may pose a threat to his agenda will come under attack and the Obama administration pulled out the big guns for this one.

The audits went much deeper than just tax analysis. IRS agents were asking for "copies of handouts for major events, names and credentials of event organizers, and names of donors and contributors." When did we become a communist country? The IRS even has its own drone program (Big brother is watching). IRS employees have received $92 million in bonuses since 2009. Apparently, it pays very well to participate in the tyranny.

It should come as no surprise that no one has come forward to accept responsibility yet. I wonder if the IRS hierarchy thought they could get away with a simple apology and resume business as usual. IRS Commissioner, Steven Miller, refused to answer questions from the press today as he was leaving his office. This is a scandal that should rock the foundations of the liberal big government machine that is now completely out of control.

Secret Seizures

May 13, 2013

When it rains, it pours. Now, in addition to Benghazi and the IRS scandal, the Department of Justice has been caught seizing Associated Press "call logs." An anonymous source with the DOJ claims they were searching for the identity of an AP reporter who allegedly leaked classified information about CIA operations in Yemen and blew the cover of a CIA agent there, compromising his ability to thwart terrorist activity in Yemen. Now that it's out in the open they are claiming their action was designed to keep the American people safe. In a CYA effort Attorney General Eric Holder emphasized the critical nature of the blown cover of an undercover CIA agent and by extension Americans safety. This excuse doesn't begin to hold water because CIA director John Brennan leaked the exact same information in a news conference the day after the AP published the story on May 7th. How could one day possibly make a difference? By design, the motivation for these seizures is to intimidate the press. Even the mainstream media is running scared because this sort of activity threatens their 1st amendment rights. It's ironic that after protecting the Obama administration for such a long time, they now find themselves under attack. They are now engaged for the first time in a very long time and are directing some very tough questions at White House Press Secretary Jay Carney. It's impossible for these seizures to take place without Attorney General Eric Holder being at the center of this but he claims he didn't know anything about it. The sheer scope of this fishing expedition is unprecedented. The DOJ obtained a sweeping subpoena for 2 months' worth of phone records that were seized for 21 phone lines used by 100 reporters with the AP. It's possible for the DOJ to make seizures of this sort if circumstances honestly warrant the need but if the DOJ fails to contact targets in advance to alert them of the pending seizures, it may not technically be illegal but it is highly unethical, especially because the scope of the seizures was so very broad. Obviously given the secrecy surrounding the seizures that took place, an advance alert did not take place. Our very right to freedom of speech as guaranteed by the 1st amendment is at stake here. The American people are now at risk! To say things are getting out of hand would be a huge understatement.

Culture of Intimidation

This government is so big they can't even keep track of how many scandals they must deal with at any given point in time. We're up to 3 now but it's altogether possible that they'll just keep coming. There are so many lies in the spin machine that the machine appears to be spinning out of control. Having said that, I believe the President is relatively immune to this level of controversy. I believe he isn't the least bit worried. President Obama has successfully established a big government monster that operates via a **culture of intimidation** and plays nothing but hardball. His non-stop campaign machine drives this mafia style form of governance which creates a completely partisan environment. Everything is political. Any political opponent who speaks out against the President's agenda will find themselves under attack, as has been the case through the course of the last 4 and ½ years. The arrogance of this administration is unsurpassed. The Obama administration would have us believe that the "trio of controversies" currently at the forefront of attention is unrelated. The fact is they are all a trickle down from President Obama's dictatorial style. The President always effectively distances himself from all controversies. The fault always lands on something or somebody else. There is a willful pursuit to hide from the truth. The truth is that everything begins at the top within the walls of the White House and everything below either falls in line or gets bulldozed out of the way. Big government works beautifully for this administration. It's time to starve the beast!

Political Circus

The President made a televised address today and spoke about the IRS scandal. Incredibly, even after the IRS had already admitted to the unfair audits and issued an apology, the President opened his statement with the word "If." After he uses the word "if" to open with, it really doesn't matter what follows. The door is already open to manipulate this issue any way he may choose. He promised to get to the bottom of this injustice, but with his lack of credibility, why bother even listening to what he says. He said he didn't know about the IRS targeting conservatives or the DOJ seizing phone records of AP reporters until he heard about it on the news. I would think the President of the United States should have some knowledge of high level actions within major divisions of our government. If President Obama doesn't know anything and Attorney General Eric Holder doesn't know anything, then who does?

Then, as if the IRS issue and the DOJ issue are not bad enough, he went on with a lame attempt to skewer the Benghazi scandal. He said the "talking points" didn't matter and that it had become a **sideshow.** He blatantly lied and said there is **no cover up.** He called the whole thing a **"political circus."** He also said **"there's no there, there"** if that makes any sense. It is common knowledge on Capitol Hill that the CIA and the Pentagon advised the President directly that the attack in Benghazi was a terrorist attack performed by an Al Qaeda affiliated group. This communication took place the day after the attack on 9/12/12. Amid the common knowledge of a cover up known by both Democrats and Republicans, President Obama decides to further stretch his lies. I'm beginning to feel sorry for Jay Carney, White House Press Secretary. Every time he turns around he finds himself in another indefensible scenario. Of course, his job is to spin and he happens to be very good at it so he may see it as just another day at the office.

Big government tyranny is alive and well. President Obama is a dictator out of control. He is so wrapped up in his own ideology that it's become his reality. I think he is beginning to believe his own lies. He seems to be oblivious to the mounting opposition that is building all around him. It's become a scramble to see who can escape blame for any number of screw-ups. The wagons are circling and whoever gets caught in the middle will wind up dodging bullets from any number of directions. Conservatives are preparing to go in for the kill and the President doesn't seem to be the least bit concerned. It's sad though that the jury for the court of public opinion is still out because so many Americans are disengaged. I suppose when you consider that the "left leaning" main stream media is so quick to provide cover for the Obama administration that it would just be too much to expect awareness at this point by the public at large. Also, the conservatives who threaten to do something about corruption within the Obama administration are all bark and no bite. They talk a good game but always fail to produce the desired results. No wonder the President is so casual about their idle threats.

Good News?

May 15, 2013

Once again, the President, in a televised statement today offered nothing of substance relating to the IRS targeting of conservative groups for extra scrutiny when they apply for tax exempt status. He intentionally waited until 6:30PM EST to address the nation so the main stream news outlets couldn't report on his statement during their 6:00PM broadcasts. He said "responsible parties will be held accountable" and that "the White House will work with Congress in their oversight role." He informed us that IRS Commissioner Steven Miller had issued his resignation to Secretary of the Treasury, Jack Lew today. Steven Miller had only held that position since November 2012 and was just an interim commissioner until June 2013, but he was Deputy Commissioner before his promotion. Miller had officially been informed of the unfair audits on May 3rd, 2012 but never revealed this practice while serving as Deputy Commissioner or acting Commissioner. Steven Millers resignation is like being kicked out of a restaurant while you are yelling, "You can't kick me out; I was leaving anyway." There was no mention today of the previous Commissioner, Douglas Shulman, who must have known at least as much as Steven

Miller. Criminal charges should be forthcoming but this DOJ with Attorney General Eric Holder leading the way will protect the Obama administration at every turn.

The President said "new checks and new safeguards" will be instituted and that he "will make sure new laws are clear with no ambiguity." President Obama has created an opportunity out of a scandal because he can now attempt to further increase the size of the IRS bureaucracy by adding even more laws that aren't even needed. He hypocritically admonished Republicans to keep politics out of this issue, when in fact the tyrannical attacks by the IRS on conservatives were totally political. Not to worry though, the President said he has "**good news**, its fixable." Does anybody really accept this kind of rhetoric? Given the gravity of the situation, the Presidents statement today was very weak. As always, President Obama appeared cool, calm, and collected today. This is another reflection of **the arrogance of power** that President Obama portrays and even enjoys. He's probably relishing the fact that there is so much for the press to deal with that it's too much for the average American to simultaneously absorb. He can hide behind the flurry of activity coming from so many different directions. Nothing this President does should come as a surprise. Today's response was sorely inadequate by design. It's really no concession but at least he's predictable.

Non-Responsive

May 16, 2013

The President made a televised appearance today along with the Prime Minister of Turkey. They had met today to discuss the escalating civil war in Syria. When the President opened the floor for questions, a Bloomberg reporter asked if the White House had direct knowledge of the unfair IRS audits which targeted several conservative groups and individuals **before** the practice was reported by the press on May 10th. The President said "I didn't know anything about **the IG report** before the IG report came out in the press." President Obama uses the, "I found out when the press reported it" excuse all too often. This lame excuse which couldn't possibly be true is so ludicrous on its face that it's difficult to understand why he employs it to such a great extent. The Presidents lame excuse didn't begin to answer the question! This is just a political ploy to say what he had already planned to say. This is an extremely important question that needs to be answered but the Presidents evasive answers to such questions make it very difficult to make any progress towards getting at the truth. Apparently, the truth is just too inconvenient to be bothered with.

Musical Chairs

May 17, 2013

A move took place today that exemplifies how the Obama administration operates. Sarah Hall Ingram, former tax-exempt organizations head at the IRS, from 2009 until 2012, during that unit's targeting of conservative groups, is now in charge of the agency's Affordable Care Act office. Joseph Grant, Commissioner of the tax-exempt office, will retire on June 3rd. Isn't it interesting that both men, Steven Miller and Joseph Grant, who supposedly fell on their swords due to the corruption in the IRS, were both already planning to leave their positions before any of the corrupt IRS actions had been disclosed. How stupid does the Obama administration think the American people are? The administration's attempt to pass off the departure of 2 bureaucrats, who were leaving the IRS anyway, as the heavy-handed blow inflicted upon the IRS to rectify their crimes is a joke! To add insult to injury, we learn that the woman who perpetrated the targeting of conservative groups by the IRS, will now be able to inflict untold misery upon the American people through the invasion of their privacy and the total control of their health care and the costs associated with that care. This is a game of **musical chairs** that lets one government bureaucrat off the hook for his over-reaching practices and rewards the other even more guilty party by promoting her to a position that gives her even more invasive power. Sarah Hall Ingram led the way to target conservative groups with outrageous invasion of privacy and denial of their most basic rights by the most powerful government agency in existence and she is rewarded with $125,000. in bonuses and a promotion to a position where she can inflict even more harm. This whole fiasco could be likened to a cheap "sleight of hand" trick.

Former IRS commissioner Steven Miller appeared before a House committee today and fielded some very tough questions. As would be expected, just like President Obama and Attorney General Eric Holder, Steven Miller either conveniently doesn't know or can't remember. The only thing he would admit to; is poor customer service. Interestingly, in the same hearing, Jay Russell George, Inspector General for the Treasury, testified that he alerted the General Council of the Treasury of the targeting of conservative groups on June 4th, 2012. Given the fact that the Treasury IG knew and the Deputy Treasury IG also knew about the targeting in June 2012, how could IRS commissioner Steven Miller for that matter Jack Lew, Secretary of the Treasury, not know? If they truly didn't know then that's an admission of incompetence and in the more likely scenario, if they did know then action should have been taken to immediately remedy the problem. Either way they dropped the ball big time!

During a very busy day in the House today, Congressmen found time to pass a measure for the 37th time to repeal Obama Care. I believe a very old adage is applicable here. "If at first you don't succeed, try try again!"

Free Press???

May 20, 2013

It became known today that Fox News Chief Washington Correspondent James Rosen has been under secret investigation by the DOJ. The effort to track the prominent reporter was part of the ongoing case against State Department security advisor, Stephen Jin-Woo Kim. The DOJ was tracking Rosen's every move inside the State Department by following scans with his government issued ID pass. The Fed's also gained access to Rosen's phone records and his personal e-mail account citing a court affidavit. The affidavit, includes a statement by FBI agent Reginald Reyes, alleging there was evidence that Rosen broke the law, "at the very least, as an aider abettor and/or co-conspirator." Fox News executive VP Michael Clemente responded today by saying, "We are outraged to learn today that James Rosen was named a criminal co-conspirator for simply doing his job as a reporter. In fact, it is downright chilling. We will unequivocally defend his right to operate as a member of what has been up until now a free press." In the past, it has been a common practice to investigate the source of a leak within the government but has never included the recipient of leaked information! We are now witnessing the **"criminalization of investigative journalism"** by the Obama administration. The Obama administration has prosecuted twice as many alleged "leakers" than all previous administrations combined.

Glen Greenwald, a reporter with the Guardian, a British newspaper, writes, "Under US law, it is not illegal to publish classified information. That fact, along with the First Amendment's guarantee of press freedoms is what has prevented the US government from ever prosecuting journalists for reporting on what the US government does in secret. This newfound theory of the Obama DOJ – that a journalist can be guilty of crimes for 'soliciting' the disclosure of classified information – is a means for circumventing those safeguards and criminalizing the act of investigative journalism itself." This creates a very scary environment that **silences sources** for fear of being monitored by the US government.

May 22, 2013

Lois Lerner, IRS head of tax-exempt organizations division, under subpoena to appear before the House oversight committee, did indeed plead the 5th today during her appearance. Prior to pleading the 5th, she insisted that, "I have not done anything wrong. I have not broken any laws. I have not violated any IRS rules or regulations and I have not provided false information to this or any other congressional committee." If this had been a court of law, her opening statement would have prevented her from pleading the 5th, but since this was a hearing before a legislative body, her attorney, William W. Taylor III, said that legality does not apply. There is strong disagreement about this assertion; therefore Ms. Lerner is not out of the woods yet. Congressman Darrell Issa is working with Congressional attorneys to re-call Ms. Lerner based on their belief that she did indeed waive her 5th amendment right by making statements that directly addressed the subject matter of the hearing as she appeared in front of the House committee before asserting her 5th amendment right. She was the IRS official who leaked and acknowledged the IRS wrongdoing at a legal conference on May 8th. Apparently, the White House had hoped that her statement would go largely unnoticed which would have enabled them to sweep the matter under the rug and move on. Thankfully this was not the case. Sarah Hall Ingram held the same position with the IRS as Ms. Lerner from 2009 until 2012. Holly Paz, Director of the office of rulings and agreements, and has served directly under Lois Lerner since May 2012, which oversees the determinations of tax-exempt organizations, was more directly involved in the corrupt actions of the IRS. Cindy Thomas, a program manager who directly answers to Holly Paz, was even more directly involved in this corruption. Holly Paz and Cindy Thomas should also be called to testify soon.

Former Commissioner of the IRS, Douglas Shulman, had made 157 visits to the White House while holding this position. In the past, an IRS Commissioner might normally visit the White House only 2 or 3 times, therefore 157 visits would be unheard of. On Tuesday 5/21, Shulman told a Senate committee that he didn't tell higher up's in the Treasury Department or members of Congress that he had learned in the Spring of 2012 that IRS workers had been improperly targeting conservative groups. Shulman, who stepped down in December 2012, said he wouldn't apologize for it and claimed no **direct** involvement. At this point we know about 2 previous IRS commissioners, 2 tax-exempt division heads, one previous and one current, one tax-exempt commissioner, due to retire on 6/3/13, one acting tax-exempt director, and one acting tax-exempt program manager who were all involved one way or another in the targeting of conservative groups with obvious political motives and none of them are coming forward with any pertinent information. They either say they don't know anything or won't talk period. In the words of Congressman Darrell Issa, "How could they be so dumb to not know so much?" It appears that Congress has only scratched the surface on this issue and that we have a long way to go to get to the bottom of this corruption.

May 23, 2013

Lois Lerner, acting head of the tax-exempt division of the IRS, was placed on **paid** administrative leave today. Ms. Lerner, who asserted her 5th amendment right to remain silent yesterday after making a statement of innocence, may be re-called to answer questions before the House oversight committee. If a judge rules that she waived her 5th amendment right when she made a statement which directly addressed the subject matter of the House oversight committee prior to taking the 5th and she then asserts the 5th again, she could go to jail.

May 28, 2013

A report came out today by Reuters that Attorney General Eric Holder personally approved a decision to subpoena Fox News telephone records for Chief Washington Correspondent James Rosen as the Justice Department investigated an unauthorized leak regarding North Korea. This directly contradicts Holder's testimony before the House Judiciary Committee on May 15th when he said he had never been involved in the potential prosecution of the press. The word **perjury** comes to mind. Eric Holder has a history of questionable testimony before Congress. His testimony regarding the New Black Panther's voter intimidation and the "Fast and Furious" gun running operation that resulted in the death of a U.S. border agent left plenty of unanswered questions due to contradictory testimony. Provided the Attorney General serves as an agent of misdirection which provides a buffer of protection for the President, I believe he will retain his position. This new development of alleged perjury has prompted a wave of speculation that it's time for Holder to step down. In a televised address, President Obama said he asked the Attorney General to investigate the allegations of misconduct within the Justice Department and to report back to him with his findings in July. It would be naïve to think that the Attorney General would investigate himself with any degree of accuracy but of course it would be inconvenient for the President to second guess his own direction. As always, the President has displayed great composure under fire while his underlying culture of intimidation is progressing with impunity.

An Arrogance of Power

Our government has shifted the polarity between America and countries around the world who oppose our freedoms to polarity between our government and the American people. While the Obama administration busily apologizes to foreign countries around the world, for what I don't know, they are actively attacking the American people at large with an agenda to remove our freedoms. Make no mistake; the American people are under attack. Americans who speak out against this tyranny find themselves under a microscope to instill fear in an intimidating effort to shut them up. Our government is out of control and is in the process of threatening all our basic civil liberties. Government officials at the highest levels claim ignorance when their corruption is exposed. If the President and the Attorney General don't know anything, then who does? They would prefer to look stupid as opposed to getting caught in a blatant lie or a criminal act or both. Our Constitution is being trampled on. There is an **arrogance of power** at work here which poses a serious threat to the American people! Our government already more closely resembles a third world communist country led by a dictator than a trusted democracy that serves at the behest of the American people. There is no precedent for the widespread corruption in the Obama administration. Corruption is the only common denominator that exists in the State Department, IRS, DOJ and the White House. Even though everything ultimately leads back to President Obama, he has strategically established several layers of protection throughout his administration. Attorney General Eric Holder is the glue that holds it all together. Holder had good reason to make a clean departure at the end of President Obama's 1st term but the President obviously convinced him to stick around. The President may find it necessary to throw Holder under the bus but that would be a last resort. The President will set up as many road blocks as he possibly can to buy time. Multiple scandals could become useful to keep investigations going in numerous directions or even in circles. All this juggling is very destructive because nothing good or productive can be accomplished with all this misdirection.

Chapter 6

In Your Face

President Obama appointed UN Ambassador Susan Rice today to succeed Tom Donilon as White House National Security Advisor. President Obama nominated White House aide Samantha Power to replace Rice as the U.S. Ambassador to the United Nations. The Rice appointment as White House National Security Advisor will not require Senate confirmation. The President had previously attempted to nominate Susan Rice as Secretary of State to replace Hillary Clinton but once it became obvious that the Senate would never confirm Rice to that position, she withdrew her nomination.

After the infamous Susan Rice tour on 5 Sunday News talk shows last September when she was appointed official White House liar to sell the lie that the deadly terrorist attack on the U.S. Diplomatic Mission in Benghazi, Libya was just a spontaneous outgrowth from protests to an anti-Muslim youtube.com video, she is being rewarded for her efforts with this new appointment as White House National Security Advisor. Suddenly I'm not feeling very secure!

I believe President Obama was enjoying every moment of the televised announcement today. This was his petty **"In Your Face"** way of sticking it to his Republican critics. The Presidents arrogance makes Richard Nixon look reserve. President Obama appears to be unconcerned over increasing criticism over the IRS targeting of conservatives, the DOJ's intimidation of journalists, or the ongoing scandal over the numerous unanswered questions surrounding Benghazi. Attorney General Eric Holder announced today during an NBC interview that he absolutely will not resign as Attorney General. This arrogant confidence on the part of the President and the Attorney General is in large part due to the huge **pass** they get from the main stream media and the large percentage of uninformed Americans.

They are free to continue their destructive actions with impunity and the blessing of the "lap dog" media. Of course, the widespread support from liberal Democrats in the House and Senate doesn't hurt. At this point, all we can expect from the President is more political posturing and lavish vacations.

NSA - National Spy Agency

The Washington Post and the Guardian reported today that a source with the NSA, National Security Agency, leaked information that a top-secret NSA program called **PRISM** exists for the collection of data directly from the servers of U.S. tech firms. They also reported that the NSA has been monitoring the phone calls of all Verizon customers (121 million people). Upon further investigation by several journalists from various media outlets, it became known that not only Verizon users were being monitored but also AT&T, Sprint, and Bell South were under surveillance. The NSA **PRISM** program collects data directly from the servers of Facebook, Google, You Tube, Paltalk, Yahoo, Apple, Skype, AOL, and Microsoft. Several denials have been made by these companies about granting "direct access" to servers. At this point, there is a lot more that we don't know about PRISM than we do. In addition to these internet providers, credit card companies and banks are also being watched. E-mails, Web searches, videos, phone calls, bank transfers and credit card transactions are all under surveillance by the NSA under a "cloak of secrecy." This is the most sophisticated and widespread spy operation in U.S. history and it's been under way for years. It all began under the Bush administration after 9/11. Keith Alexander, Director of the NSA, Chief of the Central Security Service, and Commander of the United States Cyber Command under the Bush administration, became known as the architect of high tech surveillance. The **USA PATRIOT Act** was passed by Congress and signed into law by President George W. Bush on September 26, 2001. The law allows for searches through which law enforcement officers search a home or business without the owner's or occupant's permission or knowledge; the expanded use of **National Security Letters** (demand letter in lieu of a subpoena), which allows the FBI to search telephone, e-mail, and financial records without a court order. On May 26, 2011, President Obama signed the **PATRIOT Sunsets Extension Act of 2011**, a four-year extension of 3 key provisions of the USA PATRIOT Act: roving wiretaps, searches of business records, and conducting surveillance of "lone wolves" - individuals suspected of terrorist activities not specifically linked to terrorist groups. Since its passage, several legal challenges have been brought against the act, and Federal Courts have ruled that many provisions are unconstitutional. Since the **4th Amendment** is the part **of the Bill of Rights** which guards against unreasonable searches and seizures, along with requiring any warrant to be judicially sanctioned and supported by probable cause, the **USA PATRIOT Act** does indeed appear to be unconstitutional but it was nevertheless signed into law.

Congressman Jim Sensenbrenner (R-WI) was the main author of the USA PATRIOT Act. He commented this week that the current level of surveillance far exceeds definitions set forth in the PATRIOT Act. At this point the consensus of Congress is that the Patriot Act by design, allows for investigation of suspected terrorists based on probable cause. Sensenbrenner said the USA PATRIOT Act was designed to prevent the NSA from data mining. Given this week's revelations, it appears that surveillance has progressed far beyond its original intention especially given NSA's **PRISM** program we just learned about. Surveillance has now progressed to what could be referred to as the **"Dark Side."** Data mining of phone records and the collection of **"Meta Data,"** the aggregation of bank transactions, roadway tolls, credit card purchases, and virtually everything we do that leaves a trail, is an attack on our civil liberties and a major violation of privacy. There is massive power in the collection of this amount of data. A government data storage facility is under construction in Utah which reportedly can hold up to 5 zettabytes of data or 5 Trillion gigabytes. The Utah Data Center in Bluffdale, UT. will be up and running this Fall.

The current Director of National Intelligence, James Clapper, appeared before the Senate Intelligence Committee on March 12th and denied allegations by panel members that the NSA conducted electronic surveillance and collected any data at all of Americans on U.S. soil. Intelligence collection by the CIA, the NSA or other agencies can be done inside the United States, but only if a special secret court created under the Foreign Intelligence and Surveillance Act (FISA court) approves the operation. The problem for those of us on the outside looking in is that the FISA court is a secret court that doesn't make its opinions public. It is obvious though that any court orders issued by the FISA court lack specificity. They are broad and vague designed to allow for the massive collection of data which is unconstitutional based on the 4th amendment.

President Obama, in a televised address today, said "We're going to have to make some choices." I was wondering if he had a mouse in his pocket, hence the reference to "we." I don't remember being consulted about the level of surveillance that now exists. He made no apologies for the widespread collection of data that we have just become aware of. He said he looks forward to having a national debate on this issue but the debate would take place after the fact. We weren't given any choice regarding the loss of our civil liberties. Interestingly, liberals appear to be more offended by this overreach than conservatives but members on both sides of the aisle have differing opinions among themselves. I found it interesting that so many lawmakers appeared to be so surprised by this revelation when they've surely known for some time the extent to which this practice has been exercised.

Since we're sacrificing all our privacy in the name of security, why don't I feel safe? Why didn't the NSA, CIA, or FBI utilize this vast array of data they've acquired to prevent the murder of 13 people and the injury of 30 people at Fort Hood by Major Nidal Hasan? Why wasn't it possible to prevent the Boston Marathon bombings where 4 people were murdered and 282 people injured by Tamerlan and Dzhokhar Tsarnaev? 17 deaths and 312 injuries should have been prevented if the appropriate government agencies were doing their job. Why collect all this data if it doesn't help prevent all terrorist attacks? We don't know that any attacks have been prevented and it appears that the massive amount of data at their disposal wasn't properly utilized in an intelligent manner in the case of the Fort Hood and Boston massacres. Intelligent profiling would be a most appropriate use of the data. If you look at the names of the 9/11 terrorists, the Fort Hood terrorist, and the Boston Marathon terrorists, a very good case can be made that every one of these terrorists are Muslims with names of Middle East decent. We even know that 15 of the 19 perpetrators of the 9/11 attack were Saudi's and all were Muslims. If the NSA, CIA, and FBI were to zero in on every Muslim in their massive data bank and focus intently on them, it wouldn't be out of line to suggest that every major terrorist attack could be prevented. Political correctness should go out the window in the war on terror not to mention every other aspect of our society it has a negative impact on. Millions of U.S. citizens could easily be ruled out as potential terrorists. Why must our government collect every intimate detail of data on innocent law abiding citizens under a cloak of secrecy? If 100% of the focus is directed at Muslims in America, I believe every terrorist attack on U.S. soil could be prevented. Every terrorist attack is related to Jihad! Defenders of the NSA's PRISM program site prevention of a terrorist plot targeting New York City's subway system. Najibullah Zazi, an Afghan-American living in Aurora, Colorado, was arrested in September 2009 before he could carry out his plan to bomb New York's subway. This was indeed a very important discovery which prevented what could have been a catastrophic attack. The prevention of this plot totally supports my assertion that the focus should be on Muslims in America. Unfortunately, President Obama is determined to protect Muslims in America. Since October of 2011, the FBI has been forbidden to covertly gather information or set up sting operations at **Mosques** unless they've been reviewed and approved by the Sensitive Operations Review Committee of the DOJ. The existence of this top-secret DOJ committee is an insult to all American citizens. We've all heard vague references about the politically correct police and now we see they do exist within the DOJ. If the President is so concerned about national security, why would he prevent the investigation of Mosques which would be the most likely place we would uncover terrorist plots? This is an outrage that very few Americans are even aware of. This ridiculous politically correct concern over offending Muslims is ludicrous. I've never heard of any concern that Christians may be offended by the constant barrage of attacks upon traditional Christian values in our country.

We should follow the example set by Australia where Muslims are not catered to. Australian government leaders have made it abundantly clear that Muslims must assimilate to Australian Christian values or leave. They have the freedom to leave Australia and they most assuredly have the same freedom to leave the United States. They can go and live in a Muslim country in the Middle East. The fact is though they don't want to leave. They like living in America or Australia because our modern infrastructure makes for a very comfortable standard of living but they want us to assimilate to their religion and their culture. American government doesn't have the courage or the good sense to issue the same ultimatum to Muslims as Australia does. It isn't necessary to make ourselves a door mat to be walked all over and it's a mystery to me why we do.

The entire premise and justification for the broad sweeping collection of data is to protect Americans from terrorist attacks. The USA PATRIOT Act was passed by Congress and signed into law just over a month after the 9/11 terrorist attack on New York City and it was common knowledge at the time that this was unconstitutional legislation. Now we learn that the NSA under the Obama administration has expanded the collection of data to an extraordinarily extreme extent under the guise of National security but their overall actions contradict their stated objective. The President has gone to great lengths to send the message that the war on terror is over. The Obama administration won't even call the Fort Hood terrorist murders an act of Islamic Jihad. Workplace violence doesn't begin to define Nidal Hasan's evil act of Islamic Jihad. If President Obama is so concerned about obtaining information to prevent terrorist attacks, why did he do away with enhanced interrogation and try repeatedly to shut down Gitmo? If the Obama administration is so concerned about protecting Americans, why did they reduce security for our American citizens in Benghazi and give a stand down order to Navy Seals in both Benghazi and Tripoli plus assets in Aviano, Italy and Rota, Spain who could have made it in time to make a big difference during the attack on the CIA annex in Benghazi and then lie to cover it up?

If this broad sweeping surveillance and collection of data by the NSA had become widely known prior to the revelations of IRS targeting of conservative groups, wasteful spending by the IRS on conferences, DOJ secret surveillance of reporters, and the Benghazi cover up, it may not have been so controversial but everything is adding up to an erosion of **trust**. Even the left leaning New York Times reported today that "the Obama administration has lost all credibility on this issue," this issue being the NSA's widespread surveillance. The Obama administration has indeed lost all credibility. This administration has shown time and time again that administration officials are not subject to accountability. The arrogance of power and culture of intimidation that exists in this administration has led to big government tyranny. It is indeed a sad state of affairs.

June 9, 2013

The Guardian published the identity of the NSA whistleblower who turned over top secret NSA documents that revealed the NSA's secret surveillance programs to the Washington Post and the Guardian. **Edward Snowden**, is currently employed by Booz Allen Hamilton Inc., an American consulting firm engaged in providing management and consulting services to the United States government and commercial services. Snowden's salary is $122,000. annually but he has only worked for Booz Allen Hamilton Inc. for 3 months. Snowden is a 29-year old former CIA technical assistant who recently fled to Hong Kong from his current home in Hawaii and came forward on his own volition. The Guardian reported that "Snowden will go down in history as one of the world's most consequential whistleblowers." Snowden said, "I carefully evaluated every single document I disclosed to ensure that each was legitimately in the public interest. There are all sorts of documents that would have made a big impact that I didn't turn over, because harming people isn't my goal. Transparency is. I'm willing to sacrifice all of that because I can't in good conscience allow the U.S. government to destroy privacy, internet freedom and basic liberties for people around the world with this massive surveillance machine they're secretly building." Snowden wisely ascertained that he would surely be tracked down and prosecuted under the Espionage Act so he immediately left the country. Hong Kong may not have been a good choice because Hong Kong has an extradition treaty with the United States. One would think China would be very interested to meet with him to pick his brain to learn what they can but Snowden does contend he didn't release anything that could negatively impact U.S. interests.

Given this critical leak of confidential government information, it begs the question of why does the NSA farm out the execution of top secret programs to an outside contractor? Over 500,000 outside contractors (individuals) have U.S. government top secret clearance. This doesn't appear to be a wise practice, although another school of thought could suggest that our huge "big government" bureaucracy is incompetent to handle such extensive surveillance and data collection on their own. On the other hand, individuals who work directly for the NSA may not be trustworthy either. These individuals should be vetted in either case but the vetting process could potentially break down. For what was thought to be one of the world's most top secret agencies, their practices certainly aren't very top secret now. President Obama is hopelessly confused and knows nothing of leadership. All of this also takes us back to the trust issue. The loss of trust in the U.S. government is the worst-case scenario and the Obama administration bears responsibility in large part because they know nothing of accountability. Now that trust is out the window, one must wonder how are we going to get the toothpaste back in the tube?

When this so called incriminating national-security leak is broken down, basically the information that was revealed isn't specific regarding any actual acquired intelligence. The only thing that was revealed is the fact that vast amounts of data is being collected from every conceivable source. No details or actual information was revealed about any specific top secret operation. It's not as though the names of CIA operatives working undercover anywhere in the world or the nature of any top-secret operation anywhere was revealed. When you consider the fact that Osama bin Laden knew years ago, that any form of electronic or phone communication was a bad idea, he was basically working under the assumption that any data that could be tracked **is** being collected. The only form of communication that he utilized was passed along through a communication mule who could deliver any given message in person. Why would we think the recent leaked information would be an astounding new revelation? Terrorist groups such as al-Qaeda are already taking precautions against using communication forms that can be tracked. The only problem I can detect is that huge amounts of data unrelated to terrorism is being collected by our government and law abiding U.S. citizens who reside in the United States are the target. We weren't supposed to find out that our most basic constitutional rights are being trampled on. The 4th amendment and the USA PATRIOT Act clearly require probable cause and a **specific** court order. Our government wanted us to continue in our blissful ignorance while they fill the Utah Data Center with every conceivable bit of data on all Americans. America could easily become a totalitarian state overnight. That may not be the objective today but one day we could be informed that the loss of all our rights has become necessary.

Now that we have a better idea of the extent to which the government is collecting data on us, it's clear that James Clapper, Director of National Intelligence, committed perjury during his testimony before the Senate Intelligence committee on March 12th. When Senator Ron Wyden asked Clapper if the NSA collected any data at all on millions of Americans, Clapper replied, "No Sir..., not wittingly. There are cases where they could, inadvertently perhaps, collect; but not wittingly." Instead of denying the NSA's data collection program, he should have responded by reminding the committee members that if he were to answer the question he would be revealing top secret information. Clapper's body language was quite revealing as he was scratching the top of his forehead in a very nervous manner while his head was dropped to avoid eye contact while lying to the Senate. After his March 12th outright lie, Clapper responded today to NBC news that, "I thought, though in retrospect, I was asked (a) 'when are you going to....stop beating your wife' kind of question, which is....not answerable necessarily by a simple yes or no. So, I responded in what I thought was the most truthful, or least untruthful, manner by saying, 'No'. And again, going back to my metaphor, what I was thinking of is looking at the Dewey Decimal numbers of those books in the metaphorical library. To me collection of U.S. persons' data would mean taking the books off the shelf, opening it up and reading it." What a convoluted mess of gibberish designed to cover his tracks! A statement from Senator Wyden today lamented that Senators weren't getting "straight answers to direct questions." This extreme understatement doesn't even come close to defining Director Clapper's evasive and false rhetoric.

June 10, 2013

The IRS announced today that Holly Paz, director of the office of rulings and agreements for the tax-exempt organizations division of the IRS, was relieved of her responsibilities in her present capacity. Paz had answered directly to Lois Lerner since May 2012. No mention was made about where she is being moved. Lois Lerner and Holly Paz were most directly involved in the targeting of conservative groups for denial of their requests for tax-exempt status. Lois Lerner is on paid vacation and I think it's safe to assume that Holly Paz will land on her feet most likely with a promotion. The Obama administration has a track record of rewarding those who successfully carry out their marching orders especially when it entails questionable practices that serve to advance the politically correct liberal progressive agenda of President Obama.

June 11, 2013

The ACLU filed suit against the U.S. government today citing the unconstitutional broad sweeping surveillance and data collection by the NSA on American citizens. Their law suit is correctly based on the government's blatant disregard for the 4th amendment. The ACLU complaint demands that this practice will end and all existing data be destroyed. The NSA is indiscriminately collecting data on citizens with FISA court orders which lack specificity. These are vague and general court orders with no specific details that would describe the justification for the court order. The FISA court has been around since the Carter administration but it became highly invasive once the USA PATRIOT Act became law.

"I don't know"

June 14, 2013

FBI director Robert Mueller appeared before the House Judiciary Committee today. His testimony could be characterized similarly to other Obama administration officials whose statements before Congressional hearings generally revolve around, **"I don't know."** Robert Mueller followed the lead of Hillary Clinton, Eric Holder, Barak Obama, Douglas Shulman, Steven Miller, Lois Lerner and James Clapper, all of whom didn't know much of anything regarding Benghazi, IRS targeting of conservatives, DOJ intimidation of journalists and NSA unconstitutional surveillance. Apparently, it's too inconvenient to manufacture **spin**. It's so much easier to just say, "I don't know." The Obama administration has epitomized oversimplification when it comes to **CYA**. Robert Mueller testified he couldn't even answer who the lead investigator is in the IRS investigation. He knew so little about an IRS investigation that supposedly began 2 weeks ago, that one must wonder if an investigation is under way. The only conclusion that can be drawn from these apparently ill-informed officials is that they're either **incompetent** or **corrupt**. Neither conclusion bodes well for the Obama administration. President Obama has been missing in action as of late. We haven't heard from him directly since his brief statement regarding massive data collection by the NSA on June 7th.

Summer Vacation

With all the controversy swirling around one scandal after another, President Obama has decided it's time for **summer vacation**. He's decided not only to leave the country but apparently a very remote destination is in order. Tanzania, Africa is not only of the country, it's very remote. The timing couldn't be better for the President. With so many scandals, I'm sure he figures Africa is a good place to hide even if it's only for a couple of weeks. We've seen that throughout President Obama's Presidency, he has an aversion to budgets. For the President, a budget is just one more inconvenience whether it applies to the entire country or to a Presidential vacation. This one is Presidential to the tune of $60 to $100 million dollars but who's counting. President Obama surely isn't. I learned today that a Presidential vacation to Tanzania, Africa requires 66 vehicles, 14 of which are limousines. The Transportation Secretary was probably consulted on that decision. It's an outrage that the 1st family is taking this ridiculously extravagant vacation when not a single family in the United States can tour the White House on their summer vacation. It's terribly unjust when the American people aren't allowed to tour the people's house but the 1st family is selfishly spending $100 million for 2 weeks of summer vacation. With a National debt of $16.9 trillion, this is extremely irresponsible behavior by President Obama but when did he ever let irresponsible behavior slow him down.

IRS Bonuses

June 19, 2013

Daniel Werfel, IRS commissioner, just approved $70 million in bonuses for IRS employees. Apparently, it pays to target conservatives and waste taxpayer dollars on extravagant employee conferences. All bonus payments were supposed to be discontinued due to Sequester spending cuts but Commissioner Werfel says the IRS is legally bound to issue the bonuses due to contracts with the National Treasury Employees Union and added that they are acting under guidance from the White House Office of Management and Budget. So far, the IRS appears to be bullet proof as it applies to their illegal and irresponsible actions. Lois Lerner and Holly Paz receive paid vacations and share in the IRS bonuses after illegally targeting Tea Party groups who had appropriately applied for tax exempt status. Obviously fiscal responsibility is not a priority for the Obama administration.

State Department Corruption

Aurelia Fedenisn, a former investigator in the State Department's Office of Inspector General, recently came forth with claims that Secretary of State Hillary Clinton helped cover up misconduct that occurred in the department during her tenure. Ms. Fedenisn was the whistleblower who brought forth an internal departmental memo that indicated recent investigations into misconduct within the State Department had been influenced, manipulated or simply called off despite the egregious nature of some of the alleged acts. One dropped investigation focused on allegations that members of Hillary Clinton's security detail engaged with prostitutes during "official trips to foreign countries." Another dropped investigation dealt with accusations about a drug ring facilitated by the U.S. Embassy in Baghdad that supplied U.S. contractors with illegal drugs. Ms. Fedenisn, said through her attorney that in the days following her testimony, investigators from the OIG, Office of the Inspector General, have gone to her home and interviewed her children, one of whom is a minor, without her presence. The investigators asked her children for her current place of employment and for a contact phone number. They then sat in front of her home in parked cars for hours. This serves as one more example of the "Chicago style" intimidation that is so very prevalent throughout the Obama administration.

Amnesty – Round 1

June 20, 2013

The immigration bill (Amnesty bill) is close to passage in the Senate. Once again, several establishment Republicans have taken the bait and are about to support this terrible unconstitutional bill. Establishment Republicans will never learn their lesson. How many times have Democrats baited Republicans with spending cuts if they will just agree to increase taxes first? Taxes go up and spending goes up too because when push comes to shove on spending cuts neither side of the aisle really wants to follow through. The whole scenario seems like a charade. This time Democrats are making a hollow promise to secure the southern border if Republicans will agree to amnesty first. This bill began with 847 pages and now has about 1200 pages. I would bet anything that the vulnerable Republicans who are going to support this ridiculous bill haven't even read it yet. Senator Harry Reid, Senate majority leader, is attempting to rush it through before anyone decides it might be a good idea to read it. The bill is loaded with pork such as $100 million to the State of Nevada to promote tourism. Senator Reid from Nevada is a low life, bought and paid for, politician.

Congress didn't read the 2700-page Affordable Care Act either but they passed the worst law in the history of America with the help of the Supreme Court who forgot they are not a legislative branch of government. Democrats have convinced this gullible group of Republicans that the GOP will meet its demise at the hands of Hispanic Americans if they don't pass this bill. I've got news for them. Hispanics weren't going to vote Republican anyway. The border security proviso to this bill will never happen anyway because neither side of the aisle really wants to secure the border. This bill is another disaster waiting to happen. All we need is another disaster on top of the disastrous Affordable Care Act. The Senate immigration bill is so bad it's not fixable. Republicans justification for supporting this sham bill is that the border will be secure which is just a lame attempt to make themselves look good. It doesn't matter how many border agents are placed along the border. Janet Napolitano, Secretary of Homeland Security, and President Obama will order all of them to stand down and welcome illegals to America. Article 4 Section 4 of the Constitution doesn't mean anything to the Obama administration. If this bill doesn't die in the House we will have another fiasco on our hands.

Reality Check

President Obama has now officially lost touch with reality. The President announced today that he will issue an executive order to address climate change. He spoke today as if he was single handedly saving the world. He specifically cited the Keystone XL pipeline as being a major contributor to global warming. The Presidents green energy initiative will cause energy bills to increase significantly. President Obama's thinking borders on insanity. Global warming is the least significant issue of our time. It isn't even settled science. Even if America were to make some slight decrease in carbon emissions it wouldn't even put a dent in carbon emission reduction worldwide. The Presidents total focus is on climate change, nuclear arms reduction, amnesty for illegals, gun control, and socialized medicine. These are not the issues that Americans are concerned with. Jobs and the economy are the predominate issues on the minds of all Americans but the President is doing everything possible to kill job creation, create a decline in prosperity and basically ruin the economy. The Presidents executive order will strike a terrible blow to the coal mining industry in West Virginia. The entire West Virginia economy is dependent on coal and when miners there lose their jobs they have nothing to fall back on. Obama Care alone will strike a deadly blow to the economy and now the coal industry will suffer a double blow.

The President is a joke among the world's leaders. President Obama is perceived as weak internationally not only among world leaders but also among the world population. The Presidents cat and mouse chase over NSA leaker Edward Snowden has become a chaotic disaster. Vladimir Putin thumbed his nose at the President today when he blatantly said Russia will not even consider extradition for Snowden. President Obama is an international embarrassment. The President's approval rating is at its lowest in his political career. Only 49% of Americans approve of the Presidents performance. President Obama is in dire need of a **reality check.**

June 26, 2013

DOMA gone

Today is a sad day for traditional marriage. A Supreme Court ruling today struck down DOMA, the Defense of Marriage Act, by ruling that same sex married couples are eligible to receive the same federal benefits as traditional married couples in the 12 States that have legalized same sex marriage. In addition, if a gay married couple moves to a state where same sex marriage is not legal, they will still receive their federal benefits. After ruling that Obama Care is a tax, therefore making it legal for Congress to force it on the American people, and now ruling to provide federal benefits to same sex married couples, the Supreme Court has become a political entity. Instead of interpreting existing law, the Supreme Court is now using loopholes to legislate from the bench based on their political agenda. Now all 3 branches of government are trampling all over the Constitution. Our Founding Fathers are surely turning in their graves!

IRS Corruption

IRS Deputy Director of Acquisitions, Greg Roseman, appeared today before the House Oversight and Government Reform committee and invoked the 5th amendment when asked about his relationship with Braulio Castillo, president of Washington based "Strong Castle, Inc." The Deputy Director of Acquisitions office awarded contracts potentially worth over $500 million to "Strong Castle." This was the largest contract awarded in IRS history. Castillo and Roseman met in 2003 and were close friends. "Strong Castle" had become eligible for government contracts set aside for disabled veterans and for small businesses in economically disadvantaged communities. Castillo acknowledged submitting false records to the SBA. Castillo twisted his ankle in 1984 while playing football at the U.S. Military Academy Preparatory School which he attended for one year. When applying to the Veterans Affairs Department for the "set aside program" for disabled veterans, he said his injuries were "crosses that I bear due to my service to our great country." Castillo's only connection to the military was his one year at the U.S. Military Academy Preparatory School. He later went on to play softball and college football. Castillo also rented an office in Washington's Chinatown while working and living with his wife in the "wealthy Virginia suburbs." Greg Roseman is still working in his current position for the IRS. Lois Lerner and Greg Roseman have both invoked the 5th amendment in recent Congressional hearings and both are still on the IRS payroll. Lois Lerner is still receiving full pay while on extended vacation. It appears we have only scratched the surface on corruption in the IRS.

Amnesty – Round 2

June 27, 2013

The Senate immigration bill passed today with a vote of 68 to 32 with 14 Republicans in favor. The bill will now go on to thankfully die in the House where House members will draft their own immigration bill. Speaker John Boehner will not even bring the Senate bill up for a vote in the House. This bill allows for the Executive branch to veto border security measures. Why would DHS director, Janet Napolitano, support any increased border security when she is on record as having said the border is totally secure now? The liberal reasoning for this is to force big government to get even bigger. They'll just allow the new illegals to legally work along with the existing illegal population and then begin supporting them with taxpayer funded entitlements.

The Senate bill also places limits on the number of agriculture work visas which will result in more illegal workers. Under Obama Care, if employers who employ more than 50 workers don't provide health insurance for full time employees, they must pay a $2000. penalty unless that employee is a foreign worker who recently gained legal status to work, in which case there is no penalty. This is stunning when you do the math. If all 11 million illegals who are already here are suddenly given legal status to work and they are all hired instead of the same number of American citizens; that would represent $220 billion in savings for American employers! It's bad enough that millions of workers won't receive employer provided health insurance because the penalty costs employers less than the coverage under Obama Care, but since the $2000. penalty isn't imposed on employers for foreign workers with legal work status, American citizens most likely wouldn't be hired in the first place. The Senate immigration bill doesn't even allow for any additional ICE, immigration and customs enforcement, agents who must monitor the United States plus Puerto Rico and Guam. The 5000 existing ICE agents must monitor 30 million existing green card holding immigrants in addition to dealing with the 11 million plus illegal aliens who would receive legal status to work based on the Senate immigration bill. ICE agents would then be responsible for dealing with 41 million foreign workers who would have legal work status plus all the new illegals who will begin flooding into the country. The Senate immigration bill doesn't even address illegals with 3 or more criminal offenses on record, so they would also immediately receive legal work status. This so-called comprehensive immigration bill is just a sham that is so completely flawed it's embarrassing. The House won't do any better so all of this is just a complete waste of time and taxpayer dollars.

IRS Arrogance

June 28, 2013

Daniel Werfel, interim IRS chief, appeared yesterday before the House Ways and Means Committee after submitting a report blaming management failures but saying he had no evidence of intentional wrongdoing by anyone inside or outside the agency. Members of the committee blasted Werfel saying his report is outrageous and worthless. The House Oversight Committee passed a resolution today by a vote of 22 to 17 which found that senior IRS official Lois Lerner waived her 5th amendment constitutional right to remain silent by making multiple statements claiming innocence prior to invoking the 5th. The resolution means that the committee's subpoena remains in effect. A date was not set for Lerner to appear before the committee again but it is widely assumed that she will once again invoke the 5th in which case she could be found in contempt of Congress and her case could proceed to a federal court. In the meantime, Lerner is still on paid vacation. Accountability is so elusive within the Obama administration that Lois Lerner will never answer for her corrupt practices at the IRS. President

Obama's DOJ will find a way to let her off the hook and she'll ride off into the sunset having successfully completed her hit job on conservatives.

Chapter 7

Politics as Usual

July 3, 2013

The White House announced today that the employer mandate for Obama Care will be delayed until January 2015. Businesses with 50 or more employees can now hold off until January 2015 before they must provide Obama Care Health Insurance for full time employees who work 30 hours or more a week. The delay of this mandate will prolong the need to either pay the $2000. penalty per employee if Obama Care health insurance is not provided for full time workers or provide expensive Obama Care health insurance for full time workers. This provision for Obama Care will have the greatest negative impact on the highest number of American workers because businesses will either choose not to provide health insurance coverage in which case employees will be forced to obtain Obama Care health insurance from the exchanges at their own expense or small businesses will establish a ceiling of 49 employees in which case they will fire existing employees to get down to 49. When the employer mandate goes into effect, all workers will have less take home pay if they even manage to keep their job. Small business is literally the backbone of the American economy and it isn't fair to place small business employers and employees in limbo for another year. The uncertainty is truly scary for both employers and employees. The nationwide negative economic impact will be huge once we get deeper into implementation.

The greater concern regarding this change is that it was initiated and carried out exclusively by executive action. This is unconstitutional! The legislative branch of government exists to either change existing law or to create new law. A unilateral change to existing law by the White House without involvement by Congress or the Supreme Court is unconstitutional. The merits of this recent change are not at issue. It makes no difference if it is perceived as good or bad. The problem lies in the fact that **King Obama** just unilaterally changed an existing law without Congressional involvement, not to mention the fact that his motivation is political. This is a blatant abuse of power! If this action goes unchallenged it sets a very scary precedent!

It's incredibly obvious that this was a political move by the Obama administration to postpone the negative fallout of the business mandate until after the 2014 mid-term Congressional elections. Democrats had been very worried about their re-election chances prior to the delay. Good things rarely get delayed. Everything about Obama Care is **political**. The law itself fulfills President Obama's political agenda to establish socialized medicine. The lie that this law would be a good thing was political. The Supreme Court ruling to uphold Obama Care as law was political and now the delay of the business mandate is political.

Bait and Switch

Implementation of the individual mandate is still scheduled for January 2014. There could still be impactful political fallout once the worst law in history goes into effect for individuals on January 1st. When employers and individuals would rather pay a penalty than deal with this terrible law, it's obvious that it's bad. In addition, when the President delay's implementation of the business mandate by one year to dodge the political fallout for Democrats in the upcoming mid-term elections, it's an admission that he knows it's bad. The collection of penalties will be the major source of revenue for Obama Care and that won't be nearly enough to support it. The basic premise of this law as set forth early on by President Obama could easily be characterized as a **"bait and switch."** The President deceitfully said the law wouldn't cost the taxpayer a penny. The CBO, Congressional Budget Office, has maintained that certain provisions of the law will provide the necessary revenue to sustain it. The CBO went so far as to claim the law would lower the budget deficit over time which couldn't be further from the truth. Apparently, the CBO is in on the "bait and switch" plan. The monetary burden was designed to be placed upon corporate America but this doesn't relieve the burden placed upon those who don't receive employer provided health insurance. Obama Care is all about income re-distribution. It was mathematically impossible to support from the outset but most Americans including most politicians didn't bother to do the math. The Politicians didn't even read the bill. Obama Care will eventually implode due to its unsustainable structure. Every time the American people think they've heard the worst of this law, they find there's more bad news to come.

The System Worked

July 12, 2013

Janet Napolitano announced today that she will step down as Secretary of Homeland Security in September to become President of the University of California which consists of 10 campuses including Berkeley. Napolitano, at the behest of President Obama, has played down the terrorist threat to America. Instead of speaking about the "war on terror," she would reference "man caused disasters" and any notion to reference Islamic Jihad is totally out of the question. The DHS under Napolitano's watch became a breeding ground for political correctness. As the head of DHS, the irony of her politically correct demeanor is inescapable given the fact that DHS solely exists to fight the war on terror. She is famous for her well known quote, **"The system worked,"** which she said in an interview with CNN's Candy Crowley after the failed attempt by Umar Farouk Abdulmutallab to blow up Northwest Airlines flight 253 on Christmas day 2009. Umar became well known as the "underwear bomber" due to the explosive device in his underwear that thankfully failed to explode so it was luck that saved lives that day as opposed to the system which failed. Napolitano later backed up on her initial claim and admitted that the system failed. She has also made claims that the southern border is secure. After a statement like that she has been the target of stiff criticism by conservatives. It was clear throughout her reign that President Obama micromanages DHS policy. It really won't matter who the President appoints as the next DHS head because he will continue to call the shots. After Fort Hood and the Boston Marathon bombing, the effectiveness of the DHS is questionable.

The Race Card

July 16, 2013

Liberals who love to play **the race card** are at it again. Al Sharpton, Jesse Jackson, and the NAACP have been working overtime since the "not guilty" verdict came down in the State of Florida vs. George Zimmerman murder trial. Heaven forbid they let a good crisis go to waste. Sharpton, Jackson, and the NAACP activists forced the excessive media attention for this trial that not only was undeserving of the overexposure it received but never should have gone to trial. The President even used the trial as an opportunity to re-ignite the gun control issue. President Obama went as far as to say that if he had a son he would have looked like Travon Martin who died as the result of the confrontation with Zimmerman. Attorney General Eric Holder has inappropriately fanned the flames of controversy surrounding the not guilty verdict by speaking out today at an NAACP convention in Orlando Florida. Holder is a political activist masquerading as Attorney General. He spoke out against the "stand your ground" law that exists in Florida which had absolutely no relevance regarding the verdict in the Zimmerman case. The Zimmerman defense was based solely on "Self Defense" and never cited the "stand your ground" law which states that individuals have no obligation to retreat from a confrontation and can also use deadly force if deemed necessary. Eric Holder said today that he had "the talk" with his son about life for a young black man in America which basically cautions that he will be discriminated against because he is black. AG Holder and President Obama have conveniently overlooked the fact that the FBI spent over a year conducting an in-depth investigation on the Zimmerman case and found no proof of racial profiling on George Zimmerman's part. Now Holder wants the DOJ to open yet another investigation attempting to bring federal charges against George Zimmerman by alleging he committed a "hate crime." The Obama administration never fails to play the race card to perpetrate racial tensions in America. It's a liberal ploy designed to elevate emotion on any number of issues even when race has nothing to do with an issue.

Sleeping Giant

Labor unions have finally awakened to the downside of Obama Care for union workers and they are emphatically speaking out. They've finally discovered that non-union workers will receive better health care benefits at a lower cost under Obama Care than union workers. Union workers with employer sponsored coverage don't qualify for health care subsidies issued by the exchanges. Multi-employer plans, also called Taft-Hartley plans, are health insurance benefits typically arranged between a labor union in a specific industry and small employers in that industry. About 20 million union works are covered under these Taft-Hartley health insurance plans. Obama Care regulatory changes to the small-group insurance market will drive up the cost of these plans. Small employers now have a more financially attractive alternative, which is to drop coverage and put people on the exchanges, once the existing collective bargaining agreements are up. That gives workers less reason to join a union. A big part of why working people pay union dues is because unions play a big role in negotiating health benefits.

Representatives of three of the nation's largest unions penned a letter to Harry Reid and Nancy Pelosi last week, warning that Obama Care would "shatter not only our hard-earned health benefits, but destroy the foundation of the 40-hour work week that is the backbone of the American middle class." Authors of the letter are James P. Hoffa, general president of the International Brotherhood of Teamsters; Joseph Hansen, International President of the United Food and Commercial Workers International Union; and Donald D. Taylor, President of UNITE-HERE, a union representing hotel, airport, food service, gaming and textile workers. These labor leaders are now demanding that their workers with employer-sponsored coverage also gain access to Obama Care subsidies. Without access to health care subsidies they claim their workers will be "relegated to second-class status" despite being "taxed to pay for those subsidies," a result that will "make non-profit plans like ours unsustainable" and "destroy the very health and wellbeing of our members along with millions of other hardworking Americans." Labor leaders are finally pointing out that President Obama pledged "if you like your plan, you can keep your plan," but as many before them have realized, this was a blatant lie.

It appears that labor unions are really setting the stage to negotiate for another major concession. Initial complaints by labor unions yielded an exemption from the 40% excise tax on individual plans costing $8900. or more annually and family plans costing $24,000. or more annually until Jan.1st 2018. It's evident that labor leaders are elevating the level of their complaints as they seek additional concessions. Labor unions played a major role in the passage of Obama Care. They spent a lot of money electing Democrats to Congress in 2006 and 2008, and fought hard to push the Affordable Care Act through the legislature in 2009 and 2010. Thanks to their efforts the rest of us are forced to suffer through this terrible law that we've known all along would be the worst law ever passed in the history of the United States. Labor union workers and leaders should be forced to take the medicine they so desperately wanted.

July 18, 2013

President Obama made a televised speech from the White House today in defense of Obama Care. The President blamed Republicans in the House for the results of a recent poll that revealed 66% of Americans are worried about Obama Care. He cited California, Oregon, and Washington as 3 states who have embraced the Affordable Care Act with full support. He said that "health insurance costs have been reduced by 50%" in these states." I thought to myself; did he seriously just say that? The facts are that insurance premiums have **increased** by 42 to 61% in California, 27 to 55% in Oregon, and 39% in Washington. He failed to mention that insurance premiums are up by 88% in Ohio and 72% in Indiana. The Presidents bold promise that insurance premiums for a family of four would go down on average by $2500. annually not only did not come to pass but premiums have **increased** by $2000. annually for a family of four since 2010 and that number will continue to rise. At this point 58% of registered voters in America want to see the repeal of Obama Care. The President spoke about rebates that insurance companies must pay to consumers under Obama Care when he pointed out that insurance companies must utilize at least 80% of the value of paid premiums for administrative costs and if that doesn't occur a rebate must be paid to the consumer. He cited one family who received a check for $136.00 and another who received a whopping $360.00 rebate. He failed to mention that beginning Jan. 1st, 2014, the excise tax that goes into effect at that time will effectively offset any small rebate that consumers may receive. It's obvious that President Obama will continue to beat this dead horse for the remainder of his 2nd term and beyond!

IRS targeting of Tea Party groups

The House Oversight and Government Reform committee questioned two more IRS employees in a hearing today as a part of their ongoing investigation of unfair targeting of Tea Party and other conservative groups who had applied for tax-exempt status. Carter Hull, a now retired 48 year veteran IRS senior attorney and tax law specialist, testified that he was told to send documents on Tea Party applications to the office of Chief Counsel, led by William Wilkins, as well as to an advisor for Lois Lerner, then head of the IRS tax-exempt office. At an August 2011 meeting, Hull said, someone from the chief counsel's office said additional information was needed from Tea Party applicants that Hull was dealing with, and that a second letter should be sent out requesting more information. Hull said during his testimony that the multi-level layer of review was "unusual." IRS Chief Counsel, William Wilkins, is a Presidential appointee who was nominated in April 2009 by President Obama.

Elizabeth Hofacre, a specialist in the IRS Cincinnati office, said "Tea Party groups got caught up in an atypical process in which lawyers in Washington controlled every step of the process." Hofacre testified, "I was frustrated because of what I perceived as micromanagement with respect to these applications." She said she was never able to close the cases as she awaited guidance from the IRS technical unit in Washington. "It was like working in lost luggage," she said. "I could never give applicants a clear answer."

House Oversight Committee Chairman, Darrell Issa (R-CA.) and Congressman Jason Chaffetz (R-UT.), have indicated officials will be looking at the IRS Chief Counsel's office next as their investigation continues.

Shameful

July 19, 2013

President Obama made a surprise appearance at a White House press briefing today to address controversy surrounding the "not guilty" verdict in the George Zimmerman case. It's bad enough that the media blew this case out of proportion and made it a racial issue when race had nothing to do with the situation, but for the President of the United States to even comment on it was outrageous. He attempted to give the impression of a desire to have a calming effect on the situation but he did nothing but elevate the controversy with remarks like, "If a white male teen was involved in the same kind of scenario that, from top to bottom, that both the outcome and the aftermath might have been different." He also questioned, "If Travon was of age and armed could he have stood his ground?" Liberal Democrats continue to attack the "Stand your Ground" law in Florida when it had nothing to do with the Zimmerman case. The Zimmerman defense was based solely on "Self Defense" and never referenced the Florida "Stand Your Ground" law. President Obama also said, "Travon Martin could have been me 35 years ago." The President said the nation needs to do some "Soul Searching." It looks like Hispanics like George Zimmerman don't qualify for racial consideration. After making his comments, the President made a quick exit without taking any questions from the White House Press Corp. This kind of political pandering for the benefit of liberal Democrats is totally inappropriate for the President of the United States and does nothing to ease racial tensions in America. President Obama was racially divisive in this action and fell far below the integrity that should be displayed and acted out by the President of the United States. His actions today were irresponsible, ignorant and **shameful**!

Phony Scandals???

July 24, 2013

The President delivered a long-winded speech today at Knox College in Galesburg, Illinois. Those who endured the full hour of the same empty rhetoric President Obama has espoused over the years were either sorry they wasted their time or for the dwindling die hard Obama supporters; they were propped up with more unsubstantiated "feel good" economics. Those who devoted a full hour of their life listening to this meaningless speech will never get that time back. That time would have been better spent bowling. I followed enough of it to write this segment and only found one highlight worthy of mention. The President lamented about, "an endless parade of distractions, political posturing and **phony scandals**." Apparently White House Press Secretary Jay Carney (Obama's paid liar) was instructed to utilize the same rhetoric about phony scandals which he spoke of in his comments on today's speech. There must be a calculation to measure how many gullible uninformed Americans there are who believe this stuff which becomes the deciding factor in determining if it's a good idea to incorporate such BS in a major speech. The calculation must factor in how many times President Obama must repeat a lie to get people to believe it. The President knows the scandals are real, hence the need for misdirection.

This speech offered no action plan and no details to support one hour of the same directionless and aimless rhetoric. That's the good news. The bad news is that the President is on the road and will make 5 more speeches like this one very soon. Surely there could be a more productive use of the Presidents time than spending taxpayer money to fly around in Air Force One to make more meaningless speeches. Speaker of the House John Boehner commented, "Americans are not asking; where are the speeches? They're asking, where are the jobs?"

The President went on to make another speech today in Warrensburg, Missouri, a college town near Kansas City. This speech lasted about 30 minutes and again focused on the economy. Economic growth over the course of the last 4 years has grown at a rate of 0.9% a year. This extremely slow economic growth rate is the worst since the period between 1979 and 1982 while and after Jimmy Carter was in office. Carter's plan for economic growth or the lack of one was the same as President Obama's in that they share a socialistic approach to address all the country's problems. They both believe that the solution lies in increasing the size of government and throwing federal taxpayer money at any given problem as opposed to allowing capitalism and free enterprise to do the job in the private sector. This socialistic approach is doomed to failure from the outset as we've experienced under Carter and now under the Obama administration.

Ultimately, the President is attempting to incite a revolution by creating civil unrest based on targeting the 1% of wealthy Americans for hoarding all the money. The 1% should be admired and held up as a shining example of what hard work and ingenuity can yield. The President's ridiculous re-distribution scheme is used to entice lower income Americans to establish an expectation of receiving government hand out's when they should be afforded the dignity of a good job.

Absence of Leadership

July 25, 2013

Ahead of the President's scheduled speech on the economy in Jacksonville, Florida today, Florida GOP Chairman Lenny Curry said in a statement released this morning that, "While Floridians look forward to hearing what you have to say about the economy, I know that they are much more interested in what you will do to strengthen our economy. After having the second highest jump in unemployment in the country in the four years prior to Governor Scott's inauguration, his formula of lowering taxes, decreasing regulations and creating an environment friendly for job creators has resulted in Florida having the second largest drop in unemployment in the country. I urge President Obama to take this formula of success back to Washington so that middle class families can look forward to a stronger economy instead of more rhetoric about it." Unfortunately, the President won't admit that Governor Rick Scott's proven formula for success may be a better approach than his proven failed approach or lack of any approach whatsoever other than merely talking about the problem. Governor Scott's wise and successful policies don't fit with President Obama's liberal agenda of big government control of the populous. Predictably, the President's speech today in Jacksonville consisted of the same type of pep talk that we've come to expect from such an uninspired man with a failed track record for success.

Recent polls speak volumes. 72% of Americans don't like the way things are going in the U.S. President Obama has an all-time low approval rating of 45% overall and 25% approval by independents. 54% believe the Obama administration has made the economy worse and the same percentage disapprove of Obama Care. Also, based on a NBC/Wall Street Journal poll released yesterday, their findings are that 83% of Americans disapprove of the job Congress is doing in Washington, an all-time high in the poll. President Obama has been a huge contributor to the huge divide that exists in Congress due to his lack of leadership and his total unwillingness to approach members of Congress to work with them. The President sits upon his ivory tower in the White House which has become an unapproachable island and is the major cause of gridlock in Washington. In the **absence of leadership**, a vacuum exists that creates a total breakdown in our government.

More Smoke and Mirrors

July 30, 2013

The President made the 4th speech today in a string of speeches to present his plans to address our failing economy. The highlight of his speech today in Chattanooga, TN. was a proposal to reduce corporate taxes from 35% to 28% based on concessions the President would need by Republicans in Congress to agree to a spending increase on an expanded fiscal stimulus program supposedly designed to create jobs. Once again, as in the delay of the employer mandate for Obama Care, the President wants to selectively portray the illusion of helping corporate businesses while ignoring small business and individuals. I refer to today's proposal as an illusion because while corporate tax rates would be reduced, this proposal would overhaul the tax code rather than simply cut rates, and would raise revenue on a one-time basis by eliminating loopholes and imposing fees on companies with accumulated foreign earnings.

The President slammed the Keystone XL pipeline today by saying it would only create about 50 permanent jobs which is an absurd assertion and couldn't be further from the truth. He failed to mention the 4000 construction jobs and 42000 future jobs the State Department said would be created by approval for the completion of the pipeline. These new jobs, whether permanent or not, would be very good for job recipients and local economy's. I believe the President used the context of today's speech to address this topic as a veiled threat targeting Republicans by using the pipeline as a potential bargaining chip to obtain approval for another spending increase. The President didn't even bother to present today's proposal to Republicans prior to the revelation of it through the press today. Republicans aren't taking the bait, so once again the President is just blowing smoke.

This obvious use of **"smoke and mirrors"** in the President's proposal today, designed to present the illusion of a tax break for corporate America when in fact it would simultaneously raise taxes and increase spending, is just a re-packaged ploy to increase the size of government. This President talks about helping the middle class when in fact the middle class is suffering under President Obama's initiatives. The 1% of very wealthy Americans are doing just fine. Poverty is at an all-time high in America. 42.6 million Americans or approximately 15% of the population is in poverty. The President has made sure these people have no incentive to work by making them dependent on government hand-outs and Medicaid. Actual unemployment is at about 16%. This percentage includes those who have quit looking for work. Only 8% are still looking for a job. This is proof positive that fiscal stimulus by our government, which failed to the tune of over $868 billion wasted during Obama's 1st term, **does not work.** The middle class will continue to take a beating once Obama Care implementation kicks in.

Chapter 8

Sign of Weakness

August 2, 2013

The U.S. government issued a global travel alert today, citing an Al-Qaeda threat that also caused the State Department to close 22 embassies and consulates throughout the Middle East and northern Africa on Sunday. State Department spokeswoman Marie Harf said some missions may stay closed for longer than a day. "Current information suggests that Al-Qaeda and affiliated organizations continue to plan terrorist attacks both in the region and beyond, and that they may focus efforts to conduct attacks in the period between now and the end of August," a State Department statement said. "There is a significant threat stream and we're reacting to it," said General Martin Dempsey, Chairman of the Joint Chiefs of Staff. General Dempsey said the threat was "more specific" than previous ones and the "intent is to attack Western, not just U.S. interests." The State Department statement continued saying, "U.S. citizens should take every precaution to be aware of their surroundings and to adopt appropriate safety measures to protect themselves when traveling." The alert expires on August 31st.

U.S. Embassies and Consulates are extensions of the United States and are technically sitting on U.S. soil. These U.S. missions and the U.S. citizens who serve in them should be protected in the same manner as our military would protect anything within the borders of the United States. We don't close the United States for a day under the threat of terrorism. Closing our overseas missions is viewed as a **sign of weakness** by Muslim terrorists. Islamist Jihadists strike when they perceive weakness. The U.S. military should be building a very large show of force fully prepared to effectively protect our missions in the Muslim world. Surely, we have the capability to do this. Instead, President Obama wants to stick his head in the sand and hope the threat goes away. It's a sad state of affairs when the United States of America essentially sends the message that we will act out of fear rather than out of strength. I can't help but wonder, now that we have announced to the world that we will be closed on Sunday, if the Obama administration has considered the fact that the terrorists now know to wait until Monday or a few days later. This notion should strengthen our resolve to build a strong force to protect our overseas interests rather than closing the doors for one day. The Obama administration has a very bad habit of telegraphing our military plans to the enemy which effectively removes the element of surprise that could work to our advantage. This administration needs to be schooled on the basics of military strategy 101.

Most Americans are under the impression that the closings are a good safety precaution and that everyone who works in a U.S. Mission in the Middle East or Northern Africa is safe during the closings. The fact is that all U.S. embassy and consulate workers are still at work in their respective properties. The U.S. missions are closed for regular business with residents and politicians of the respective countries where they're located but the buildings are full of the regular workers. It appears the Obama administration is only concerned with foreigners who live in the countries where closings are being observed but the U.S. citizens there can only hope they aren't attacked. All U.S. Ambassadors and staff workers are still at risk but that little detail was conveniently left out of the recent closing announcement.

The Obama administration is responsible for this new threat because this administration purposely allowed the attack on our consulate in Benghazi, Libya on 9/11 last year for political reasons and failed to do anything to find and kill the perpetrators of the attack. The CIA, NSA, FBI, and DHS know who they are and where they are but no action has been taken to retaliate for their attack and murder of 4 U.S. citizens. These Muslim terrorists have been emboldened by our failure to seek justice for the murder of Ambassador Christopher Stevens and 3 other Americans. The successful murder of a U.S. Ambassador is a huge notch in their guns and it gives them big time motivation to strike again.

August 6, 2013

In his first public comments about the recent terror threat, President Obama made an appearance on "The Tonight Show" with Jay Leno today. I suppose it's a good way to insure softball questions to spin a very serious situation any way he may like for his initial statements on this threat. The President remarked, "It's a reminder that for all the progress we've made, getting Bin Laden, putting Al Qaeda between Afghanistan and Pakistan back on its heels, that this radical, you know, violent extremism is still out there, and we've got to stay on top of it." He just can't bring himself to specifically talk about Islamic Jihad. Apparently "violent extremism" is an extremely vague reference for Islamic Jihad but who really knows for sure. His failure to reference Islamic Jihad or Islamic terrorism for exactly what it is speaks to his weak character that is now widely recognized globally.

The President and Leno went on to discuss the NSA surveillance program and President Obama described it as a "critical component to counterterrorism." He went on to say, "We don't have a domestic spying program." I never cease to be amazed at how calmly and deliberately President Obama lies to the American people. It's common knowledge at this point that the NSA collects all data on every Americans phone calls along with extensive data contained in our e-mails, texts, and social media. The Obama administration has attempted to tell us they only collect meta-data, nothing more than headers with no actual content. Anyone who actually believes this stuff is extremely naïve'. This extreme unconstitutional government overreach goes far beyond the amount of surveillance it would take to effectively search for potential terror threats. We should narrow our search down to profiling Muslims because Muslims are always the perpetrators of Islamic Jihad. It shouldn't come as a surprise that the President's approval rating based on the August Fox News poll is 42% approve and 52% disapprove.

August 7, 2013

The U.S. has filed sealed criminal charges against Ahmed Abu Khattala for the attack on the U.S. Consulate in Benghazi, Libya which took place on 9/11/12. U.S. officials are prohibited by law from discussing matters that are under seal in a court. CNN recently interviewed Khattala, who Libyan and U.S. officials have described as the Benghazi leader of the Al Qaeda affiliated militia group, Ansar al-Sharia, one of many groups that filled the vacuum of authority after the overthrow of Muammar Gaddafi in Libya.

Congressman Jason Chaffitz, R-UT, demanded today to know why investigators have not captured or killed any of the suspects in the attack pointing out that CNN found the man who some say was the ringleader in the assault that left the Ambassador and three other Americans dead. Eight GOP lawmakers are asking that incoming FBI director James Comey brief Congress within 30 days about the investigation. They say the administration's inquiry into the September 11, 2012 attacks in Libya has been "simply unacceptable," based on a draft letter obtained by CNN.

Everything about the way the Obama administration has handled the Benghazi attacks is suspect; from the initial and ongoing cover-up to the failure of officials to exact justice. Eleven months after the attacks the FBI has nothing to show for their supposed investigation other than charges filed today against one individual. It's no wonder that Al Qaeda groups around the Middle East are boldly preparing for future attacks on other U.S. missions.

August 8, 2013

CNN reported today that 7 suspected U.S. drone strikes have been reported to have occurred in Yemen in the past 2 weeks alone. The strikes have killed 29 militants and 2 civilians based on reports from Yemeni officials. These same Yemeni officials have confirmed that most of the slain militants were linked to Al Qaeda.

I have been very critical of the Obama administration in recent days for the lack of a response to terror threats directed at U.S. missions in the Middle East and northern Africa so I must applaud the recent drone strikes as a very appropriate response to recent threats. I do also believe that the U.S. must develop a more comprehensive strategy to combat global Islamic Jihad. Drone strikes alone are sorely inadequate. We must devise strategies to educate people on the negative aspects of Muslim ideology regarding how it will threaten their overall quality of life. Radical Islam thrives on the exploitation of impoverished people whose poor living conditions make them easy targets for recruitment as Jihadists. This is obviously a daunting challenge but we must stay the course to fight the war on terror on numerous fronts.

More of the Same

August 9, 2013

The President held the first White House press conference since April today. There was no news associated with this press conference. It was just **more of the same** and a complete waste of time. This press conference was scheduled for 3:00PM on a Friday afternoon in August as an appeasement to the White House Press Corp since the President made an appearance on the Tonight Show earlier in the week. How very thoughtful of him. He made an initial statement about government surveillance and then took 8 questions from the White House Press Corp. The press conference lasted about an hour. The President utilized his usual strategy of mini filibusters when answering questions (over 6-minute average answer time per question). It's an effective strategy to minimize the need for damage control. There wasn't a single question asked about the IRS targeting of conservative groups even though an IRS agent testified today before the House Ways and Means Committee that this unfair targeting is still going on. The agent testified that he has been instructed to automatically submit Tea Party tax-exempt status applications for Political Advocacy secondary screening even though there is no evidence of political wrong doing. The absence of accountability within the bureaucracy of the IRS is a crime. How very thoughtful of the lap dog media to give the President a pass on the IRS scandal. The main stream media also gave the President a pass on the stagnant economy. The awful record of 0.9% average annual GDP growth for 4 consecutive years should be worth addressing. I suppose it's just too much to expect for a Friday afternoon in August.

The Presidents initial statement covered 4 steps to improve NSA surveillance. He suggested the need to work with Congress to increase oversight and insure that phone records aren't being listened to without a warrant citing section 215 of the Patriot Act. He then suggested additional safeguards for oversight and constraints with changes to the secret FISC court (Federal Intelligence Surveillance Court created by the Federal Intelligence Surveillance Act of 1978) to insure security and privacy for American citizens. He went on to suggest increased transparency with the appointment of a full time civil liberties and privacy officer and finally he suggested the establishment of an outside source to study new surveillance technologies to develop better ways to implement surveillance. Does anyone really buy this patronizing rhetoric? Most of us know that none of these initiatives will ever see the light of day and even if they were instituted it would just expand bureaucratic big government and we'd see no better results. The NSA and the Obama administration have been walking all over the 4th amendment and section 215 of the Patriot Act since President Obama took office. Both the 4th amendment and section 215 of the Patriot Act cite the need for probable cause and a specific warrant to spy on any American. Section 215 of the Patriot Act also narrows it down to strictly overseas communications that are subject to surveillance with probable cause and a warrant. We now know that all domestic communication is being illegally collected with no probable cause or specific court order.

The President was asked about the upcoming appointment of the next Federal Reserve Chairman. He acknowledged that this would be the most important economic decision of his Presidency. He said he was considering a range of outstanding candidates with 2 at the forefront. Larry Summers and Janet Yellen are at the top of the list. He said criteria for his decision consists of a dual mandate. First, the need to keep inflation in check with a sound dollar and no artificial bubbles. Second, the need for full employment with his admission that we have had too much long-term unemployment. He said he will make an appointment this fall.

Most Americans don't realize that the Federal Reserve is not an official U.S. government agency. The Federal Reserve is a private banking organization although its leadership is appointed by the President and must be confirmed by the Senate. The Federal Reserve is led by the Federal Reserve Chairman, Vice-Chairman and the Board of Governors. The Board of Governors has 7 members and they serve for a term of 14 years. The Chairman and Vice-Chairman are usually selected from the Board of Governors. They oversee the 12 district Federal Reserve Banks. The Federal Reserve Banks represent the 12 districts the Federal Reserve has divided the nation into. Their job is to help implement monetary policy as established by the Federal Reserve's Federal Open Market Committee. The Open Market Committee focuses on establishing interest rates and dealing with the nation's money supply. They also oversee the Federal Reserve's purchase and sale of U.S. Treasury securities. The district Federal Reserve banks help regulate the banks in their area.

The Federal Reserve was created in 1910 by a group of powerful east coast bankers. Its creation was justified under the ruse that a central banking system could prevent money panics and runs on banks. A bank run was underway in 1910 which paved the way for the creation of the Federal Reserve. There is significant validity for the need to prevent bank runs but the real reason was to establish control over interest rates, money supply, and basically to establish a banking monopoly that would stifle free enterprise within the overall banking system. The Federal Reserve has managed to maintain a secure foundation for the economy over the years but they are presently allowing the U.S. Treasury to print so much money that the dollar which is the world's reserve currency has been significantly devalued. Also, since the government is spending about $1 trillion a year over its actual revenue stream, it must support printing more money and selling Treasury bonds to offset the deficit. The dollar and the bonds are declining in value as we continue down this path. The question on everyone's mind is how long can this practice continue.

The next question in today's press conference asked the President to detail specific plans to improve government surveillance. He reiterated the need for additional oversight and audits with more transparency. He emphasized his intent to do nothing other than look for terrorists and said he is confident there is no abuse. He said we should follow technological advances with an eye to establish embedded technology which would prevent unnecessary snooping. He went on to suggest that we advance the conversation of how we can make people more comfortable with surveillance and to have discussions on how we can do it better. Enough of the patronizing rhetoric already!!!

He was then asked about his earlier statements asserting that Al Qaeda has been decimated and is on the run. He said core Al Qaeda has been decimated and is on its heels and is broken apart and very weak but that AQAP, Al Qaeda in the Arabian Peninsula, can still pose a threat. He said we need to pay attention to potentially manageable regional threats and that it is an ongoing process. He did say we will never stop terrorism. When asked about the failure to capture the perpetrators of the Benghazi attack he said there is an ongoing effort in place to do just that and reminded us that it took him 11 months to find and kill Osama bin Laden. I suppose efforts by the Bush administration for 7 years to find Bin Laden doesn't count. Had it not been for the groundwork laid by the Bush administration, President Obama would not have been positioned to complete the task. To compare the hunt for Bin Laden to the search for the Benghazi perpetrators is totally unjust because we've known for some time that Ahmed Abu Khattala was the ringleader of the Benghazi attack and we know exactly where he is. A sealed criminal indictment was recently issued by a U.S court directed at Khattala. It remains to be seen where that will lead.

Ed Henry with Fox News asked about the government's preparedness to begin Obama Care implementation on October 1st. President Obama refused to admit to any problems that may exist even though he was reminded of the delay to the employer mandate by one year. He insisted that 85% of Americans presently have health care insurance and that the remaining 15% will be able to sign up for affordable below market value health insurance on October 1st. He rambled on covering the same talking points we've heard repeatedly such as coverage young people up to the age of 26 still at home, rebates, senior discounts for prescription medicines, and new availability for preventative checkups. Based on his comments today it should come as no surprise that he will stick to his signature health care program until it implodes under its own unsustainable weight. Nothing was mentioned about the President's recent executive order to continue the federal employee health plan for the Obama administration and Congress who will continue to receive the 75% health care subsidy they presently receive. There's something terribly wrong about having ineffective and unaffordable socialized medicine crammed down our collective throats while lawmakers and federal employees within the Obama administration are not subject to the same unaffordable coverage everyone else must live with. They should be forced to take their own bad medicine as they had no problem forcing it on us. Low income Americans who qualify for either Medicaid or government subsidies are the only group who benefit financially but the quality of their health care is terrible if they can even find a Doctor who will accept their inferior health care plans.

The President went on to aggressively attack Republicans and said they want to make sure people can't get health insurance. He said it is their "holy grail" and number one priority to make sure 30 million people won't have health care and that Republicans criticism of Obama Care has no basis in fact. He said Republicans have no agenda for health care and that they shouldn't be so combative as he went on to add that Republicans need to rise above it and work with Democrats. One reporter asked if the President would allow a government shutdown to prevent defunding Obama Care. He took a final shot to attack Republicans when he turned the question around and said it would be a bad idea for Republicans to force a government shutdown in their effort to defund Obama Care. Heaven forbid the possibility of a government shutdown might be his fault. The President is standing on the assumption that government is the only entity that can provide health insurance. President Obama has never even considered the private sector because his major objective is to increase the size of already big government. Republicans haven't offered any sort of specific replacement plan for Obama Care so they need to get to work on one. They keep talking about it but haven't presented anything yet.

A final question was asked about immigration reform. The President defended the Senate bill by saying it would improve the economy and increase border security by using new technology. This President has not credibility to make such a claim as he supports open borders and the notion that the Senate bill will improve the economy is absurd. He urged the House to act and get a bill on the floor soon.

Overall, nothing new was covered. It was a regurgitation of recycled lines that have led this President to a place where many American's have lost confidence in him and don't trust him. Not to worry though; it's time for the President and family to head for Martha's Vineyard for yet another super expensive vacation.

Arbitrary Waivers

August 13, 2013

It was revealed today that the Obama Care "out of pocket" cap for annual health care costs will be delayed until 2015. It isn't clear who made this revelation known today but it wasn't the

White House. The Obama Care provision to cap annual out of pocket expenses at $6300. for individuals and $12,700. for families, has now been delayed by the President until 2015. Computer systems for health insurance companies are not prepared to aggregate or synchronize medical and prescription costs based on Obama Care regulations so they can't accurately calculate total costs to reconcile out of pocket costs, hence the delay. This is just one more example of the endless complications associated with 20,000 pages of Obama Care regulations. Since the Affordable Care Act is a law, Congressional involvement is necessary to make changes to the law but the Imperial President prefers to **arbitrarily manipulate** changes at will by executive action. The legality of an executive order in this instance is highly questionable. This President has abused executive orders like no other. It's not about the number of executive orders; it's about the excessive overreach associated with President Obama's executive orders. So far, the President has unilaterally delayed the employer mandate and now the out of pocket cap for Obama Care until 2015. The Presidents lawless and unconstitutional actions stem from his insistence to govern by dictatorial standards that suit his self-designed Imperial Presidency.

It's clear now that individuals will be hammered with excessive health care costs throughout 2014 and beyond. Premiums for coverage and now "out of pocket" costs will be considerably higher than anything that could be considered affordable for many American individuals.

Stonewall

August 20, 2013

Secretary of State John Kerry has determined that the 4 State Department officials placed on administrative leave by Hillary Clinton after the terrorist attack on the U.S. Diplomatic Mission in Benghazi do not deserve any formal disciplinary action. Secretary of State Kerry has asked these people to return to work at the State Department today. These 4 scapegoats had been on paid administrative leave to give the appearance that action was taken to reprimand these 4 as if they bore some responsibility. I'm not sure why Hillary even bothered with such a weak attempt to keep up appearances. These officials who returned to work today are no more culpable than the State Department cleaning crew. Hillary Clinton and President Obama were the only government officials with the power to bear responsibility for this terrorist attack which absolutely could have been prevented. After Hillary Clinton's failed White House bid in 2008, she aspires to run again in 2015, 16. This incompetent and corrupt woman has no business even thinking about being POTUS.

Gregory Hicks who did everything he possibly could from his station in Tripoli is still suffering through his undeserved demotion. Why wasn't he re-instated to his former position today as Deputy Chief of Mission in Libya along with the 4 inconsequential individuals who merely work at the State Department in Washington DC? The answer to that question is that he is being punished for his testimony before the House Oversight and Government Reform committee which was damaging to Hillary Clinton. The truth is once again too inconvenient for the Obama administration. The **"stonewall"** that has been set up to protect Hillary Clinton and President Obama is very strong but must be torn down to pave the way for accountability. Speaker Boehner should have appointed a House select committee with subpoena power by now to investigate this scandal because the oversight and government reform committee hasn't made any progress. A select committee would have a single and specific mission to reveal the corruption at the center of this scandal. Apparently, John Boehner doesn't have the courage to appoint such a committee.

The Perfect Storm

August 27, 2013

The Perfect Storm is brewing. With the debt ceiling to deal with and the need for yet another CR, continuing resolution, to fund the government by October 1st, our government is facing some tough economic decisions in addition to some serious foreign policy concerns. October 1st is also the deadline for Obama Care exchanges to be up and running. The current debt ceiling is @ $16.699 trillion. Raising the debt ceiling is a very controversial action in Congress. Congress hasn't even passed a budget for 2014 yet but they must now act on the debt ceiling because the government will default on its financial obligations by mid-October if the debt ceiling isn't raised. Our government will literally lose its ability to pay government bills without the ability to borrow more money. Congress must not only pass legislation to raise the debt ceiling but they must also pass another continuing resolution to fund the government. Funding for Obama Care becomes an integral factor in that debate. If our government were acting responsibly, we wouldn't be facing these fiscal problems. It's entirely possible for the legislative and executive branch to work together to reduce crippling government regulation on business to grow our economic base thus providing the additional revenue needed to pay our bills without the need to borrow money. The fact is our government has proven to be incapable of fiscal responsibility and prefers the easier method of just borrowing our way into financial oblivion.

As turmoil in Egypt continues to escalate we are now seeing the most extensive use of chemical weapons by the Assad regime in Syria. Six days ago, on the 1st anniversary of the day President Obama declared that the use of chemical weapons in Syria would represent the crossing of a red line, the Obama administration still doesn't have a plan for a strategic response. Today, Secretary of State John Kerry spoke out and strongly condemned the use of chemical weapons in Syria. He said UN inspectors on the ground in Syria have confirmed the use of chemical weapons and he eluded to a possible military response. The President, in a televised PBS interview today, spoke about "a shot across the bow" to describe the military response he has in mind. President Obama is viewed as weak and indecisive on the global stage which is a reputation he has earned but in the case of Syria, a unilateral decision by the President to lob a few missiles at Syria to justify his red line declaration is not a viable solution. After a vote in Parliament, the UK has opted out of possible participation in a missile strike on Syria. Without a coalition of at least a few NATO countries (an alliance of 16 sovereign Euro-Atlantic countries) working with the United States, our position is severely weakened. Secretary of Defense, Chuck Hagel, said the tentative plan is to fire 200 Tomahawk cruise missiles at various Syrian military installations. Each Tomahawk cruise missile costs $1.5 million so the missile cost alone would total $300 million plus operational costs. We can't target chemical weapon sites because we could inadvertently unleash deadly chemicals that could feasibly kill thousands. We can't target Bashar al-Assad because he is a moving target as is a lot of his most used weaponry including the WMD. The civil war in Syria does not present a national security or territorial threat for America. There is absolutely no possibility for a good outcome if President Obama orders a limited missile strike. We also place Israel at risk for no good reason but to allow the President to check the box that he acted even though this action would accomplish very little if anything at all. A missile strike on Syria could also have a negative impact on the stock market and the economy in general here at home. The fact is that our enemies are killing each other in Syria and any action by the U.S. would benefit one side or the other when neither can be viewed as a victory for America. President Obama's first mistake was drawing the red line in the first place. He never should have made an idol threat that we weren't prepared to act on. The Obama administration is swirling in the middle of a **perfect storm** of economic crisis at home and failed foreign policy initiatives abroad.

Black Budget

August 29, 2013

"U.S. spy network's successes, failures, and objectives detailed in **'black budget'** summary" is the title of a Washington Post article published today that reveals the $52.6 billion black budget for fiscal 2013 which was obtained from former intelligence contractor, Edward Snowden. The 178-page black budget maps a bureaucratic and operational landscape that has never been available for public scrutiny until now. The National Intelligence Program budget details the successes, failures and objectives of the 16 spy agencies that make up the U.S. Intelligence community. The summary describes cutting-edge technologies, agent recruiting and specific ongoing operations. The Post is withholding some information they obtained from Snowden but China and Russia clearly had access to every detail of the black budget from Snowden which could represent the most damaging leak of U.S. Intelligence in our history. This classified information that is now out there can provide insight for foreign intelligence sources to discern our top national priorities, capabilities, sources and methods that allow us to obtain information to counter threats. The initial Snowden leak which described extensive NSA surveillance on Americans in the U.S. was general information that wasn't really damaging but the black budget summary is different. Now that we know that Russia and China have specific detailed intelligence on where and how money is allocated within the CIA, FBI, NSA, and every other U.S. spy agency, we are exposed in ways that will haunt us and weaken us for some time.

Indecision

August 31, 2013

After a Friday night meeting with White House Chief of Staff Denis McDonough, the President has had a change of heart and in a televised Rose Garden address on Saturday he said he will seek congressional authorization before deciding to order an attack on Syria. He emphasized his authority to act without Congress but went on to make the case that a strike would carry more weight if Congress is behind it. This President has always struggled with important foreign policy decisions. His **indecision** is systemic of his inability to lead. He appears to be following the UK's lead after Prime Minister Cameron sought the approval of Parliament to stand with the U.S. in a strike on Syria. President Obama may be hoping for a different outcome with the U.S. Congress than the negative vote by Parliament in the UK. I think the President is looking for shared responsibility especially if the outcome of a missile strike on Syria backfires on him. With so much time to prepare and move key targets around, Assad is setting the stage to boast that a failed limited strike by the U.S. had little negative impact for his regime and has only served to strengthen his resolve to act with impunity.

The decision to seek Congressional approval for a strike is one thing but to wait several days until they return from summer break instead of calling them back for an immediate vote is another sign of **indecision**. At this point, even if the President ultimately orders a strike, we still appear weak on the global stage. The only good outcome of this delay would be to take the time to develop a strategy for an end game which doesn't exist yet. The United States must have a goal of exactly what we hope to accomplish with a missile strike and a well thought out next step with several potential retaliatory scenarios under consideration. We must be fully prepared for any number of responses from Syria and even the potential for intervention by Iran. So far, the Presidents response appears to be nothing more than a political exercise which shouldn't come as any great surprise. His decision to defer to Congress is clearly political because it's so out of character. This is the dictatorial Imperial Presidency that only chooses to utilize Congress as a last resort to provide cover for the feckless foreign policy of the Obama administration.

Chapter 9

Saving Face

September 6, 2013

President Obama made a televised appearance today at a press conference in St. Petersburg, Russia during the G-20 summit. Syria was a major topic of international discussion during the summit and the President took the opportunity to garner support for a strike on Syria. Based on his statements today it sounds like the consensus of nations attending the summit is that they have no problem with the U.S. mounting a strike but there was no offer to join in. The President stands by his position that a missile strike is necessary to deter the use of chemical weapons by the Assad regime. Here at home it appears that any hope of support from Congress is rapidly dwindling. The Senate may ultimately approve a missile strike with the absolute provision that there will be no "boots on the ground" as the situation evolves. Support in the House is cratering which would put a nail in the coffin of Congressional approval.

The President has been hoping to **save face** for his "red line" ultimatum by obtaining Congressional approval for a missile strike on Syria. Even though he was basically forced to defer to Congress for approval as a last resort, that move may prove to be a greater risk than even suggesting the attack in the first place. This President can't stand working with Congress so seeking their support now must be a tough pill to swallow. The President's hole is getting deeper! He needs to stop digging but he seems to be at a loss when it comes to his next move. If the President orders a strike without Congressional approval he would be making a huge mistake. White House Deputy Security Advisor, Tony Blinken, made a statement that the President will move forward with a strike even if he fails to obtain Congressional approval. In the face of this possibility, Senator Rand Paul asserted that it would be a constitutional disaster and that the vote itself would be nothing more than a political circus. Once the backlash began in response to Blinken's statement, he backed up big time but his vague retraction was too little too late.

America has nothing to gain by attacking Syria and everything to lose. The motive is one of emotion over the use of chemical weapons but wars are fought for strategic ends, not emotionalism. The American people have come out in a solid stand against military action. The American people are war weary and have zero appetite for an attack which could possibly escalate to "boots on the ground" based on the unknown response by Syria and even Iran. In the absence of a missile strike on Syria, the compromise of arming rebel militia groups also fails the test of effective action on the part of the United States. Many of the rebel militia groups are too heavily infiltrated by Al Qaeda elements so these groups can't be trusted. There are actually many varied factions of rebel militia groups, both Shiite and Sunni, in Syria so it's difficult to assess where their allegiance lies and which ones can be trusted. Many Syrian rebels/Jihadists are killing Christians who refuse to denounce Christ and convert to Islam. If chemical weapons were to fall into the hands of Syrian rebels/Jihadists, the much greater problem of terrorists possibly using WMD on Israel would be a terrible result. The solid outcry from the American people to refrain from military action in Syria has the Obama administration running around in circles. Confusion is running rampant at the Pentagon due to 50 revisions so far to strike plans by the Obama administration. The problem is that the Obama administration doesn't have a plan. Any tentative plans being formulated change based on political winds. Everything is political with this President because he has no idea how to lead.

The only productive military action the U.S. should take now would be to attack nuclear facilities in Iran with the support of NATO nations but forming such a coalition is much easier said than done and it would be a huge mistake for the United States to go it alone. President Obama is clueless when it comes to foreign policy and utilization of our military which he has weakened to a very great extent. His political decision to pull all troops out of Iraq leaving no residual force behind was disastrous. Iran stepped in to fill the vacuum and took control of Iraq with Assad as a willing partner. Every sacrifice our fighting men and women made in Iraq including the loss of life and limb was wiped out. The WMD we didn't find in Iraq was surely moved to Syria. Bashar al Assad was a General under Saddam Hussein in Iraq. Saddam Hussein killed thousands more people with chemical weapons in Iraq than Assad has in Syria. The Presidents failed policy in Iraq is a precursor to the disaster just waiting to happen in Syria.

Lifeline

September 9, 2013

In response to remarks made today by Secretary of State John Kerry during a London news conference, Russian Foreign Minister Sergei Lavrov suggested Syria hand over their chemical weapons and place them under international control. When Kerry was earlier asked by a reporter what the U.S. could do to avoid a strike on Syria, he said the U.S. would stand down if Assad would "turn over every single bit of his chemical weapons to the international community in the next week." He immediately added, "but he isn't about to do that," basically saying "when pigs fly." It was shortly after those remarks that Kerry was caught off guard when his suggestion became a serious proposition as Syria's Foreign Minister, Walid Moualem, said Syria "welcomes Russia's initiative." Based on the Presidents numerous attempts to buy time while he flails around making up his ill-conceived non-existent strategy on the fly, this dubious gift falls in his lap. He immediately embraced his unexpected **lifeline** and began to spin this opportunity for diplomacy as the best course of action. While President Obama hangs on to his political lifeline as a needed reprieve, all the Middle East and the rest of the world see America as weak. A follow through on his "red line" declaration in the form of an "unbelievably small limited kind of effort" (in John Kerry's exact words) would only make us look weaker. This is what happens when the President of the United States fails to lead.

In the absence of an American strategy, Vladimir Putin has 3 very clear cut objectives in play. First, Russia will take the lead in the removal of chemical weapons from Syria while keeping Assad in power and second, they will protect their naval/air base in Syria and third, Russia will demand the U.S. agree to forego military force on Syria as a key provision to a chemical weapons removal agreement. As Russia succeeds in accomplishing these objectives, they appear strong while making America look weak. Putin is playing with Obama and enjoying it every step of the way. President Obama is unwittingly playing along out of political necessity while allowing Russia to buy time which the President sees as a good thing. Putin has also rendered Congress unnecessary in this situation. While most of Washington DC is breathing a collective sigh of relief with the delay of military action, Russia is making us look stupid while they lead the way.

Meanwhile, very little thought has been given to the fact that the removal of Assad's chemical weapons is a very complicated proposition no matter who the players are. The feasibility of removing all the chemical weapons and destroying them with full verification is not good. Hillary Clinton further muddied the waters today when she spoke out and said Syria must immediately turn over their chemical weapons with no excuse for delay and no obstruction of the process. There is no realistic hope that Assad's huge cache of chemical weapons can be cleared out of Syria in a few days. If Syria ultimately agrees to Russia's initiative, it could take months to comply and even then, it's very unlikely that 100% of Syria's chemical weapons would be eliminated. Syria's new found willingness to cooperate could easily be very short lived because it's most likely just a ploy they've worked out with Russia to buy time. After a month or so of negotiations we'll just be back at square one. I'm getting dizzy just following the circles of deception. President Obama's "Keystone Cops" act is tiring everyone out including Secretary of State John Kerry who is just along for the ride!

Nothing New

September 10, 2013

The President addressed the nation this evening from the east room of the White House. The speech lasted 15 minutes. It was a speech in search of a purpose. The American people have seen that leading from behind has left a power vacuum in front that Russia has rushed in to fill in Syria. The President's speech didn't offer any clear statement of our objectives so he failed to get out in front. The shaky plan for a military strike has now taken a back seat to diplomacy based on Russian manipulation. Now that Congress is out of the equation, the President appears to have renewed hope for a UN Security Council resolution that will demand Syria to submit their chemical weapons to International control. A timeframe of about 15 days was placed on the diplomatic effort. The UN is the wrong entity to place hope in. There are too many variables that work against effective UN involvement.

The President spoke about a targeted strike on Syria but in Senator Rand Paul's words, "he didn't offer a plan for victory so the goal must be for a stalemate." President Obama said a targeted strike would make Assad think twice about using chemical weapons in the future but that just opens the door for more questions and no answers. The Presidents answer to the danger of retaliation is that Assad isn't capable of significant retaliation and that Israel can take care of themselves. It occurs to me that the President is making a case for an attack that he has no intention of ordering. He even said tonight that the U.S. is not the world's police. At this point our military is being instructed to forget about a plan to fire missiles and simply plan for time. In the end this evening, it's clear that **nothing new** was presented so the President has done nothing to restore his credibility which he never really had in the first place.

Russian roulette

September 15, 2013

Based on Russia's leverage over Syria, Secretary of State John Kerry and Russian Foreign Minister Sergei Lavrov have reached an ambitious tentative agreement calling for an inventory of Syria's chemical weapons within one week. The agreement calls for the removal from the country or destruction of all Syria's chemical weapons by mid-2014. The Syrian government has yet to issue an official statement on the agreement. The deal was met with cautious optimism in Israel where leaders expressed satisfaction that Syria could be stripped of their chemical weapons but also pessimism about whether Bashar al-Assad will comply. Israeli Prime Minister Benjamin Netanyahu said, "The determination the international community shows regarding Syria will have a direct impact on Syria's ally Iran. Iran must understand the consequences of its continued defiance of the international community by its pursuit toward nuclear weapons." He went on to say that, "if diplomacy has any chance to work, it must be coupled with a credible military threat." Israel has its own intelligence assessments of Syria's weapons which they will compare to the inventory submitted by Syria in a week so the international community will know if Assad's intentions are serious or just deception. Secretary of State John Kerry stressed that the deal is a framework and not a final agreement.

The Obama administration is playing **Russian roulette** with the international community in brokering this shaky deal with Russia. The deal places a lot of undeserved trust in Assad's compliance. The world is watching carefully to see how this situation plays out and given

President Obama's lack of credibility, expectations are low. A lot is riding on the good will of Russia's leadership which must be met with a certain degree of skepticism. The United States is playing Russian roulette with a rather reluctant international community while Vladimir Putin is playing chess with Barak Obama. Putin is wisely playing several moves ahead while President Obama isn't sure what his next move is. The end game will find its way back to Iran who is ultimately the most dangerous player.

Let the games begin

September 20, 2013

The House voted today to keep the government open through mid-December but only if Congress strips funding from Obama Care. The vote was 230 to 189 with 2 yes votes coming from Democrats. The GOP measure would fund the government through December 15th, at current funding levels. Congressman John Culberson (R-TX) said, "Today, the constitutional conservatives in the House are keeping their word to our constituents and our nation to stand true to our principles, to protect them from the most unpopular law ever passed in the history of the country, Obama Care, that intrudes on their privacy and our most sacred right as Americans to be left alone." House Speaker John Boehner said, "You've got businesses all over the country who are not hiring because of the impact of this law. You've got other businesses who are reducing the hours for their employees because of this law. And so, our message for the United States Senate is simple: the American people don't want the government shut down and they don't want Obama Care."

House Republicans and their constituents who favor repeal or at the very least delay of the health care law can celebrate a very short lived and merely symbolic victory today. As Senate Majority leader Harry Reid likes to remind everyone as often as possible, the House bill is dead on arrival in the Senate. Senator Ted Cruz is committed to blocking a procedural Senate vote for cloture on the House approved spending bill, saying that Senate Democrats would have too much leeway to add in funding for Obama Care. "Any vote for cloture, any vote to allow Harry Reid to add funding to Obama Care with just a 51-vote threshold, a vote for cloture is a vote for Obama Care," Senator Cruz said today. He went on to say, "And I think Senate Republicans are going to stand side-by-side with Speaker Boehner and House Republicans, listening to the people and stopping this train wreck that is Obama Care." Senators Ted Cruz and Mike Lee have threatened a filibuster in the Senate which could lead to a government shut-down if Harry Reid fails at his attempt for cloture. If this were to occur, House Republicans would breathe a sigh of relief because the blame for a government shut-down would fall on Senate Republicans. This would take unification of Republicans in the Senate which doesn't exist to a great enough extent yet. Too many old guard Republicans don't want to risk the blame for a government shut-down to fall on their shoulders. If the bill is bounced back to the House, Republicans in the House could concede defeat and choose to fund the government or at the suggestion of Senator Cruz, the House could start by passing incremental continuing resolutions to fund each department of the government separately. "If Harry Reid kills the bill in the Senate, the House should hold their ground...start with smaller continuing resolutions," Cruz said. "Start with the military. Send it over, see if Harry Reid is willing to shut down the military." The semantics are quite different for each side. The more aggressive and savvy Republicans speak in terms of Harry Reid and President Obama as those who will cause a government shut-down but Democrats speak strictly in terms of Republicans wanting to shut down the government.

Let the games begin between the House and Senate and between deeply divided Republicans in the Senate. The President can't wait to enter the fight if it comes his way for a veto. He's already participating in the war of words. This is political gamesmanship being played for very high stakes. The American people will be the losers and the irony is that they are merely sitting on the sidelines. The American people must wait for the 2014 mid-term elections to speak. The only realistic hope to save the American people from the disaster that is Obama Care is the very likely prospect of self-implosion but it's difficult to nail down the timeframe on implosion should that be the ultimate demise of this law. There are so many logistical problems with implementation that the nightmare of implementation could sink the ship which would come as a huge relief to many Americans and make them the ultimate winners in the short term. Even if Obama Care implodes, we are still left with a less than desirable existing health care system. Health care insurance reforms will still be needed but socialized health care via Obama Care is clearly not the solution. A move toward health care savings accounts with supplemental catastrophic coverage should be part of the solution and would be a step in the right direction. This can be achieved through the private sector with minimal government oversight and should be handled by each individual State. There is no need for any involvement by the federal government. Americans bear a personal responsibility to manage their health care. Federal bureaucrats have no business dictating the vehicle by which Americans obtain health care insurance.

September 24, 2013

The first procedural vote on the House-passed continuing resolution will take place in the Senate tomorrow. If the motion to proceed passes, Senators will have 30 hours of debate on the measure to fund the federal government at current funding levels of $986.3 billion through December 15th and to defund Obama Care. As of this evening, Senator Ted Cruz (R-TX) continued to speak on the Senate floor going into his 10th hour, elaborating on his opposition to the Affordable Care Act aka Obama Care. This old-fashioned filibuster by Senator Cruz has been a great opportunity to stand up and do the right thing to raise awareness and oppose funding for the worst law ever passed in the history of the United States.

This afternoon, Senate majority leader Harry Reid said he will substitute the House version with his own amendment that would strip the defund language that passed in the House and shorten the funding period from December 15 to November 15. He also said the final vote on the continuing resolution would likely take place on Sunday, though he was waiting to see if Republicans would agree to end debate early.

Yesterday Senator Harry Reid filed cloture on a motion to proceed on the CR which sets up a series of procedural votes, the first to be held on Wednesday. Following this vote, Senators will have 30 hours to discuss and debate the CR. On Thursday, Harry Reid is expected to file another procedural motion that will continue the formal debate on the CR into Saturday. On Saturday, the Senate will hold another vote to cut off debate and any attempts to filibuster the CR. If Harry Reid gets past the 60-vote threshold needed for cloture, he will schedule a final simple majority vote on his alternative amendment to the CR, and if it passes, the CR goes back to the House striped of the defund Obama Care language. House Speaker Boehner and the Republican leadership will then have to decide whether to accept the Senate CR or pass yet another version and risk not meeting the September 30 deadline when current temporary funding for the government runs out. They could also very likely attempt to push the date of the vote to fund the government until the middle of October at which time they would deal with the CR and the Debt Ceiling at the same time. Senator Harry Reid can put a check in the win column for this key part of the battle. Harry Reid and Senate Democrats win if House Republicans concede defeat and make a choice to fund the government with no interruption and they also win if House Republicans force a government shut-down to extend the fight. There is an up-side for Republican opponents of Obama Care which is the fact that Congressional Democrats will have confirmed their ownership of Obama Care. Their confirmed defense of this very unpopular law will come back to haunt them when the 2014 mid-term elections roll around.

September 26, 2013

"The IRS is unable to account for $67 million spent from a slush fund established for Obama Care implementation," based on a Treasury Inspector General for Tax Administration report released today. The report goes on to say "The Health Insurance Reform Implementation Fund was tucked into Obama Care to give the IRS money to enforce the tax provisions of the healthcare law. The fund, totaling some $1 billion of taxpayer money, was used to roll out enforcement mechanisms for the approximately 50 tax provisions of Obama Care." This report adds fuel to the fire of skepticism over our government's ability to implement this disastrous health care law and the role of a scandal ridden IRS in the process.

Senator Ted Cruz (R-TX) wrapped up his historic appeal to Democrats and establishment Republicans in the Senate as he argued at length, the need to pull out all the stops in the fight against implementation of Obama Care. He spoke on his feet for over 21 hours straight. Senate majority leader Harry Reid called it a waste of time and establishment Republicans appeared to be reluctantly inspired. I characterize the Republican response as such because finding themselves at a loss for criticism of Senator Cruz's passionate oratory, they found themselves applauding the effort with moderate enthusiasm. These old guard Republicans who don't have the courage to fulfill their campaign promise to do everything possible to save the American people from Obama Care are afraid they will be blamed for a government shut-down. They can't negotiate from a position of strength when it's so apparent that they will cave. They argue that a vote against cloture is a vote against the House bill that they all support. They fail to mention the fact that their yes vote for cloture has them voting with every Democrat in the Senate. Their position defies logic. Voting yes along with every Democrat enables Senator Harry Reid to amend the House bill by adding funding for Obama Care. The long term disastrous effects of socialized health care by implementing Obama Care will be devastating to Americans for years to come. Compared to a short-term government shut-down, years of suffering with Obama Care is much worse. Fearful establishment Republicans will have their opportunity to disgrace themselves tomorrow when the cloture vote occurs on the Senate floor.

As the saga continues with the need to fund the government with a short-term CR along with the attempt by courageous Republicans to defund Obama Care, battle-lines are already being drawn on the Debt Ceiling crisis which must be dealt with by mid-October. For now, Democrats will continue to focus on a government shut-down and responsible Republicans will focus on an Obama Care shut-down.

September 27, 2013

The Senate voted on cloture today which was invoked by Senate majority leader Harry Reid to end debate on a bill to defund Obama Care. The vote was 79 for and 19 against. 27 establishment Republicans voted for cloture which is technically a vote in support of Obama Care because cloture enabled Harry Reid to strip out the defund Obama Care piece of the bill which is exactly what he did in very short order. 27 Republican Senators backed away from their campaign promise to do everything possible to save the American people from the disaster of Obama Care. These Republican Senators lack character, integrity, and courage. They're so concerned with passing the buck onto House Republicans to make sure they bear responsibility for a short-term government shut-down which now appears to be inevitable, that they let their constituents down. The House bill included a mandate to take Obama Care funding out of mandatory spending to completely defund it. Even though the likelihood of total success to defund Obama Care was slim to none, those 27 Republicans should have stood their ground in support of the House bill as a show of strength and unity but their rush to concede defeat reflects fear and weakness. They have no fear for their personal health care insurance needs because they will receive a 72% subsidy to offset the cost of their excellent coverage. While our government inflicts pain upon the American people, they selfishly took care of themselves. Obama Care was never about affordable health care for the American people. It's always been about control of the American people by making big government bigger with an income redistribution scheme. The countless mandates included in the law are restrictions on the American people that create power and control for big government.

Nuclear fallout

Just when Americans thought Congressional dysfunction couldn't go any further downhill, the President decided to take that downhill path and exercise his greatest weakness; Foreign Relations. He must have decided that since we've neglected Iran since 1979, it's time to throw them a bone. I use the word neglect with great sarcasm. President Obama must have forgotten the reason for our frosty relationship with Iran. The Islamic Republic of Iran is a terrorist state and is the largest State sponsor of terrorism in the world. They provide funding for Palestinian terrorists, Hamas, Hezbollah, and others of the same ilk. Anyone who believes their nuclear pursuits are exclusively energy related is extremely naïve. In a phone conversation between President Obama and Iranian President Hassan Rouhani today, President Obama suggested the possibility of an agreement that would initiate a winding down of the crippling economic sanctions on Iran. After President Obama was basically snubbed by Rouhani at the UN in New York earlier this week, his response is to initiate unsolicited negotiations with a bunch of terrorists. It's like High School romantic posturing. Rouhani plays hard to get and then Obama takes the bait. World leaders throughout the Middle East see that President Obama is weak and Rouhani sees an easy mark so why not take a shot. In the short span of about 2 weeks President Obama has been played by Putin over Syrian chemical weapons and now he's being played by Hassan Rouhani. It's embarrassing!

President Obama said, "The very fact that this was the first communication between an American and Iranian President since 1979 underscores the deep mistrust between our countries, but it also indicates the prospect of moving beyond that difficult history. I do believe that there is a basis for a resolution." The President said both men had directed their teams to work expeditiously toward an agreement on the nuclear issue. As President of Iran, Rouhani is the head of the government but has limited powers. Supreme Leader Ayatollah Ali Khamenei is the ultimate authority in Iran with final say on domestic and foreign policy, though Rouhani says he has been given full authority to negotiate on the nuclear issue.

President Obama went on to say, "I've made clear that we respect the right of the Iranian people to access peaceful nuclear energy in the context of Iran meeting its obligations. So the test will be meaningful, transparent and verifiable actions, which can also bring relief from the comprehensive international sanctions that are currently in place."

To begin, it's insane that the President of the United States is anxious to negotiate with a terrorist regime in Iran over their nuclear weapons program and with Russia over chemical weapons in Syria but he flatly refuses to negotiate with the Congressional branch of the United States regarding meeting the needs and desires of the American people. He's willing to force a government shut down over his signature health care law so he can use that scenario as a hammer to politically pound Republicans. His narcissistic personality has become dangerous. His stonewall tactics will cause irreparable harm to the American people in numerous ways.

The **nuclear fallout** from making a deal with Iran to lift economic sanctions while allowing them to become a nuclear power will bring the world to the brink of destruction and the United States doesn't even get anything out of the deal. The President has literally lost touch with reality. May God help us.

Chapter 10

All in

President Obama and Senate majority leader Harry Reid, along with every Democrat in the Senate, have just shut down the U.S. government. The President and Senate Democrats have refused to negotiate with the House. Last week the House passed a bill to completely fund the government at current funding levels with a provision to defund Obama Care. The Senate flatly rejected this bill. The Senate striped the defund language from the House bill and bounced it back to the House late Friday evening 9/27. Congressmen in the House worked Friday night and all day Saturday on a compromise bill. They passed a bill on Saturday to once again completely fund the government but this bill contained a provision to delay the individual mandate for Obama Care by 1 year and it contained another provision to do away with the medical device tax associated with Obama Care. The President and Senate Democrats not only refused to negotiate on this new bill but they also refused to come to work Saturday evening or Sunday. The President played golf on Sunday. When the Senate showed up on Monday, they rejected the new House bill and sent a message that they will only accept a clean CR with no additional provisions. They also reiterated their position saying they will not negotiate under any circumstances. It's interesting to me that the ACA was passed without a single Republican vote and now the Democrat controlled Senate is once again pulling a completely partisan play to reject a bi-partisan opportunity to not only make reasonable changes to the ACA but also to shut down the government with a hyper partisan political move.

The House went to work and began sending over individual CR's to fund specific departments of the government. They began with the military and the Senate refused to fund the military. They continued all day and one by one the Senate refused to fund every single individual CR. Finally, the House passed a measure to reconstruct the original Obama Care bill adding every provision back in that the President had unilaterally and unconstitutionally removed. The House agreed to fund the government and re-insert The Affordable Care Act in the complete form it was in when it became law and when the Supreme Court upheld it as law. This time the President and Senate Democrats rejected Obama Care in its original form and once again refused to negotiate with the House.

Senator Harry Reid and the President placed all blame for the shut-down on Republicans in the House even though it's the President and Senate Democrats who refuse to negotiate while Republicans in the House sent over compromise after compromise to the Senate. Republicans in the House have worked very hard for a bi-partisan resolution while the President and Senate

Democrats stonewall. Senate Democrats and the President are bluffing with a bad hand but their bets are still **all in.**

Shut Down

October 1, 2013   10:00AM

Republicans used every conceivable tactic and came up short. It's time to throw in the towel and regroup to fight another day. Republicans need to prepare for the upcoming debt ceiling battle where they have a chance to gain the upper hand. If they concede and send a clean CR to the Senate today which will end the government shutdown in short order, they can stop the bleeding and won't be hurt. If the government is shut down for only one day it will be easily forgiven by the American people but if it lasts for 2 weeks or more, Republicans will take a hit. Democrats are elated and will milk the shutdown for everything they can get out of it. Christmas came early for the President and every Democrat. The main stream media is having a field day with this and they're very effectively doing the bidding of the President who in their eyes can do no wrong. Nobody is talking about the fact that 85% of the government is still being funded during the shutdown due to mandatory spending. Social Security benefits are being paid, the mail is moving, and the military is still being funded along with several other areas of government but the rhetoric being passed along by the main stream media is that government has been severely crippled. The stock market hasn't even been impacted. The Dow dropped a few points on Monday and then shot back up today. Investors know this so-called shutdown is no big deal.

The Obama Care exchanges opened for enrollment today. Millions of low income Americans and Americans with pre-existing conditions went online today to sign up for low cost health care insurance. It wasn't exactly smooth sailing. Countless glitches in the system created chaos and confusion. Error messages were abundant and actual people with a pulse weren't available to talk to on the phone. It will take weeks if not months to smooth out the bumps in the road. It will also take time to determine what percentage of people successfully enrolled today and in the days to come. We do know that younger Americans along with middle and upper income Americans didn't go online today and won't be rushing to their computers to do so any time soon because they know they will be faced with higher premiums to pay for those who might receive affordable health care insurance. When low income people who don't qualify for Medicaid see that their premium is affordable due to the subsidies but that their deductible will be about $6000. for a bronze plan, they won't be happy campers. That cheap health insurance premium won't do much good when they can't cover the deductible.

Republicans must shift the focus from the government shutdown to the numerous problems associated with Obama Care enrollment. These initial enrollment problems are merely the tip of the iceberg. As problematic enrollment attempts continue and other implementation problems arise, Republicans need to find their way out of the corner they've painted themselves into and shine a very bright light on the countless problems associated with Obama Care implementation as they unfold.

Dug In

October 2, 2013

The President ordered some national parks employees who weren't furloughed due to the shutdown to go to the World War II memorial to set up barricades to keep Americans out. He used the same pain seeking tactic when the Sequester became law and he closed the White House to tours. A group of about 100 World War II veterans from Mississippi and Iowa had flown in on an honoree tour and were initially kept out. Word of this ridiculous shut out reached Republicans in the House and several went to the memorial and had the barricades removed. Some of the parks employees who were ordered to keep people out are veterans who readily helped to remove barricades and allowed the group of 80 and 90-year old veterans, most of whom were in wheel chairs, to spend as much time as they wished at the memorial. It's disgraceful to barricade an open-air memorial to keep out the men who fought courageously for our freedom. I'm sure the President has given considerable thought to covering the Statue of Liberty and Mt. Rushmore with huge tarps. The barricades surrounding the World War II memorial will become one of the most viewed optics of this shutdown but just as the White House has remained closed, the President will stand his ground on this ridiculous order to inflict maximum pain for political leverage.

It appears at this point that the Republican strategy is to stand firm on the government shutdown and tie it to the debt ceiling debate which is underway and will reach critical mass by October 17th. Both sides are so **dug in** that the partial shutdown will most likely continue until the 11th hour when it becomes necessary to raise to debt ceiling. Only time will tell.

End Game

October 3, 2013

As it turns out, my poker analogy isn't completely applicable to the game been played out between Senate Democrats and the President on one side and House Republicans on the other. The rules in poker are black and white and set in stone. Once you've lost on a bad hand it's time to pay up and move on. It doesn't work that way in political games. The rules are essentially made up as the game goes along. Thus far, the House has run the gamut from no Obama Care to 100% original Obama Care, all of which has died in the Senate. In our current scenario, House

Republicans have raised the stakes and decided to play out their questionable hand. Their strategy is to continue sending over individual bills to fund national parks, the VA, and other popular parts of the government with no Obama Care provisions attached. This initial strategy of passing mini funding bills in the House hasn't produced any results but none were really expected. It's a tactic to make Senate Democrats look bad because none of these funding initiatives have any ties to Obama Care and they benefit some of the most important political patrons of the Democrat Party: unionized government workers. This may eventually yield some positive results for Republicans but the main stream media isn't reporting on the details surrounding Republican funding initiatives so most people aren't aware of them. The only message most people are getting is that the government is shut down and it's the fault of those nasty Republicans. As we approach the debt ceiling deadline the stakes grow higher and Senate Democrats will be feeling more pressure. Moderate Republicans are growing anxious to end the stalemate but House Speaker Boehner has deployed House Budget Committee Chairman Paul Ryan and Ways and Means Committee Chairman Dave Camp to encourage their fellow conservatives to hold the line in hopes of striking a bigger deal that might include entitlement reform, changes to Obama Care, and an overhaul of the federal tax code. It's obviously still a very fluid situation with no **end game** in play.

The President is using scare tactics and campaign style rhetoric to attack Republicans. He appears to be thoroughly enjoying himself. He issued a warning to corporate America that we are headed for default over the debt ceiling. This very un-presidential tactic designed to disrupt the stock market is dangerous and stupid. Director of National Intelligence James Clapper warned of a serious national security threat due to the government shutdown. Clapper's assertion was a low blow to the CIA and NSA which brings his reputation to an all-time low. This fear mongering designed to place blame on Republicans could negatively impact financial markets and unnecessarily instill fear in the hearts of Americans. Corporate CEO's around the country are only concerned with raising the debt ceiling. If the debt ceiling isn't raised by October 17th, the value of U.S. Treasury Bonds could fall and the U.S. credit rating could also fall. This could have serious economic implications. If an economic downturn were to occur, responsibility could fall directly on the Presidents shoulders. Blame for a serious economic downturn rarely falls on Congress but since the President has the main stream media in his back pocket he may be in the clear. As we approach October 17th, the President will feel more and more pressure to finally negotiate with Republicans. Negotiating doesn't fit President Obama's dictatorial style but as inconvenient as the narcissist will see it, he will be forced to yield to some extent. For now, he is standing on principle. Republicans could possibly gain some ground by simply dropping the word negotiate. If they change the language and work more behind the scenes, they may be able to strike a deal while allowing the President to save face.

The repeated debt ceiling debates could end if a serious effort were in place to cut spending and reduce our debt. The Obama administration is addicted to routinely piling on debt by out of control spending. We can only hope for a miracle of fiscal responsibility to break out within the executive branch and the Senate. Short of that miracle we are doomed to repeated fiscal cliff scares over the debt ceiling. It's totally ironic that it's referred to as a ceiling because ceilings are generally immobile. The lofty heights of debt aspired to by the Obama administration is dangerous to economic stability.

Sticker Shock

The glitches and kinks associated with the opening of online Obama Care exchanges continue to escalate. Californians were greeted with a blank screen today. Few people successfully enrolled but they got deep enough into the plan descriptions and pricing that enrollment would have been the last thing anyone would have been inclined to do. Premiums and deductibles have doubled and even tripled in most cases over everybody's existing health insurance. The main stream media has conveniently ignored the fact that many States turned down Medicaid expansion which would be critical to potential low income enrollees. I received an e-mail from Congressman Walter Jones who is the representative for the district where I reside in eastern North Carolina. He related some actual experiences of North Carolinians who attempted to sign up for Obama Care health insurance during initial enrollment currently underway. One individual from Pender County reported that his monthly rate is more than doubling from $465. to $1095.97. A gentleman from New Bern said he was told that his premium will skyrocket from $7500. to over $15,000. annually. A healthy family of 5 in Dare County reported they had just received a notice that their premium would go from $6000. to over $12,000. a year.

In Congressman Jones words, "Washington DC needs to hear the stories of real people like these who are suffering the consequences of President Obama's ill-conceived government takeover of the healthcare system." These rate increases have been anticipated by many and haven't necessarily exceeded their expectations but now that they have become reality, its eye opening to say the least. **Sticker shock** doesn't even begin to describe the disaster that is unfolding before our very eyes. The real-life consequences of Obama Care will wreak havoc throughout the American population and the destruction has only just begun!

Battle Lines

October 7, 2013

At this point the **battle lines** have been clearly drawn. House Speaker Boehner has been forced to increase his strong stand because the majority in the House demand it. Republicans are still divided but conservatives in the House are in the minority. Senate Democrats have become less vocal in the interest of self-preservation but the President continues to ramp up his rhetoric and has recruited Treasury Secretary Jack Lew to join in as a fear monger over the debt ceiling debate.

The President is using the government shutdown as leverage and House Republicans are using the debt ceiling as leverage. It's too early to predict the outcome but one thing is certain. The President's firm stand on the Obama Care individual mandate is set in stone. He knows that implementation will totally break down if both the employer and individual mandates were to be delayed. Every day that goes by reveals another problem. There is nothing good to report after the first week of enrollment and one of the more impressive revelations is the extremely low volume of enrollment. One year of dismal results would sink the ship. The dirty little secret of extremely high deductibles hasn't been revealed to a great enough extent yet. Insurance companies will do everything possible to maintain a low profile on high deductibles because their profits depend on it. Most people still don't realize that older women will be paying for maternity benefits they don't need and people who have never done illegal drugs or consumed alcohol to excess will be paying for drug and alcohol rehabilitation benefits. These items don't even begin to scratch the surface of the income redistribution scheme that is Obama Care.

Debt Ceiling Debate

October 8, 2013

The President made a televised address to the nation today and made some inflammatory statements and outright lies. He said that the deficit has been cut in half since he took office. I asked myself; did he seriously just say that? The US government has been running on $1 trillion plus annual deficits since Obama took office. The national debt has increased by nearly $7 trillion since he took office. During President Obama's first term the deficit by year is as follows: 2009 $1.4 trillion, 2010 $1.3 trillion, 2011 $1.3 trillion and 2012 $1.9 trillion. In 4 years, the spending addicted Obama administration increased our debt by $5.9 trillion which is the largest increase for any single Presidential term. At the end of the 3rd quarter of 2013 the deficit is $759 billion. The Sequester spending reductions forced by Republicans is the only reason the deficit hasn't increased as much for 2013 as previous Obama administration years. When the President asserted he had cut the deficit in half he must have isolated the first 3 quarters of 2013 and it's ludicrous for him to take any credit. Senate Democrats and the President hate the Budget Control Act (Sequester) which has effectively reduced out of control spending. Each year under the Obama administration the government has been taking in about $2 trillion in revenue while they spend over $3 trillion. The national debt is at $17 trillion dollars. The country's slow economic growth is a major contributor to the deficit because lower incomes translate to less revenue. The President said raising the debt ceiling does not increase our debt.

Raising the debt ceiling is all about how much money the government can borrow therefore it is of course about increasing debt. Does the President think we aren't paying attention or that we are incapable of simple math?

He went on to say that he is willing to work through all the issues that the House is concerned with but in the same breath said he will not negotiate with them. He says the House is holding him hostage when in fact he is holding the House hostage. The truth is that Republicans can't in good faith towards their constituents raise the debt ceiling without spending reforms. The President went on to preach doom and gloom over the debt ceiling from his bully pulpit to scare the American public and even financial markets over his obsession to demonize Republicans. He said countries around the world are concerned but that they understand "the messy process of American Democracy." As I've said before, Democracy is just too inconvenient for this Presidents Dictatorial Imperial Presidency.

He went on to say that Democrats give and give and give while Republicans won't give on anything. These statements he's making today go well beyond rhetoric; they are outright lies and they don't help toward making any progress. The President did seem to open a very small door when he said he may consider agreeing to a short-term CR and raising the debt ceiling for about 2 to 3 weeks and then negotiate during that time. Even though Republicans and Democrats in Congress are not inclined to do this, it appears to represent a minimal indication of movement of some sort on a possible extension of the debt ceiling.

One very interesting development during this news conference was that not a single question was asked about Obama Care. Even though this is true to form for the lap dog media, it's such a glaring oversight that it presents another great example of the main stream media's desire to do this President's bidding and when combined with the President's bully pulpit, it becomes a powerful weapon in the President's arsenal. The President's priority today was to scare the hell out of Americans and to trash America in the process.

The only way our government defaults on our debt would be a failure to pay interest on treasury bonds. The President was throwing fuel on the fire over a default that will not occur. Treasury Secretary Jack Lew did the same thing this last weekend. Our leaders should be calming the environment but this President continues to ramp up his negative rhetoric. The Dow fell 160 points today and about that same amount yesterday. Fear and panic reigned among America's financial markets today due to the President's scare tactics. This doesn't need to happen.

House Speaker John Boehner made a televised appearance today in response to the President's news conference. He said the President's position is not sustainable. He went on to say that there will eventually be a negotiation. He pointed out the fact that over the last 40 years the debt ceiling was used 27 times as a bargaining chip to negotiate on policy changes to reduce spending. Given this precedent and the fact that we can't continue to borrow money and live beyond our means without spending limits; it's not unreasonable to negotiate before any sort of agreement is made on the debt ceiling.

Foreigners Welcome

Americans, not so much

While every monument and the mall in DC are closed and inaccessible due to barricades, the mall was opened today for over 10,000 illegal aliens to hold a rally celebrating immigration reform. Several Democrat members of Congress were present to welcome the illegal aliens to the mall which is shut down to American citizens. A few reporters attempted to interview some of the rally participants but they couldn't even speak English.

This is beyond shameful! American war veterans were standing outside the World War II memorial, Viet Nam War memorial, and the Korean War memorial unable to enter the memorials paid for by their tax dollars to honor them while 10,000 illegal aliens were having a big time on the mall. One reporter cornered Congresswoman Nancy Pelosi (D-CA.) on the mall while she mingled with the illegals and asked her to go to the memorials to greet the veterans. She replied that she doesn't grandstand but there she stood grandstanding on the mall to promote Amnesty and open borders for illegals. Her presence on the mall standing with thousands of illegal aliens while American War veterans were being denied entry to their memorials was appalling. Nancy Pelosi, Barak Obama, and others who promote and support amnesty and Obama Care are stabbing Americans in the back. American citizens will suffer under government mandates while illegal aliens will receive a check.

Despicable

October 9, 2013

We learned today that death benefits are being denied to the families of 5 American combat men and women who were killed in Afghanistan on Sunday. The Gold Star families of these brave Americans who gave their lives fighting for our freedoms would normally receive $100,000. in death benefits but even though the House, Senate and the President passed a law last week to pay our military during the partial government shutdown, lawyers at the Pentagon blocked the death benefits for 5 Gold Star families who lost their loved ones in Afghanistan. President Obama could easily step in and insure payment of death benefits with a pen stroke but he hasn't lifted a finger to honor our countries promise to meet the immediate financial needs of our nation's grieving military families. These Gold Star families are America's families who have suffered enough. This outrage represents one more example of the Obama administration's strategy to inflict pain on Americans and blame Republicans. This was totally intentional and **despicable** to use the Gold Star families of these brave men and women, who gave their lives for our country, as pawns in a political game. I can only wonder how much further downhill things will progress while President Obama does everything possible to inflict maximum pain on Americans in his quest to destroy the Republican Party.

Punt

October 17, 2013

The proverbial can has once again been kicked down the road. Congress passed a bill today to fund the government for another 3 months and allow the government to borrow more money until February 7th 2014. Now that the debt ceiling has been raised again and the partial government shutdown has ended, Americans can focus on the colossal failure of Obama Care enrollment. After 17 days, it is still impossible for most people to log on and even get past the account set up page for the online exchanges. Error messages continue to abound with no end in sight. After spending $634 million on the web site, it's nothing short of disaster. Data within the system is unreliable due to website architectural problems. Over 5 million lines of faulty software code has been identified. Major errors have occurred such as individuals enrolling in multiple plans and spouses showing up as children. Insurance companies make decisions based on this unreliable and outright false data. These companies will surely be forced to backtrack and make adjustments that will negatively impact American consumers. So far less than 1% of those who logged onto the site successfully registered and couldn't even complete the enrollment process. This is just the beginning of the mounting problems associated with Obama Care implementation that will plague the American people in the weeks and months to come.

The vote to raise the debt ceiling in the Senate was 81 – 18 and the House vote was 285 – 144. The President signed the bill shortly after midnight so the Apocalypse predicted by Senate majority leader Harry Reid was averted. This should provide a short reprieve from the inflammatory scare tactics that continually flowed from Senate Democrats and the President. Republicans were branded as hostage taking, bomb wearing anarchists and that's the abbreviated version.

In addition to the CR and debt ceiling extensions, the bill includes income verification for Obama Care subsidies and the formation of a budget committee who will be expected to miraculously construct the framework for a budget resolution that will garner bi-partisan support. This represents the 3rd attempt at the formation of a bi-partisan committee to find a solution to our budget woes. Congress must be hoping the 3rd time will be the charm but don't hold your breath.

Everybody took a hit over the government shutdown. The American people are disgusted with the political dysfunction we are seeing from Congress and the President. Our war veterans will never forget this debacle. The Republican Party is in complete disarray. The blame for this fiasco will cross party lines. There's plenty of blame to go around. Nobody can claim victory because there isn't one. After all the pain that was intentionally inflicted on Americans by the White House and all the drama in Congress, nothing of substance was accomplished. No political victories were won and Congress failed to do their job. Even though blame is evenly shared throughout Congress, the President bears the ultimate responsibility. The President of the United States should lead by working with members of Congress on both sides of the aisle. He openly refused to negotiate which shouldn't be an option for the President. In addition to his refusal to negotiate, President Obama was the worst perpetrator of divisive rhetoric.

Despite major divisions in the Republican Party, Tea Party Republicans are energized big time. They make no apologies for their stand on principle. They fully realize that the Republican Party took a hit in the polls for now but they are in for the long haul. They look upon establishment Republicans like John McCain, Lindsey Graham and others as defectors who need to be ousted during the primaries leading up to the 2014 midterm elections. As the Republican Party is more divided than ever and Tea Party Republicans face strong criticism, the Tea Party is committed to their conservative beliefs and will continue to fight the good fight.

The best our government could do today was to **punt** to buy time to get back to the same place we just arrived at. Today's bill may be a done deal but a real solution to our government's budget struggles isn't even close to being formulated much less instituted and the closer we get to the 2014 midterm elections the needs of the American people will continue to take a backseat to politics.

Salesman in Chief

October 20, 2013

The President made a televised address from the Rose Garden today flanked by 13 people who supposedly had successfully enrolled online for Obama Care health insurance. We later learned that only 3 of them were enrolled and the others had only made it through the account setup page. The President did his best to defend the initial "enrollment rollout" of his signature health care law. He reluctantly admitted to some kinks in the system. He must have decided the use of "glitches" had grown tired at this point and that "kinks" would help to update the spin. After a very brief acknowledgement of problems with the website he transitioned into a lengthy sales pitch. He espoused some false statistics on enrollment numbers and went on to preach that the product is good. He said the prices are good too. He went on and on until I thought sure he would offer a free set of steak knives with every plan purchased. At the point when the embarrassment factor was reaching a climax he offered an 800 number to call for enrollment help since the website had failed. He apologized for the antiquated use of an 800 number but guaranteed the enrollment process could be completed over the phone. The **Salesman in Chief** must have failed to test the 800 number prior to making his guarantee because once several news commentators called the number they were all told that nothing could be done over the phone and that they should go to the website. Apparently, the President has an aversion to testing. He'd rather cross his fingers, hope for the best and deal with the fallout after the fact. The fallout has only just begun! We still don't know how many people have successfully signed up and completed the purchase of Obama Care health insurance. 7 million individuals including at least 2.7 million healthy young people must sign up by March 2014 to sustain full implementation. If this were to occur, it would be nothing short of miraculous.

Now that the Tsunami of negativity associated with Obama Care has engulfed large numbers of Americans, the inevitable backlash is building steam. The most significant backlash will come from the Insurance industry. If Obama Care doesn't deliver the millions of desirable customers the President has promised, widespread rate shocks soaring higher than those already reported could cause more insurers to dump customers and even get out of the business altogether. "Florida Blue" which is Florida's largest health insurance provider, has already dumped 300,000 people from their health insurance plans due to Obama Care mandates. The Texas Insurance Pool, which offers insurance to those who cannot qualify under a regular plan, has informed its 94,000 customers they have until December 15th to purchase another plan under Obama Care. Kaiser Permanente CA. recently dropped 160,000 people. United Health Care completely pulled out of California. These are just a few examples of many. President Obama promised in no uncertain terms on numerous occasions this would not happen. Hundreds of thousands of Americans have been blindsided with health insurance cancellation letters that offer replacement policies at double to triple the cost of the insurance they were perfectly happy with. This should never happen in America and thankfully it's only a matter of time before the bottom falls out and the Affordable Care Act implodes.

Death Spiral

October 28, 2013

Megan Kelly reported today on her Fox News program, "The Kelly File," that an IRS regulation that was created due to a new HHS regulation on Obama Care, would lead to an estimated fallout of millions of Americans who would be unable to keep their existing health insurance plan under the Affordable Care Act. Megan Kelly was holding a copy of the IRS form in her hand that revealed the fact that the White House knew as early as August 2009 that up to 67% of Americans who purchase health insurance on an individual basis would lose their existing plans.

We're talking about approximately 15 million Americans who the President knew would lose their coverage when he adamantly declared in 2010 and again in 2012 that "if you like your plan you can keep your plan; period!" and "if you like your Doctor you can keep your Doctor; period!" He also promised that premiums would drop by $2500. a year for a family of four. The President occasionally used the "guarantee" word as he repeated his explicit promises on numerous occasions. There appears to be no end to President Obama's blatant lies! Worst of all, this was a calculated and strategically designed part of the President's plan to force these Americans out of their existing plans and into the exchanges. HHS created a regulation that redefines the Grandfather clause in these individual plans. The regulation negates the Grandfather clause if any change, no matter how minor, is made to the plan. All individual plans change in minor ways from year to year. The new HHS regulation essentially voids the Grandfather clause from all individual health insurance plans allowing for increases to premiums and deductibles contained in the new plans that Americans will be forced into. Since the IRS is the enforcement arm for Obama Care, this new HHS regulation became a new IRS regulation inserted in the IRB, Internal Revenue Bulletin. The new regulation that voids the Grandfather clause in existing individual plans was by design. It was inserted to force approximately 15 million Americans into the Obama Care exchanges and into one of only 4 available plans which is another way to strip Americans of their liberties and freedom of choice.

The White House is blaming insurance companies for the cancellations. Once again it appears the disastrous rollout of Obama Care was preconceived as a ploy to possibly move Americans into a single payer health care system. While it's still nearly impossible to enroll for Obama Care coverage on the failed website, the late-night talk show hosts and "Saturday Night Live" are having a field day joking about the useless website. In the handful of States with State launched websites that partially function, 95% of enrollees are applying for Medicaid and the rest are sick people with preexisting conditions. Secretary of Health and Human Services, Kathleen Sebelius, was asked about calls for her resignation during a press conference yesterday and her reply was, "Calls for my resignation are from people I don't work for." She went on to explain that she only answers to her boss, the President. How could she make such a stupid and thoughtless comment? The American people pay her inflated salary. What happened to "government by the people, for the people, and of the people," which Abraham Lincoln so aptly articulated government's responsibility to the people. The Obama administration is telling Americans they're stupid and that government knows better what is good for the public at large.

The White House announced today that it will waive tax penalties for anyone who signs up by March 31st 2014, in effect granting a limited grace period. This somewhat helpful concession is totally unconstitutional as are all the other changes and delays unilaterally ordered by the President. CMS administrator Marilyn Tavenner, who heads up the Centers for Medicaid and Medicare Services appeared before the House Ways and Means Committee today. She opened with a weak apology over the failed website that she directly oversees but she refused to reveal the actual number of Americans who have successfully enrolled for Obama Care health insurance so far. She stood by a statement that an agreement had been reached to wait until mid-November before revealing that information. The number must be embarrassingly low. The latest joke in Washington is with all the data available through WikiLeaks, the only secret left in Washington is the number of people who have successfully enrolled in Obama Care. Obama Care enrollment has indeed entered a **death spiral** of continual embarrassing gaffs. Seniors are being dropped from Medicare Advantage plans because $716 billion was siphoned out of Medicare and channeled into Obama Care funding which ultimately increases funding for Medicaid. We aren't hearing about changes to employer provided health insurance because of the strategic delay of the employer mandate by the President. The employer mandate was conveniently delayed past the 2014 mid-term elections because all hell will break loose when the largest segment of the population begins feeling the pain of the drastic changes to plans which employers will pass along to their employees. Those changes will consist of higher premiums and deductibles that employers cannot absorb for their employees therefore the increased cost will fall on the backs of hard working middle class Americans who are currently living payday to payday. Now that the spin machine at the White House has spun out of control from continual use, this administration is finally getting beat up. The main stream media has jumped ship for the most part on the health care issue and Red State Democrats are beginning to take the leap too. The dominoes have only just begun to fall! Even though the President is taking a serious hit over the botched rollout of his signature health care plan, he will retain most of his core supporters but once Obama Care degrades to an even greater extent it will be very interesting to see how many hang on to the end.

October 30, 2013

Secretary of Health and Human Services, Kathleen Sebelius, testified before the House Energy and Commerce Committee today. The Healthcare.gov website is completely down today as it has been in large part since its debut on October 1st. Secretary Sebelius accepted responsibility for the rollout debacle and issued an apology to the American people. Her testimony went downhill from there. Congressman Mike Rogers (R-AL) grilled her over security failures on the website. Rogers presented paperwork from one of the website contractors confirming that basic end to end security testing had not been performed prior to the Oct. 1st rollout. When asked about this serious failure, Sebelius refused to directly answer and only said people didn't need to worry about it. She might have a different opinion if she experienced identity theft and found her bank account cleaned out and her credit cards maxed out. Secretary Sebelius was asked repeatedly about the Presidents promise that individuals could keep their existing plan and Doctor. Her answer throughout the hearing was that it's only 5% of the total market and that these individuals will be able to purchase better plans than the ones they were perfectly happy with before. Democrat Representatives did everything they could to support her and echoed her response on the cancelled individual plans. The American people are intelligent enough to know they are being told that government knows better than they do when it comes to the type of health insurance plan they need. The Democrat defense is based totally on their claim that the more expensive new plans are better than the plans that people lost due to Obama Care mandates. They completely ignore the fact that people never would have purchased the plans they are now losing if they didn't want them. The President made an address in Boston today and spoke of substandard plans that people purchased which are now being cancelled due to the new law. He said you've got to replace them with quality coverage. The take away from the Presidents statements is, we've got a more expensive plan with a huge deductible that will be so much better for you. If you're a single 27-year old man who earns about 50 grand a year, we've got a plan for you with maternity benefits, pediatric care, and mental health coverage which we're going to make you buy and if you don't buy it we're going to hit you with a tax penalty. What's wrong with this picture? Big government will screw the people at every turn! We may need that mental health coverage after all.

Secretary Sebelius was challenged on her personal federal health insurance plan which has nothing to do with Obama Care. When asked if she would be willing to go into the exchanges to obtain her health insurance she said she wouldn't because it would be illegal which is not the case. As the questioning dragged on for 3 and ½ hours we heard one lame excuse after another. She did absolutely confirm that the website will be fully operational by November 30. If this promise isn't kept, things will go further downhill for Secretary Sebelius and the President.

On a humorous note, Vice President Joe Biden said in a statement to CNN today that he and the President aren't technology geeks and that they **assumed** everything would be OK with the rollout on October 1st. No wonder they keep Uncle Joe locked away for the most part! He occasionally gets out and about and when he does it's always good for a laugh.

Chapter 11

Damage Control

November 4, 2013

The President was in **damage control** mode again today. He spoke at an "Organizing for Action" event in Washington DC and lied about his previous lies! As the fallout continues to mount over the Presidents dishonest pledge that "If you like your plan you can keep your plan, **period**"; he decided to dig a deeper hole and lied once again when he said today, "What **we** said was, you could keep it, **if** it hadn't changed since the law was passed, but if the insurance company changes it, then what we're saying is they've got to change it to a higher standard." **That isn't what he said** 24 times between 2010 and 2012! That's a very big **"if"** in his revised statement. What could he be thinking now that he's added this lengthy caveat and wants us to believe that his revision mirrors his initial promise? For once, the American people are paying attention because hundreds of thousands have been directly affected with cancelled health insurance plans and notification of much higher premiums, deductibles, and co-pays under Obama Care mandates. His lies about Fast and Furious, IRS targeting of Tea Party groups, and Benghazi were terrible and didn't go unnoticed but the Obama Care lies took a direct hit on the bank accounts of many Americans! Now that his Obama Care lies are front and center due to the negative impact already felt by hundreds of thousands of Americans, everybody is paying attention.

November 5, 2013

The President opened the White House for tours today after having been closed to tours since March. Closing the White House to tours was one of the Presidents pain inflicting initiatives to emphasize the effect of Sequester spending reductions. Now that he's under fire with approval ratings at an all-time low, opening the White House for tours is obviously a desperate move to ease tensions. This must be a blow to his huge ego. Sequester spending reductions are still very much in force so nothing has changed, yet suddenly the President has found funding for security to make White House tours possible. The people's house should never have been closed to tours but things change when political winds change direction. The Presidents downhill spiral has only just begun so throwing the people a bone by opening the White House for tours will only help for today.

Open Mouth, Insert Foot

November 7, 2013

In an interview with Chuck Todd of NBC News, the President voiced a weak apology to Americans who lost their existing health insurance he promised they could keep. "I am sorry that they are finding themselves in this situation based on assurances they got from me," he said. He was basically saying, I'm sorry you believed me. He went on to remind us that the cancelled plans are "a lot of subpar plans" affecting a "small amount of the population." All things considered, the so-called subpar plans were much better than the overpriced ACA plans being forced on folks and the number of people affected were many more than characterized by the President. He said, "we weren't as clear as we needed to be" but that ultimately Americans will receive "better care at the **same cost or cheaper**." Another huge lie! When Chuck pressed him on the November 30 deadline promised for a fully functioning healthcare.gov website, the President said "I'm confident the website will be better" and that "If there are any roadblocks, we will make sure those roadblocks are removed," and finally he declared, "Given that **I've been burned** already by a website, …. well, more importantly, the American people have been burned by a website." As the President was pulling his foot out of his mouth he managed to segue from the first person to the American people. It's all about him and his political agenda!

As painful as his apology must have been, when followed by a series of "buts", he negates any semblance of sincerity he may have initially attempted to portray. His huge understatement, "we weren't as **clear** as we needed to be," was an insult to the intelligence of his audience. "If you like your plan you can keep your plan; period" is about as **clear** as it gets. The apology itself falls flat because it doesn't provide a solution. Nothing short of a complete solution restoring the desired coverage's that were cancelled based on regulations designed to assure their cancellation, could make up for the intentional insertion of said regulations. The "buts" kept coming until they reached a crescendo of his true feeling that it was he who had been burned. The Presidents rationalizations wouldn't have been complete without a good solid lie. After thousands of first hand examples have been recently revealed of much higher premiums and deductibles based on Americans personal experience, his blatant lie of "better care at the same cost or cheaper" flies in the face of every American targeted by the Presidents income redistribution scheme called Obama Care. Mr. President, if you like your apology you can keep your apology; period!

President Obama did tread carefully when speaking of the website deadline, basically giving every assurance that it won't be ready for prime time on November 30. His reference to being "better" and talk of roadblock removal after the fact was attorney language for, it won't be ready. Apparently, he's at least learned a partial lesson regarding declarations about his signature law but the ever-present lie is just too tempting to pass up.

Death Spiral

November 14, 2013

HHS Secretary Kathleen Sebelius announced enrollment numbers for Obama Care today covering the first 6 weeks since October 1st. It was reported that a whopping 26,794 people have enrolled on the Healthcare.gov website since 10/1. Another 79,391 people have enrolled on the State run websites. Most of these people haven't purchased plans but have merely placed plans in their shopping cart. In addition, Secretary Sebelius refused to disclose a breakdown of the demographics for these supposed enrollment numbers because it's very unlikely that any significant percentage of these people are young healthy people who are desperately needed for Obama Care math to work. Medicaid enrollment topped the charts with 396,000 who will receive health care that our tax dollars must pay for. The most distressing number wasn't reported by Secretary Sebelius today. During the same 6-week timeframe, 5,026,000 people have lost the health insurance plans that they were perfectly happy with. If the total enrollment number of 106,185 people so far is correct, then that number is 2% of the total number of people who have recently lost their health insurance. It's easy enough to conclude at this point that this trend will continue to snowball in which case the results will be disastrous. History will record this trend as the Obama Care **"death spiral"** because the worst is yet to come. Democrats are heading for the hills out of necessity because they must put as much distance as possible between themselves and the President as we approach the 2014 midterm elections. Senator Diane Feinstein (D-CA) isn't even up for reelection next year and she has jumped ship because over 1 million of the cancellations to date are in California. Jay Carney, White House press secretary, announced that the President is working on a proposal to fix the problem. That will be very interesting because it's laughable. Nothing short of repeal of the law will prevent further cancellations. The President and his fellow Democrat conspirators can't put the toothpaste back in the tube. Harry Reid, Nancy Pelosi, and President Obama will watch their ill-conceived plans unravel as they spin themselves into oblivion.

The White House is spiraling out of control as they attempt to spin the impossible scenario they've worked themselves into and as the Obama Care death spiral winds down into the abyss of political suicide that they unwittingly committed. The Obama administration, based on the direction of their fearless leader, thought they could slip the Republic into Socialism without anyone noticing or caring. Their plan vanished while only the tip of the iceberg is showing. They're scrambling to restore order but they're only digging a deeper hole. They've painted themselves into a corner and the only way out will be extremely messy. I could relate an endless number of metaphors on their dilemma but I think I've made my point. They're screwed and they will twist in the wind until we witness the complete collapse of the progressive liberal movement. This won't happen overnight. While President Obama is in office his administration can spin as they explain away the pain they've inflicted on the middle class. Even if Congress were to successfully pass legislation to repeal the ACA, the President would simply veto it. The only thing in question is the timeframe but this socialistic income redistribution scheme will unravel and implode.

Administrative Fix

November 14, 2013

The President muddied the Obama Care waters big time today. He made a political move to protect Democrats from the fallout over millions of cancelled existing health insurance plans. The Presidents talk began with a statement that he is, "offering an **idea** that will help." The President declared, "Insurers **can** extend current plans that would otherwise be cancelled **into** 2014." The words "**can**" and "**into**" make this an empty and vague promise. He did make it clear that State Insurance Commissioners hold ultimate authority over plan extensions. It's also important to note that extensions are nothing more than a delay to the inevitable cancellation of policies. He went on to say, "This won't solve every problem for every person," and that "we will do everything we can." What he won't do is waive the tax penalty that will be assessed if by some miracle people may be able to keep their existing plan for one year. President Obama's **administrative fix** is creating chaos. He has been unilaterally and illegally re-writing the law for some time. The delay of the employer mandate is the centerpiece of his executive actions and significant exceptions for Unions keep coming. Once the President lost the House, he lost his appetite to work with Congress. He's used executive privilege so often that nobody thinks to question it. This time he's instilled false hope in the hearts of millions of Americans in his quest to offer political cover for Democrats in Congress. His so-called fix passes the buck to State Insurance Commissioners so he can shift blame on them for cancelled policies. The level of cooperation by State Insurance Commissioners is uncertain at this point although commissioners in Washington State, Arkansas, and Indiana have already declined to reinstate any of the cancelled plans and in addition to no reinstatements California confirmed increased premiums. The infrastructure of Obama Care is contingent upon individuals losing their existing plans and going into the exchanges, hence the hollow promise the President made today. Today's promise was all about making a scapegoat out of the insurance commissioners and providers.

The Presidents muddled, illegal and disruptive promise does little to protect embattled Democrats. It is a political band aid at best. Why would we want to take his word for it anyway?

His credibility or lack of it doesn't exactly instill confidence in his empty promises. The American people now see right through him. Obama Care is doomed to fail. The famous axiom, it's not a question of **if**, but a question of **when,** is applicable in the case of Obama Care. It's become more and more apparent that the demise of Obama Care will occur sooner rather than later.

November 15, 2013

The Presidents primary motivation for his illegal administrative action yesterday was to head off the vote in the House on Fred Upton's (R-MI) "Keep your health plan act." If over 100 Democrats were to vote in favor of this bill it would have been extremely embarrassing and politically damaging to the Obama administration. This bill passed today by a vote of 261 – 157 with 39 Democrat votes in favor. It could have been much worse for the President. The President's action to undermine this bill did in large part produce the desired effect because 39 Democrat votes in favor won't hurt him to a great degree although he certainly isn't out of the woods yet. Congressman Upton's bill is largely symbolic because it's widely understood that Harry Reid will squash it when it reaches the Senate. It won't see the light of day in the Senate. There will be no debate and no vote in the Senate and the President announced yesterday that if the bill were to reach his desk he would veto it. House minority whip Nancy Pelosi called the bill "poisonous." She has interestingly defended the ACA with a lot more enthusiasm than even the President. Her insistence to beat a dead horse is really above and beyond the call of duty. She would be better served if she were to retreat and maintain a low profile for some time along with most of her colleagues. The downhill trudge of the ACA will be long and painful for Democrats who sold it as the "holy grail" of health care reform.

Rolling Collapse

November 19, 2013

Henry Chao, Deputy Chief Information Officer for CMS, Centers for Medicare and Medicaid Services, was back on Capitol Hill today testifying before the House Energy and Commerce Committee. Congressman Cory Gardner (R-CO) asked how much of the website is still left to be built and Chao's response was, "I think it's – uh, just an approximation, we're probably sitting somewhere about 60 and 70 percent." Later in the day Chao told "Buzzfeed" that the numbers were reversed and clarified that 30 to 40 percent still need to be constructed, so his original statement apparently referred to the percentage that had already been completed. Either way, 10 days out from the second self-proclaimed deadline, HHS, Health and Human Services, obviously has a long way to go toward completing construction on the Healthcare.gov website. Chao went on to explain that, "The back-office systems, the accounting systems, the payment systems, they still need to be built." Those systems include one that makes government subsidy payments directly to insurance companies on behalf of consumers who qualify. The fact that construction hasn't even begun on the payment mechanism with 10 days left on the second deadline is just one more example of the incredible incompetence displayed by HHS Secretary Kathleen Sebelius.

The most enlightening aspect of this disclosure is that the already dismal numbers of Obama Care enrollees won't even possess valid coverage on January 1st because they won't be able to make a payment online. Even if they mail their payment they still may not have valid coverage because the government can't pay the insurance companies. Yesterday White House Press Secretary Jay Carney said the Obama administration would consider the effort successful if four out of five consumers could successfully enroll in insurance plans. While the White House continues to lower the bar, enrollment numbers are inconsequential because no policy is valid without the ability to make a payment. While the White House and HHS continue efforts to repair the flawed website, this **rolling collapse** will continue to spiral out of control. The Obama administration is unwilling to embrace the only solution which is to completely scrap the existing website and start over from scratch.

Security concerns continue to elevate as Henry Chao was grilled by several Congressmen about an internal CMS memo written just days before the start of open enrollment which concluded that "the threat and risk potential" to the website "is limitless." Chao testified that he had never seen such a memo. The memo went on to reference the possibility of identity theft; unauthorized access; and misrouted data. "Due to system readiness issues, the SCA, security control assessment, was only partly completed," said the internal memo from CMS. The memo went on to say, "This constitutes a risk that must be accepted and mitigated to support the Marketplace Day 1 operations." Not to worry though as Chao claims the administration plans to have it all fixed by May 31, 2014...or by February of 2015. A security expert testified before a Congressional subcommittee that "the [Healthcare.gov] website has been hacked already or will be soon." Four experts who testified before the subcommittee said that, because of the security issues, Americans shouldn't even be using the site at present. Apparently, the problem is that security wasn't built into Healthcare.gov from the beginning. Website security should have been paramount in the minds of the architects.

November 20, 2013

A hearing was held in the Senate today to address concerns over the effects of Obama Care on small businesses with 50 or fewer employees. There are approximately 7 million small businesses in America that fall into this category. The American Enterprise Institute projects that about 66% of all small business health insurance plans will not grandfather and will therefore cancel. They project that over 100 million Americans will lose existing health insurance that was previously provided by their employer. The small business owners who testified before the Senate today claimed they will not be able to continue to provide health insurance for their employees due to Obama Care mandates that cause the cost to skyrocket. This is a ticking time bomb that will explode in October 2014 at the worst possible time for Democrats up for re-election in November 2014. These Democrats are seething behind closed doors at this point but they will begin to openly switch sides and turn on the President in the very near future out of necessity.

After two halfhearted apologies, the President placed blame on Republicans today for problems associated with Obama Care implementation because he claims they are invested in failure. His narcissistic behavioral tendencies just won't allow for the acceptance of responsibility. Republicans had nothing to do with implementation efforts. If their warnings had been heeded, we wouldn't be in this mess. The President and Democrat political appointees bear total responsibility for the implementation failures. A CBS poll out today revealed a 37% approval rating for the President and 31% approval for Obama Care. This is an all-time low for President Obama and does not bode well for prospects of accomplishing any of his 2nd term initiatives.

Power Grab

November 21, 2013

Senate majority leader Harry Reid and 52 Democrats invoked the nuclear option today and ended a 225-year precedent to make a huge Senate rule change by a vote of 52 - 48. The nuclear option brings an end to bipartisanship in the Senate as it applies to judiciary nominations and other executive appointments. It ends the filibuster which allows for a 60-vote majority on judiciary and other executive appointments. Supreme Court appointments are still subject to the filibuster. A simple majority will rule under the nuclear option so only 51 votes will be required in the Senate for judiciary and other appointments to top posts. Harry Reid broke the rules to change the rules in an end run around a long-standing Senate rule. It's a raw and desperate **power grab** by Harry Reid and Senate Democrats. The Senate was once a great deliberative body but will now be ruled by a simple partisan majority. Republicans called it a sad day in the history of the Senate. In a statement addressing the Senate rule change, the President said the "unprecedented pattern of obstruction" in Congress has left Americans more frustrated with Washington than ever. Frankly, Americans are probably more concerned with the "McRib" sandwich being dropped from McDonald's menu today than a major change to Senate rules.

It's been suggested that Harry Reid chose to follow through on the nuclear option today as opposed to past threats to do so because it's an attempt to distract focus from Obama Care failures. If that was his motivation I've got news for Senator Reid which is; this small blip on Americans radar screen will barely be noticed by most people unlike Obama Care woes that are having such a dire and direct effect on their lives.

I believe Harry Reid received his marching orders from the White House. The President is desperate to complete implementation of Obama Care along with some green initiatives he'll ram through with the help of the EPA and liberal controlled courts before Republicans can take control of the Senate. Democrats want to paint Republicans as obstructionists but it will backfire on them in 2015 when Republicans gain control of the Senate. Senate Democrats know they will lose the Senate next November due to the colossal failure of Obama Care so they only have one year to ram through as many liberal judicial appointments as possible. Since they can't legislate the Presidents liberal agenda they will utilize the judicial process to do it with the Presidents corrupt appointees. The United States Court of Appeals for the District of Columbia Circuit is arguably the most important inferior appellate court as it controls decisions and rulemaking of many federal independent agencies of the U.S. government. There are 11 judgeships in this court and currently there are 2 vacancies. Changes to existing seats are based on either retirement, death, or reassignment. The President is responsible for filling vacant seats. This is the court to watch in the days and weeks to come. We may also see some replacements in the President's Cabinet. Kathleen Sebelius, HHS Secretary, may as well start cleaning out her desk because she could be replaced overnight. This abuse of power by Democrats is disgraceful and they will live to regret it. If Republicans take control of the Senate after the 2014 mid-term elections, they could pass legislation to reverse the nuclear option rule in the Senate but this would require an outbreak of highly ethical behavior on the part of Republicans in the Senate.

Historic Mistake

November 24, 2013

At the behest of President Obama, a nuclear deal was made with Iran Saturday night that will go down in history as, in the words of Israeli Prime Minister Benjamin Netanyahu, a **historic mistake!** The United States, Great Britain, Russia, China, Germany, France, and the EU collaborated on negotiations that led to this undeserved deal. "What was reached last night in Geneva is not a historic agreement, it is a **historic mistake**," Netanyahu said. The Israeli Prime Minister went on to say, "Today the world became a much more dangerous place because the most dangerous regime in the world made a significant step in obtaining the most dangerous weapons in the world." President Obama and Secretary of State John Kerry called it a "1st step" toward a final deal to prevent Iran from becoming a nuclear power. The deal allows for a 6-month window to test Iran's willingness to comply with the stipulations of this deal but significant skepticism exists regarding our ability to verify Iran's compliance. John Kerry called it a "test of good faith." The coalition of nations who conspired to make this deal should have agreed to increase sanctions but Russia and China have too much to gain by lifting sanctions. They can now resume trade with Iran on oil and weapons based on the limitations of the deal and they will never agree to the reinstatement of sanctions if Iran is noncompliant. While Iran is shouting that they have an inalienable right to enrich uranium, we are giving in by acknowledging that right. Iran knows the Obama administration is weak and they are spiking the ball in the end zone because they know they can act with impunity, as they have been doing, without concern over consequences. They just became the beneficiaries of a deal that pays them billions in sanctions relief in exchange for minor temporary cosmetic changes to their nuclear program.

In the wake of President Obama's desperate need to take the focus off Obama Care failures, he has created a nuclear arms race in the Middle East. Saudi Arabia, Kuwait, Turkey, the United Arab Emirates, and Egypt will now be highly motivated to develop their own nuclear weapons in response to the possibility of a nuclear Iran. The suckers deal that was made guarantees Mullahs in Iran stay in power. The deal has no provision for any dismantlement of their 19,000 existing centrifuges or dismantlement of their advanced ARAK plutonium heavy water reactor. This deal sets a lower bar than existing U.N. Security Council resolutions. The President failed to include a provision for the release of Rev. Saeed Abidini, an American being held prisoner in Iran for practicing his Christian faith. This was a huge oversight!

The relaxed sanctions will generate billions in renewed revenue for Iran. They will immediately receive $4.2 billion in cash relief and additional sanction relief will come from trade in Gold, Automobiles, and Petroleum. This is only the beginning of the cash windfall that Iran will receive due to the elimination of sanctions. Iran will ultimately receive $150 billion from frozen Iranian assets as part of the sanctions relief. This is a lot of money that the largest State sponsor of terrorism will surely use to fund terrorist activity around the world. Iran will be allowed to enrich uranium up to 5% and will not be allowed to activate 8000 new centrifuges and can't operate their existing centrifuges if they follow the agreement. IAEA inspectors will be allowed daily access to camera footage at 2 uranium enrichment locations. Iran also agrees to dilute uranium that has already been enriched to 20% which is well beyond civilian energy usage levels. Secretary Kerry emphasized that this deal is a 1st step toward a comprehensive agreement.

1st step or not, any negotiation with Iran assumes on some level they can be trusted. Iran clearly cannot be trusted and they go out of their way to make it clear that the complete destruction of Israel is their goal. Israel considers a nuclear-armed Iran a threat to their very survival, citing Iranian calls for Israel's destruction, its development of long range missiles capable of striking Israel and Iran's support for hostile terrorist groups along Israel's borders. Prime Minister Netanyahu voiced what he called Israel's right to self-defense, and said, "I want to clarify that Israel will not let Iran develop nuclear military capability." It is so wrong on so many levels that the United States would fail to support our most important ally in the Middle

East and leave them to fend for themselves even though they are highly capable of a devastating military response to nuclear aggression. Our relationship with Israel should have been our priority but President Obama has snubbed Israel at every turn.

America should have increased sanctions to drive Iran to a breaking point. In addition, we need to increase domestic oil production to lower our reliance on Middle East oil. Sensible business minded solutions have always been above and beyond the competence level of the Obama administration. Their blind commitment to the radical left wing agenda of their political base will drive America to the brink of disaster!

Small Stuff

November 27, 2013

Late this afternoon as most Americans were leaving work and beginning preparations for the Thanksgiving Holiday, the White House announced the delay of Obama Care online enrollment for small businesses with fewer than 50 employees until November 2014 in the 36 states that must utilize the Federal Healthcare.gov website to purchase health insurance for their employees. There are over 7 million small businesses in America. The American Enterprise Institute has projected that 66% of existing small business plans will not grandfather and will therefore be cancelled. Over 100 million small business employees will lose their employer provided health insurance due to Obama Care regulations.

Small business employers must now utilize an insurance broker and work through extensive paperwork to buy Obama Care approved health insurance for their employees. These small business employers aren't mandated by the law to provide health insurance for their employees but the SHOP exchanges were supposed to offer more options for employers who wanted to offer health insurance for their employees as a benefit. Now their options are limited and they won't have the promised convenience of online enrollment through the SHOP exchanges. The message the Obama administration is sending to these small businesses is, don't sweat the **small stuff**, as if their now limited options and inconvenient purchase process is no big deal. Given the limited options and higher costs, many small business employers with fewer than 50 employees may not choose to provide health insurance for their employees in which case these Americans would find themselves in the incredibly expensive individual marketplace. This is likely the desired outcome the Obama administration was looking for because they need the numbers to reach the 7 million individuals needed to enroll by March 1st for the overall monetary equation to work.

Clearly the Obama administration has made this large group of Americans their last priority. There seems to be no end to the broken promises associated with this disastrous law. Given the timing of this announcement, I suppose we weren't supposed to notice because after all; it's just **small stuff** in the eyes of the Obama administration. Millions of Americans have been branded as being insignificant in the eyes of the Obama administration as they're rendered a mere footnote to the law that was supposed to help them. Not to worry though because these employees can now join all the other individuals who don't have access to employer provided health insurance and must then go to the healthcare.gov website that doesn't work, to attempt to buy insurance they can't afford.

Chapter 12

Hand Grenades, Horseshoes and Obama Care

December 2, 2013

The Obama administrations 2nd self-proclaimed deadline to have the Healthcare.gov website fully functioning has now past and the President is claiming success. The American people have learned that President Obama's measure of success is like **hand grenades and horseshoes** in which case close still counts. Centers for Medicare and Medicaid Services Spokeswoman Julie Bataille said of the website, "Today, we're now 'more in the zone of about' 80% of users being able to do that same process successfully." The words "in the zone of about" certainly leave plenty of wiggle room. She went on to say that not all Americans will feel comfortable signing up by the website, and could seek help by phone or in person. That suggests that the vague 80% number includes all forms of signing up for insurance, not just through the website. Can you imagine if Amazon.com or any other major private sector website only worked for 4 out of 5 people? They would be out of business in short order.

Enrollment numbers are the least of the website woes. Construction on the back end of the website that communicates with Insurance companies and Doctors isn't even finished yet. Construction hasn't even begun on the payment mechanism. The Obama administration just announced a "workaround" and Reuters reported, "Health plans will estimate how much they are owed, and submit that estimate to the government. Once the system is built, the government and insurers can reconcile the payments made with the plan data to 'true up' payments." Anyone who thinks insurance companies will reimburse the government for payment overages is extremely naïve. Karen Ignagni, President of America's Health Insurance Plans, told the New York Times, "Until the enrollment process is working from end to end, many consumers will not be able to enroll in coverage." The Washington Post just reported that nearly one-third of the Obama Care applications sent to prospective insurers have errors. The errors include, "failure to notify insurers about new customers, duplicate enrollments or cancellation notices for the same person, incorrect information about family members, and mistakes involving federal subsidies." The bad news continues with the websites lack of security. The administration's decision to completely ignore security has made the site a prime target for hackers. We are literally hearing of hundreds of daily hacking attacks. Once these deficiencies are digested it's difficult to swallow the President's claims of success. The Presidents credibility, as well as Elvis, "has left the building." Close may count with **hand grenades and horseshoes**, but the Presidents claims of success obviously don't even come close.

Poised to Fail

December 4, 2013

President Obama addressed the Liberal Center for American Progress today and spoke of Obama Care and the economy. As the President spoke to one of his most liberal audiences he was quite comfortable speaking of his opinion that there's a need for more redistribution of wealth to deal with income inequality. The President has made no secret of his central aim of shifting wealth throughout his time in office. The reality is that the Presidents law is based on a social-engineering mission that turns insurance companies into vehicles for redistribution. As the President continued his theme of success with Obama Care enrollment he said, "over a half million people are now **poised** to have health insurance." He must think we all miss those misleading key words. The truth is that the American people are **poised** to be screwed, against their will, by the biggest bait and switch scam ever perpetrated. Even the poor who will receive Medicaid coverage for the first time will find that government provided health care is risky business. The government funded care they may or may not receive will be so inadequate that it could literally cost the lives of those who are seriously ill. This law was never about providing affordable health care for the American people. It's always been about income redistribution and a means to an end that will move America closer to single payer health care or basically an expansion of Medicare for all Americans of every age. In more general terms, the Obama administration's motive is to destroy private sector health care to set up government controlled health care. Doctors and Hospitals aren't the only private sector targets for destruction. Pharmaceutical companies are targeted due to the very limited lists of drugs that will be covered under Obama Care health insurance plans. This will have a devastating impact on many critically ill Americans and the harm done to major Pharmaceutical companies will have a negative impact on the economy.

Obama Care is **poised to fail** because Democrats were determined to shove it down the collective throats of Americans by making a big power grab of one-sixth of the American economy. If they had proceeded on an incremental basis, they may have made progress over time toward the successful implementation of their liberal agenda. Their greedy all-inclusive power grab will cost them dearly and it will be a slow and painful decline over the course of the next 3 years that will strike a huge blow to the liberal progressive movement in America.

Hired Gun

December 10, 2013

White House Chief of Staff Dennis McDonough made a move to bring in John Podesta as a White House counselor for one year. Podesta was Bill Clinton's Chief of Staff and was best known for performing clean up duties after the Monica Lewinski affair. Podesta is a very wealthy DC lobbyist and is a well-connected DC insider. His ideology is very far to the left and his tough guy reputation precedes himself. It's very safe to assume that he will be called into service to hammer Republicans, especially over Obama Care. The 65-year old **hired gun** was basically brought in to bat clean up as the Presidents credibility and ratings in the polls have hit an all-time low.

Don't Bring a Knife to a Gun Fight

Congressman Paul Ryan and Senator Patty Murray announced today that they've reached a budget deal that could bring an end to the endless CR's, continuing resolutions, and allow Congress to establish appropriations and function within the confines of an actual budget for the next 2 years. Their work in conference with the budget committee will potentially end the "crisis to crisis" fiscal management style that has reigned under the Obama administration for almost 5 years. The deal cancels about $63 billion in across the board Sequester spending reductions and offsets the restored spending with about $85 billion in more targeted spending cuts spread over a decade. The largely symbolic $22 billion deficit reduction is nothing more than a trivial rounding error that won't come to fruition anyway. These numbers may appear to be marginally reasonable but when the $63 billion is spent quickly in less than 2 years and then most of the $85 billion in supposed cuts go away because Congress has 10 years to play shell games with it, the deal as it stands today will be long forgotten. Congressman Ryan spoke of smart targeted reforms that replace autopilot Sequester spending cuts and emphasized there will be no tax increases. He said it is a 1st step to rebuild trust on both sides of the aisle.

It's widely thought that the deal will pass through the House and Senate even though Democrats won't get the unemployment benefit extension or corporate tax loophole cuts they were looking for and Republicans won't get entitlement cuts they wanted. The deal saves a looming $20 billion cut to Pentagon spending which the Sequester cuts would have called for that would have severely affected military readiness. The deal also saves drastic domestic discretionary spending cuts to Education, Medical Research, Defense Jobs, Transportation and National Parks of which Democrats are most concerned with. There will nevertheless be some political grandstanding on both sides in protest to key parts of the deal but Republicans don't have the appetite for another government shut-down and Democrats are still reeling from Obama Care failures so both sides must put their differences aside and agree to this bipartisan deal.

The President praised the deal as a good first step and urged lawmakers on both sides to follow up and "actually pass a budget based on this agreement so I can sign it into law and our economy can continue growing and creating jobs without more Washington headwinds." Of great importance is the fact that an actual 2-year budget deal will provide certainty for the business community and retains the power of the purse in Congress where it belongs. The continual string of CR's over the course of the last 5 years has placed too much power in the hands of the executive branch.

That said, make no mistake, this is a terrible budget deal and true Conservatives have every right to be upset. $63 billion in Sequester spending cuts mandated by law went out the window. These Sequester cuts were the only driver that had recently brought about an actual deficit reduction. Spending addicted Democrats aren't even happy with the $63 billion which would be restored if this budget becomes law. These Democrats won't be happy until they spend us into oblivion. Ultimately, Americans can't lose sight of the fact that we have $90 trillion in unfunded liabilities and with $17.2 trillion in debt, America is headed for disaster. The misconception that many Republicans espouse is that this is the best that can be done with divided government but that's a very weak excuse. It wasn't that long ago that Republicans controlled the Executive Branch along with both chambers of Congress and spending was wildly out of control. It is possible to make bipartisanship work. If Republicans were united on Conservative principles, they could accomplish much more than they have and frankly John Boehner has been weak on too many issues during his 3-year span as Speaker and it's too late for him to get tough and be believable and effective in the process. Tip O'Neil never would have found himself in the weak position that John Boehner is in now. When going up against an unethical thug like Senate majority leader Harry Reid; well, **'don't bring a knife to a gun fight'** comes to mind. Also, suffice it to say that President Obama is the most divisive and incompetent President in the history of the United States so he most assuredly exacerbates the process but Republicans have done a terrible job of playing out the hand they were dealt.

December 18, 2013

For the first time since President Obama took office the U.S. government has a budget. After 5 years of Continuing Resolutions the Senate passed the Ryan/Murray budget today by a vote of 64 to 36. The budget recently passed in the House by 332 to 94. The President has indicated that he will sign the budget into law but this will require running him down in Hawaii where he is normally found this time of year spending an obscene amount of taxpayer dollars. The irony associated with this budget deal is inescapable because on one hand, Congress must be commended for its rare bipartisan work to pass this legislation that provides the first budget in 5 years but on the other hand the substance of this budget leaves a lot to be desired. Of the many deficiencies, one of them defies logic. $6 billion over 10 years will be taken away from military retirees, including wounded warriors. The baffling aspect of this provision is that an amendment proposed by Senator Jeff Sessions (R-Ala.) called for $6 billion to be taken from illegal alien welfare benefits and in turn appropriated to restore the Veterans benefits that were slashed in the budget deal, but the amendment was blocked by Democrats. This shameful move by Senate Democrats is beyond disgraceful. To take from the Americans who served our country with distinction and give instead to people who entered our country illegally and have not only done nothing to serve America but are bottom feeders who depend on our generosity is incomprehensible.

On the damage control front, the President announced the appointment of Katie Beirne Fallon as director of legislative affairs. Fallon is a veteran Capitol Hill insider who maintains deep relationships with Democrat lawmakers and is highly regarded as a policy and political strategist. She replaces Miguel Rodriguez, a lawyer and former foreign policy aide who was relatively unknown among congressional leaders. Fallon will be expected to coordinate the Presidents climate control agenda and manage legislative strategy around immigration reform and the health-care law. In a statement announcing Fallon's appointment, the President said, "She has the deep expertise and strong relationships required to build on the progress we've made this year and advance my top priority; creating jobs and expanding broad-based growth and opportunity for every American." Coming from the President, this is a very confusing and misleading statement, but then why would we expect anything else. His reference to progress is nothing short of delusional. The Fallon appointment is just one more desperate move to regroup and move the Presidents ill-advised agenda forward over the course of the next 3 years.

Obama Care Hardship

December 19, 2013

The President made his 12th unilateral executive order late this evening to once again change the ACA aka Obama Care. The latest in the now rather lengthy list of waivers makes an exemption to the individual mandate by allowing individuals whose existing health insurance was cancelled due to Obama Care mandates to purchase bare bones catastrophic coverage which previously didn't meet the requirements of the law. Basically, individuals will make a self determination as to whether they were placed in a **hardship** position due to the cancellation of their existing health insurance. Interestingly this is easily seen as an admission by the administration that Obama Care has imposed a **hardship** on all individuals. The newly created plans which came as a surprise to insurance companies, will create an offering of minimal catastrophic coverage that will surely cause an increase in premiums for everyone. These minimal coverage plans still cost at least twice as much as comparable plans that existed prior to Obama Care. Premiums for the new bare bones plans will cost about $185. a month with a deductible of about $8000. for most individuals when premiums were previously about $92. a month with lower deductibles. The Bronze plan is only slightly more @ about $210. a month with the same kind of high deductible. This most recent unilateral change to the law by executive order, which is totally unconstitutional just like the previous changes, will undermine the risk pools and create a logistical nightmare for insurance companies. If insurance companies hadn't been guaranteed a government bail out in the very likely event of the disastrous implosion of Obama Care, they would be bailing out of the health insurance market as fast as possible. The United States government bears all risk which you and I will ultimately pay for.

December 20, 2013

The President made his year-end appearance before the White House press corp. today right before boarding Air Force 1 for his annual Hawaii vacation. The healthcare.gov website conveniently crashed right before he took the podium. He had to field a few tough questions but since he remains unencumbered by the constraints of truth and accuracy, he managed to calmly work his way through what would otherwise have been a very uncomfortable press conference. At one point, he said "things aren't as bad as people think they are." In his opening statement, he said over 1 million people have selected Obama Care coverage and again referred to this group as being poised to be covered. The President's 1 million number sounds high when compared to the HHS number of about 325,000. Given the fact that nobody has paid any money to an insurance company yet and can't because the payment mechanism doesn't even exist yet, it's difficult to see how anyone will be insured on January 1st. The President also failed to mention the other 1 million who have enrolled in Medicaid for government provided health care at no cost to this group of individuals. He also failed to mention the 5.9 million whose existing health insurance was cancelled and are yet to obtain new coverage. He still falsely maintains that this group was either grandfathered in or found better insurance at a cheaper cost but conveniently ignores the math which doesn't even come close to supporting such a ridiculous claim. When asked about his most recent accommodation he said "it's no big deal because not many people are affected." He spoke of about 500,000 people who will benefit from his latest waiver but it's difficult to reconcile that number with the 5.9 million who lost their existing coverage. When asked, what was his biggest mistake, he did at least accept responsibility for the failed website roll out.

The President appeared to be tired and beat up as the few tough questions were posed. He was probably thinking let's just get this over with so he could make his escape to Hawaii and chill out for 2 weeks. Aloha and Mahalo Mr. President! You may want to think about staying there and just let Uncle Joe fade the heat for the next 3 years.

Chapter 13

Income Inequality

January 10, 2014

As we enter the New Year, Democrats are making the President's call for higher taxes and increased government spending to combat **"income inequality"** the centerpiece of their 2014 strategy. Raising the minimum wage and extending unemployment benefits for 1.3 million Americans are the initial priorities for the President. It would cost $6.4 billion to extend unemployment benefits for another 3 months. These same so-called emergency benefits have already been extended 11 times while these Americans have been out of work for over 2 years. Democrats aren't at all concerned with the source of the $6.4 billion needed to extend these benefits but Republicans will insist on a definite source for the money. The concern conservatives have is that it's much more difficult for workers to re-enter the workforce when they've been out of work for an extended timeframe because their skills atrophy and employers question their work ethic. This concern is at the center of the conservative conclusion that enabling this group of long term unemployed workers to remain unemployed is not in their best interest. December jobs numbers just out from the Labor Department show that U.S. employers added a paltry 74,000 jobs in the final month of 2013 which represents the lowest number of new jobs in 3 years. This number is nowhere near the more than 200,000 jobs the economy must add each month just to keep pace with population growth. Over 347,000 job-eligible adults dropped out of the labor pool in December taking the total unemployment number to 13.1% with 1 out of every 5 American men unemployed. The Obama administration continues to tout an unemployment number of 6.7% which doesn't include Americans who have quit looking for work. At this point 62.8% of the unemployed have quit looking for a job. It's been over 35 years since this many people have dropped out of the workforce. The President also continues to claim that economic recovery is real and will leave nobody behind but recent jobs numbers and the need to further extend unemployment benefits for the 12th time doesn't remotely support such a claim. 5 years of increased government spending on economic stimulus has led to the worst economic recovery in history. Many Americans are finally beginning to understand that big government can't create jobs and that government spending hinders economic growth. Once we add the extensive damage done by Obama Care to small business and the entire middle class, we see a depressing picture of economic woes that will persist under the Obama administrations failed economic policies.

It shouldn't even make sense for the words income and inequality to be combined in the same phrase. The implication is that income is a right and doesn't necessarily need to be earned. **Income inequality** perpetuates the notion that people should rely on government to meet their needs as opposed to the rewards of hard work which leads to earned success and dignity. The battle cry of income inequality will continue to be heard over the next 3 years predominately as a diversion to take the focus off Obama Care failures.

Defense Gate

January 14, 2014

Robert Gates, President Obama's first term Secretary of Defense, has shaken things up in Washington and disrupted the Presidents intended narrative for the midterm election year with the release of his new book, "Duty: Memoirs of a Secretary of War." Gates, who also served as Secretary of Defense for the George W. Bush administration, claims that President Obama was skeptical about his own policy on the war in Afghanistan and was "outright convinced it would fail." Gates writes, "With Obama, however, I joined a new, inexperienced President determined to change course – and equally determined from day one to win re-election. Domestic political considerations would therefore be a factor, though I believe never a decisive one, in virtually every major national security problem we tackled." One of Gates most enlightening statements from his book is, "I felt that agreements with the Obama White House were good for only as long as they were politically convenient."

Gates certainly didn't overlook former Secretary of State Hillary Clinton or Vice President Joe Biden. On Clinton, he writes about her decision to oppose the 2007 "Iraq Surge," a strategy from the Bush White House that effectively turned the tide in that war. "Hillary told [Obama] that her opposition to the [2007] surge in Iraq had been political because she was facing him in the Iowa primary…. The President conceded vaguely that opposition to the Iraq surge had been political. To hear the two of them making these admissions, and in front of me, was as surprising as dismaying." While Gates had a few good things to relate about Clinton and Obama, Joe Biden didn't fare as well. Gates did call Biden "a man of integrity," but his praise for Biden ended there. On Biden, Gates writes, "I think he has been wrong on nearly every major foreign policy and national security issue over the past four decades." In a January 14th appearance on "Fox and Friends," Gates said of Biden, "Starting with voting against the aid package for South Vietnam in the mid-1970's, he opposed virtually every element of President Reagan's defense program and approach to the Soviet Union and he voted against the first Gulf War."

The Wall Street Journal had this to say about Gates book; "The Gates book may be most troubling for what it says about the three long years left in Mr. Obama's second term – which also makes us wonder why he didn't go public sooner, at the time he left office. He describes a President who knows he must invoke the traditional rhetorical markers of U.S. foreign policy – a strong defense, credibility with allies, democracy and human rights – yet whose every impulse is to leave the world to its own devices."

Preventable

January 15, 2014

The Senate Intelligence Committee issued a report today finding that the September 11, 2012 attack on the U.S. diplomatic outpost in Benghazi, Libya was **preventable** and was, in fact, carried out by Al Qaeda affiliated groups. The committee report, offered by Chairwoman Diane Feinstein (D-CA), blames the State Department, then headed by Clinton, for not bolstering security at the compound, despite repeated warnings of imminent attacks. In an appearance on CNN, Senator Feinstein said, "We know there were training camps around that area, and it is something that I think the State Department has to really come to grips with."

Senator Marco Rubio (R-FL), a member of the Senate Select Committee on Intelligence, issued the following statement today in response to the release of the committee's report.

"This report will contribute to the overall examination into those attacks. However, this is not a complete report, and it only sheds light on part of the overall picture. The American people deserve the truth when it comes to the Benghazi attacks, and more work needs to be done."

"Specifically, the Senate Foreign Relations Committee has yet to seriously examine these attacks that resulted in the death of four Americans, including the U.S. Ambassador to Libya, Chris Stevens. The committee should reexamine former Secretary of State Clinton's failure to provide adequate security for our deployed personnel in Benghazi, as well as what actions she and others, including the President, took in the hours and days that followed the attack."

"Throughout this investigation, the Obama administration was more of a roadblock than a contributor to committee efforts to analyze the root cause of these attacks. This is especially troubling given that no one at the State Department, which has direct responsibility for the safety of U.S. diplomatic posts overseas, has been held accountable."

"Despite many promises of ensuring justice for those behind this attack, that has not happened. This complete absence of accountability is unacceptable, and it is my hope that this administration will finally commit the intelligence, diplomatic and military resources to bring those responsible for these attacks to justice."

The Senate Intelligence Committee stopped short of placing blame on any specific individual such as Hillary Clinton or even Barak Obama and instead made it a general indictment on the bureaucracy. Make no mistake, Hillary Clinton as Secretary of State at the time and the

President, are ultimately responsible for this disaster because they deliberately refused to provide the necessary security that was pleaded for by Ambassador Stevens so they could maintain the re-election narrative that the war on terror is over and Al Qaeda is on the run. Clinton and Obama gambled with the lives of American diplomats in Benghazi at stake and lost.

Accountability is a dirty word as far as the Obama administration is concerned. No one has been held accountable for any of the numerous failures and scandals of this administration. Heads of the IRS, HHS, DOJ, State Department and NSA have escaped accountability for targeting conservative groups with intense scrutiny (IRS), Obama Care failures (HHS), "Fast and Furious" (DOJ), Benghazi (State Department) and illegal surveillance of U.S. citizens (NSA) to name just a few. The scandalous Obama administration will go down in history as the least accountable and most corrupt administration the American people have ever experienced.

New Yorker Profile

January 21, 2014

A lengthy interview with the President in New Yorker magazine paints a revealing picture of the President's state of mind one year into his second term. It's somewhat surprising that he would agree to a 17,000-word high profile interview while his administration and agenda are mired in failure after failure but his narcissistic persona can't resist the spotlight. New Yorker editor David Remnick conducted the interview and offered his view of the President as, "He is said to be a reluctant politician: aloof, insular, diffident, arrogant, inert, unwilling to jolly his allies along the fairway and take a 9-iron to his enemies. He doesn't know anyone in Congress. No one in the House or the Senate, no one in foreign capitals fears him. He gives a great speech, but he doesn't understand power. He is a poor executive. Doesn't it seem as if he hates the job? And so on. This is the knowing talk on Wall Street, on K Street, on Capitol Hill, in green rooms." This is certainly a strong indictment coming from the editor of such a liberal publication.

When asked, what he wants to accomplish in the next 3 years – Obama replied, "I will measure myself at the end of my presidency in large part by whether I began the process of rebuilding the middle class and the ladders into the middle class, and reversing the trend toward economic bifurcation in this society." He went on to describe himself as "a relay swimmer in a river full of rapids."

At this point the President appears to be defeated and disillusioned. This is certainly understandable given the fact that he hasn't accomplished anything he led us to believe he wanted to accomplish. He succeeded in forcing socialistic health care on us but the numerous failures associated with Obama Care make it a dubious accomplishment at best. Conservatives can find some relief in the Presidents failure to advance his multipronged destructive agenda but President Obama still leaves a wake of destruction following his path of misguided socialistic goals. Since destruction by deceit is at the core of this President's agenda we must consider the frightening notion that the destruction is intentional so that America may be rebuilt as a socialist nation. He doesn't have sufficient time left for the rebuilding aspect of this notion so he must be counting on a successor to complete his misguided task. I'm sure Hillary Clinton would love to grab the socialistic baton to finish the task of taking this nation down.

Train Wreck

January 22, 2014

As we approach the end of open enrollment for Obama Care at the end of March, problems are mounting and it's become increasingly obvious that this law is indeed a **train wreck**. Admissions of failure by the Obama administration are gradually finding the light of day beginning with documents released by HHS and CMS to justify a no-bid contract with Accenture after firing CGI as the lead contractor for the construction of the disastrous healthcare.gov website. The documents offer a rare glimpse into the administrations worst fears saying the problems with the website puts "the entire health insurance industry at risk… potentially leading to their default and disrupting continued services and coverage to consumers." The documents went further saying if the problems were not fixed by mid-March, "they will result in financial harm to the government." The documents added that without the fixes "the entire health care reform program is jeopardized."

It's important to note that Toni Townes-Whitley, Senior Vice-President of CGI, the Canadian company who landed the no bid contract worth $93 million to build the healthcare.gov website so far costing $678 million, was a classmate of Michelle Obama at Princeton. Apparently, no American companies were even considered to build the website and there's nothing to point to in defense of awarding CGI the contract. CGI's most notable previous job was building a gun registry for the Canadian government which resulted in CGI being fired by the Canadian government for cost overruns that cost Canada $100 million.

Shortly before CGI was fired, HHS Secretary Kathleen Sebelius gave Fox News an upbeat account saying, "I'm thrilled that we're going to have millions of people for the first time that have health security." This woman is in so far over her head that I'm beginning to feel sorry for her. It's painfully obvious that there is no room for optimism because what is known as the "back end" of the website, which allows for communication between HHS and the insurance companies, hasn't even been constructed yet. Insurance companies are dealing with massive confusion, missing information on who's signed up and what subsidies they get. Sebelius insisted today that it will all come together as she said (concerning the insurance companies), "I mean we will get them paid," and added, "There is no question about that, so we are on track."

To express such confidence in a system that relies on estimates, basically the honor system, coming from the insurance companies who are only concerned with their own survival, is a clear sign of the extreme incompetence at play here that will yield disastrous results.

Aetna CEO Mark Bertolini told CNBC today that so far, Obama Care has just shifted people who were insured in the individual market to the public exchanges where they could get a better deal with a subsidy for coverage. "We see only 11% of the population is actually people that were firmly uninsured that are now insured. So [it] didn't really eat into the uninsured population." He related that for Obama Care to work better, it needs more flexibility and choice of insurance programs.

January 23, 2014

Moody's investors services downgraded its outlook for the U.S. health insurance sector today to negative from stable, because of the uncertainty created by Obama Care. "While we've had industry risks from regulatory changes on our radar for a while, the ongoing unstable and evolving environment is a key factor for our outlook change," Moody's Senior Vice-President Stephen Zaharuk said in a statement. He added, "The past few months have seen new regulations and announcements that impose operational changes well after product and pricing decisions were finalized." Moody's said sluggish enrollment by young adults also contributed to the downgrade. Only 24% of enrollees so far in the individual insurance exchanges are in the 18 to 34-year old group, Moody's noted. That number may have to rise to 40% to keep premiums from going up, it says. "We find that after accounting for subsidies and cost-sharing, six out of seven uninsured, young adult households will find it financially advantageous to forego health coverage, and instead pay the mandate penalty and cover their own healthcare costs" in 2014, the study noted.

The bad news continues with the revelation that heirs of Medicaid recipients will now be on the hook for their parent's health care bill. The government is tracking all health care expenses of Medicaid enrollees and heirs will be shocked when they discover a lien on the estate left by their parents. Heirs simply won't have access to their inheritance, provided there is one, until the health care bill for their parents is paid in full.

Illegal Snooping

In a 3-2 ruling, the Privacy and Civil Liberties Oversight Board said the federal government violated the Patriot Act by stockpiling Americans' phone records and the phone companies are violating other federal laws by turning over the information to the federal government. The board is an advisory panel and doesn't carry the force of law but it did go on to say that the government should destroy all records it has. Patricia M. Wald, a former senior federal judge and one of the privacy board's members, said "It's the fact that the government has this mass of information. Even if it doesn't use it in any way detrimental to anybody, it changes the power structure." The Patriot Act gives the government power to collect "relevant" records and the privacy panel's majority said collecting all records goes well beyond that. The panel also said that demanding the records from the phone companies is illegal because the Electronic Communications Privacy Act prohibits companies from turning over information except in limited circumstances. The Patriot Act is not one of those exceptions, the panel concluded. The President addressed the nation on January 17th in a 45-minute speech about NSA surveillance after which it was difficult to conclude anything of substance. The speech was a long and rambling dissertation that was extremely vague and open ended. He merely spoke on principle and in the end deferred to Congress and the DOJ.

State of the Union

January 28, 2014

The President delivered the State of the Union address this evening in a speech short on substance but basically harmless overall. There was no passion in the Presidents delivery and he failed to express any sense of urgency. He didn't introduce any new initiatives in what could be characterized as a very dull speech. The Presidents sense of defeat was evident but he plowed ahead as best he could, speaking about the same failed policies he made no progress with in 2013. His speech writers could have just gone on vacation, handed him a copy of last years' speech and he, along with the rest of the Country, probably wouldn't have noticed. The speech was heavy on rhetoric and light on specifics about how we can move the Country forward in 2014. His repeated threat to utilize executive orders as opposed to working with Congress to legislate initiatives became the resounding theme for action in 2014 as the President expressed confidence that 2014 will in fact be a year of action. The joke of the night was when the President said we have a broken health care system and we're in the process of fixing it. Speaker Boehner, who could be seen behind the President throughout the speech, managed to refrain from any facial expression during the speech until that claim and for a moment his expression was priceless.

The President didn't even bring up his signature health care law until 40 minutes into the speech when he briefly brought up "insurance reform." He went on to say, "More than 9 million Americans have gained insurance under the law." The Obama administration claims that 6 million people have been determined to be eligible for Medicaid and 3 million have signed up for private health insurance coverage. At this point we have no way to verify these numbers other than just taking the administrations word for it but their definition of "signed up" is questionable. They consider people who have gone on the website and put a plan in the shopping cart as a bona fide "sign up" as opposed to people who have made their first payment. Also, we have no way of knowing how many of the Medicaid enrollees would have obtained Medicaid coverage even without Obama Care and the total number of enrollees who signed up for private coverage because they lost their existing insurance is not clear either.

Aside from the questionable number of people the President claims to have enrolled in Obama Care, he shared some other whoppers. He claimed we have the lowest unemployment in 5 years, deficits have been cut in half, and climate change is a fact. He failed to mention we have the lowest labor force participation since 1978 with 1 out of 6 Americans on food stamps. The budget deficit was reduced during a 9-month period in 2013 due to spending limitations mandated by the Budget Control Act (Sequestration) but that inconsequential reduction pales in comparison to the rising $17.3 trillion National Debt which the President ignored in his speech. The Presidents certainty on climate change could be a relief since we've learned to believe the exact opposite of anything he says. That brief feeling of relief went out the window when the President cited the EPA as one of the beneficiaries of executive orders to regulate energy resources and he even threatened to invest more money in solar energy, this after the disastrous results of the Solyndra investment. Climate change or global warming isn't even settled science but the President expects the American people to accept it as fact when there is absolutely no proof of its existence. The assertion, by a few scientists who are bought and paid for, that climate change exists simply isn't sufficient proof. The President's determination to go back to the well of failed initiatives is incredible. He promised to close Guantanamo this year, a promise he's failed to live up to for 5 years now because there's very little support to do it and for good reason.

The President went on to talk about other tired and even dead initiatives such as long term unemployment insurance, high quality Pre-K education, raising the minimum wage, women's inequality in the workforce, government job training programs, nuclear negotiations with Iran, immigration reform and a general reduction to our military. On the military front, he spoke of a troop draw down in Afghanistan which would leave only a small contingent to deal with the Taliban and Al-Qaeda after a significant troop withdrawal takes place. After experiencing disastrous results from doing the same thing in Iraq, common sense would dictate an avoidance of making the same mistake in Afghanistan but unfortunately this administration is short on common sense. He said we must move off a permanent war footing and promised no more large scale deployments. As the President was promising a decimation of our military in the Middle East, the television camera's focused on the joint chiefs in the audience and their obvious disapproval was easy to detect. This administration has significantly damaged our relationship with Israel, indirectly supported Iran's nuclear program, decimated all progress made in Iraq, set the stage for disaster in Afghanistan and sacrificed any respect we once enjoyed throughout the Middle East.

The Presidents year of action will consist of a series of unconstitutional executive orders which will accomplish little and unlike Congressional legislation his executive actions can just as easily be wiped out by the next President. This Presidents failure to lead the nation will insure more of the same disastrous results that we've experienced for the last 5 years. The promised year of action in 2014 will most likely consist of ducking for cover as one failure after another unfolds throughout the year and beyond. The very real issues such as Obama Care failures, IRS targeting of conservative groups, the hidden truths about Benghazi, "Fast and Furious" gun running by the DOJ, unconstitutional NSA snooping on all U.S. citizens, and most importantly our stalled economy, will continue to be swept under the rug with the hope that Americans will shift their attention to the inconsequential distractions outlined in tonight's speech.

Chapter 14

Super Bowl Sunday

February 2, 2013

Right before the Seattle Seahawks punished the Denver Broncos in the Super Bowl, Fox News journalist, Bill O'Reilly, interviewed the President in a high profile face off that gave us more to talk about than the game. President Obama ducked and dodged while refusing to give a straight answer to Bill's questions. Bill focused on the Obama Care debacle, the IRS scandal, and Benghazi, all topics that the main stream media intentionally ignores because the President has them in his back pocket. The biggest and most obvious lie came when Bill was grilling the President on IRS targeting of conservatives. As Bill was drilling down on the illegal IRS actions targeting conservative groups (predominately Tea Party groups) who had applied for tax exempt status, the exchange went as follows:

O'Reilly: You're saying no corruption?

Obama: No

O'Reilly: None? No?

Obama: There were some -- there were some bone-headed decisions....

O'Reilly: Bone-headed decisions?

Obama: -- out of – out of a local office...

O'Reilly: But no mass corruption?

Obama: Not even mass corruption, **not even a smidgeon of corruption,** I would say.

Given the fact that the IRS investigation is an open investigation with no official conclusion or decision, the President's lie of no corruption is premature to put it lightly. The IRS commissioner at the time, Douglas Shulman, was cleared in and out of the White House 157 times, more than any cabinet member and far more than any previous IRS chief in history. Apparently, there was some serious plotting under way to wage war against the Presidents political enemies leading up to the November 2012 Presidential election. Even though the investigation is on-going we know more than enough to conclude that conservative groups and only conservative groups were singled out and refused tax exempt status which they clearly qualified for while liberal groups were approved in short order. When you have Lois Lerner, the head of the tax-exempt division of the IRS at that time, take the 5th and refuse to testify in a Congressional hearing and shortly after that resign and take early retirement, plus the Treasury Department's Inspector General for Tax Administration, J. Russell George, who concluded on the record that conservative groups were targeted and described this practice as "inappropriate," clearly the IRS and the Obama administration are evading the truth. The corrupt practice of targeting conservative groups was revealed in an admission by Lois Lerner during a press conference in May of 2013 when she said IRS agents singled out dozens of organizations for additional reviews because they included the words "tea party" or "patriot" in their exemption applications. She went on to say that in some cases groups were asked for lists of donors which violates IRS policy in most cases. Once this admission became a major news story, the White House fired back and said it was just some low-level employees in the Cincinnati office who committed this action and that no one in management or at the White House was aware of it until months after it occurred. We've since learned enough from the Inspector General and Congressional hearings to know that this action originated in Washington DC from very high levels of government.

It's important to note that presently the investigation is being led by Barbara Boserman who donated $6750. to the Obama 2012 re-election campaign. This so-called investigation is a sham because none of the targeted groups have even been interviewed by the FBI. Conservative groups like the "Tea Party Patriots" in Sarasota, FL. have been waiting for a ruling on their tax-exempt status for over 3 years with no answer to this day when the process originally took only 3 to 4 weeks, so as the President attempts to convince us that the situation is resolved and that there was no corruption, we have groups who continue to be strung along by a corrupt IRS in the middle of a corrupt investigation.

On Benghazi, after a drawn out back and forth of dodging by the President, it came down to this:

O'Reilly: It's the fog of war...

Obama: -- people-- that's -- people don't know at the very moment exactly why something like this happens. And when you look at the videotape of this whole thing unfolding, this is not some systematic, well organized process. You see...

O'Reilly: Well, it was heavy weapons used...

Obama: -- You...

O'Reilly: -- and that...

Obama: -- what you...

O'Reilly: -- that's the thing...

Obama: -- what you see -- Bill...

O'Reilly: -- heavy weapons coming in.

Obama: -- Bill, listen, I -- I -- I've gone through this and we have had multiple hearings on it. What happens is you have an attack like this taking place and you have a mix of folks who have an ideological agenda.

O'Reilly: All right.

Obama: You have some who are affiliated with terrorist organizations. You have some that are not. But the main thing that all of us must take away from this is our diplomats are serving in some very dangerous places.

The Presidents claim that the attack was not systematic or well organized and his claim about a mix of folks with an ideological agenda doesn't make sense when we know that it was a highly-organized terrorist attack by an Al Qaeda affiliated group who were using sophisticated military hand signals, knew the exact whereabouts of the Ambassador and were firing mortars with great skill and accuracy. How could anyone reasonably conclude that it was a spontaneous response to a U-tube video when all the facts point to a highly-coordinated terrorist attack? Mike Morrell, former CIA Deputy Director, changed the original talking points which were apparently closer to the truth, and inserted the ridiculous video story. Morrell told Senators Lindsey Graham (R-SC) and Kelly Ayotte (R-NH) during a private Senate meeting that the FBI changed the talking points but when Graham checked with the FBI they vehemently denied Morrell's assertion and Morrell was forced to admit he had done it. The identity and the whereabouts of the perpetrators of this terrorist attack are known by the CIA and the FBI but nothing has been done to capture or kill them. One can only conclude that this administration is still concerned with maintaining the campaign narrative that Al Qaeda has been decimated and is on the run when we know that there are at least 5 Al Qaeda franchises now operating in 12 Countries.

On Obama Care, the President said the healthcare.gov website is now working the way it's supposed to and 3 million people have signed up but O'Reilly immediately pointed out that just last week there was an Associated Press report about people who went to the website and only 8% of them feel that it's working well. The President didn't even bother to refute Bill's point. Bill went on to press the President on the fact that no one has been held accountable for the roll out fiasco and asked why Kathleen Sebelius, Secretary of HHS, hasn't been fired but the President dodged the question and didn't even begin to answer it.

Given the time constraints, Bill O'Reilly did a very good job of holding the Presidents feet to the fire and didn't allow him to filibuster which he is particularly adept at. When the televised portion of the interview went off the air, Bill had more time with the President and Bill asked if he had always treated him fairly and the President immediately responded that he hadn't but that he still liked him. Then the President went on to say, "We've just run through an interview in which you asked about health, uh, health care not working, IRS where – were we, uh, wholly corrupt, Benghazi…. they're defined by you guys in a certain way…. I think regardless of whether it's fair or not, uh, it has, uh, it has made Fox News very successful…. what are you gonna do when I'm gone?" Sounds like someone has a bit of an ego problem! The latest Quinnipiac poll on trustworthiness might quell the Presidents enthusiasm for self because it finds that 49% of Americans do not find the President to be trustworthy.

Stuck

February 3, 2014

The Washington Post revealed a new Obama Care problem today when they reported that about 22,000 consumers are **stuck** with Obama Care errors because the mechanism to correct errors hasn't even been constructed yet. These consumers have been told that the healthcare.gov computer system is not yet allowing federal workers to go into enrollment records and change them based on accounts by individuals inside and outside the government who are familiar with the situation. As these consumers search for a resolution to their dilemma they've been told to print out a 7-page form, complete it and mail it to a government contractor in Kentucky where…. nothing will happen. The Washington Post's Amy Goldstein reported that, "For now, the appeals are sitting, untouched, inside a government computer."

Senator John Thune (R-SD) said today, "The President's State of the Union address was notable for one thing: the almost total absence of the President's signature health care law…. The worst possible thing we could do is saddle businesses with new taxes and regulations that discourage hiring and expansion and encourage cutting jobs and hours. Yet that is precisely what the President's health care law does. The health care law has been a disaster from the start, devastating family budgets and the entire economy. Every Democrat who voted for this law owes the American people an explanation…. and Americans will demand one at the ballot box." I couldn't agree more! We may be **stuck** with Obama Care but we don't have to like it and we can and will speak when we cast our vote in November.

Trillion Dollar Farm Bill

February 4, 2014

The $1 trillion 1000-page Farm Bill passed in the Senate today by a landslide vote of 68 – 32. The bill passed in the House on 1/29 by a vote of 251 – 166. The billion-dollar-per-page bill makes a small reduction to food stamp spending while continuing generous subsidies for the nation's farmers. House conservatives originally sought a $4 billion reduction to food stamp benefits but settled for $800 million in food stamp cuts. The CBO, Congressional Budget Office, projects that the bill will save about $1.65 billion annually overall even though it's loaded with pork. The President is set to sign the bill into law on Friday 2/7.

Poverty Trap

February 5, 2014

The CBO, Congressional Budget Office, released a report today that asserts approximately 2.3 million people will lose their full-time job and be forced into part time work due to Obama Care regulations and that Obama Care will add $10 trillion to federal deficits by 2024. The report coming from the non-partisan CBO detailed how millions of workers could accept fewer hours or opt out of the job market entirely because of benefits under the health law. CBO Director Douglas Elmendorf testified before the House Budget Committee today to answer questions on the report. While being questioned by Committee Chairman Paul Ryan (R-WI), Director Elmendorf said, "the act will create a disincentive for people to work because more people would opt to keep their income low to stay eligible for federal health care subsidies or Medicaid." Ryan clarified that the CBO report found not that employers would lay people off but that more people would choose not to work. "As a result....that [lower] labor supply lowers economic growth," Ryan said. Elmendorf answered, "Yes, that's right." Ryan vehemently declared that this would mean fewer people would be "joining the middle class." "It's adding insult to injury," Ryan said. "As the welfare state expands, the incentive to work declines -- meaning grow the government, you shrink the economy."

It's the latest indication that "the Presidents health care law is destroying full time jobs," said Rep. John Kline (R-MN), chairman of the House Education and Workforce Committee. "This fatally flawed health care scheme is wreaking havoc on working families nationwide," he said. The training, habit, and dignity of work, is under attack by the law. The Wall Street Journal reported today that 1 out of 6 men between the age of 25 and 54 don't have a job. It should come as no surprise that we are seeing the lowest labor participation rate in 5 years when 17% of the population who should be at the height of productivity are without a job. When January 2014 job numbers came out we saw only 113,000 jobs added in January when 194,000 jobs were added for the same month last year and the labor participation rate has fallen to 63%. It's no wonder that the latest Quinnipiac poll finds that 60% of Americans oppose the health care law and a recent Fox News poll finds that 59% of Americans disapprove of the Presidents performance on the economy.

The White House spin asserts that people will have more time with their family and that the law creates "choices" for Americans because it allows people to work less. The law means people "will be empowered to make choices about their own lives and livelihoods," said White House Press Secretary Jay Carney today. Carney went on to say that the law "creates the opportunity for more entrepreneurship." Health care shouldn't be the driving force in determining the content or size of the labor force. The reality is that we're dealing with a government dependency Ponzi scheme that deliberately establishes a **poverty trap** so that more and more Americans are forced into dependence on the government. Safety Net programs such as Medicaid and Food Stamps also create a disincentive to work, so now we have a huge expansion of Medicaid and millions of Americans forced into part time employment which brings about a huge expansion of the welfare state. Wealth redistribution has been at the heart of this administrations goals and Obama Care is successfully playing a major role in helping the Obama administration realize their goal. Government subsidies don't just fall from the sky. Americans who don't qualify for the subsidies are the people who are paying for the subsidies. This is wealth redistribution 101.

February 6, 2014

A Duke University study revealed today finds that 44% of U.S. firms have cut back on health care benefits for their current workers due to Obama Care regulations. 55% of Americans obtain their health insurance through their employer so it's no surprise that the study also finds that over 30 million workers are on track to lose their existing employer provided coverage. At this point it's abundantly clear that the loss of existing health insurance coverage by as many people possible was by design to force as many as possible into the exchanges.

27th time's the charm

February 10, 2014

The President just changed his signature health care law by executive order for the 27th time today. This latest unconstitutional change is a big one. It delays the employer mandate one more time for companies with 50 to 99 employees. This 2nd delay to the employer mandate gives companies with 50 to 99 employees another year, until Jan.1st 2016, before they are faced with a $2000. fine per employee if they fail to provide Obama Care health insurance for their employees. Employers will be faced with a scary requirement though because they will be forced to sign an oath on an IRS form that they will not lay off any employee due to Obama Care regulations. This is just one more example of government overreach afforded by a huge government bureaucracy that strikes another blow to free enterprise in America by placing burdensome requirements on employers that affect their ability to show a profit. This 2nd delay to the employer mandate for mid-size companies will provide some relief for these companies as we approach the 2014 mid-term Congressional election, but it's important to understand that this unconstitutional delay is a purely political action designed to protect Democrats who are up for re-election in November and is one more admission by the administration that Obama Care mandates impose unreasonable hardships upon employers which in turn harms employees of these companies.

No previous President has displayed such blatant disregard and disrespect for the Constitution. The imperial presidency of the Obama administration has boldly bypassed Congress in an unprecedented attack on the Constitution by issuing executive orders that surpass his authority. Law suits have been filed to address the President's illegal activities by unilaterally changing law but the administration will prolong the legal process through appeals that should buy the President sufficient time to leave office before facing accountability for his illegal activity. While the President provides relief to corporate America, individuals are still subject to Obama Care fines so individuals will suffer while special considerations are protecting businesses to satisfy the political needs of Democrats. The American people are now aware of the unfair and illegal nature of this President's practice of changing law to satisfy political needs and they will express their outrage at the polls in November.

Historic Law Suit

February 12, 2014

Senator Rand Paul announced today what he described as one of the largest class-action law suits in history, taking President Obama and top intelligence officials to court over NSA surveillance. The suit, joined by conservative advocacy group Freedom Works, was filed in U.S. District Court in the District of Columbia. The suit specifically named the President, Director of National Intelligence James Clapper, NSA Director Keith Alexander and FBI Director James Comey. The suit alleges the NSA program that sweeps up and stores massive amounts of telephone "meta-data" -- which includes where and when calls are made, but not the contents of the calls – violates the fourth amendment. The suit asks the court to rule the program unconstitutional and forbid the government from continuing it. "There's a huge and growing swell of protest in this country of people who are outraged that their records would be taken without suspicion, without a judge's warrant and without individualization," Paul said, at a press conference in Washington. He said hundreds of thousands have joined, and predicted the suit could, "conceivably represent hundreds of millions of people who have phone lines in this country." The lawsuit argues that the bulk metadata that is routinely collected nevertheless "reveals a wealth of detail" about Americans personal and professional associations "that are ordinarily unknown to the government."

Republican Leaders Surrender

February 13, 2014

While the national debt has risen to $17.3 trillion, Congressional Republican leaders made a strategic move to **surrender** on the debt ceiling and set the stage for both chambers of Congress to pass a bill to increase the debt limit. The House passed the bill on Tuesday by a vote of 221 – 201 (only 28 Republican votes) and the Senate passed the bill today by a vote of 55 – 43 (no Republican votes). The measure passed due to strategic maneuvering by Speaker of the House, John Boehner, and Senate minority leader, Mitch McConnell. Speaker Boehner allowed a vote in the House on a clean bill to increase the debt limit with no strings attached relying on minority leader Nancy Pelosi (D-CA) to pass the measure on the strength of Democrats against strong objections by Tea Party Republicans and Mitch McConnell did essentially the same thing in the Senate by avoiding a 60-vote filibuster threshold which Ted Cruz (R-TX) tried to force. The strategy that won out among Republicans was to avoid any fall out from another potential government shut down or even another blow to the credit rating of the U.S. government and to run exclusively on the Obama Care debacle in November with an eye on retaining the House and gaining a majority in the Senate. The severe beating Republicans took last October was enough to convince enough Republicans to cave on shutting down any future government funding measures because the 16-day partial government shut down that took place in October 2013 brought about a significant blow to GOP poll numbers. Raising the debt limit permits Treasury to borrow regularly through March 15th, 2015, putting the issue off until after the November elections and setting it up for the new Congress to handle next year.

Global Warming Hysteria

February 17, 2014

The Obama administration has recently engaged in a full court press on what they call climate change. Climate change, formerly known as global warming, has always been a part of the Obama administration's liberal agenda but they have recently turned up the volume to drown out Obama Care woes. While we're in the middle of the coldest winter on record in years, global warming is sounding more ridiculous than ever before, hence climate change, as if nobody would notice the new label which is even more ridiculous than global warming. The President is in Fresno, California touting a $1 billion "climate resilience fund" which he recently proposed knowing that the House would kill such an initiative the second it reaches that chamber of Congress. The President has already pushed the envelope on executive orders to change the Obama Care law so he knows he isn't in position to issue an executive action to order a $1 billion initiative on such a ridiculous proposition as climate change, not that he hasn't seriously considered it. Over the weekend, Secretary of State John Kerry leaped into the fray big time when he declared, "Climate change can now be considered another weapon of mass destruction, perhaps the world's most fearsome weapon of mass destruction," during a speech in Indonesia. He went on to mock those who deny its existence or question its causes, comparing them to people who insist the earth is flat. He said, "We should not allow a tiny minority of shoddy scientists and science and extreme ideologues to compete with scientific facts." James P. Pinkerton, former Deputy Assistant to the President for policy planning under George H.W. Bush, countered Kerry's assertions and said, "Does John Kerry really believe that carbon dioxide is a bigger threat than Al Qaeda? Or Iran? If so, maybe the House Foreign Affairs Committee could inquire as to whether State Department diplomacy now reflects the Secretary's priorities."

Global warming, climate change, or whatever liberals want to call it, is the furthest issue from the minds of Americans. The American people, who live in the real world, something Obama administration officials know little about, are not concerned with the weather. The American people are dealing with a very weak economy which has yielded the lowest labor participation rate in decades, 3% lower than 5 years ago, and even widespread poverty with 47 million Americans on food stamps and other welfare programs designed to create dependence on big government. The American people want the dignity of a job, not a government hand-out, therefore they are much more concerned with initiatives that effectively address our stalled economy as opposed to some ridiculous climate change fantasy. Americans have been slammed by Obama Care mandates and won't be fooled into taking their eye off the ball of the most unpopular law ever thrust upon them by lies and manipulations perpetrated by power hungry liberal politicians. The President has already displayed his utter incompetence in dealing with the economy when his $868 billion economic stimulus fell flat after his first term. The so-called economic stimulus was loaded with pork and fraud and not only didn't accomplish anything but unemployment peaked at 10%, not including those who had already dropped out of the work force, at the height of the stimulus and now two thirds of Americans believe we are still in a recession.

News Police

February 21, 2014

At the urging of the White House, the FCC, Federal Communications Commission, set out to establish a newsroom monitoring program citing a study they call CIN, critical information needs, designed to control the flow of information through the media which basically creates a re-distribution of information. The Obama administration's idea of information re-distribution calls for less reporting on Obama Care problems, Benghazi, IRS targeting conservatives, and other recent scandals while more attention would be directed at climate change, immigration reform and numerous forms of misinformation designed to promote the Presidents socialistic agenda. Ajit Pai, one of 5 FCC Commissioners, wrote an op-ed piece in the Wall Street Journal last week revealing this latest attempt by the White House to intimidate and control newsrooms. This blatant violation of the 1st amendment reflects a significant threat to news outlets because the FCC wields tremendous power over broadcast licensing. The program is allegedly voluntary but news organizations understand full well that a snub directed at the FCC could jeopardize their license to operate.

FCC Chairman Tom Wheeler is behind this latest push to wage war on free speech which should come as no surprise coming from an Obama campaign donor. The proposed actions by Tom Wheeler's "thought police" come disguised as an FCC research project, as if it's a harmless study merely asking questions with the answers being stored away for posterity. The Presidents war on freedom of the press can be traced back throughout his Presidency where we have seen attacks on Fox News and radio talk show hosts like Rush Limbaugh and even spying on AP journalists and Fox News journalist, James Rosen, by the Justice Department under Eric Holder's direction. If it hadn't been for Fox News and Ajit Pai we wouldn't have even seen this coming because the main stream media has been completely silent on the issue. NBC, ABC, CBS, CNN, MSNBC and The New York Times have not reported on this dismantling of the 1st amendment because they are perfectly willing to go along with it.

After Fox News launched a reporting blitz on this issue, the FCC backed down and issued a statement that they are suspending the program, but respectable news outlets like Fox News and American citizens need to keep their guard up because the Obama administration won't give up so easily on an initiative to silence those in the press who do their job by reporting on government overreach as opposed to those who suck up to the President.

Lawless

February 25, 2014

Attorney General Eric Holder addressed the National Association of Attorneys General today and effectively gave the green light for states to stop defending bans on gay marriage. He told his state counterparts that they do not have to defend laws against constitutional court challenges if they consider them discriminatory. Holder said, "In general, I believe that we must be suspicious of legal classifications based solely on sexual orientation." Several Democrat Attorneys General have already taken the unusual step of abandoning their defense of state gay marriage bans after section 3 of the federal Defense of Marriage Act was struck down by the Supreme Court last year when they ruled sec.3 unconstitutional under the Due Process

Clause of the 5th amendment. Members of the Republican Attorneys General Association blasted Holder's remarks in a statement Tuesday afternoon. "A state Attorney General has a solemn duty to the state and its people to defend state laws and constitutional provisions against challenge under federal law. To refuse to do so because of personal policy preferences or political pressure erodes the rule of law on which all our freedoms are founded. A government that does not enforce the law equally will lead our society to disrespect the rule of law," Alabama Attorney General Luther Strange said. Ed Whelan, President of the Ethics and Public Policy Center, said "state attorneys general are obligated to defend state marriage laws." He added, "It's unfortunate and outrageous that Attorney General Holder doesn't understand that, but it's hardly surprising."

This is just one more example of the **lawless** nature of the Obama administration. No previous administration has trampled on the constitution to the extent that this administration has. We've seen continual attacks on the 1st, 2nd and 4th amendments by the Obama administration. President Obama was a professor of constitutional law so he understands the **lawless** nature of his actions but obviously doesn't care. This President treats the bill of rights as though they're just a list of suggestions. Attorney General Eric Holder supports the President's lawless dictatorship so it's no wonder that he abuses executive privilege to such a great extent. The President and the Attorney General have effectively worked together to make up law as they go along and the success of this partnership has emboldened their efforts over time. This team has boldly gone where no previous President and Attorney General have gone before.

Horror Stories

February 26, 2014

President Obama's henchman, Senate Majority Leader Harry Reid, took to the Senate floor today and claimed, "There's plenty of **horror stories** being told; **all** of them are untrue but they're being told all over America." Reid went on to say, "Those tales turned out to be just that; tales, stories made up from whole cloth, lies distorted by the Republicans to grab headlines forming political advertisements." Several of his Democrat Senate colleagues and even White House Press Secretary Jay Carney joined in the chorus to advance their strategy of calling most Americans liars. Senator Reid's statement wasn't a spontaneous or emotional response to anything that just occurred on the Senate floor because he was obviously reading a prepared statement. Senator Reid went on to make it clear that his statement targeted ads funded by Americans for Prosperity, a conservative group, backed by the billionaire Koch brothers. Americans for Prosperity President Tim Phillips, in response, said Reid had effectively 'attacked the character and integrity of every American who had the courage to share how they're being hurt by the president's health care law.' Reid dug himself an even deeper hole when he went on to say he believes Americans for Prosperity hires actors in their ads to tell fake stories about cancelled policies, higher premiums and ruined lives under Obama Care.

Democrats in Congress have found themselves to be in a very difficult situation, especially those who are up for re-election in November, so they've adopted a desperate strategy of lies to combat growing criticism fueled by actual true life experiences of Americans who have lost access to their current Doctors, Hospitals and critically needed prescription drugs. Americans are paying at least twice as much compared to the previous plans they were forced out of due to Obama Care regulations for inadequate coverage that could, in some instances, cost them their life. The very true **horror stories** have only just begun to be heard. As even larger numbers of Americans lose their existing coverage, which they were perfectly happy with, when the employer mandate kicks in later this year, the horror stories will grow to unimaginable numbers. Multiple polls have revealed that most of the currently uninsured who Obama Care was supposed to help don't even want Obama Care coverage because it's become increasingly obvious that the new expensive plans are sorely inadequate. They're paying for pediatric dental care, maternity care, and mental health care whether they need it or not but the Doctors, Hospitals and Prescription Drugs they do need aren't covered. Democrats will pay for their folly when they lose the Senate in November.

Chapter 15

Russian Aggression

March 3, 2014

The President's failure to act on his "red line" statement regarding Syrian chemical weapons and other weak foreign policy positions is coming back to haunt him. President Obama is living in a fantasy world. He sees the world as he wants to see it; not the way it really is. He doesn't even understand that Vladimir Putin is our adversary. He thinks we have common interests with Russia and Syria when in fact we do not. When President Obama lifted sanctions on Iran and got nothing in return he displayed his complete incompetence to deal with any threat coming out of the Middle East. He thinks global warming is our biggest threat and it doesn't even exist. This President is not only unconcerned about America's superpower status in the world; he is actively working to take us down a couple of notches to level out American dominance on the world stage and to establish some level of moral equivalence in the world. He sees American exceptionalism as a bad thing. President Obama doesn't understand that America holds a special place in history and on the global stage due to our innovation, determination and courage. The Presidents moral equivalence thought process began with the apology tour early on during his first term. The notion that America has anything to apologize for on the world stage is ludicrous and anti-American.

The President sacrificed all progress we made in Iraq and is now ready to do the same thing in Afghanistan. If he does away with Bagram Air Base in Afghanistan we lose our ability to police most of the Middle East and the Taliban will immediately re-establish their presence in the region. President Obama's recent announcement that he is proposing a reduction to military personnel in the Army as part of his 2015 budget has fueled the fire of skepticism by the rest of the world over America's superpower status. The President wants to reduce the Army's combat force from 522,000 to about 440,000 which is the lowest post World War II level we've seen. He's already taken $487 billion out of our military since he took office. 50% of Sequestration spending reductions came out of the military when it only represents 18% of our total budget. This gutting of our military has placed us in a very dangerous position.

President Obama's weak and indecisive character invited the Russian invasion of the Crimean Peninsula in Ukraine which Ukraine declares as a Russian declaration of war. Five years of President Obama's naïve and incompetent view of foreign affairs brought us to this place. He should have actively sought to bring Ukraine into NATO years ago. President Obama's Mr. Nice Guy strategy employed throughout his time as President is so naïve it's incomprehensible and of course has failed miserably. His idea of a re-set with Russia was to cancel the sanctions imposed by George W. Bush over Russia's invasion of Georgia which sent the message loud and clear that he is weak and can easily be trampled upon. The President set the stage for Ukraine's demise. His miscalculation of Putin's intentions will prove to be disastrous. Putin knows President Obama is nothing but a community organizer who is in way over his head.

When we cancelled our missile defense complex in Poland in 2009 Putin was further emboldened. President Obama and then Secretary of State Hillary Clinton convinced our NATO allies to abandon the missile shield as an act of appeasement with the hope of establishing friendly relations with Russia. This was a terrible miscalculation. The absence of a U.S. ballistic missile shield in Europe opens a huge hole in defense capability for our allies in Western Europe. We must resume this project as soon as possible and it should remain our top priority along with pulling out all the stops to become not only energy independent but also a major energy supplier to Western Europe.

Ousted Ukraine President Viktor Yanukovych disappeared and then showed up in Russia where Vladimir Putin condemned Ukraine's removal of Yanukovych declaring it an unconstitutional coup to justify his invasion of Crimea when in fact Putin is on the move because he knows President Obama doesn't know how to respond. Putin also claims Russian Nationals are at risk in Ukraine and that the exiled Yanukovych invited Russia's invasion of Crimea. The time for action by President Obama has come and gone so at this point our options are extremely limited. President Obama made a statement from the White House today and said he has held talks with leaders throughout Europe and discussed a wide range of economic and diplomatic actions designed to isolate Russia. The EU will need to play a major role in these actions. He said Russia is in violation of multiple international treaties and that Russia is on the wrong side of history. He said this will be a costly proposition for Russia. He's correct in that the Russian stock market is down 10% over the weekend which represents a cost of $58 billion (U.S. dollars) to Russian investors. President Obama was referencing an imposed cost by America and our NATO allies which is still questionable at this point. Sanctions cut both ways and would cost the EU more than they may be willing to withstand. Germany will be especially reluctant to act against Russia but Great Britain, France and the rest of the EU aren't far behind. It would be necessary to immediately expel Russia from the G8 because they would otherwise veto any action by the G8. The U.K. and the U.S. have an obligation to protect Ukraine under treaty. President Obama pledged a billion dollars in economic aid to Ukraine and called upon Congress to take a unified position to support him in that endeavor. The EU pledged $15 billion in aid to Ukraine. Ukraine officials have advised that they will need about $35 billion in foreign aid over the course of the next 2 years to avert a financial collapse.

The G8 summit in Sochi, Russia is scheduled for June. America may pull out of the summit which could be likened to a pin prick in the grand scheme of things. The President should act to freeze assets held by Russian Oligarchs that exist outside of Russia. Wealthy Russians wouldn't like this but Putin has the last word so the Oligarchs would be forced to go along with him if he dictates that they must live with it. Putin himself is one of Russia's Oligarchs but he is willing to take the personal financial hit. America and the EU would need to destabilize Russia's economy by imposing sanctions on Russian banks to crush the Ruble which is already weak and move to expel Russia from the World Trade Organization, the G8 and NATO. These actions can't be done overnight and it could take months to persuade the EU to participate but they may ultimately decline to act. America should immediately position war ships in the Black Sea but the absence of a contingency plan that should have been worked out with NATO a long time ago makes it a difficult proposition at this point.

Russia has established complete control over the Port of Sevastopol in Crimea where the Russian Navy already had a strong presence. The Port of Sevastopol is a critical warm water port on the Black Sea which gives Russia a strong position to defend their ambitious interests in the region. Putin has deployed 16,000 troops to Crimea in addition to the 2000 original invaders to solidify his presence there. These troops are void of Russian identification and are wearing black masks. He's also positioned Russian war ships in the Black Sea to tighten his grip on Crimea. The question now becomes; will Russia expand their invasion to Kiev (Ukraine's capital) and the rest of eastern Ukraine. Putin wants to expand his empire. He is a Russian imperialist with eyes on Moldova, Estonia and other Baltic States. Vladimir Putin is prepared to withstand any negative economic impact on Russia as the result of his aggression in Ukraine. Putin is an aggressive dictator whose interest lies in the acquisition of power and if he must pay an economic price to gain power he will gladly do so. Putin is a former KGB agent who relates more to the era of CZAR's and doesn't believe the cold war ever ended. He has successfully overtaken Crimea and there's nothing that can be done about it. He's already successfully done this in Georgia while George W. Bush was in office and when the dust settled, Russia retained 2 provinces in Georgia which they still control and occupy to this day. He won't stop until he's reconstructed the Russian empire to its original state. President Obama's weakness and incompetence will prove to be very dangerous as it relates to U.S. security. The President has created a leadership vacuum in the world and Putin has stepped in to fill it. Americas only hope for the future is to fully utilize our natural resources at home to further develop energy sources that can not only meet all our own needs but also the needs of Western Europe. 35% of the EU's energy imports of oil and natural gas come out of Russia and all the pipelines that transport natural gas to European countries run through Ukraine. The problem is that President Obama doesn't remotely understand the power of energy independence. He won't even authorize completion of the Keystone XL pipeline and he doesn't understand the importance of fracking (hydraulic fracturing). America must fully develop our energy resources at home and then work towards exporting American oil and natural gas to the EU and beyond. 34% of natural gas used in the EU comes from Russia. The United States should be developing LNG, liquid natural gas, to export to EU countries. America could single handedly devastate Russia's economy by becoming the EU's primary supplier of natural gas. This would weaken Russia's position with the EU as America steps in to level the playing field.

March 4, 2014

The President announced today that he will not attend the G8 summit in Sochi, Russia this June. President Obama spent one hour on the phone with German President Angela Merkel today and just like his hour and a half phone conversation with Putin yesterday, nothing was resolved. The President of the United States shouldn't spend 90 minutes on the phone with a ruthless dictator. He should have taken 5 minutes with Putin to demand Russia's withdrawal from Crimea and then used some strong diplomacy with Merkel to convince her that Germany should make some sacrifices and agree to sanctions on Russia which may hurt for a while but with an eye to the future that this kind of aggression will not be tolerated. Nothing was reported today that any discussion of sanctions on Russia took place during the President's conversation with Chancellor Merkel. So far today the U.K. and Germany have folded on sanctions, France went out on a limb and called for mediation with Russia and Italy really took the plunge when they threatened to suspend preparations for the G8 summit. Our friends have thrown us into the deep end of the pool and ran the other way with the life preservers.

Secretary of State John Kerry spoke from Kiev today and said that Putin's unwillingness to agree to a retreat is a sign of weakness. Putin has successfully invaded Crimea without firing a shot and he's there to stay. That doesn't sound very weak, particularly when he did it with no consequence. I'm sure Putin is shaking in his boots from all the rhetoric being thrown his way. He's so shaken up that he test-fired a long range intercontinental ballistic missile today amid rising tensions. President Obama took time out of his busy schedule today when he interrupted his visit to a Washington DC school and spoke from a kindergarten classroom on an alphabet rug to convince us that strong diplomacy will do the trick. The optics were really threatening coming from a community organizer in a kindergarten classroom.

A new Fox News poll of registered voters out today revealed the President's approval rating has hit an all-time low. The poll revealed that only 38% of registered voters approve of the President's performance while 54% disapprove. Another Fox News poll from the same group revealed only 33% approve of the President's performance on foreign policy. Historically, when a President's approval ratings are as low as President Obama's in an election year, members of the President's political party have great difficulty winning an election. Democrats up for re-election for Congressional posts in November are in trouble. The President's low approval rating, Obama Care woes, and the weak economy will be very difficult for Democrats to overcome.

Shock and Awe Budget

The President determined to explode his 2015 budget proposal on the scene today with **shock and awe** as he presented a $3.9 trillion tax and spend budget to Congress. The President's budget proposal is designed to make Republicans say no and get Democrats re-elected in November. So far, Republicans have done a good job of staying quiet on this inconsequential proposal other than Speaker Boehner. John Boehner spoke out and said it's the most irresponsible budget yet. This budget proposal is so ridiculous that it will indeed raise some eyebrows but the printed copies will soon find their way to the trash. This proposal raises taxes by $1.75 trillion and offers no deficit reduction. It calls for $302 billion for infrastructure spending and another $56 billion for job training and early childhood education. It has the Buffett tax, named for Warren Buffett, which raises taxes on the wealthy. The proposal is a "wish list" of liberal "tax and spend" initiatives that will never see the light of day.

Delay Du Jour

The President offered his **delay du jour** today but didn't find any Republican's interested in placing an order. Today's special Obama Care delay was cooked up to entice voters to support Democrats who are up for re-election in November. The Obama Care law has been unilaterally changed and delayed so many times that most of us have lost count but we're hovering around 30 illegal changes so far. These unconstitutional changes are purely political. This delay once again pushes back mandates for individuals so Americans will be free to keep the plans they had prior to Obama Care for 2 more years even though they don't meet Obama Care mandates but as with the previous delay State regulators and insurers have the option to allow this or not. The White House was very deliberate in their defense of vulnerable Democrats who are up for re-election this year giving them credit for their role in granting this illegal extension. These same Democrats who now support extending health insurance plans which they've repeatedly defined as substandard were adamantly opposed to a 1 year extension of these same plans previously proposed by Republicans in the House during the debt ceiling debate last year. To hear it from Democrats it was as though the sky is falling. Funny how these plans are now completely acceptable to Democrats for not just 1 more year but 2.

Wrist Slap

March 17, 2014

The President took to the airwaves today to announce his response to Russia's referendum on Crimea which took place after a vote in Crimea with 97% voting in favor of annexation by Russia. Of course, the legitimacy of the Crimea vote is questionable but it stands whether it was corrupt or not. President Obama announced that America will levy sanctions on 11 Russian

Oligarch's who serve as Putin's top advisors. The President went on to declare that the referendum for the annexation of Crimea by Russia would not be recognized internationally and that we will work with our NATO allies to determine the next step.

That's it! Obama responds with a **wrist slap.** The Russian stock market shot up directly after the President's announcement of sanctions on 11 Oligarch's. This reflects Russia's confidence that President Obama's weak response is nothing to be concerned with. President Obama seems to be more concerned with filling out his NCAA "March Madness" bracket than dealing with the crisis in Ukraine. No sanctions were placed on Putin personally and no U.S. banking sanctions were imposed. The 11 Russian's who were hit with sanctions had sufficient time to move assets offshore where they would be safe from any U.S. action. Their now frozen accounts were surely depleted and transferred to protected accounts in other countries prior to the freeze. These 11 Russians won't be able to enter the U.S. because their VISA's were pulled so they will be vacationing in Sochi, Russia instead of Palm Beach or Las Vegas. I'm sure they are severely traumatized by this inconvenience but they won't have a problem with vacationing in Sochi to display their loyalty to mother Russia. Barak Obama is so wildly incompetent to deal with such an act of aggression by Russia that Putin has been further emboldened to take his next step and invade the rest of eastern Ukraine in addition to Crimea. Russian forces have already seized Ukraine's naval headquarters in Crimea. No sovereign nation has been invaded and annexed by another country since World War II.

U.S. banking sanctions directed at Russia would be the only somewhat effective action that the U.S. could take on our own in the short term but President Obama didn't think to do the one thing that we could do now without NATO cooperation. Any energy related restrictions would require participation by the EU which they have no appetite for now. The only thing that will get Putin's attention would be to hit Russia where it hurts by attacking their economy through banking and energy related sanctions which would require cooperation by the EU. It may take Russian acquisition of eastern Ukraine before the EU wakes up to the threat they face and decide to make the necessary sacrifices that they must endure to hit Russia where it hurts. Putin understands brute force but his weakness lies in his limited ability to protect and even advance Russia's economy. Since military action by the U.S. and our NATO allies is out of the question, economic and energy related actions are our only recourse but they could be extremely effective once we have the cooperation of the EU. Our own energy independence should be our highest priority but again the President doesn't understand the power and economic advantages associated with energy independence. Putin will not stop with Crimea and will not be satisfied until the whole of the Soviet Union is re-established and the cold war is once again in full swing. He knows he has at least 3 years to accomplish his mission because President Obama is too weak and incompetent to stand up to him. America survived Jimmy Carter and we will survive Barak Obama. With a real leader at the helm America will once again become the superpower we once were before President Obama although Hillary Clinton will most likely take another run at the White House in 2016 and if she were to succeed this time the consequences could be disastrous for America.

March 20, 2014

As Russia ramps up their military presence in Crimea, President Obama announced a new executive order today that gives the U.S. authority to impose sanctions on key sectors of Russia's economy and sanctions on more senior officials in Russia. This weak and vague response is a joke. The authority to impose sanctions is not the same as the actual establishment of sufficient sanctions that will change Russia's calculus on a deeper invasion into Ukraine. The sanctions that have been imposed fall far short of the degree of sanctions that would be effective.

Blitzkrieg

March 29, 2014

Russia has now amassed between 80,000 and 100,000 troops on Ukraine's eastern border. Russia is preparing for a real blitzkrieg or multi-pronged attack on eastern Ukraine which will surely incorporate ground troops, tanks and air support to overwhelm Ukraine's weak and ill-prepared military as they prepare to take control of eastern Ukraine in addition to Crimea. President Obama was in Saudi Arabia yesterday when Putin called him and they spoke for about 50 minutes on the phone about the developing invasion of Ukraine by Russia. Putin was strategically going on record that his concern is for the interests of Russian speaking people in eastern Ukraine. President Obama made the following statement after the phone conversation with Putin; "It may simply be an effort to intimidate Ukraine, or it may be that that they've got additional plans," Obama said. "And in either case, what we need right now to resolve and de-escalate the situation would be for Russia to move back those troops and to begin negotiations directly with the Ukrainian government, as well as the international community." President Obama still doesn't understand the difference between what Russia should do and what they will do. He must think his suggestions carry some weight. Vladimir Putin laughs at President Obama's suggestions while he acts on Russia's interests with no regard for President Obama's philosophical reasoning. Putin is aware of President Obama's reasoning that America should take a step back so the rest of the world can step up. This insane philosophy will continue to take a toll on America's superpower status in the world while Russia, China, Iran, and North Korea build their strength in contrast to a fearful EU and an erosion of America's power in the world. President Obama's fictional "international community" also reveals his naïve understanding of how the world works. There is no international community. The United Nations is a joke and NATO is only as powerful as the leaders of each NATO country with leadership from America as their backbone. President Obama has no backbone, so NATO is void of meaningful leadership. Angela Merkel in Germany and David Cameron in the UK are unable to fill the void that President Obama leaves in his wake. Putin is aware of President Obama's 2015 budget proposal that proposes a huge cut to U.S. Army combat forces to the lowest level since World War II and the surrender of the Tomahawk missile program by cutting $128 million from the program in 2015 and complete elimination by 2016. Thank God these are only proposals but they are a sad indictment on our President's ability or desire to insure our national security. China, Iran and North Korea are paying close attention to the evolving situation in Ukraine and will adjust their playbook accordingly based on what President Obama does or does not do.

Chapter 16

Victory Lap

April 1, 2014

President Obama addressed the nation today from the Rose Garden to report on Obama Care enrollment numbers. Initial enrollment ended yesterday at midnight and the White House is reporting 7.1 million have enrolled for Obama Care health insurance. The 7.1 million number is highly questionable because the Obama administration won't reveal the breakdown that would clear up the validity of their number. We still don't know how many sign ups have paid their first premium, how many were previously uninsured and how many are young and healthy. Any number is meaningless without this breakdown but the President nevertheless was taking a proud **victory lap** today when he should have just yelled, "April Fools." Considering the celebratory atmosphere at the White House, you would think we had just witnessed a major victory on multiple fronts but there is nothing victorious about questionable numbers on an even more questionable major government program. Insurance companies are reporting that about 80% of the sign ups have paid at least their first premium which translates to only about 5.6 million actual enrollees. Once the widely predicted "premium default" occurs when premiums become even more unaffordable, this socialistic endeavor will begin to further unravel to the point that insurance companies will line up for the promised bail out of taxpayer dollars.

The President was joking around seemingly having a lot of fun. HHS Secretary, Kathleen Sebelius, was nowhere to be found near the President. She was in the audience not feeling the joy and probably realizing just as Dorothy and Toto learned; she's not in Kansas anymore. The former Kansas Governor was totally snubbed by the President. She will be rendered to waiting in the wings until the time comes for her to take the fall for Barak Obama. Vice-President Joe Biden stood with the President near the podium grinning when President Obama declared, "the debate is over," as if that's our cue to move on and accept the terrible hand we've been dealt by our incompetent President and the Democrats who conspired with him to upend 1/6th of the American economy. Commenting on the enrollment number, Tonight Show host Jimmy Fallon said it's amazing what can be done when a government program is made law, a penalty of 1% of a person's income is imposed if you don't enroll and when key aspects of the law are delayed for months. He makes a compelling point but the President sees those details as a mere footnote to the big picture. He may be basking in the light of his faux victory now but he'd better brace himself for the dark days ahead.

Benghazi 18 months later

April 2, 2014

Michael Morell, former CIA Deputy Director and former acting CIA Director, testified before the House Intelligence Committee today to defend his revisions to the White House talking points on the Al Qaeda terrorist attack on the U.S. diplomatic mission in Benghazi, Libya on 9/11/12 in which 4 Americans were murdered by terrorists including Ambassador Christopher Stevens. This was Morell's 1st appearance in an open hearing after having appeared in 2 closed classified hearings on Benghazi. He vigorously defended his decision to deceive Americans on his politically motivated removal of key aspects of the attack from the original talking points. Morell's changes to the now discredited talking points were not minor adjustments as he literally changed 50% of the original document.

After the State Department sent out 2 cables during the attack confirming there was a terrorist attack in progress by Ansar Al Sharia and a CIA memo dated 9/15/12 issued by the CIA Station Chief in Tripoli confirming the attack was not the result of a protest, Morell proceeded to remove these facts from the talking points with full knowledge that his action was deceptive and political but he testified that any discrepancies were merely bureaucratic mistakes. References to a terrorist attack in the talking points were changed to violent demonstration before the document went to the Office of Congressional Affairs. Morell testified that he thought the CIA Station Chief's "on the ground" assessment was speculative and not credible so he chose to go with the assessment of analysts in Langley. Any notion that analysts in Langley had a better handle on the situation as opposed to the CIA Station Chief on the ground in Libya is ludicrous. He said at the time he never thought the terrorist attack and a supposed protest in response to a video was mutually exclusive. He also claims he didn't know who removed any reference to Al Qaeda from the talking points. When asked if he was suggesting that a terrorist attack could evolve into a protest, Morell answered yes, which I for one find to be incredible. After the Regional Safety Officer in Benghazi, Chief of Base in Benghazi, Chief of Station in Tripoli, and other political officers on the ground in Libya confirmed it was a terrorist attack and not a protest in response to a video, Morell still moved forward with changes to the talking points that he confirmed were solely based on the assessment of analysts in Langley. Morell removed the word Islamic from the talking points which was in front of the word extremists. When asked about this he said he was afraid of inflaming the Muslim world and he testified that the threat today from Al Qaeda is very significant and growing.

We now know that Susan Rice who was the U.S. Ambassador to the U.N. at the time was privy to all information confirming it was a terrorist attack and not a spontaneous response to an anti-Islamic video prior to going on 5 Sunday morning talk shows (ABC, FOX, CNN, NBC, and

CBS) on 9/16/12 and boldly proclaimed the video story. It's common knowledge that Morell was in receipt of an e-mail from the CIA Station Chief in Tripoli on the Saturday morning before the Susan Rice appearances on the Sunday morning talk shows. That e-mail confirmed there was no protest and that it was a terrorist attack. Morell testified today that he removed any reference to a terrorist attack from the talking points because he thought it might appear that the CIA was attempting to shift blame to the State Department. He said there was significant concern over possibly embarrassing policy makers and State Dept. leadership. I question why the CIA appeared to be more concerned with protecting the State Dept. than even the State Dept. was.

Morell's testimony was filled with contradictions. His testimony didn't fit the timeline beginning with the attack itself on 9/11/12 and running through the Sunday after the attack on 9/16/12. He defended Susan Rice's evaluation on the 9/16 Sunday morning talk shows saying she was working with information they had at the time. Susan Rice who is now National Security Advisor, appeared on NBC's "Meet the Press" on 2/23/14 and defended her earlier remarks on 9/16/12. Rice conceded some of her statements may not have been correct, but insisted she did not mislead the public and was speaking based on information she had at the time. Her arrogance in standing by the false narrative she proclaimed on 9/16/12 after that narrative has been totally discredited as being false is disgraceful. Morell admitted to making significant substantive changes to the talking points but testified he was not instructed to do so by the White House. Senators Ayotte, McCain, and Graham who as members of the House Intelligence Committee had been present for the 2 classified hearings said Morell's testimony was at best misleading but more accurately lying by omission.

Morell testified that we still don't know the motivations of the attackers to this day because they haven't been apprehended. We all know their motivation is Jihad; kill the infidels; attack the great Satan, the United States. What part of that doesn't Morell understand? We now know that the CIA and FBI have known exactly where to find the perpetrators of the Benghazi attack for some time. Since nothing has been done to apprehend these terrorists one can only conclude that the Obama administration doesn't want to apprehend them which of course makes no sense but we've learned the Obama administration is notorious for actions or inaction that make no sense. Morell said the CIA shouldn't be involved in providing information for public consumption and that they are not good at public relations, which is finally something I can agree with him on. Morell is currently employed by Beacon Global Strategies, a Washington insider strategic communications firm which has deep ties to former Secretary of State Hillary Clinton. With an ongoing motivation to protect Hillary Clinton, Michael Morell is understandably biased in his relationship with her.

The unspoken mystery in the search for truth on the Benghazi terrorist attack remains as no Republican or Democrat seem to be willing to corner Leon Panetta who was Secretary of Defense at the time of the Benghazi attack and extract his full knowledge of the events. Leon Panetta was in a position as Secretary of Defense to have full access to all the intelligence but for some mysterious reason major Republican players involved in seeking the truth such as Congressman Jason Chaffetz (R-UT) who has been one of the most outspoken Congressmen on the falsehoods perpetuated by the White House and State Department falls silent when Leon Panetta's name is even mentioned. Congressman Mike Rogers (R-MI), Chairman of the House Permanent Select Committee on Intelligence, also clams up at the mention of Leon Panetta's name in relation to Benghazi. Panetta did testify in a Senate hearing on 2/7/13 and defended the DOD on their role in decisions made on the Benghazi attack but was perfectly willing to throw President Obama and Hillary Clinton under the bus when he testified that both were missing in action after 5:00PM EST in Washington DC during the critical hours of the attack. I believe Panetta would be willing to testify before the House Committee on Intelligence now because the most important questions remain unanswered but for some unknown reason he seems to be off limits. The only thing we know for sure regarding the unanswered questions on the Benghazi terrorist attack is that those questions remain unanswered. Congressional hearings have proved to be sorely inadequate to get at the truth. These hearings begin with a lengthy statement from the committee chairman, then a statement by the ranking member of the opposing political party of the committee chairman, and then a lengthy statement by the person called to testify. At that point members of the committee are allowed 5 minutes each to question the person called to testify. These 5 minute intervals generally begin with a statement by the committee member who, cognizant of the television cameras, is often more interested in building themselves up for their viewing constituents than asking a question and the committee member of the opposing political party asks some completely unrelated question. When a question finally comes out, the person testifying can easily stall and offer evasive testimony while time runs out. The need for a select committee to investigate primarily Benghazi and the IRS has been understood by many for some time but for some unknown reason Speaker Boehner and for a known reason Senate majority leader Harry Reid, have not called for a select committee to investigate these scandals. Only time will tell if the critically needed answers to the many unanswered questions will be revealed.

Ugly

April 8, 2014

Attorney General Eric Holder appeared today before the House Judiciary Committee and it didn't take long for things to get **ugly**. Holder was called to testify before the committee by its chairman Bob Goodlatte (R-VA) with the objective of oversight on the Department of Justice.

The Attorney General has had a contentious relationship with several Republican members of Congress since the House found him in contempt of Congress in 2012 for failing to turn over certain documents tied to the "Fast and Furious" scandal involving botched firearms sting operations, despite a Congressional subpoena seeking those documents. Considering Holder's lack of respect for contempt charges, Rep. Louis Gohmert (R-TX) said, "I realize that contempt is not a big deal to our Attorney General, but it is important that we have proper oversight." A visibly upset Holder, leaning back in his chair, shot back, "You don't want to go there, buddy. You don't want to go there, O.K." As Holder argued that assumptions shouldn't be made that it's not a big deal to him, Gohmert pressed the issue when he said, "There have been no indications that it was a big deal, because your department has still not been forthcoming in producing the documents that were the subject of the contempt." Gohmert went on to add, "I don't need lectures from you about contempt," and Holder responded, "And I don't need lectures from you either." It's scary when an Attorney General threatens a Congressman and refers to him as "Buddy." It reeks of Chicago style crime boss behavior which is completely unbecoming for the Attorney General of the United States of America.

The documents at issue are from the months after the public learned that an investigation had been opened by the Bureau of Alcohol, Tobacco, Firearms, and Explosives examining the operation called "Fast and Furious" that put guns into the hands of criminals in Mexico. When ATF officials realized that they would have to retract a letter to Congress denying any such thing happened, Republican lawmakers subpoenaed the Justice Department for internal e-mails dated after Feb 4, 2011. President Obama then asserted executive privilege over the documents, and Republicans filed suit in federal court.

Even though Republicans in Congress obviously have good reason for concern over the Justice Department's failure to comply with subpoenas, they are frequently called out by the Attorney General and the President for their supposed concern over these Congressional investigations. In keeping with the frequency of firing back at Republicans, the Attorney General did just that the next day after the House Judiciary Committee hearing when he appeared at an Al Sharpton function for his organization, "National Action Network" and committed the predictable act of throwing the race card. Holder spoke of, "unprecedented, unwarranted, **ugly** and divisive adversity" during the last 5 years that he asserts he and the President have been subjected to. He went on to ask, "What other Attorney General has had to deal with that kind of treatment?" He then asked, "What other President has had to deal with that kind of treatment?" He must have forgotten about John Mitchell, Attorney General under Nixon, who served 19 months in prison (1977 – 1979) for his role in the Watergate scandal and he was white. Just because Holder hasn't been found guilty of his crimes yet, doesn't exclude him from comparison to Mitchell.

Holder offered his customary pat answers to questions today when he would say things like, "I can't comment on that because the investigation is ongoing," or simply "I don't know," and the infamous "I'll check on that and get back to you." Eric Holder is an embarrassment to the office of Attorney General and an embarrassment to responsible African American's who see right through the race allegations and fully understand these claims are without merit.

April 10, 2014

Holder's unwillingness to dispense justice is cause for further concern over the unresolved scandals relating to the botched gun running scheme Fast and Furious, the doctored White House talking points on the Islamist terrorist attack on the U.S. Diplomatic Mission in Benghazi, the Justice Departments snooping on journalists including Fox News James Rosen, NSA domestic surveillance policies, and the IRS targeting of conservative groups. The House Ways and Means Committee issued a "letter of criminal reference" to the DOJ yesterday citing former IRS official Lois Lerner's refusal to testify after she made 17 different supposed factual assertions of innocence during a hearing last year before she asserted her 5th amendment right to silence. She's beginning to learn it doesn't work that way. The House Oversight Committee found Lerner in "contempt of Congress" today and of course this action goes to Eric Holder's corrupt DOJ as well. House Ways and Means Committee Republicans aren't ruling out use of the chamber's 'inherent contempt' authority if Attorney General Eric Holder refuses to act on the panel's accusations against Lerner. The House 'inherent contempt' authority under the Constitution was initially exercised in 1795 during the first Congress and on multiple occasions thereafter. Under 'inherent contempt' Lerner could be held behind bars until January 2015 when a new Congress is seated, which could issue another subpoena and throw her in the slammer again if she still refuses to testify.

Obama Care 4.0

April 11, 2014

On the heels of yesterday's AP report that Kathleen Sebelius is set to resign, the HHS Secretary appeared with the President, Vice-President, and her nominated successor in the Rose Garden to formally announce her resignation from the beleaguered bureaucracy that has and will continue to wreak havoc upon the economy, the health care system, and the American people. Her rocky reign over HHS during the disastrous roll out and subsequent questionable implementation of the ACA will be remembered by all as the catastrophe it was and continues to be. As Sebelius read a prepared statement we were reminded of the inept nature of her management style when she approached the end and verbally admitted the last page was missing so she had to wing it from that point forward. Sebelius acquired a lot of experience with 'winging it' during her time as HHS Secretary as she along with the rest of us were met with one surprise after another. Her time with the Obama administration was characterized by incompetence. In her final good-bye e-mail to her HHS co-workers, Sebelius misspelled the name of her successor. The e-mail read as follows, 'As you've no doubt heard by now, in the coming months I will be passing the baton to my friend and colleague, Sylvia Bur**rell**…. I've worked closely with Sylvia in her role as director of OMB.' Government bureaucrats like Sebelius and Obama will never succeed at the business end of their job because they know nothing about running a business.

The President named OMB Director, Office of Management and Budget, Silvia Mathews Burwell as Sebelius's successor. With her background as budget director, her nomination sends a clear signal that the White House is more interested in the numbers relating to Obama Care than actual management over health care for Americans. Wouldn't it make more sense to nominate a Doctor? Burwell is surely headed for a tough Senate confirmation hearing as Republican Senators will seize the opportunity to drill her on the unknown breakdown of the Obama Care numbers. In an election year, Republicans must shine a light on the still broken aspects of the President's signature health care law at every turn. It's widely believed though that Burwell will ultimately be confirmed as the new HHS Secretary. It's difficult to imagine why anybody would want the job considering the existing mess and the likely rocky road ahead. Burwell's business background will give her a leg up toward her attempt at the unfinished implementation job but she's still walking into mission impossible.

As recently as the end of March, Sebelius had talked about staying on board until sometime in November but the President must have formulated a new plan once 7.5 million people supposedly enrolled in the new health insurance program. The still highly questionable number has energized the Obama administration and it appears they see an opportunity to re-launch their socialistic health care plot with the goal of single payer. Yes, Medicare and Medicaid for everybody is the light at the end of the tunnel for Democrats. Of course, the re-launch required a new scapegoat, I mean leader, to sell it to the American people. As the administration continues to claim victory, their vision for the launch of **Obama Care 4.0** is at the forefront of their agenda. The new and improved version will be touted until the existing cracks in the mortar plus new ones break loose and the whole thing goes to hell in a hand basket setting the stage for single payer. Silvia Burwell had better brace for one hell of a ride while Kathleen Sebelius begins writing her memoirs and the Obama administration braces for increasing failures associated with this socialistic income re-distribution scheme that was doomed to fail from the beginning!

Tax Day

April 15, 2014

New taxes to fund Obama Care's insurance subsidies kicked in today for many Americans. New income taxes on top earners, an increase in federal payroll taxes and new taxes on investment income will help pump an estimated $20.5 billion into the Presidents socialistic health care program. The new health care law also restricts write offs for medical expenses. The threshold that must be reached before medical expenses become deductible was raised from 7.5% to 10% of gross income. 20 new Obama Care taxes will cost taxpayers over $500 billion over the next 10 years. New taxes on companies such as the controversial medical device tax and a plan tax on insurance companies are among the new taxes. The GAO reported that 45,000 jobs are at risk due to the new medical device tax. After 36 unconstitutional unilateral changes to the law by the President, the national debt will balloon to an even greater extent than it otherwise would have. The Obama administration's decision to delay scheduled cuts to the popular Medicare Advantage program will make a significant contribution to the substantial increases in our debt. The Washington Examiner's Phillip Klein said last week that, "according to the Government Accountability office, if Obama Care's Medicare cuts don't get implemented, instead of decreasing deficits, the law would increase long-term deficits by $6.2 trillion." The Tea Party's acronym 'Taxed Enough Already' is growing in relevance as taxes associated with the ACA spiral out of control.

The tax code has also reached an entirely undecipherable and unintelligible level! It's so complex that even the most accomplished tax preparation experts are beginning to doubt their ability to submit totally accurate tax returns for middle and upper income Americans who are the only people who even pay federal taxes. Former Secretary of Defense Donald Rumsfeld posted a picture on Twitter of the letter he sent to the IRS, saying he had submitted his tax return by Tuesday's deadline but that he had "absolutely no idea whether our tax returns and tax payments are accurate." This despite his being a College graduate and having paid an accounting firm to prepare his return, he said.

As of 2013, the top 10% of taxpayers now pay over 70% of all federal income tax and the top 1% pay 30% of the total while the remaining 90% of Americans pay just under 30% of all federal income tax. 47% of all Americans pay hardly anything at all while the bottom 20% not only don't pay anything but they receive payments from the federal government by claiming more in credits than they owe in taxes, giving them a negative tax rate. There's surely a better way for the federal government to collect income tax but a simplified method like a flat tax would be received by special interest groups and most lobbyists with great criticism because their interests wouldn't be served to their satisfaction. Since most politicians are beholden to these special groups, the likelihood of any change to the complicated tax code is slim to none.

Keystone Cops

April 18, 2014

The State Department quietly issued a statement late today, as is the customary method of unpopular revelations coming out of this administration, advising further delay of a decision to finish construction on the Keystone XL pipeline. The Obama administration just happened to pick Friday afternoon of Easter weekend to announce delay of the Keystone XL pipeline until late this year after the mid-term elections in November. Apparently, the State Department needs more time to assess the non-existent environmental threat posed by the pipeline. After 5 years, the State Department and the President just can't figure out if it's better to safely and rapidly flow oil through a pipeline from Canada to the Gulf of Mexico or if the current slower less environmentally friendly method of Trucks and Rail would be best. The President and the State Department are terminally indecisive on this issue. The only thing the Obama administration knows for sure is that huge Democrat campaign donors such as Tom Steyer, a wealthy environmentalist whose political advocacy group, NextGen Political Action, will be contributing $50 million of his own money and another $50 million raised from other donors to Democrats who support climate regulation, hence the decision to stonewall completion of the oil pipeline. Jeffrey Katzenberg, film studio executive and film producer, is another of these wealthy environmentalists who are disrupting America's ability to become energy independent. The Obama administration and several wealthy environmentalists are playing **Keystone Cops** to block the Keystone XL pipeline and their incompetence surpasses that of the **Keystone Cops** featured in silent film comedies of the early 20th century. When the special interests of wealthy campaign donors stifle job creation and threaten national security it's obviously bad for America.

Rob Collins, executive director of the National Republican Senatorial Committee, believes Democrats will regret giving climate activists an outsized role in the elections. "Extremism in general-election politics is always a dangerous thing, especially when it's in the hands of a small group of people with a lot of money," Collins said, adding that donors are less politically experienced than party operatives. Polls have shown the American people support the pipeline 3 to 1. 11 Democrat U.S. Senators also support the pipeline but the President has left them out in the cold. That cold shoulder could prove to be very costly for these Democrat Senators in November.

Terry O'Sullivan, general president of Laborers International Union of America (LIUNA), called the President's move "gutless" and a "low blow to the working men and women of our country." Labor unions were formerly major Obama supporters but now that Obama Care and environmental initiatives have done significant harm to the labor union work force, they are speaking out and aren't pulling any punches.

Gary Doer, Canadian Ambassador to the United States, has been extremely outspoken in defense of the pipeline. Doer cites 4 major reasons why the Keystone XL pipeline should be completed. Job creation, Public Safety, Cost and the greenhouse gas effect of current truck and rail transportation as opposed to the more environmentally friendly pipeline are 4 very strong reasons to support completion of the pipeline. He points out that the oil is still making its way to Port Arthur, TX. via truck and rail but that the more efficient and faster flow of oil through the pipeline would in turn displace some of America's dependence on oil from Venezuela and the Middle East. I find it incredible that the President would deny job opportunities for thousands of Americans in Nebraska, Kansas, Oklahoma and Texas just to maintain his unsustainable position to protect extreme environmentalists who don't understand the importance of U.S. energy independence.

Pernicious Ignorance

April 29, 2014

Secretary of State John Kerry told a room of influential world leaders on Monday 4/28 that if there's no two-state solution to the Israeli-Palestinian conflict soon, Israel risks becoming "**an apartheid state**." "A two-state solution will be clearly underscored as the only real alternative. Because a unitary state winds up either being **an apartheid state** with second class citizens – or it ends up being a state that destroys the capacity of Israel to be a Jewish state," Kerry told the group of senior officials and experts from the U.S., Western Europe, Russia and Japan. Based on the 1998 Rome Statute, the "crime of apartheid" is defined as "inhumane acts…. committed in the context of an institutionalized regime of systematic oppression and domination of one racial group or groups and committed with the intention of maintaining that regime."

Kerry went on to make other controversial comments during his remarks to the Trilateral Commission in a recording obtained by the Daily Beast. He lashed out against Israeli settlement-building in the west bank. Kerry said that both Israeli and Palestinian leaders share the blame for the current impasse in the talks. He also said at some point, he might unveil his own peace deal and tell both sides to "take it or leave it." State Department spokeswoman Jen Psaki told the Daily Beast that Kerry was simply repeating his view, shared by others, that a two-state solution is the only way for Israel to remain a Jewish state in peace with the Palestinians. Kerry began to back away from his comments today when he said he shouldn't have used the word apartheid but failed to make an actual apology.

The response on Capitol Hill was quick, strong and came from both sides of the aisle. House Majority Leader Eric Cantor urged Kerry to "apologize to the Israeli government and people." "Reports that Secretary Kerry has suggested Israel is becoming an apartheid state are extremely disappointing," Cantor, who is Jewish, said in a statement. Cantor went on to say, "The use of the word apartheid has routinely been dismissed as both offensive and inaccurate, and Secretary Kerry's use of it makes peace even harder to achieve." Late Monday, Senator Barbara Boxer (D-CA) tweeted, "Israel is the only Democracy in the Middle East and any linkage between Israel and apartheid is nonsensical and ridiculous." Shortly after Cantors call for an apology, Senator Ted Cruz (R-TX) called for Kerry's resignation on the Senate floor. "Mr. President, it is my belief that Secretary Kerry has thus proven himself unsuitable for his position and that before any further harm is done to our alliance with Israel, he should offer President Obama his resignation," Cruz said. "And the President should accept it." Senator Marco Rubio (R-FL), a member of the Senate Foreign Relations Committee, voiced it best when he said, "These comments are outrageous and disappointing. Incendiary name calling does not change the fundamental fact that Israel does not currently have a viable partner for peace. I urge Secretary Kerry and the administration to focus on pressing challenges in the Middle East such as ending the humanitarian catastrophe in Syria and preventing Iran from acquiring a nuclear weapon instead of pressuring Israel to make additional concessions to partners who have now chosen to align themselves with a terrorist group."

While not confirming whether Kerry warned that Israel could become an apartheid state, State Department spokeswoman Jen Psaki said, "The Secretary does not believe and did not state publicly or privately that Israel is an apartheid state, and there's an important difference there." Secretary Kerry's **pernicious ignorance** is disgraceful. He obviously doesn't understand that there will never be peace between the Nation of Israel and the Islamists who are squatting on God's land which he provided for Israel. Israel is the only God ordained land in the world!

President Mahmoud Abbas of the Palestinian Authority, which was originally formed by the Father of Modern Terrorism, Yasser Arafat, made it clear recently that his alliance with Hamas is solid. These terrorists make no apologies for their well-known desire to wipe the Nation of Israel from the map. The Palestinian Authority and Hamas epitomize apartheid as they seek to advance their agenda of ethnic cleansing; to murder Jews in their homeland. The unshakable alliance between the Palestinian Authority led by Abbas and Hamas in Gaza makes peace in the Middle East impossible and the ignorant naivete of President Obama merely exacerbates the problem. The Obama administration has blatantly snubbed Israel for 5 years by giving millions to the Palestinian Authority, appointing known Jewish haters like Secretary of Defense Chuck Hagel and UN Ambassador Samantha Powers and attempting to force Israel's hand to align themselves with known Islamist terrorists who only wish to obliterate the Nation of Israel from the Earth. The only hope for peace in the Middle East is Christ's promised return in great power and glory as the Lion of Judah when everything will change!

Smoking Gun

April 30, 2014

The White House just released over 100 pages of documents to the conservative watchdog group Judicial Watch as part of a Freedom of Information Act lawsuit. The documents are all related to the Benghazi terror attack of 9/11/12. Several e-mails were among the documents, some of which point to involvement by a senior White House aide who played a key role in preparing former US Ambassador Susan Rice for her infamous appearances on 5 Sunday morning talk shows the Sunday after the attack, where she conveyed false information relating to the Benghazi attack.

A September 14, 2012 e-mail from Ben Rhodes, Deputy National Security Advisor for strategic communications, was sent to a dozen members of the administrations inner circle, including key members of the White House communications team such as Press Secretary Jay Carney. The e-mail focuses on the anti-Islamic video that Susan Rice proclaimed to be the motivating factor behind the attack. The e-mail covers several strategic goals, two of which are particularly incriminating. The first goal reads, "To underscore that these protests are rooted in an internet video, and not a broader failure of policy." The second goal reads, "To reinforce the President and Administration's strength and steadiness in dealing with difficult challenges."

Judicial Watch President Tom Fitton said, "The goal of the White House was to do one thing primarily, which was to make the President look good. Blame it on the video and not the President's policies." The 9/14/12 e-mail from Ben Rhodes is significant because it's the first solid evidence that the video story originated from the White House and not the CIA talking points. The e-mail coupled with the fact that former Deputy CIA Director Michael Morell testified in an early April 2014 Congressional hearing that the video was not part of the CIA analysis. "My reaction was two-fold," Morell told members of the House Intelligence Committee, regarding Rice's appearances. "One was that what she said about the attacks evolving spontaneously from a protest was exactly what the talking points said, and it was exactly what the intelligence community analysts believed. When she talked about the video, my reaction was, that's not something that the analysts have attributed this attack to."

As a follow-up, 3 leading Republicans sent letters to the House and Senate foreign affairs committees on Monday night 4/28/14 asking them to compel the administration to explain who briefed Rice in advance of the Sunday talk shows and whether State Department or White House personnel were involved. "How could former Ambassador to the United Nations Susan

Rice, during the 5 Sunday talk shows on September 16, 2012, claim that the attacks on our compounds were caused by a hateful video when Mr. Morell testified that the CIA never mentioned the video as a causal factor," said the letter, from Senators Lindsey Graham (R-SC), Kelly Ayotte (R-NH) and John McCain (R-AZ).

White House press secretary Jay Carney made an incredible statement today in response to the Ben Rhodes e-mail. He told the press that the e-mail was not specifically about Benghazi but instead it was about general unrest in the overall region. One of the bullet points in the e-mail read: To show that we will be resolute in bringing people who harm Americans to justice, and standing steadfast through these protests. Benghazi was the only location in the region where Americans were harmed so Carney's assertion that the e-mail referenced general unrest throughout the overall region doesn't hold water. The White House will continue to spin until their dizzying lies look more and more ridiculous. They will continue to evade the truth at all costs because the cost of accountability is high. This White House and State Department have the blood of 4 Americans on their hands. Ambassador Christopher Stevens, Sean Smith, Glen Doherty and Tyrone Woods lost their lives so President Obama could maintain the campaign narrative that GM is alive, Osama Bin laden is dead and Al Qaeda is on the run. The first two parts of the narrative are quite true but the last part couldn't be further from reality and Barak Obama's insistence to stick to his story turned out to be deadly. The subsequent cover up to avoid accountability is shameful and may eventually blow up in Hillary Clinton and Barak Obama's face. They are undoubtedly deserving of dire consequences. The recently unveiled Ben Rhodes e-mail is a **smoking gun** that will haunt the President and the State Department for some time.

Chapter 17

Dude

May 1, 2014

Tommy Vietor, former National Security Council spokesman, appeared on Fox News "Special Report" with Bret Baier this evening. Vietor helped to brief Susan Rice prior to her appearances on 5 Sunday morning talk shows on 9/16/12. Baier asked Vietor if he changed "attack" to "demonstrations" in the Benghazi talking points and he replied, "Maybe, I don't really remember," so when Baier pressed him on his non-answer, he said, "**Dude**, this was like 2 years ago," so Baier fired back, "Dude, this is what everyone is talking about," and Vietor went on with a vague rant that still didn't answer anything but did happen to mention that he was in the situation room at the White House during the attack. Baier quickly seized the opportunity and asked Vietor if the President was in the situation room during the attack and he answered, "No." It didn't take Vietor long before he realized he'd just answered a huge question that countless people have tried to find the answer to for some time, so when Baier's subsequent questions drilled down for more detailed information on the President's absence in the situation room, Vietor attempted to back up and said the President wasn't in the room he was in as if there's more than one room in the situation room but Baier reminded him that he's been in the situation room many times and that it is only the one fairly small room so Vietor had to concede his lame retraction attempt with no further debate.

Retired Air Force Brigadier General Robert Lovell, former intelligence director of AFRICOM, testified before the House Oversight Committee today and clearly indicated more could have been done militarily to respond to the terrorist attack on the U.S. Diplomatic Mission in Benghazi on 9/11/12. Gen. Lovell was in Stuttgart, Germany during the attack. Lovell's demeanor during questioning reflected his frustration that the order for military action never came. During Lovell's prepared statement before questioning began, he said military officials knew "early on that this was a hostile action." "This was no demonstration gone terribly awry," he said. During questioning by Congressman Jason Chaffetz (R-UT) Lovell said that soon after the attack began, he believed they were attributable to Ansar al-Sharia, an Al Qaeda affiliated group. Chaffetz asked Lovell, "Was it a video that sparked a protest?" Lovell answered, "No sir." Lovell added, we may have possessed the ability to save four Americans that died and added, "but we'll never know."

House Select Committee on Benghazi

May 8, 2014

House Speaker John Boehner announced the formation of a Select Committee yesterday to engage in a thorough investigation aimed at answering the numerous unanswered questions surrounding the 9/11/12 terrorist attack on the U.S. Diplomatic Mission in Benghazi, Libya. Speaker Boehner resisted this action for over a year since several House members began calling for such a committee last year. The Ben Rhodes e-mail that revealed the White House as the origination point of the video story in the talking points used to prep Susan Rice for her 5 Sunday morning talk show appearances on 9/16/12 was the straw that broke the camel's back. The fact that this e-mail had previously been withheld by the White House when under subpoena by Congress was more than sufficient reason to establish the select committee. The House held a vote today to establish the committee and it passed 232 to 186 with 7 Democrats voting in favor. Speaker Bohener appointed Congressman Trey Gowdy (R-SC) to head the panel. Rep. Gowdy's initial statement was, "This resolution equips the select committee with the scope and tools necessary for the seriousness of this investigation. We are charged with a clear mission: uncover all the facts and provide answers to the American public."

Speaker Boehner said the make-up of the committee will consist of 7 Republicans and 5 Democrats reflecting the Republican majority in the House. House Democrats are very upset about the establishment of this committee. House minority leader Nancy Pelosi (D-CA) said, "This is a stunt, this is a political stunt." House Democrats have repeatedly pointed to 7 previous hearings held by 5 different House committees as having been sufficient probing and have threatened to boycott the select committee. The fact is that the previous hearings were fragmented and limited in scope which made it extremely difficult to drill down and obtain pertinent information from the people who were called to testify. The select committee will have unlimited subpoena power to obtain documents that may hold all the answers. In addition to Rep. Gowdy as the committee chairman, Speaker Boehner appointed Jim Jordon (R-OH), Susan Brooks (R-IN), Martha Roby (R-AL), Peter Roskam (R-IL), Mike Pompeo (R-KS) and Lynn Westmore (R-GA) as the Republican members of the committee. This select committee is tasked with the daunting responsibility of revealing the truth about that fateful night in Benghazi. Only time will tell if their probe results in accountability for those responsible for the unnecessary death of four fine Americans.

Contempt

May 8, 2014

The House Ways and Means Committee has been attempting to obtain all Lois Lerner e-mails in relation to IRS targeting of conservatives who were denied tax exempt status for over a year now but the IRS has finally released the Lois Lerner e-mails to Congress. House GOP members also report today that in addition to denial of tax exempt status to conservative groups, the IRS audits 10% of Tea Party campaign donors as opposed to audits on only an average of 1% of ordinary Americans. The House voted yesterday to find Lois Lerner in **contempt** of Congress by a vote of 231 for and 187 against with 6 Democrats voting in favor. Unfortunately, the **contempt** charge goes to Eric Holder's corrupt DOJ where it's unlikely that it will go anywhere but because of "shall language" the charge might go to a grand jury. The charge says the U.S. District Attorney "shall" take it (not can or may take it) to a grand jury but Washington DC U.S. District Attorney Ronald Machan works for the corrupt Attorney General who has also been found to be in **contempt** of Congress. A grand jury would surely pass the charge on to a judge but the charge must find its way to a grand jury first.

The House also held a vote to call for Special Counsel to investigate the IRS. This measure passed by a vote of 250 for and 168 against with 26 Democrats voting in favor. This measure also goes to the corrupt DOJ and when we consider Barbara Bosserman, a trial attorney within the IRS Civil Rights Commission who is a maxed-out Obama campaign donor is leading the internal investigation, it's unlikely that this will go anywhere either. Regarding the Lerner e-mails, House Ways and Means Committee Chairman Dave Camp (R-MI) said, "We believe she violated people's Constitutional rights to due process, and that's actually criminal in nature, so this is very serious." Camp went on to say, "We want to find how far this goes, and we're going to follow these e-mails wherever they lead us."

Cooking the Books

May 15, 2014

Veteran Affairs Secretary Eric Shinseki testified before a Senate panel today to answer questions about tactics being used at VA medical centers around the country to hide huge appointment backlogs. Reports of the practice go all the way back to 2010 but recent VA whistleblowers have blown the lid off this scandal. Dr. Samuel Foot of the Phoenix, AZ. VA medical center sounded the alarm last week and since then Dr. Jose Mathews, Chief Psychiatrist at the St. Louis, MO. VA and Dr. Richard Krugman of the Harlingen, TX. VA have come forward to report scandalous practices that have sparked renewed investigations. Dr. Mathews was fired as soon as he spoke out about undeserved bonuses. Apparently, government employees can be fired after all and quickly too. A series of reports by the GAO, Government Accountability Office, the VA Inspector General and Shinseki's own internal medical investigators documented the existence of bogus waiting lists and other paperwork tricks at VA hospitals nationwide.

Dr. Samuel Foot of the Phoenix, AZ. VA reported that 40 patients died there while waiting for appointments that were on a hidden list and held up until 14 days prior to the time they could be seen so it would appear that patients were being seen promptly. Bonuses for VA directors are based on timely execution of appointments. Phoenix VA Director, Sharon Helman, received a $9000. bonus last year while she was **cooking the books** and causing patients to die. Secretary Shinseki dodged questions during the Senate hearing while he insisted on getting the results of the IG's investigation and his own internal review of what happened in Phoenix before offering conclusions or taking disciplinary action. Senator Richard Burr (R-NC), the ranking Republican on the Committee, pressed Shinseki on prior reports as he went through a list of previous investigations, all of which found records were being falsified at veterans' medical centers to hide the appointment backlogs and the subsequent lack of care. Senator Burr fired on Shinseki while he said, "VA's leadership has either failed to connect the dots or failed to address this ongoing crisis, which has resulted in patient harm and even death." Burr went on to say, "The question we must answer today is, even with all the information available to the secretary, starting over a year and a half ago, and specific instances of patient harm and death directly related to delays in care, why were the national audits and statements of concern from VA only made this month."

Dr. Robert Petzel, Under-Secretary for health, was seated next to Shinseki during the hearing and said the agency does try to root out inappropriate scheduling practices. "It's absolutely inexcusable," Petzel said. Rep. Jeff Miller (R-FL), chairman of the House Committee on Veterans Affairs, first revealed the practice of secret waiting lists being kept in Phoenix. Miller said there were credible reports that two sets of books were kept at the Phoenix hospital to hide wait times that were longer than allowed in agency policies, and that as many as 40 patients died due to delayed care.

The Obama administrations answer to problems at the VA has been to throw money at it. The total VA budget for 2009 was about $100 billion which was increased to $140 billion by 2013. The VA budget this year is $158.6 billion. After increasing the VA budget by over 50% in 4 years, patient care has declined. Granted we've seen a large increase of wounded warriors returning from Iraq and Afghanistan in recent years but when a 50% increase in funding doesn't even come close to improving care for our veterans, we are experiencing a serious management failure that is inexcusable. President Obama, who hadn't so much as run a lemonade stand prior to becoming President, has no idea how to manage major government entities much less the entire country. VA Secretary Shinseki may have a distinguished military background but he too has no idea how to properly manage the Veterans Administration. The VA spent $500 million on new office furniture last year so they could carry on their corrupt practices in style. Calls for Shinseki's resignation will grow louder and louder as we approach Memorial Day weekend.

May 16, 2014

Dr. Robert Petzel, Under-Secretary of Health for the VA, resigned today amid controversy surrounding corrupt practices at VA medical centers around the country. This faux consequence over corruption at the VA is a joke because Petzel had already announced his retirement last September and was set to leave anyway in just 2 more weeks. His replacement, Jeffrey Morowski, was announced 3 weeks ago. Nobody inside the Obama administration bothered to mention Petzel's previous retirement announcement today as that would have watered down their show of action over corruption at the VA. Fox News however was not remiss in pointing it out. The main stream media was also quiet on Petzel's earlier retirement announcement. VA Secretary Shinseki is the person who should resign but that would spoil the administrations perfect record on accountability which is that accountability is non-existent with this administration. Shinseki's resignation alone will do nothing to fix the problems at the VA. The bureaucratic structure of the VA must be overhauled from top to bottom. This daunting task calls for a dedicated leader who has the courage to oversee sweeping changes which must be supported by Congress and the President but Senate majority leader, Harry Reid and President Obama are too closely associated with the problem therefore it's unrealistic to think they could contribute to the solution.

We're seeing a harbinger of big government health care in action as we witness the domino effect of the systemic problems at the VA. Obama Care will be worse because the size of the problems and the amount of corruption will be directly proportional to the size of the bureaucracy. Socialistic big government health care administered by the IRS is a ticking time bomb of catastrophic proportions. The sheer incompetence and inability to perform by this administration is causing irreparable damage to the American people. If the people elect an actual qualified leader as President in 2016 we can reverse the wake of destruction left behind by the Obama administration but presently we are rendered virtually helpless while this President's hapless agenda wreaks havoc throughout the country.

The Presidents response to the VA scandal, as conveyed by White House Press Secretary Jay Carney, is oddly reminiscent of his response to IRS targeting of conservatives and the DOJ's "Fast and Furious" scandal. It seems the President learned of the scandalous actions of all 3 bureaucracies through the media. Really, …. Is that the story he wants to go with? We know from briefing materials obtained by the Washington Times back in 2008 through the Freedom of Information Act that the President was duly warned about VA directors who were gaming the system as revealed in this transition briefing memo for the incoming Obama administration. "This report and prior reports indicate that the problems and causes associated with scheduling, waiting times and wait lists are systemic throughout the VHA."

White House Chief of Staff Denis McDonough told CBS News that the President is "madder than hell" over the situation at the VA. We heard the same response to IRS targeting of conservatives before he went silent. It seems the strategy is to stick their collective heads in the sand until these problems go away as they rely on the main stream media to move on and honor their silence. For those of us who are paying attention this strategy is completely ineffective but for those who rely on the main stream media for their news, they will blindly go on about their everyday business as their freedoms are being systematically stripped away.

We are now dealing with a President who is disengaged. He thought being President was about traveling around the world in Air Force 1 making philosophical speeches as he left the business of running the country to a bunch of big government bureaucrats. He appointed people to high level cabinet positions who held the same philosophical ideologies as his. Now that his idealistic world is unraveling faster than he can make speeches to address the problems, he's shut down and left people like White House Press Secretary, Jay Carney and White House Chief of Staff, Denis McDonough, to carry on with the strategy of messaging over action and critical partisan attacks targeting the opposition. The opposition is beginning to creep into his own party as political survival instincts are kicking in among vulnerable Democrats. The thought of over 2 more years of watching the President duck for cover while Congress is stalled in gridlock is unimaginable. Congress will most likely be freed up when Republicans take control of the Senate next year but the President's veto pen will shut down every effort to clean up the mess.

Misdirection

May 21, 2014

Nancy Pelosi (D-CA), House minority leader, announced her appointment of 5 Democrats to the House Select Committee charged with investigating the alleged White House and State Department cover up of their missteps in response to and leading up to the terrorist attack on the U.S. Diplomatic Mission in Benghazi, Libya on 9/11/12. After 13 days of indecision regarding Democrat participation on the select committee, Pelosi explained Democrats concluded in the end they needed to be at the table to provide balance. Pelosi appointed Elijah Cummings (D-MD), Adam Schiff (D-CA), Linda Sanchez (D-CA), Tammy Duckworth (D-IL) and Adam Smith (D-WA) to the committee. Elijah Cummings who fought vigorously with Darrell Issa (R-CA) on the House Oversight panel said Trey Gowdy told him that he was "hopeful that we would be able to have a situation where there would be fairness." Cummings went on to say, "We need someone in the room to defend the truth." Unfortunately, Gowdy's definition of fairness and truth vs. Cummings definition of fairness and truth will surely conflict given Cummings ignorant and belligerent attitude. On a more positive note, Trey Gowdy is capable of intelligent, articulate and aggressive diplomacy that will frustrate Cummings attempts at **misdirection**.

Period

May 22, 2014

The House passed a bi-partisan bill today to authorize dismissal of VA administrators for corrupt practices. The bill is designed to enable top level VA management to fire administrators in the field immediately for corrupt scheduling practices in lieu of long drawn out review processes. The bill passed 390 to 33 and will now go to the Senate.

The President finally addressed the nation yesterday to offer his response to allegations made by VA whistleblowers. His demeanor was that of a bad actor who was attempting to show the appropriate amount of indignation. The Presidents forced disdain came several days late. His familiar promise of punishment for offenders fell flat as he said, "If these allegations prove to be true, it is dishonorable, it is disgraceful and I will not tolerate it – **period**." The emphatic "**period**" at the end of his statement is reminiscent of his Obama Care statements that promised we could keep our plans and Doctors - **period**. We all know how that turned out! The Presidents attempt at "hurry up and wait" is also a familiar tactic which is utilized as his administration hopes the situation will just blow over and become old news. The President is sadly mistaken if he thinks problems at the VA will just fade away. Too many Democrats are all over this one and its gaining momentum daily with 26 VA facilities under investigation. Memorial Day weekend is on the horizon which will place a laser focus on the VA debacle.

Systemic

May 30, 2014

Veterans Affairs Secretary Eric Shinseki resigned today while under fire from all directions. There was no hiding from the **systemic** failures that have plagued this corrupt big government bureaucracy. As should be expected from this administration, both Shinseki and the President claimed they knew nothing of the bad news about secret wait lists at VA facilities around the country. They must have conveniently overlooked the 18 specific IG reports since 2010 that reveal the corruption. The inconvenient truth is that both Shinseki and President Obama knew full well that corruption existed but it was easier to continue with business as usual even though our veteran's lives were hanging in the balance. After resigning, Shinseki admitted to **systemic** problems at the VA and apologized while he claimed, "I was too trusting." He said he trusted reports that he should have been suspect of. Deputy Secretary Sloan Gibson will take over as interim Secretary. Gibson is relatively new to the VA so it's hoped that his hands are clean and that he can lead the initial charge to clean things up. Rep. Jeff Miller (R-FL), chairman of the House Veterans Affairs committee, appears to be taking an extremely hands on approach to dealing with the clean-up.

Back in 2010 some bureaucrat came up with the bright idea to link employee bonuses to maintaining appointment wait times to 14 days. That's all it took for other bureaucrats down the line to figure out that if they kept appointment requests on a secret wait list until they knew they could meet the 14 day criteria and subsequently transfer these veterans to the real appointment list at that time, they would qualify for a nice bonus. No wonder greed is one of the 7 deadly sins because these sins were indeed deadly. We recently learned from one IG report that approximately 1700 veterans were kept on secret lists with an average wait time of 115 days for an appointment. The most recent IG reports wouldn't have been called for if it hadn't been for brave whistleblowers like Dr. Katherine Mitchell of the Phoenix VA who just joined in with the initial whistleblowers. Dr. Mitchell's bravery was rewarded with a reprimand by her boss who was subsequently fired by Shinseki on his way out along with other directors in Phoenix. Dr. Mitchell raised eyebrows when she said she knew of one IG who slanted his report in favor of the VA. As of today, the number of VA facilities under investigation has grown to 42.

Chapter 18

Deal with the Devil

June 1, 2014

President Obama's desire to close Guantanamo has now resulted in desperate, dangerous and illegal action. His latest unlawful unilateral move has left most of the country in shock. He's broken America's decade's long tradition of not negotiating with Terrorists in a precedent setting trade of 5 Taliban Commanders we've held captive at Guantanamo 12 years for 1 American deserter held captive for 5 years in Afghanistan by the Haqqani network of the Taliban. He made the trade against the advice of his military advisors and he did not consult with or even notify anyone in Congress. President Obama signed legislation into law that requires the executive branch to give Congress 30-day notice for the release of any Guantanamo detainee. On June 21, 2013, White House Press Secretary Jay Carney addressed the White House Press Corp and said the Obama administration would never release a Guantanamo detainee without consulting Congress and without being in accordance with U.S. law. The President broke this law when he secretly made this trade without notifying Congress. The Obama administration made the assertion that Army Sgt. Bowe Bergdahl was in serious failing health and that their decision to move quickly was due to the need to get him out before he died but the Taliban released a video of the actual hand off in Afghanistan where a Blackhawk helicopter flew in to pick Bergdahl up and he appeared to be in great shape while he walked with ease on his own power and looked quite healthy. Once again, the Obama administration is caught twisting the truth due to an unanticipated propaganda video released by the Taliban. Senator Diane Feinstein (D-CA), chairman of the Senate Intelligence Committee, had previously advised the President in writing that she could not support the release of these 5 Taliban Commanders under any circumstance so the President had a "heads up" that Congress would not approve this trade and moved forward on his own in violation of the law. Senator Feinstein made a statement after the trade became known to express her concern and disgust for the Presidents violation of the law, and this coming from a Democrat supporter of the President. We've seen a bi-partisan uprising from several members of Congress over the Presidents ego driven violation of the law. The imperial President strikes again in a move that was purely political.

On June 30, 2009 Army Sgt. Bowe Bergdahl abandoned his post while on duty in far eastern Afghanistan. He was serving in a brigade size platoon at the time consisting of about 2000 soldiers. He slipped under the wire with a change of clothes, a cell phone, food, water, a knife, and a compass. He left a note that read, "I'm leaving to start a new life." An Army investigation conducted shortly after he left revealed that he had denounced his U.S. citizenship in writing and that he wanted to join the Taliban. Army code dictates that a search must be mounted for any soldier missing in action even in the case of desertion so this platoon's entire mission statement changed to a search mission for Bergdahl. Sgt. Evan Buetow, Bergdahl's platoon squad team leader, appeared on Fox News shortly after the trade had been announced and said that upon Bergdahl's departure, IED's were immediately making direct hits under Humvee's when previous IED attacks were not accurate. Sgt. Buetow said only an insider could have supplied such accurate information so it became clear to them that Bergdahl was collaborating with the enemy. At this point we have solid information from several soldiers in Bergdahl's platoon that 6 brave soldiers died in the search for Bergdahl during the 5 years of his time with the enemy. Numerous other sources have confirmed these deaths now that the trade has become public knowledge including a few parents of the fallen. Sgt. Buetow also revealed that they knew from radio chatter that Bergdahl was trying to find the Taliban. Buetow said Bergdahl had made 3 specific inquiries prior to his departure which he didn't think much of at the time but upon reflection after Bergdahl's desertion it all began to make sense. Bergdahl had asked his leader about obtaining money and asked about mailing his computer home along with other personal items and finally inquired what would happen if sensitive items such as night vision goggles, weapons, etc. went missing.

The search for Bergdahl has been under way since his departure 5 years ago. Now we learn that high level negotiations have been under way with the Taliban to secure Bergdahl's release in violation of America's long standing credo to never negotiate with terrorists because once we set that precedent, the enemy will be ignited with a heightened motivation to capture Americans for ransom. Now that a very dangerous precedent has been established, every American in the Middle East and many other locals around the globe are in danger of being captured and held for ransom. Apparently, negotiations for Bergdahl's release were very one sided in favor of the Taliban because they got exactly what they initially asked for without conceding anything. They asked for the 5 highest profile Taliban Commanders being held at Guantanamo and that's exactly what they got. Here's the breakdown of the Taliban Dream Team:

1. Khair Ulla Said Wali Khairkhwa - Khairkhwa was Taliban Interior Minister from 1994 until his capture in Jan. 2002. He is a major opium drug lord.
2. Mullah Mohammad Fazi - Fazi was Chief of Army Staff under the Taliban regime. He had been held at Guantanamo since Dec. 2001.
3. Mullah Norullah Noori - Noori is a Taliban Commander who has also been held at Guantanamo since 2001
4. Abdul Haq Wasiq - Wasiq was Deputy Chief of the Taliban's Intelligence Service. He also served as an Intelligence officer for Al Qaeda.

5. Mohammad Nabi Omari - Omari was the Taliban's Chief of Communication. He was also associated with Al Qaeda and another militant group called Hezb – e – Islami Gulbuddin.

These high-profile terrorists have been condemned by the UN and are classified as war criminals who have beheaded hundreds of Muslims for violating Sharia law. These evil men are now living in Dohar, Qutar where they are supposed to reside for 1 year as a condition of their release. Qutar's government is serving as mediator and overseer of this conditional provision for their new-found freedom. I doubt these lowlifes have a problem with living in the lap of luxury in one of the wealthiest cities in the World for a year before they return to their role as logistical masterminds of Jihad in Afghanistan or anywhere else in the Muslim World where their expertise can be utilized to terrorize the Great Satan who held them captive for over a decade.

The President appeared in the Rose Garden day before yesterday with Bowe Bergdahl's parents who live in Idaho where Bowe grew up. At the time, the President saw this as an opportunity to appear as though he was the hero who had just rescued the only remaining captive U.S. soldier in Afghanistan. The President proudly announced details of Bergdahl's release and then yielded the podium to Bergdahl's emotional Mother. With knowledge that it would be some time before she would be physically reunited with her son due to his debriefing by the Army, she issued a passionate statement directed to her son expressing her delight over his release and her great desire to see him soon. Next, Bowe's father took the podium while the viewing audience wondered why he sported a very long beard that any Muslim would be particularly proud of. Robert Bergdahl's odd appearance didn't dampen his confident demeanor as he rambled on heaping emotional praise on his son and said, "Most of all, I'm proud of how much you wanted to help the Afghan people." His sympathetic commentary toward the people of Afghanistan gave way to a message addressed to his son in the Pashto dialect and ended praising Allah in Pashto. If this came as a surprise to the President, he nevertheless seemed to take it all in stride but one can only wonder if he knew of Robert Bergdahl's sympathetic leanings toward Muslims. Over the weekend, we've learned that Robert Bergdahl tweeted that all Guantanamo detainees should be released. We also learned that Rolling Stone magazine had published e-mails that Bowe Bergdahl had sent to his parents while serving in Afghanistan. These e-mails revealed Bergdahl's disgust for American policy in Afghanistan and in one e-mail he even said he was ashamed to be an American.

Now that Americans have had a day to process the Rose Garden fiasco, National Security Advisor Susan Rice appeared on a Sunday morning talk show to add insult to injury. Sunday morning talk show appearances aren't exactly her forte. It's difficult to imagine why the Obama administration would send her out with ridiculous talking points on the recent prisoner trade after her infamous appearance on 5 Sunday morning talk shows on 9/16/12 to present the quickly dismissed video story/lie in a feeble attempt to explain the highly coordinated Al Qaeda terrorist attack on the U.S. Diplomatic Mission in Benghazi, Libya on 9/11/12 that resulted in the deaths of 4 Americans including Ambassador Chris Stevens. Today she unbelievably and inexplicably had the unmitigated gall to say that the deserter, Sgt. Bowe Bergdahl, served his country with "honor and distinction." You can't make this stuff up!

The Presidents **deal with the devil** will haunt him big time in the days to come. I believe most Americans stand by the maxim that America leaves no soldier behind and that every reasonable effort should have been exhausted to get Army Sgt. Bowe Bergdahl out of Afghanistan but the terrible deal that was made by negotiating with terrorists and turning over the 5 most dangerous high profile terrorists being held at Guantanamo to secure Bergdahl's release was unlawful, inexcusable and just plain stupid. Efforts to extract Bergdahl militarily had been under way for the 5 years since he deserted his post and were still underway. This effort could have been escalated to whatever extent necessary to successfully extract Bergdahl in lieu of negotiations with terrorists for the first time in U.S. history. Bergdahl was being held by 200 Taliban terrorists at a rag tag Haqqani outpost in far eastern Afghanistan. My guess is that the current extraction mission was being conducted with less than maximum enthusiasm after 6 had already died during the effort and given the fact that they were searching for a deserter. Given the opportunity to choose between the terrible deal that was just made and a full-blown escalation of the military mission, I believe our military leaders, excluding the Commander and Chief, would have made the choice to escalate the military mission to the extent necessary to achieve success but that choice was not offered.

Blowback

June 5, 2014

Fox News journalist James Rosen reported today on secret documents he obtained that were generated by "Eclipse", a private intelligence company and Pentagon sub-contractor. The Eclipse "sitrep" intelligence reports offer the most detailed account of Bergdahl's time with the Haqqani's who held him captive for 5 years. Much of the information was obtained by former CIA officer Duane R. Clarridge. Rosen reported that an unnamed former Senior Intelligence officer confirmed the Eclipse reports and it is known that General Robert Ashley, former Chief of Intelligence for Sitcom, did in fact receive the reports. General Ashley is now the Commanding Officer at Fort Huachuca in Arizona. The Eclipse "sitreps" (situation reports) are real time dispatches that cover a timeframe from 2009 until 2012 and contain the actual names of the men who controlled Bergdahl. The reports reveal that Bergdahl did attempt to escape after a year and was loose for 5 days before he was recaptured. Upon his return to the Haqqani outpost a cage was constructed to house him in 2010. The reports revealed that circumstances changed dramatically for Bergdahl by 2012. At this point in August of 2012 it's reported that Bergdahl converted to Islam and referred to himself as a Mujahid (warrior of Islam) of the Mujahadin. He participated in AK-47 target practice with his captors and they allowed him to carry a weapon. He also played soccer with them. The documents also revealed that the Haqqani network preferred a ransom over a prisoner exchange but that wouldn't have served the Presidents objective to release every terrorist detained at Guantanamo.

June 6, 2014

Sgt. Evan Buetow, Bergdahl's squad team leader, and 6 other soldiers who served alongside Bergdahl in Afghanistan appeared last night and again tonight on "The Kelly File", Megyn Kelly's prime time Fox News program. All 7 men confirmed the fact that Bergdahl is a deserter and that 6 men died in the search for him after he voluntarily abandoned his post while on duty at the remote Army Platoon post in far eastern Afghanistan. All 7 men said they would have died for their fellow soldier. They expressed their disgust over the Rose Garden ceremony with Bergdahl's parents and the President where Bergdahl was portrayed as a hero whom we should all welcome home with thanksgiving. When Megyn asked them if they thought Bergdahl should be tried as a Deserter and Court Marshaled, they unanimously agreed he should. They also agreed upon their desire to see Bergdahl rescued and returned home but not by releasing the 5 most high level Taliban Commanders held at Guantanamo in trade. They also confirmed their unanimous belief that the remaining troops in Afghanistan are now at great risk of capture for ransom due to the Presidents terrible decision to set the precedent that America now negotiates with terrorists.

Obama supporters have attempted to make the case that prisoner trades go all the way back to a trade made by George Washington plus other trades that have been executed since but they fail to understand the difference which is that those were not negotiations with terrorists. Once the war on terror began, everything changed because no other war compares to it. The President continually speaks of his accomplishment of ending the war in Afghanistan and Iraq but he too fails to understand that the war on terror won't end until Christ returns in all powerful glory. Just surrendering in Iraq and Afghanistan doesn't count for anything other than paving the way for the enemy to regroup and attack us on American soil again.

The President was in Brussels, Belgium earlier this week for a G7 summit and is in Normandy, France today to commemorate the 70th anniversary of the historic Normandy invasion that saved France from Nazi occupation and changed the tide of World War II but at the very high cost of over 10,000 American, British and Canadian soldiers lives that day on Omaha beach. The President did make a moving speech there today but of course that's the one and only thing that he's good at. It's become apparent that the President never anticipated the huge amount of **blowback** over his terrible political decision to make a prisoner trade and over the Rose

Garden debacle that he planned to make himself appear to be the hero. It was a terrible miscalculation that he is paying the price for in Europe as reporters are acting like a dog with a bone that they won't turn loose of. The President has been slammed with unanticipated questions over the prisoner trade which has limited his intended messaging basically designed to brag and make himself look good for our allies in Europe. When asked about the controversy back home he said, "I'm never surprised by controversies that are whipped up in Washington." When pressed more specifically on the prisoner swap he declared, "We saw an opportunity and I seized it and I make no apology for that." He impressed upon the crowd that we leave no man behind. His "whipped up" reference is reminiscent of the "phony scandal" label he came up with over the Benghazi, IRS, and NSA scandals. His unapologetic position isn't surprising given his extreme narcissism. The **blowback** over the prisoner trade is gaining momentum here at home so the President has only just begun to experience the consequence of his sins.

Squandered Sacrifices

June 12, 2014

A radical Islamic medieval style Caliphate is forming in the Middle East and Osama bin Laden's vision is being realized as the largest Jihadist State in history is being formed in northern Syria and northern Iraq. The Civil War in Syria contributed to the April 2013 formation of the Islamic State of Iraq in Syria (ISIS) aka Islamic State of Iraq and the Levant (ISIL). President Obama's hollow red line ultimatum over chemical weapon use by Assad allowed ISIS to organize and grow in Syria. When the President made the decision to pull out all troops in 2011 we left Iraq with no intelligence capabilities which left both Iraq and the U.S. blind in the region. Support for moderate Sunni rebels in Syria has been quite controversial because of concern that we would inadvertently be helping terrorists. CIA operatives on the ground in Syria may be able to distinguish between Sunni terrorists affiliated with Al Qaeda and moderate Sunni rebels but this is questionable. Both groups oppose Assad and our fight is predominately against the Sunni terrorists so It is indeed complicated. The ISIS extremists along with another group called Jabhat al-Nusra have successfully hijacked Syria's more moderate majority Sunni-opposition and went on to do the same thing in Iraq where Sunni's are the minority. These moderate Sunni's in Syria and Iraq are the least of all evils in the region so they may be the group we need to support in our effort to prevent the nightmare we now face. Iraq's Prime Minister, Nouri al-Maliki, has been aligned with Iraq's Shi'ite majority for years and has always been heavily influenced by Iran's Shi'ite ideology which will set Iraq up to become a client state of Iran. Iran took advantage of American inaction in Syria last year to strengthen their influence there and they will do the same thing in Iraq to an even greater extent because Maliki will be easy to manipulate.

Once American troops made their complete departure from Iraq 2 and ½ years ago, Maliki established an authoritarian rule that has repressed the Sunni minority in western and northern Iraq by pushing them out of political power. This fueled the Sunni insurgency and forced them to look to the extremists for protection and power. If a residual force of American soldiers (about 10,000 to 20,000) had been left behind to work in non-combat roles they could have provided a crucial stabilizing factor to restrain Maliki and to bolster support for Iraq's military in their effort to fight off the Sunni terrorists but negotiations between Obama and Maliki broke down in large part due to a lack of engagement by the White House. President Obama has been frustrated with Maliki's sectarian rule in Iraq but an ego driven stand-off doesn't accomplish anything. The vast long standing differences between Sunni's, Shia's and Kurds in Iraq will always exist so it's unrealistic to think we can bring them together but they did agree on the one issue of support for an American residual military force to be left behind as a stabilizing force.

The population in Iraq breaks down with 60% Shi'ites, 20% Sunni's and 20% Kurds. President Obama has made it clear that U.S. military help is contingent upon the Shi'ites, Sunni's and Kurds forming a coalition government they can all live with. Ideally, a coalition government that allows for an autonomous role for each of the 3 sects would be the best scenario but it's also very unlikely this will occur. Maliki is more likely to make a deal with Iran for their military support which would set the stage for Iran to take control of Iraq. If a status of forces agreement had been established between the U.S. and Iraq before we pulled out in 2011 it would have prevented the now near collapse of Iraq as a country. The complete U.S. departure from Iraq left a vacuum which is rapidly being filled by radical Islamic Jihadists.

A powder keg of catastrophic proportions is developing in Iraq and Syria as insurgent groups capture and gain control over key cities and infrastructure in the region. ISIS is building an Islamic Jihadist State to organize and attack America first and then obliterate Israel. ISIS spawned from Al Qaeda but they are much more violent than Al Qaeda. Abu Bakr al-Baghdadi is the 42-year old leader of ISIS and claims to be a direct descendent of Mohammad. He makes Osama bin Laden look like a choirboy. He was in U.S. custody in Iraq in 2009. When he was released he told a U.S. soldier, "I'll see you in New York." At this point, ISIS has captured and controls Fallujah which occurred 6 months ago, in January. This should have been a wake-up call but the White House and State Department act as though the ISIS offensive is a complete surprise. They went on to capture Mosul, Iraq's second largest city of 2 million people. When ISIS took control of Mosul they captured and now control the Turkish embassy there so Turkey now has a stake in the fight. The rapid advance of the battalion type structure of ISIS militants took control of the oil-refinery cities of Baiji, Kirkuk and Tikrit as they continue their quest for domination in the region leaving a trail of decapitated Iraqi's who resisted. Oil prices have already begun to spike with a 4.1% increase this week to $106.91 a barrel and gas prices are about to reach $4.00 a gallon nationwide as oil companies speculate over an interruption in the flow of oil coming out of Iraq which is OPEC's 2nd largest producer and the 5th largest oil producer in the world. Iraq's military is in no shape to stop or even slow down the ISIS advance because Maliki systematically weakened their security force by placing political cronies and hacks in high level military positions. He basically gutted the Iraqi army. Iraq's hollowed out military has a manning rate of 50% due to desertions. Iraqi soldiers are literally dropping their weapons where they stand and heading for the hills while ISIS militants are picking up U.S. supplied weaponry including 72 tanks, 700 Humvees and 2 helicopters for their own use. When ISIS gained control of Mosul they stole $400 million from Iraq banks there so they are quickly becoming a powerful force to be reckoned with as their army is quite sophisticated. They are now worth a total of $2 billion with 6000 fighters in Sunni areas of Iraq and 4000 in Syria. They utilize social media very effectively with videos on You Tube and rants on Twitter, Instagram and Facebook. ISIS is now positioned to tap Muslim westerners with U.S. and European passports who have traveled to Iraq to join the jihadists. These new recruits armed with their passports will be an invaluable resource for ISIS which is a sinister and evil force with a long term strategic plan that is America's worst nightmare.

President Obama's naïve assertion that Al Qaeda is on the run and his inability to adjust to the fact that Al Qaeda and their affiliates do in fact move and expand beyond Afghan and Pakistani borders has severely jeopardized America's national security. At this point Al Qaeda has 39 affiliates around the world. If the Obama administration remains true to their pattern of ignoring reality while maintaining the political narrative that Al Qaeda is on the run, Iraq is doomed to become a terrorist state with ISIS in control of Sunni's in the north and west and Iran in control of the southern Shia region. ISIS terrorists are so vile that Al Qaeda won't claim them as their own. They institute strict Sharia law in every city with amputations for robbery and the mandate that women must stay indoors. They have decapitated countless Iraqi's who they've declared to be in violation of Sharia law. They've killed 1700 Iraqi soldiers in just a few days. President Obama and many other liberals here at home are attempting to make the case that Iraq bears complete responsibility for their defense and that they should no longer look to the United States for help but this naïve position doesn't consider that America's national security is at risk if a Jihadist State is formed out of Iraq and Syria with Afghanistan in their sights once we pull out there. We've already missed our opportunity to effectively quell the rise of ISIS in Syria and Iraq along with Iran's increased influence over the Shia's in Iraq. The terrorists will now have a huge staging area to train recruits and formulate plans to attack the Great Satin on U.S. soil and to also attack Israel.

June 13, 2014

At this point, Iraq is sorely in need of sophisticated intelligence gathering assets plus air support that the U.S. could provide but President Obama announced today that he will wait several days before any decision is made to step in and assist Iraq while his national security team accesses the situation with an eye to the safety of personnel at the U.S. embassy in Baghdad. National Security Advisor Susan Rice will head up the effort to analyze the situation in the days to come which isn't very reassuring. Yesterday he said, "All options are on the table" but quickly added the proviso that there will be no American troops on the ground. The key factor that the President either fails to understand or refuses to accept is that air support, whether manned or unmanned drones, is worthless without ground intelligence to assist in locating and identifying targets while working to minimize unintended civilian deaths and more importantly we've already missed our opportunity to strike without being perceived as either being aligned with Iraqi Shia's and by association aligned too with Iran which will alienate moderate Sunni's and Kurds in Iraq and ultimately do more harm than good. The terrorist's oldest trick in the book is to mix in with the civilian population and use them as human shields so the collateral damage of civilian deaths further complicates an already extremely complicated scenario. U.S. air strikes should have occurred months ago, when ISIS made their initial advance into Iraq before they had the opportunity to infiltrate the moderate Iraqi Sunni's. Now that the divisions between Iraqi Sunni's, Shi'ites and Kurds are deeper than ever the best scenario of the 3 sects cohabitating in relative peace is further than ever from becoming reality. Any U.S. intervention at this point will be conceived as siding with one of the 3 sects and therefore alienating the other 2. It is indeed a very complex situation.

The President has ignored all the blood and treasure sacrificed in Iraq with the death of over 4500 U.S. soldiers and tens of thousands wounded at the financial cost of $1.7 trillion. The huge U.S. investment in Iraq designed to bolster our own national security has become a **squandered sacrifice.** If America could form a coalition with our Arab league allies in the region designed to mount a coordinated effort with a sustained tempo to quell the rising ISIS army we might be positioned to attack ISIS without the appearance of specific alignment with any single group but such a move is likely the furthest thing from President Obama's incompetent mind. That incompetence is what got us into this terrible situation to begin with.

About 2000 Iranian Revolutionary Guard troops are now on the ground in southern Iraq. They were surely dispatched to help defend Shia's there because of Iran's alliance with Maliki and Iraq's Shi'ite Muslims. Their initial concern is to protect historical Shi'ite Shrines in southern Iraq but ISIS doesn't even have an interest in attacking the Shi'ite holy lands. Iran's Revolutionary Guard will take control of the situation in southern Iraq. They will help to fire up Iraqi troops who sorely need the support but Iran has their own agenda to establish a strong foothold in Iraq so they shouldn't be looked upon as White Knights coming to the rescue.

The White House considers evacuation of the U.S. embassy in Baghdad to be "too politically sensitive." This embassy is a $1 billion fortress with 5500 Americans housed in it but without U.S. forces there to defend it we could see a scenario unfold that would make Benghazi look like a minor incident. The U.S. has increased drone surveillance over Iraq so we'll be able to at least watch while our people there are slaughtered if ISIS were to launch a successful attack on Baghdad. ISIS terrorists will most likely dig in where they are for several days to consolidate their wins and build in defenses as they prepare for what would be a tougher fight over Baghdad. Even if they never capture and control Baghdad, they already control more than enough territory to establish a terrorist state and pose a huge threat to Europe, Israel and the United States.

As the historical invasion of Iraq by ISIS terrorists unfolds, the President is playing golf in Palm Springs. While in California the President made a hyper partisan speech at UC Irvine where he focused on Climate Change aka global warming and as usual was highly critical of conservatives who don't buy into the concept. While the President plays golf, American Civilian contractors are leaving Iraq in droves. Evacuation efforts for defense and oil contractors plus NGO workers are in full swing with charter aircraft going out yesterday and today.

June 15, 2014

The Pentagon is finally beginning to react to the highly volatile terrorist offensive in Iraq as ISIS forces have now taken control of Tal Afar, a city of 200,000 near Mosul. We just learned that ISIS terrorists may have up to 100 U.S. stinger missiles that may have been left behind for Iraq but we don't have absolute confirmation of this yet. These are extremely accurate shoulder fired missiles that are effective against counter measures and can easily bring down aircraft. Secretary of Defense Chuck Hagel has ordered 4 naval vessels into the Persian Gulf at this point including the aircraft carrier, "George H.W. Bush." The "Mesa Verde" has 550 Marines on board along with Osprey aircraft. The White House reported that the Vice-President is in close contact with Prime Minister Maliki. It's a scary prospect when you consider Joe Biden and Chuck Hagel calling the shots while the President is playing golf in Palm Springs, but when you add Barak Obama to the equation things don't improve much if any at all.

June 16, 2014

Secretary of State John Kerry just announced that U.S. drone strikes may commence soon as we attempt to stave off the ISIS advance on Baghdad. Drones will only be marginally effective because these drones can only fire 2 to 3 hellfire missiles per sortie and each drone can only fly 2 to 3 sorties daily and without special-forces troops on the ground to coordinate targeting, it will be very difficult to effectively strike intended targets. Collateral civilian deaths could reach a high level without accurate targeting coordinated from the ground. Secretary Kerry has now announced that the U.S. may begin talks with Iran to discuss strategies to contain the ISIS attacks. The possibility of forming a coalition with Iran to utilize their ground forces already on the ground in Baghdad to help coordinate U.S. air attacks will be discussed. Former CIA director Mike Morrell has already advised against this. U.S. air strikes could help Iran to gain control of Iraq and considering that Iran has been actively engaged in killing Americans for 30 years and that Iran trained Shia militia in Iraq for years who then killed countless Americans in Iraq should be more than enough to make the decision to go it alone. The White House confirmed today that up to 275 U.S. military personnel will be sent to Baghdad. About 150 are Marines who will focus on protection of the U.S. embassy in Baghdad and about 100 to focus on air field management. The State Department announced that 1000 of the 5500 U.S. embassy personnel will be evacuated.

June 19, 2014

George W. Bush predicted the now unfolding situation in Syria and Iraq back in 2007 and Mitt Romney echoed the Bush prediction while on the campaign trail in 2012. They understand the evolution of Islamic Jihad. The definition of the name Al Qaeda is "the base" in Arabic meaning that Al Qaeda was formed as the base for the 39 affiliate groups that now exist around the world. ISIS is now advancing the movement to a medieval style Caliphate of Islamic Jihad.

Oil is a central aspect of this entire situation which can't be ignored. The United States doesn't rely on Iraqi oil but the EU does and if an interruption to the flow of oil out of Iraq occurs the EU's need to go elsewhere to meet their oil demands will drive the price of oil up everywhere. Fortunately, most of Iraq's oil production is in the South which Iraqi Shi'ites and Iran will fight tooth and nail to protect but if the worst scenario were to play out and ISIS gains control of the entire country of Iraq, oil could easily go way up to an unimaginable price per barrel which would create a disastrous ripple effect around the world.

The United States and our allies in the Middle East have 3 main areas of concern. First is overall stability in the region which includes the need to prevent Iran from becoming a nuclear power. Next, there must be no ungoverned spaces but this has already basically occurred in northern Syria and northern and western Iraq. Finally, oil must continue to flow.

The President addressed the nation today and announced that there will be no combat operations in Iraq but that 300 military advisors (Special Forces) will be sent to Iraq in addition to the approximately 270 already committed to. He said there are no immediate plans for air strikes but left the door open to that possibility in the future. He qualified any possible air strike scenario as one that can't appear to be supportive of Shia's over Sunni's. The President emphasized the point that we can't allow ISIS to gain a broader footprint in the region which basically concedes the ground they've already gained. He said Secretary of State John Kerry will be dispatched to Baghdad in a few days to work diplomatic channels. Overall the President was sending a message to Iraqi Prime Minister Nouri al-Malaki that he is basically on his own.

The 300 Special Forces military advisors being sent to Iraq are problematic at this point because Malaki's force in Baghdad is nothing more than a Shi'ite militia allied with Iran. By supporting Malaki's Shi'ite militia in Baghdad, we are essentially helping Iran but we don't yet know how the U.S. troops will be dispersed in the region so it's difficult to predict how this will play out. There are only a few good options open to us at this point but the Obama administration isn't open to any of them. The time to act effectively without sacrificing a great deal of blood and treasure has long since passed

June 22, 2014

The ISIS army just captured Al Qaim, a border crossing town on the Iraq/Syria border. This is a primary border crossing for the flow of goods and commerce between Syria and Iraq. Now that ISIS controls this border crossing they have access to a very important route to transport troops and weaponry between Syria and Iraq.

Secretary of State John Kerry is in Baghdad today with the media in tow so photo ops are all we're seeing. Kerry has probably had some strong and even threatening discussions with Malaki sending the message that he could be forced out of power if he doesn't shape up and pull all 3 Iraqi sects together with some semblance of a unified front so at least the appearance of a solid government can be portrayed. The chances of this actually coming to pass are slim to none and pushing Malaki out after being in power for 8 years is problematic because it's not clear if a politician even exists in Iraq who can accomplish the impossible mission of patching together a coalition government representative of Sunni's, Shi'ites and Kurds. Nevertheless, John Kerry is sending a clear message that Iraq's leaders, whoever they may be, must lead the way to establish peace.

Border Crisis

June 16, 2014

Tens of thousands of children from Central America are being transported through Mexico to the Texas border by Mexican criminal organizations and once across the U.S. border they're left for U.S. Border Patrol agents to deal with. While ill-prepared border agents are busy processing children and even changing diapers, the drug cartels are moving drugs in behind the children because they know border agents are overwhelmed dealing with illegal children. These Mexican criminals are making about $5000. per child to transport them from Central America to the American side of the U.S./Mexico border. The corrupt Mexican government is getting a piece of the action so their hands are far from being clean. Once the unaccompanied children are across the border they wait out in the open for border agents to pick them up while cartel members literally transport drugs across the Rio Grande on jet skis. Over 48,000 children have arrived in the last 2 weeks and they continue to arrive at the rate of about 1000 daily. About 240,000 adults from Central America have entered the U.S. illegally since April in addition to the thousands of children. The main entry point is McAllen, Texas but they don't have adequate facilities to handle this huge influx of illegal children, so many children are being flown on charter planes to Nogales, AZ. because they're better equipped to process larger numbers there. One group was even flown to Massachusetts. Others are bused to Oklahoma and from Arizona many are bused and flown to Riverside County California. The small town of Murrieta, Ca. (pop. 106,000) is bearing the brunt of the illegal child dump. Mayor Allan Long said they received no advance notification that hundreds of illegal children would be dumped in his town and his attempts to contact the Governor of California have been to no avail. He said many children must go straight to the emergency room at the hospital as soon as they get off the bus due to various diseases they have and that they are ill equipped to handle this crisis. The only facility available to house these children in Murrieta is a jail. Murrieta Mayor Allan Long understands that this problem can only be addressed at the federal level but the federal government won't even communicate with him.

Word is being spread throughout Central America by the media that now is the time to go because the U.S. border is wide open and unaccompanied children won't be returned because of a 2012 executive order by President Obama known as the Dream Act. The Dream Act reinforces the 2008 child trafficking law and mandates that any child from a non-contiguous country who enters the U.S. must have a deportation hearing and are entitled to an immigration attorney. Some of these children are attempting to re-unite with their parents who are already here. The children are given a notice to appear before a judge for their hearing in 90 days before they're turned loose. It's difficult to imagine why border agents even bother with the notice because it surely won't be adhered to as most of these children will never show up for their hearing. Disease is a major problem as many of these children arrive with various kinds of disease such as scabies, measles and lice that can easily spread. Four cases of tuberculosis have been identified which is of course extremely serious and highly contagious. The CDC is on alert for Swine Flu, Ebola and Adult Chicken Pox. It's been reported that medical workers on the border have been told by HHS and DHS that if they speak out about the serious health issues posed by these illegal children they will be severely dealt with, so the cover up is in full swing.

A document issued by DHS back in January revealed that this mass influx of children was anticipated and actively planned for. The Jan. 14 document was an order for UAC services to shop for contractors to handle transportation services for up to 65,000 unaccompanied children. HHS is referring to the transportation of these illegal children to various locations around the country as refugee resettlement. DHS is calling it a reunification project because these children are supposedly coming to join their parents who we're told are already here but when the children are questioned while being processed they say their parents are still in Central America and they want to go home. Texas Governor Rick Perry has authorized $1.2 million a week to fund action by various Texas agencies to deal with the problem. No financial support has been offered by the federal government. Governor Perry hasn't even heard from the President on the problem. The White House and Democrat legislators are using the 2008 Child Trafficking Law, passed under the Bush administration, to justify their refusal to immediately deport the children. This law which was passed unanimously by Congress was designed to address sex trafficking and it does require that a deportation hearing must take place before any possible deportation of Central American children. These children are given special immigrant juvenile status and then turned over to ORR, Office of Refugee Resettlement. The children are under ORR care for an average of 35 days before most will be allowed to stay in the United States. Only a small percentage is being deported which is probably a smokescreen by the Obama administration to make it look like their doing something right.

U.S. Congressman Jim Bridenstine (R-OK) went to Fort Sill in Lawton, Oklahoma where 1200 illegal children are currently being housed to assess the situation. When he approached the heavily guarded compound where the children are he was denied access to the facility. He informed the guards that he is the U.S. Congressman for that district in Oklahoma and that surely, he of all people as a federal official should be allowed to enter. After the guards consulted with their superiors they informed Congressman Bridenstine that he would not be allowed access but that he could return in 3 weeks for a highly-restricted visit if he sets up an appointment. This kind of secrecy by our government is highly suspect particularly when a U.S. Congressman is the one being kept in the dark. This is a government sanctioned invasion of our country that is wrong on so many different levels that it's criminal.

Liberal Democrats understand that many of these illegal children will eventually become registered voters who will surely vote for Democrats because of the open borders policy of Democrats. Texas is already on the verge of becoming a blue state because of the large numbers of Mexicans who have been there long enough to become registered voters. Democrats are highly motivated to facilitate the arrival of illegal immigrants who may eventually receive amnesty to facilitate their desire to create a Democrat majority in Texas.

Article 4 Section 4 of the Constitution states that the U.S. border must be secured. The federal government is blatantly imposing their will upon local governments who have no choice in the matter. This unconstitutional action by our federal government is extremely destructive but the

Obama administration obviously doesn't care because their political priorities always trump the Constitution which Obama has trampled on since he took the oath that he would protect it.

The dog ate my homework

June 13, 2014

The IRS advised Dave Camp, House Ways and Means Committee Chairman, that they've lost Lois Lerner e-mails for the timeframe of Jan. 2009 until April 2011. Camp was told a computer glitch caused the disappearance of 2 years of Lerner's e-mails all of which were outgoing communications to entities outside the IRS like the White House. Apparently, all internal correspondence is still available. This highly convenient development for the IRS has many Republicans on Capitol Hill in an uproar. These e-mails must be archived somewhere but if all else fails surely the NSA has them along with every other U.S. e-mail in existence.

The nature of the computer glitch was that Lois Lerner's hard drive crashed and coincidentally the hard drives of 6 other IRS individuals whose e-mails were also under subpoena also crashed. This miraculously coincidental and convenient development provides an unexpected twist to the investigation that will make it extremely difficult for Republicans to get to the bottom of this scandal. Not only did all 7 hard drives simultaneously crash but the IRS claims they recycled the hard drives and have no idea of their whereabouts so all e-mails in question are un-retrievable. How unbelievably convenient! The miraculous and coincidental disappearance of Lois Lerner's e-mails over the exact 2-year timeframe the investigation is focused upon represents corruption at the highest levels of the U.S. government. If you're kid ever used **"the dog ate my homework"** excuse, you may have thought you had heard it all but this IRS story trumps that one.

June 19, 2014

IRS commissioner John Koskinen appeared before the House Ways and Means committee today and was grilled by Republicans while Democrats on the committee did their best to deflect the heated attacks. Republicans fired off tough questions over the allegedly lost Lois Lerner e-mails while Koskinen maintained an arrogant, smug and defiant demeanor. His answers to Republicans questions were pure spin while Democrats either lobbed soft balls or praised him for tolerating the abuse dished out by those nasty conspiratorial Republicans. In a very heated exchange between Paul Ryan (R-WI) and Koskinen, Ryan said, "I don't believe you; nobody believes you." Koskinen defiantly answered that no one had ever said such a thing to him in all his many years of service and Ryan once again answered, "I don't believe you." Koskinen's spin lacked creativity because in one statement he claimed, "Not a single e-mail has been lost since the start of this investigation." Chairman Camp had to answer that ridiculous claim by reminding Koskinen that the e-mails in question were from the time frame prior to the start of the investigation. Finally, after it had become abundantly clear that Koskinen would continue stonewalling, Camp told Koskinen that the one thing they hadn't heard from him was an apology and Koskinen replied, "I don't believe an apology is owed."

June 20, 2014

Round 2 took place today when IRS Commissioner John Koskinen was back on Capitol Hill to appear before the House Oversight and Government Reform Committee. Koskinen's arrogance was on par with yesterday's performance. Today we learned the time frame relating to the supposed hard drive crashes. Lois Lerner reported that her hard drive crashed on 6/13/11 just 10 days after House Ways and Means Committee Chairman Dave Camp made his initial inquiry into IRS targeting of conservative groups. Then on 7/20/11 Lerner claimed she was told the data couldn't be recovered. The IRS then abruptly terminates their 5-year contract with Sonasoft, an archiving company that backs up IRS servers. In addition, today we learned that Lois Lerner's missing recycled hard drive was destroyed but Koskinen claims the other 6 hard drives are simply missing and he has no idea where they are. It's difficult to imagine how anyone could see this as anything other than a cover up and a weak one at that.

Commissioner Koskinen offered that about 2000 hard drive crashes have occurred at the IRS since 2011. I'm not sure why he thought this would help his case particularly since he offered no proof that this happened but in response he was reminded that the IRS has a $1.8 billion annual technology budget. Serious money like that should support a very sophisticated IT department that could prevent 2000 hard drive crashes and insure multiple backups in the event of any crashes at all. Koskinen continually referred to an investigation underway being conducted by a Treasury Inspector General. The Obama administration seems to think the IRS can effectively conduct an internal investigation and that everyone will just accept the easily manipulated findings from one of their own. It's doubtful that we'll ever get to the truth about the political targeting of conservative groups by the IRS but nobody has thrown in the towel just yet.

The media should be demanding accountability for this criminal enterprise but their silence has been deafening. It's common knowledge by now that the President has the main stream media in his back pocket. If a Republican like Richard Nixon were in the White House while a pattern of corruption by the IRS became known, all hell would break loose. The media would be all over it and impeachment proceedings would be well under way. In this case the main stream media is complicit in the corruption by their failure to report on it. If not for Fox News we would all be in the dark. Congress has called for an independent special investigator but Eric Holders corrupt DOJ would be responsible for such an action so everyone knows this won't happen.

Trigger happy

June 25, 2014

A Lois Lerner e-mail chain just surfaced that revealed Lerner had targeted Senator Chuck Grassley (R-IA) for a possible audit back in Dec. 2012. Lerner had inadvertently received an invitation intended to go to Senator Grassley inviting him to speak at a seminar that Lerner had also been invited to attend. Lerner noticed that Grassley's wife, a DC lobbyist, was not only also invited but that the group holding the seminar was offering to pay her travel expenses. **Trigger happy** Lerner saw an opportunity and fired off an internal e-mail suggesting an audit. "Looked like they were inappropriately offering to pay for his wife. Perhaps we should refer to exam?" Lerner wrote this e-mail on Dec. 4, 2012 and sent it to several individuals at the IRS. An IRS official, Matthew Giuliano, replied, "Your and Grassley's invitations were placed in each other's envelopes. Not sure we should send to exam. I think the offer to pay for Grassley's wife is income to Grassley, and not prohibited on its face."

As it turns out, Grassley and his wife did not attend the event. Grassley offered the following statement today, "This kind of thing fuels the deep concerns many people have about political targeting by the IRS and by officials at the highest levels. It's very troubling that a simple clerical mix-up could get a taxpayer immediately referred for an IRS exam without any due diligence from agency officials."

House Ways and Means Committee Chairman Dave Camp offered the following statement, "We have seen a lot of unbelievable things in this investigation, but the fact that Lois Lerner attempted to initiate an apparently baseless IRS examination against a sitting Republican United States Senator is shocking. At every turn, Lerner was using the IRS as a tool for political purposes in defiance of taxpayer rights."

Unanimous

June 26, 2014

The Supreme Court slammed the President today in a **unanimous** decision that limits the Presidents power to fill high-level vacancies with temporary appointments. The President had made a unilateral move in 2012 when he made appointments to the NLRB (National Labor Relations Board) while the Senate was in pro-forma session. President Obama took advantage of a 3-day break to make the appointments but he intentionally overlooked the fact that the Senate decides when they are in session, not the President, and in this case the Senate was technically still in session when the President made the NLRB appointments.

Justice Stephen Breyer said in his majority opinion that a congressional break must last at least 10 days to be considered a recess under the Constitution. "Three days is too short a time to bring a recess within the scope of the Clause. Thus, we conclude that the President lacked the power to make the recess appointments here at issue," Breyer wrote. At the same time, the court upheld the general authority of the President to make recess appointments.

The Obama appointees must now be replaced or re-appointed by the President with Congressional approval. The new Senate rule that only requires a simple majority for appointment confirmations should make it relatively easy for the President to make the replacement appointments that he desires but all NLRB decisions made since 2012 by the unconstitutional appointees will be rendered null and void so the new appointees must reconsider everything done for the last 18 months at great expense to taxpayers.

This is the 12th time in the last 18 months that the President has been shut down by the Supreme Court in unanimous 9 – 0 decisions which have overturned executive overreach on his part. This President believes that if he must trample on the Constitution to advance his liberal agenda then so be it because he thinks it's in the best interest of the Country. His dictatorial outlook ignores the fact that the United States government is made up of 3 distinct branches so that checks and balances exist to prevent the kind of dictatorial power grabs that this President is so fond of. This President sees the Constitution as nothing more than an inconvenience.

Chapter 19

Mexican Stand Off

July 8, 2014

As Central American women, children and teenagers continue to stream across the border at the rate of about 1000 daily, the White House has decided it's time to throw some money at the problem. A lot of money! The President is asking Congress to appropriate $3.7 billion to fund processing costs for the huge influx of illegal aliens who have invaded our southern border. The President is referring to his request as "emergency funding" to pay for the large number of immigration attorneys and judges needed to start moving cases. The White House is exploiting the 2008 child trafficking law that requires due process for any child from Central America who manages to cross our border and enter the country. The law was passed to protect Central American children from sex trafficking and requires a deportation hearing before any of these Central American children can be deported. The President issued an executive order in June of 2012 known as the Dream Act that more specifically detailed the necessity of a deportation hearing for any OTM child (other than Mexican) who make it into the United States. This was obviously a calculated action designed to close any loopholes in the 2008 law that could have allowed for quick deportations under appropriate circumstances. The President could rescind his June 2012 executive order and modify the 2008 child trafficking law by executive fiat to allow for rapid deportations based on emergency circumstances but that would undermine his true motivation to keep the children here. Approximately half of the children are 15 to 17 years old but are technically classified as children since they're under 18. Many of these teenagers were gang members in Guatemala, El Salvador and Honduras which presents a serious security threat for the communities they will eventually reside in.

Senator Diane Feinstein (D-CA) issued a statement confirming the 2008 law allows for executive action under emergency circumstances to deport these illegal immigrants without a hearing but the White House has offered no such remedy nor is the President willing to send National Guard troops to the border as a deterrent to illegal border crossings. The National Guard could guard the border while border agents apprehend and process illegals. The Presidents unwillingness to change the 2008 law by executive order and to send the National Guard to the border confirms his desire to allow as many of these illegal immigrants to stay here as possible. President Obama and other liberals clearly have designs on creating a large block of future Democrat voters. Defenders of the Presidents policy maintain this can't be the case because it would take about 15 years before this group could achieve legal status and become voters but they don't speak about the high probability of amnesty which would speed up the process big time. If plane loads of these children began arriving back in Central America it would send a clear message that they're wasting their money to pay coyotes ($5000. to $7000.) to transport their children through Mexico to the U.S. and the influx would come to a screeching halt.

July 9, 2014

The Presidents most recent Democrat fund raising trip was kicked off in Colorado yesterday and moved on to Dallas, Texas today. For some crazy reason the President thought the optics of shooting pool and drinking beer with Colorado's Governor yesterday was a good idea but it didn't appropriately set the stage for his subsequent visit to Texas today. Texas Governor Rick Perry had more serious business on his mind when he met with the President in Dallas today. Fund raising was the only thing on the President's agenda for his Texas trip but his hand was forced when Governor Perry pressed for a joint trip to the border to get an up close and personal view of the unfolding crisis. When the President declined on the border visit his advisors must have convinced him that the least he could do was to meet with Governor Perry in Dallas. The President held a press conference after his meeting with Governor Perry and offered what he called a simple solution to the problem. His two-fold simple solution consisted of Congressional approval for the $3.7 billion he had requested and that the House must pass the Senate immigration reform bill which we all now know to be amnesty for 11 million illegals who already reside here. He explained that he didn't need to personally visit the border because DHS Director Jeh Johnson had already made 6 separate trips to the border and was keeping him thoroughly apprised of the situation. He also said he wasn't interested in photo ops on the border which didn't play very well after all the photo ops in Colorado while he was having fun drinking beer and shooting pool. Governor Perry said he pushed the President to send the National Guard to the border immediately but his pleas were answered by the Presidents promise to give it some consideration which we all know to be nothing more than a brush off.

House Republicans have sent a clear and consistent message for over a year now that they will not act on any form of immigration reform until the border is secure. The current crisis has served as a stark reminder that the border is wide open and that the President has no intention to do anything to secure the border which is in violation of Article 4 Section 4 of the Constitution. What we have is a "**Mexican stand-off**" between the President and House Republicans and neither is remotely close to the beginnings of a compromise. The Presidents absolute refusal to secure the border is blocking any hope for progress on this crisis. His strategy is to hold out for the $3.7 billion which the White House now calls the "supplemental" as if the "humanitarian situation" (another diluted label) will just pass soon and everything will be fine. Once again, the Presidents monumental incompetence is wreaking havoc in the face of a humanitarian crisis that could be brought to a quick conclusion by immediately deporting these illegal immigrants who have no respect for U.S. law and never will. Americans do have compassion for these people and understand the terrible circumstances they are fleeing from but we are a nation of laws and cannot sacrifice our sovereignty by opening the door to every human being facing tyranny and poverty in their homeland. It would be Central America today followed by Africa and all the rest in short order. We welcome immigrants but they must follow the law and the process currently in place if they want to take advantage of our freedoms. We need to take care of our own first and many Americans are now speaking out to remind politicians that our limited resources must first be directed to helping existing American citizens before we take on the rest of the world's downtrodden.

36,000 illegal minors entered the United States last year and only 95 were ultimately deported. We're up to 60,000 illegal minors who have made it into the country this year and we're on track to reach a total of about 100,000 in 2014. Only 40 of these illegal minors have been deported this year! 230 of these illegal aliens were polled in El Paso, Texas recently and 219 out of the 230 polled, said they came because they heard they would receive a "permiso" or free pass to enter the United States. This perception is reinforced by the coyotes who are getting rich transporting these illegal minors through Mexico to the U.S. border.

The White House is orchestrating an operation that is shrouded in secrecy as they process the illegal aliens and transport them around the country to dump them on unwitting recipients when they least expect it. Unmarked planes land and off load the children at predetermined locations which they deem to be adequate. Local authorities receive no advance notification so they can't mount a defense or protest to the unsolicited arrivals. Citizens in Oracle, AZ caught wind of just such a dump on their community and immediately mounted a protest that discouraged the arrival of 120 illegal children. To avoid the bad press associated with such a protest, the children were presumably sent to a different location where they could catch citizens off guard. Nebraska Governor Dave Heineman said 200 illegal minors were dumped in his State with no warning. Iowa Governor Terry Branstad is speaking out and giving the federal government notice that he will do anything necessary to prevent illegal minors from being dumped in his State. Oklahoma Governor Mary Fallin has expressed her concern over 1200 of these illegal children who were brought to Fort Sill in Lawton, OK. and said that half of them have already been released to unidentified people in her State who are presumably illegal alien family members of these children.

July 29, 2014

The House passed a bill today to address the border crisis. The bill allows for $659 million for enhanced border security and calls for accelerated due process to deport illegals. Even though everyone knows the bill is dead on arrival in the Senate, House members didn't want to give Democrats any ammunition to bolster criticism for inaction and perceived justification for executive action by the President to unilaterally address immigration reform which he has threatened. The House bill passed at the last minute prior to the August recess for Congress. House Republicans feel they can now go home and face their constituents with the message that they did act.

Iron Dome

July 29, 2014

Hamas terrorists have once again launched an offensive against Israel by firing rockets from Gaza into Israel. This offensive which began on July 10th is the most aggressive attack by Hamas to date because they are firing longer range missiles supplied by Iran and are targeting Tel Aviv. Israel's **Iron Dome** missile defense system is catching 95% of the rockets being fired upon Israel but the 5% that land can do considerable damage and the resulting need for Israeli citizens to rush to bomb shelters on a frequent basis is maddening for them. Israel developed the Iron Dome missile defense system predominately with U.S. provided funds. The U.S. gives Israel about $3.2 billion annually in foreign aid. Israeli leaders are always careful to give the United States due credit for Iron Dome in statements to the media. Israel initially countered the attacks by Hamas with carefully targeted air strikes on Gaza but once Hamas terrorists were spotted in Israel as they emerged from tunnels they built from Gaza into Israel, the Israeli military mounted a ground attack on Gaza utilizing 58,000 Israeli soldiers to find the tunnels and destroy them along with taking out rockets and rocket launchers. Israeli soldiers found that Hamas was storing and launching rockets from civilian locations such as hospitals, schools and UN sites. In addition, Hamas is using civilians as human shields which is standard operating procedure for these terrorists. Prior to any air strike or ground attack, Israel distributes leaflets, sends e-mails and text messages to Palestinian civilians as a warning to evacuate any targeted site but Hamas terrorists have been directing civilians to the targeted sites and threaten to kill them if they attempt to flee. Hamas terrorists want to run up the body count which now stands at 1300 civilian deaths in Gaza. Israel has lost 43 soldiers and suffered 2 civilian deaths so far. Israeli Prime Minister Benjamin Netanyahu said, "Israel is using missile defense to protect civilians while Hamas is using civilians to protect their missiles." While Israel mourns the death of any civilian whether Palestinian or one of their own, Hamas celebrates the death count on both sides.

These attacks have been erupting about every 2 years but given the escalation by Hamas in this current attack, Israel has reached the conclusion that it's time to end the cycle by completely eradicating Hamas in Gaza along with their arsenal of rockets and rocket launchers. Israeli soldiers have found 35 tunnels built by Hamas which must also be destroyed because they provide access to Israeli neighborhoods for Hamas terrorists to kill or kidnap Israeli citizens. So far, they've destroyed 15 of the death tunnels so they must continue their mission to take out every tunnel. Israel just activated 16,000 of their military reserve force to complete the ground initiative in Gaza. Israel's determined effort to demilitarize Gaza and shut down the death tunnels has come under attack by anti-Semites throughout Europe and in the United States. Anti-Semitism has existed for thousands of years and will continue to exist until Christ returns. This is an unfortunate fact of life that is fueled by evil forces of darkness. True Christians understand this reality and will always support God's chosen people even though most Jews don't acknowledge Jesus as Messiah. Barak Obama is one of those anti-Semites and his position has been reflected throughout his time as President. After only weeks in office he began giving significant financial support to the Palestinian Authority which doesn't even qualify for U.S. foreign aid because they are not a sovereign country and they are a terrorist organization. The President has snubbed Israeli Prime Minister Benjamin Netanyahu at every turn even though he occasionally speaks favorably of Israel which is purely political.

During the current crisis in Israel the President has acknowledged Israel's right to defend itself but there is always a "but" in such statements which flips the focus to a critical stance against Israel. President Obama continually cautions Israel about the civilian death count in Gaza as if the placement of civilians as human shields in Gaza is Israel's fault. The President speaks with an expression of moral equivalence between Hamas terrorists and Israeli's which couldn't be further from reality. This position permeates throughout the Obama administration. Secretary of State John Kerry made an unsolicited trip to the Middle East under the guise of a peacemaker but when he met with officials from Qatar and Turkey to develop a cease fire proposal, the result was disastrous. To begin, John Kerry knows both Qatar and Turkey are major supporters of Hamas and that any recommendations on their part would be totally skewed in favor of Hamas which was in fact the result. The Kerry proposal gave Hamas everything they wanted. Kerry should understand that Israel must stay the course until they achieve total demilitarization of Hamas in Gaza and his proposal didn't even mention disarmament. Israeli columnist Ari Shavit who writes for Haaretz, Israel's leading liberal newspaper, was very critical of Kerry's proposal. He wrote, "U.S. Secretary of State John Kerry ruined everything. Very Senior officials in Jerusalem described the proposal that Kerry put on the table as a strategic terrorist attack." Both Kerry and State Department spokeswoman Jen Psaki began walking back Kerry's proposal when criticism became overwhelming saying that it was just a draft not intended for public consumption. Kerry finally said, "Any process to resolve the crisis in Gaza in a lasting and meaningful way must lead to the disarmament of Hamas and all terrorist groups." Kerry and the President make statements like this to sound as if they are truly supportive of Israel but their actions tell a completely different story. If they were serious about supporting our most important ally in the Middle East, they would stop attempting to negotiate a peace that will never exist due to the Islamist commitment to Jihad and the destruction of Israel. What they could do is immediately fund needed replenishment for the Iron Dome missile defense system and to stop giving money to the Palestinian Authority because those funds inevitably go towards building new tunnels and more rockets to fire at Israel.

July 30, 2014

The House passed a resolution to sue the President today for excessive overreach specifically for his executive action to delay the employer mandate for Obama Care by one year. There are several other executive actions that are also considered to be beyond the constitutional boundaries for Presidential executive orders but the House chose to narrow the lawsuit for the sake of clarity and focused on the employer mandate delay for Obama Care. Democrats were hoping for impeachment proceedings because they felt Democrats would win in the court of public opinion but cooler heads prevailed in the House and Republicans chose to go with the lawsuit as opposed to impeachment proceedings. The vote was 225 to 210 to move forward with the lawsuit.

August 1, 2014

Israel and Hamas agreed to a 72-hour cease fire brokered by Egypt yesterday that was set to begin this morning. Hamas broke the cease fire after only 3 hours when they killed 2 Israeli soldiers and apprehended another.

Genocide

August 7, 2014

The Nineveh plains Christians in Iraq who have lived in and around Mosul for over 2 thousand years have fled to Irbil seeking the protection of the Kurdish Peshmerga army/militia. There are over 100,000 Christians in northern Iraq who are being persecuted by the ISIS terrorists. Many have already been beheaded, raped, mutilated, stoned, and even crucified. All of them have been issued an ultimatum to either convert to Islam, pay the exorbitant Muslim Jizya tax, leave or die. Even though most of these Christians have now made their way to relative safety in Irbil, they are now refugees who have lost their homes, businesses and churches. Another large group of religious minorities mostly comprised of Yazidi's are stranded on Mt. Sinjar facing dehydration and starvation because they have no food or water left. There are about 40,000 Yazidi's on Mt. Sinjar whose ancestors have occupied the sacred mountain for hundreds of years. Yazidi's practice a unique religion based on Zoroastrianism but are still considered to be infidels by the Muslims because their religion doesn't recognize Islam. These days most live at the base of the mountain but had to flee their homes to higher ground once ISIS took control of the area. ISIS has also seized Iraq's largest dam that controls most power in northern Iraq and could be used to flood large areas around Mosul. If the Mosul dam is blown up millions of people could die. Baghdad is also dependent upon this dam for most of its water supply.

August 8, 2014

With the possibility of a huge **Genocide** looming, the President is finally acting. U.S. air strikes have commenced as 4 FA-18's, launched from the U.S.S. George H.W. Bush, dropped 500 lb. laser guided bombs which destroyed an ISIS mobile artillery truck near Mosul. U.S. humanitarian relief in the form of air drops of food and water are also under way as 1 C-17 and 2 C-130 cargo aircraft dropped 72 large bundles of food and water consisting of 5300 gallons of water and 8000 pre-packaged meals. The President addressed the nation after the air strikes and food drops had begun. He was very detailed and dramatic as he outlined the very limited and specifically targeted attack. He emphasized that there will be no U.S. boots on the ground even though we presently have 800 U.S. troops in and around Mosul and Irbil who must be wearing tennis shoes. The President is obviously very uncomfortable with any military involvement due to his earlier declaration of success in Iraq and his promise of complete withdrawal but under the circumstances he's been forced to act although his calculation is totally political and insufficient.

August 9, 2014

As ISIS is poised to make a move on Kurdistan, the President has stepped up air strikes in northern Iraq. Additional air drops of food and water for the Yazidi's on Mt. Sinjar are in process. President Obama addressed the nation today and said it's a situation that will take weeks to address. He continued to promise no boots on the ground but said air strikes will continue. He also emphasized the need for the Iraqi government to get its act together with a major push to unify Kurd's, Sunni's and Shiites. These groups have been split for centuries so the call to form a unified government in Iraq isn't just a tall order, it's mission impossible.

August 10, 2014

The White House issued a statement today detailing the need to protect the U.S. Consulate in Irbil and a reminder that the humanitarian crisis on Mt. Sinjar is still a major concern and will continue to be addressed. We've now dropped a total of 74,000 MRE's (meals ready to eat) and 15,000 gallons of water for the Yazidi's on Mt. Sinjar. Iraq's Prime Minister Malaki was finally a target of criticism by the White House. Even though we're seeing some action by the President in Iraq to address the dire situation there, he's still failed to develop a meaningful strategy for the region. We should have plans for a sustained air offensive in Iraq and Syria but the President is taking a fragmented approach with no long-term strategy in place. The President and his political base continue to hold strongly to the notion that Iraq must step up and defend themselves militarily but the President still hasn't acted to provide needed weaponry especially for the Kurds who are anxious to defend themselves but are ill equipped to do so. The Mosul dam and the Haditha dam further south of Mosul are still major areas of concern and ISIS is also presently conducting attacks in Kirkuk and Tikrit. ISIS is also attacking south of Baghdad for the first time.

August 11, 2014

The U.S. is finally beginning to supply weaponry to Kurds in the north and Shiites in Baghdad are finally calling for Malaki to step down to pave the way for a new Prime Minister. The U.S. supplied weaponry going to the Kurds consists of very old small arms which falls far short of the heavy weaponry needed to effectively defend themselves from ISIS terrorists who possess sophisticated heavy weaponry originally issued to the Iraqi military by the U.S. but was abandoned in northern Iraq when the Iraqi army fled from ISIS not long ago. President Obama addressed the nation today from Martha's Vineyard where he's begun his August vacation. He said Iraq's new President Fuad Masum has announced a new Prime Minister appointee as Haider al-Abadi. He once again spoke of Iraq's need to form a unified government but didn't mention Malaki who still hasn't agreed to step down. He said air strikes are still underway to protect Irbil because of the U.S. Consulate located there and the Americans who are still there. A joint mission is underway by the Kurdish Peshmerga on the ground and U.S. Naval aviation and Air Force from the air. The immediate focus is to clear the Sinjar area of ISIS forces to enable the rescue and resettlement of the Yazidi's.

U.S. air strikes have been extremely limited in scope. They've conducted only 2 small targeted strikes each day for the last 4 days. These air strikes are nothing more than defensive pin pricks. Hundreds of Yazidi's have already been killed by ISIS fighters and many women have been taken captive and used as sexual slaves.

August 12, 2014

Secretary of Defense Chuck Hagel made a statement today and acknowledged the threat posed by ISIS. He said additional military personnel will be sent to northern Iraq. Deputy National Security Advisor Ben Rhodes clarified Hagel's statement and said a limited number of military advisors will be sent in to assist on the ground in the north with the evacuation of Yazidi's from Mt. Sinjar. Rhodes acknowledged the challenge of getting the Yazidi's off the mountain and to a place of relative safety. He said the long-term strategy is to help Iraq establish a new government and to provide military equipment to the Kurdish Peshmerga and Iraqi military forces.

ISIS has changed their operation from a strategic military force operating out in the open to blending in with the civilian population for cover. This tactic is limiting the effectiveness of U.S. air strikes.

August 13, 2014

Iraqi Prime Minister Nouri al-Malaki has finally agreed to step down and he endorsed President Masum's appointee, Haider al-Abadi, as the new Prime Minister. Abadi is a Shiite, Masum is Kurdish and the Iraqi Parliaments Speaker, Mr. Jubouri, is a Sunni. All 3 emerged from Iraq's Parliament where they worked together over the last decade to pass legislation and defuse numerous crises. They face many difficult challenges but it appears this group may have the best chance to unify Iraq's government. President Masum has charged newly designated Prime Minister Abadi with forming a cabinet which will be critical to the effectiveness of the newly formed Iraqi government.

ISIS has grown to a force of over 10,000 fighters and they control an area in Syria and Iraq that is about the size of Belgium. They control key resources such as oil, weaponry and a lot of money. They are presently worth about $2 billion but their net worth is on the rise as they are bringing in about $3 million daily selling smuggled oil. They're selling about 80,000 barrels of oil a day on the black market at prices well below market value. ISIS has their eyes on oil fields in southern Iraq and even Saudi Arabia. They can't be allowed to gain control over increasing amounts of oil production in the region because they'll become too powerful. Thousands of new fighters are showing up in Iraq and Syria to join the jihad. Many ISIS fighters hold EU passports and about 100 have U.S. passports. The UN classifies ISIS as a level 3 threat which is their highest threat level. Over 1 million Iraqi's have been forced to flee their homes as ISIS terrorists continue to escalate their reign of terror.

August 17, 2014

U.S. air strikes around the Mosul dam continue with 14 air strikes today and 9 yesterday. They took out 10 armed vehicles, 7 Humvees, 2 armored personnel carriers and 1 checkpoint. U.S. military supplies are still flowing to Kurdish Peshmerga fighters and Iraqi security forces as they continue the fight on the ground to reclaim Mosul dam. There are still over 5000 Yazidi's trapped on Mt. Sinjar but the President is nevertheless claiming victory over the humanitarian crisis in northern Iraq. He did say there is more to be done but his premature victory lap was political and highly inappropriate given the ongoing **Genocide** of religious minorities in Iraq by ISIS.

August 20, 2014

The fight for Mosul dam has largely been won by Kurdish Peshmerga and Iraqi security forces on the ground. The ground forces have been quick to acknowledge the key role of U.S. air strikes for the success of the mission. 170 IED's were found attached to the dam so the threat by ISIS to blow it up was indeed very real.

American journalist James Foley who has been held captive in Syria since 2012 was executed yesterday by an ISIS terrorist. Foley was beheaded on camera and the video went out on You Tube and Twitter for the world to see. The President took time out of his vacation on Martha's Vineyard to address the nation on the brutal Foley murder. He said we must "contain" ISIS which falls far short of taking them out. He was back on the golf course ten minutes after addressing the nation and was photographed smiling and fist bumping with his golf buddies which was terribly insensitive toward the grieving Foley family. The Obama administration dug themselves a deeper hole when they leaked intel of a failed rescue mission to save James Foley from his captors. This stunning breach of security was totally unnecessary and purely political. As the President becomes increasingly disengaged, he's beginning to draw criticism from his own political base. Secretary of Defense Chuck Hagel and Joint Chiefs Chairman Martin Dempsey held a press conference from the Pentagon today and had much stronger words on ISIS for the American people. Dempsey confirmed the need to attack ISIS in Syria in addition to Iraq and Hagel said ISIS is very sophisticated and far beyond any terrorist group we've ever dealt with. He also said, "They marry ideology with a sophistication of strategic and tactical prowess." The President probably called Hagel after hearing his comments and told him to dial it back on the factual-intel.

The State Department is requesting more security personnel in Iraq. They're asking for 300 more troops to be sent to Baghdad which would take the total number of boots on the ground in Iraq to 1100. The U.S. "no name" operation in Iraq is growing out of sheer necessity. The Kurdish Peshmerga is still outgunned and in serious need of more U.S. supplied weaponry. The Kurds were supportive of our troops when they were in Iraq and are solid allies to this day but our Commander in Chief doesn't recognize how useful the Kurds could be to help bring stability to the region if the U.S. would only supply them with the heavy armament they need to fight ISIS.

Feckless

August 28, 2014

Webster's defines **feckless** as:

1. Ineffective; unable or unwilling to do anything useful.
2. Unlikely to be successful; lacking the thought or organization necessary to succeed.
3. Synonyms: incompetent, spineless, feeble, useless

I can't think of a better single word best suited to describe President Obama than **feckless** and based on its frequent usage by several Republican Senators, Congressmen and Pundits of late, it appears they agree. Our President has never lived up to this definition better than his performance today as he addressed the nation wearing an un-presidential tan suit that just added to the weirdness of today's televised appearance as he announced to the world that he has no strategy for dealing with ISIS in Syria. He said, "I don't want to put the cart before the horse; we don't have a strategy, yet." Any other nations President or Prime Minister with half a brain knows better than to tip your hand to the enemy that you have no idea what you're doing. He could just as well have addressed ISIS directly and said, bring it on because we're totally unprepared. It was an invitation that ISIS terrorists will surely act upon very soon. Islamist jihadists strike when they smell weakness and our President wreaks of it. He not only announced that he has no strategy to deal with ISIS in Syria but he went on to basically announce that his strategy to deal with Putin is to do nothing. He said Russia is hurting itself and that he will wait until after the NATO summit meeting scheduled for next week where he plans to confer with our allies about Russian aggression in eastern Ukraine. Procrastination is a natural inclination for our President. His complete inability to be decisive is crippling the nation. We've never been more vulnerable! President Obama is only interested in advancing his agenda on global warming and amnesty for illegal aliens. He's already threatened executive action on both which is surely forthcoming but he's been sidetracked by the rapid growth and aggressive advances by ISIS in Syria and Iraq. His narcissistic personality tells him that this wasn't supposed to happen to him because he was supposed to be the guy who led us out of Iraq and who would then go on to concentrate on his liberal domestic agenda. He sees those pesky terrorists as a major inconvenience that just won't go away. The November mid-term elections may also delay executive orders on his "green initiative" and amnesty for about 5 million illegal aliens who have been in the U.S. for over 10 years. Looks like it's time for the President to hit the links and the fund-raising circuit until after the November elections.

August 29, 2014

UK's Prime Minister David Cameron addressed the British people today and made the speech that Obama should have made yesterday. He announced that the UK's terrorism assessment center just increased their terrorism threat level from substantial to severe (the 2nd highest level) and he went on to make it abundantly clear that the threat is indeed a serious one that must be addressed. He said he will address the House of Commons on Monday and will recommend revoking passports of individuals who they've identified as a potential threat. ISIS just slaughtered 160 Syrian fighters they had captured and they just captured 40 U.N. peacekeeping members in the Golan Heights. They're like a machine that just doesn't stop or even slow down. Saudi King Abdullah just echoed Prime Minister Cameron's strong warnings on ISIS aggression which just heightens the embarrassment over President Obama's **feckless** foreign policy.

August 30, 2014

As the President is focused on what he won't do in Syria and Iraq, Tom Fitton, President of Judicial Watch has issued a warning that ISIS has expanded their relationship with the Mexican Drug Cartels based in Juarez, Mexico to establish a base of operations near the U.S. border that they can utilize to launch attacks such as car bombings and suicide bombings in the U.S. homeland. President Obama is in denial of the grave threat that ISIS poses to the United States homeland. We're learning more about the organizational structure of ISIS in that they've established a bureaucracy with a hierarchy of leaders consisting of high level commanders, regional leaders and deputies along with a public relations arm. They've developed a synergistic organization with solid bases of operation mainly in Syria and definite supply lines that run between Syria and their bases of operation in Iraq. They carefully document their attacks so they can track their progress and measure their success. The U.S. is continuing with air strikes in Iraq as they successfully targeted ISIS operations near Amirli, Iraq (pop. 15,000) today but these pinprick attacks fall far short of what's needed. President Obama's minimalistic approach is better than nothing but as ISIS is poised to attack major cities such as Aleppo, Syria and Baghdad, Iraq, not to mention the U.S. homeland, President Obama is staring at his naval.

Chapter 20

Reign of Terror

The 2nd beheading of an American journalist by ISIS took place today. American freelance journalist, Steven Sotloff, was beheaded by ISIS today and in the same fashion as the James Foley beheading, ISIS posted the video of the beheading on social media (You Tube, Twitter ...) and included a strong warning with the promise of future beheadings of more Americans. "Our knife will continue to strike the heads of your people, just as your missiles strike our people." The video bore the title, "2nd warning to America" and there's no question that they will keep their promise of future beheadings. President Obama must see this as just another inconvenient interruption to advancing his domestic agenda because on the heels of yesterday's Labor Day speech where his 3-pronged focus was, "join a union", "choose hope" and "raise the minimum wage", he was silent today after the Steven Sotloff beheading. The President should have taken to the airwaves today and pounded the podium with the promise that America will annihilate ISIS for their barbaric slaughter of American citizens and he should have made a formal declaration of war against ISIS but all we got was silence. We didn't even hear from top cabinet members such as Secretary of State John Kerry or Secretary of Defense Chuck Hagel but instead we get weak statements by White House staffers. The Presidents absolute refusal to use the terminology "Islamic terrorism" or "Islamic Jihad" is very telling. He likes to use "extremist" whatever that is. His defense of Islam is a tough pill to swallow given the barbaric acts of ISIS, Al Qaeda, Boko Haram, Hamas, Hezbollah, the Taliban, al Shabab and the Muslim Brotherhood. President Obama is either delusional or he harbors some perverted notion that America deserves these brutal attacks for our dominance over the years which I suppose is one in the same. He truly believes America doesn't have the moral right to interfere abroad so he maintains a passive approach to the extreme threat we all face. A former Pentagon official just confirmed that the President has been briefed on ISIS for over a year having received specific intelligence on their movements and growing infrastructure but he continues to cling to his official position that he's the guy who ended the war in Iraq and having done so it's a closed book. He's only allowed the occasional drone strike to take out a specific terrorist leader so he can maintain the appearance that he's doing something but he's also fully aware that a replacement leader is waiting in the wings to step in and continue their jihad and that it's like swatting a hornet's nest as it further motivates the terrorists to advance their **reign of terror**.

Manageable Problem

September 3, 2014

President Obama addressed the nation today during his first stop for the NATO summit in Tallinn, Estonia. The focus of the summit is to address Russian aggression in eastern Ukraine and to form a coalition of NATO countries to combat ISIS in Iraq and possibly Syria. President Obama began his address with some strong language regarding a response to ISIS but walked it back once he went off teleprompter. His conflicting remarks began with, "Our objective is clear; to degrade and destroy ISIL," then he went on to denounce their barbaric cruelty and said we will bring ISIL to justice but his next key statement made while off teleprompter was watered down. He went on to say we must "**shrink** ISIL's sphere of influence, military capabilities, effectiveness and financing to the point where it's a **manageable problem**." The key words in his 2nd statement, **shrink** and **manageable problem**, are quite conflicting in contrast to degrade and destroy. If this was his idea of digging out of the hole he dug when he said we don't have a strategy, he didn't succeed because he just dug a deeper hole with his conflicting statements. Many people frequently acknowledge the President as a brilliant orator but when off teleprompter his foot can wind up in his mouth in short order. He also said the ISIL threat began when they took Mosul but that was 5 months after they took Fallujah and long after they had established their command and control center in Raqqa, Syria.

President Obama is a cerebral President because everything takes place in his mind but rarely translates to effective action. **Manageable problem** is the talk of the community organizer that he is. When he opens with, "our objective is clear," that's your first clue that his stated objective will be anything but clear. President Obama is never "all in" regarding foreign policy, especially regarding winning or victory in war. He hates to use the word victory because he can't stand American dominance and he won't use the word war because he was supposed to be the guy who led us out of Iraq first and Afghanistan next. He will say he ended war but he won't allude to an aspiration of victory in war or a declaration of war. His language is very telling particularly when it comes to prefacing extremism with "Islamic," which he refuses to do. President Obama was raised as a Muslim by his step Father and refuses to clearly denounce the factions of Islam that take their command to "kill the infidel" literally. Is there a certain number of beheadings of Americans that is manageable? The Presidents political identity is so wrapped up in complete withdrawal from Iraq that he can't bring himself to command the necessary action needed to fight ISIS. The world has disappointed him and his frustration translates to confusion and a lack of direction on foreign policy. For example, he won't deal directly with the Kurds who could be key players on the ground in Iraq. He can't accept the fact that Iraq's fledgling government in Baghdad is still refusing to accept Kurdistan as an entity that should be allowed a certain amount of autonomy and have a strong say in issues that affect them independent of Baghdad. The Kurdish Peshmerga could be a valuable force on the ground in Iraq if they were armed with the same kind of heavy armament that ISIS is using against them but President Obama won't issue the command to supply them with heavy arms. If he does decide to supply heavy arms for the Kurds, he'll insist on working with Iraq's flailing government in Baghdad with the expectation that Prime Minister Haider al-Abadi will do the right thing and take care of the Kurds but there's no assurance he'll do that. If it weren't for the over 150 air strikes by the U.S. in Iraq aimed at ISIS targets in recent days, the Kurds would have been in very bad shape but if Kurds were properly equipped to advance a strong ground initiative combined with ongoing U.S air strikes we could effectively push the enemy back on their heels and take the upper hand in the fight. In addition, the U.S. and our NATO allies should be targeting ISIS funds and their financial transactions to dismantle their considerable financial holdings. Prime Minister David Cameron of the U.K. has begun revoking passports of U.K. passport holders who have traveled to Syria and joined ISIS but President Obama has failed to follow his lead and do the same thing with the over 100 American passport holders that are known to be fighting for ISIS in Syria and Iraq.

September 8, 2014

The President's September 5th address from the 2nd stop of the NATO summit in Wales contained more vague language that fell short of the kind of strong commitment that needs to be made if President Obama were to take a leadership role that would spur our NATO allies into serious action. He said we must dismantle ISIL and push them back. "Degrade and destroy" was modified to "degrade and ultimately destroy" which hints at a long drawn out initiative. Later in the speech he used "degrade and defeat" and he also spoke of "effective partners on the ground to help." "Dismantle", "push back", "ultimately destroy" and "defeat" is language that falls far short of a commitment to completely decimate or annihilate ISIS which would be necessary to put an end to the threat they pose. Just pushing ISIS back, defeating them or dismantling them doesn't put an end to them. We must take the head off the snake just as they took off the heads of 2 American journalists.

The President appears academic when he addresses the world regarding ISIS. He displays no passion and when he's seen on the golf course 10 minutes after speaking to the nation about the James Foley beheading on August 17, the optics are very weak. He even made a rare admission of fault when he said, "I should have anticipated the optics," and "The theatre of the Presidency doesn't come naturally to me." These strange admissions don't help and when he's silent for a day after the Steven Sotloff beheading, he's once again displayed weakness and an inability to lead. When he finally spoke to the Sotloff beheading, 48 hours after it occurred, he once again displayed no passion. Only weeks ago, the President was referring to ISIS as the "JV team" but on 9/7 when Chuck Todd pressed him on that comment during an interview on

"Meet the Press," he tried to spin it or more accurately Politico reported he lied and based on the Washington Post fact checker who gave him 4 Pinocchio's for his denial, his new assertion that he was really referring to terrorists in the region generally just doesn't pass the smell test. A new Washington Post/ABC poll reveals that 57% think he's a weak leader, 52% believe his Presidency is failed, 40% say he's too cautious on foreign policy and his overall approval was at 40%. Only 26% believe we're safer since 9/11/01 and 47% believe we are less safe since 9/11/01. The latest Gallup poll has his approval rating at only 38% and when he makes vague statements that fall short of an all-out commitment to take ISIS out he runs the risk of falling deeper into the abyss of inaction and falling poll numbers.

Prime Time

September 10, 2014

The Presidents practice of leading from behind has rarely been more apparent than what we've seen in recent days. He likes to react as opposed to lead so he generally waits until he has a firm grip on public opinion and then he shapes his response to fit public opinion instead of leading and shaping public opinion by making a strong case to the American people to lead them where we need to be collectively as a country. At critical times when the largely uninformed public may not have it right and doesn't understand what's best for the country the President must lead and make a case for the best course of action. The Presidents tendency to lead from behind was on display tonight when he made a **prime-time** address to share his limited vision on the challenge we face in Syria and Iraq to combat ISIS. Instead of presenting a clear strategy to destroy ISIS, the President was all over the board as he described a counterterrorism campaign in very general terms to push ISIS back. He even refuses to clearly define ISIS as an army of Islamic Jihadists. He said, "ISIL is not Islamic; no religion condones killing innocents and it certainly is not a state." He called them a terrorist organization and insisted, "The United States is meeting threats with strength and resolve." The Presidents refusal to acknowledge Islam as the driving force behind the Islamists motivation to wage jihad is very troubling. It speaks to his sympathetic position regarding Islam if not his complete yet subtle support for Islam.

The Presidents **prime time** address was filled with half measures designed to placate the American people and to respond to pressure from some of our NATO allies in the Middle East such as King Abdullah of Saudi Arabia who has been pressing the U.S. to arm the free Syrian army for 3 years now. President Obama reinforced his position that there will be no American boots on the ground and confidently spoke of a broad coalition of partners who will do the heavy lifting on the ground but the Presidents reluctant coalition of 9 countries who are yet to make a firm commitment to offering up ground forces to combat ISIS in Iraq and Syria is weak by comparison to the 38-country coalition and the 48-country coalition formed by Bush 41 and Bush 43 respectively. The CIA is now reporting that recent ISIS recruitments have increased their numbers from about 10,000 fighters to as many as 31,500 in Syria and Iraq and they're signing up about 500 additional new recruits daily. As ISIS continues to strengthen their ground force, the U.S. and our coalition partners must get serious about forming a strong ground force of our own. King Abdullah II of Jordon has offered ground forces but says he won't commit until he's asked to do so by the U.S. which hasn't happened yet. Turkey and Saudi Arabia could make a significant contribution to the ground force but they've been reluctant to commit. It's incomprehensible that the Free Syrian Army, Kurdish Peshmerga and Iraqi Security Forces will be able to handle the heavy lifting on the ground without help from other coalition countries. The Free Syrian Army is far from being ready to hit the ground running as 5000 of their force must undergo training in Saudi Arabia that could take months. The U.K. hasn't even committed to air strike participation much less boots on the ground.

The only specific measure outlined in the President's address was that the U.S. will begin air strikes over Syria but everything else was general and ill defined. He made strong statements like, "If you threaten America you will find no safe-haven," and went on to say we will go after their finances and their ideology but statements like that are so general that the President has left himself a back door to escape through as his notoriously weak follow through leaves us wondering what happened to his portrayal of strength and resolve. Just one year ago today he made his red line declaration over chemical weapons use by Assad in Syria but he failed to follow through on his hollow threat so why would we believe he'll follow through on his promise to degrade and destroy ISIS? He still doesn't have a clear strategy to deal with the daunting challenges presented in the Middle East. The main stream media is isolating his stronger statements and spinning with commentaries that make the President look strong so the politics of addressing public opinion with spin but with little effective follow through is in full swing. The President has been careful to remind the American people that this is an initiative that will take time so he can continue with half measures until he leaves office in just over 2 years. President Obama fails to consider that ISIS may have a much different timeline in mind which is most likely on a much faster track than he's counting on. It's very likely that the Presidents hand will be forced in the future by a serious domestic terrorist attack and he'll find himself in the undesirable position of having to take decisive action that he's very uncomfortable with. Decisive action is not in the Presidents foreign policy playbook. His administration is struggling to define the fight against ISIS as war which was apparent in Secretary of State John Kerry's statement that, "we're engaging in a very significant counterterrorism operation" and went on to clearly say that we are not at war with ISIS but White House Press Secretary Josh Earnest said we are at war with ISIS as did Pentagon spokesman, Rear Admiral John Kirby but the President continues to search for a different word than war to appease his left wing base.

The President claims to want Congressional "buy in" but has refrained from seeking clear Congressional authorization for the war against ISIS. If President Obama were to go to Congress to ask for authorization it would necessitate presenting a clear strategy with a definite timeline attached but that would require a clear and definite commitment to the war and would effectively close the President's back door to escape responsibility for his actions. The White House is relying on the use-of-force resolution approved by Congress in 2001 to act without Congressional authorization but opposition is mounting in Congress noting that the use-of-force resolution was directed specifically at Al Qaeda and that the President is embarking on a long-term commitment to wage war against ISIS in Syria and Iraq. Sooner or later the Presidents hand will be forced and Congressional authorization will need to be obtained for a war that the President himself has said will last at least 3 years but Congress may not press on their war powers prerogative until after the November mid-term elections so the President has some time to procrastinate which is standard operating procedure for him.

Headless

September 13, 2014

Islamic State terrorists carried out another high-profile beheading and produced a sophisticated video of this horrific act which has been seen around the world. David Haines, a British aid worker, was the victim and another British aid worker, Allan Henning, was introduced as the next captive who will soon be **headless**. Islamic Sharia law demands beheadings so they are following their religious law which is sacred to these Islamic radicals. U.K. Prime Minister David Cameron left a wedding he was attending and went right to work on his response while President Obama played golf. Prime Minister Cameron has engaged in an abundance of tough talk condemning ISIL but has only offered up surveillance aircraft to address the crisis so his actions don't line up with his rhetoric so far, although UK's Parliament is the stumbling block that's holding Cameron back. Secretary of State John Kerry has been traveling throughout the EU and the Middle East attempting to strengthen the coalition of countries banding together to take on ISIS in Iraq and Syria. The number of countries who've agreed to join the coalition is up to 26 but most have only committed to share in the cost of humanitarian efforts and none have committed the necessary ground troops.

After-hours sorting session

Former Deputy Assistant Secretary of State, Robert Maxwell, served at the State Department for 21 years and is highly respected among his colleagues. Maxwell was a leader in the State Department's Bureau of Near Eastern Affairs (NEA), which was charged with collecting e-mails and documents relevant to the Benghazi probe. Maxwell came forward today to report that

Hillary Clinton confidants were part of an operation to separate damaging documents before they were turned over to the Accountability Review Board investigating security lapses surrounding the 9/11/12 terrorist attack on the U.S. Diplomatic Mission in Benghazi, Libya. Maxwell claimed the after-hours session took place over a weekend in a basement operations-type center at State Department headquarters in Washington D.C. He said, "I was not invited to that after-hours endeavor, but I heard about it and decided to check it out on a Sunday afternoon." He said Cheryl Mills, Chief of Staff to Hillary Clinton, was present along with Deputy Chief of Staff, Jake Sullivan, and that both were directing the sorting process. The Select Committee charged with investigating the administrations failures surrounding the Benghazi terrorist attack which is headed up by Congressman Trey Gowdy (R-SC) will surely be taking a careful look at the **after-hours sorting session** at the State Department.

Pinprick

September 17, 2014

The President addressed the nation from U.S. Central Command headquarters at McDill AFB in Tampa, FL. today. After meeting with General Austin and other senior military commanders there he took to the podium where he strongly declared, "We will degrade and ultimately destroy ISIL through a sustained counter-terrorism campaign," and he went on to emphasize his commitment that there will be no combat mission for U.S. troops in Iraq. He said he will not commit our troops to another ground war in Iraq and we will lead a broad coalition of partner countries, continue air strikes and train Iraqi, Syrian and Kurdish forces to serve as the ground force in the region. He said Australia and Canada will provide trainers and the U.K. and Australia will conduct surveillance flights. He went on to remind us that 30 nations have provided humanitarian support so far and that training exercises will be conducted in Saudi Arabia to train 5000 members of the Free Syrian Army. It's estimated that it will take 1 year to effectively train Free Syrian Army members. The President announced that retired Marine Gen. John Allen will serve as special presidential envoy for the State Department to coordinate and lead the coalition of partner countries. Allen had been the top U.S. Commander in Afghanistan before his retirement.

The President basically described a plan to fail. He's been widely criticized for announcing to the enemy that we will not commit U.S. troops to fight on the ground. The coalition consists of a decent number of countries but their individual contributions are extremely weak and none will commit to providing ground troops. The air strikes so far have been crafted to take out buildings and military vehicles but very few ISIS fighters have been killed. These **pinprick** strikes aren't remotely getting the job done. President Obama is reacting to public opinion and doing as little as possible as he attempts to make it look like he's doing something that will make a difference. Few Americans are impressed with the President's actions so far and polls are showing that most Americans will support sending U.S. ground troops to assist in targeting for air strikes and to root out the enemy from urban areas where they blend in with civilians but the President isn't committed to destroying ISIS. Americans would be much more supportive of a powerful initiative designed to destroy ISIS as opposed to a slow-moving campaign designed to fail which is exactly what we've witnessed so far.

Khorasan

September 18, 2014

Congress passed a bill today to fund the government by a continuing resolution (CR) and the bill also approved additional funding needed to arm and train moderate Syrian rebels. The House passed the measure by a vote of 273 to 156 and the Senate passed the bill by a vote of 78 to 22. Congress now considers their work for the year to be finished as they likely will not reconvene until after the 1st of the year due to the mid-term congressional elections on Nov.4. It's amazing what can be accomplished when they want to leave town for 3 months.

September 19, 2014

France dove in head first today as they conducted their first and only air strike over Iraq. I hope they didn't hurt themselves over this underwhelming single air strike that ISIS probably didn't even notice. The Obama administration is boasting the formation of what has now grown to a 40-country coalition to fight ISIS but if the recent contribution by France is any indication of the kind of help we can expect to receive from our coalition partners, we should come to terms with the fact that we will, in large part, be going it alone. This shouldn't diminish the importance of having a multi-country coalition to fight ISIS because at the very least it strengthens our justification for being in this war. We need to get our own house in order though because we've seen growing frustration between the Pentagon and the White House over the President's reluctance to fully commit to a strategy that would be effective. The President is continually placing limitations to the loosely formed plan so the Pentagon is basically fighting with one hand tied behind their back because they're not receiving authorization for the necessary resources needed to fight ISIS effectively. We must eventually have special ops troops on the ground to take out ISIS leadership and to provide accurate targeting for air strikes but the President can't or won't accept the reality that ground troops are critical to accomplish the goal of degrading, defeating and destroying ISIS.

September 23, 2014

The U.S. and 5 of our Arab allies in the region began air strikes and missile attacks on ISIS and Khorasan targets in Syria at 9:00PM their time yesterday. At the cost of $1.5 million each, 47 tomahawk missiles were fired from the USS Philippine Sea and the USS Arleigh Burke and hit 22 targets of ISIS and Khorasan command and control facilities in Raqqa and Aleppo (14 ISIS targets in Raqqa and 8 Khorasan targets in Aleppo). Saudi Arabia, Bahrain, UAE, Jordan and Qatar are the Arab countries who took part in the air strikes. Ironically these are 5 Sunni countries who fired on the Sunni enemy. Turkey was noticeably absent from the countries who participated in the strikes.

The President addressed the nation in a brief statement that took under 5 minutes and offered no details of what to expect next. The U.S. did not coordinate with the Assad regime before or during the attacks and Assad was silent during and after the attack which for the most part was expected. The stealth F-22 Raptor was utilized for the first time during this attack and is said to have performed beautifully. This was the first we've heard about the **Khorasan** group. As it turns out, **Khorasan** is a group of seasoned Al Qaeda veterans. **Khorasan** is a term for an area including parts of Pakistan and Afghanistan where Al Qaeda's main council is believed to be hiding. The leader of the Khorasan group, Muhsin al-Fadhli, was a close confidant of Osama bin Laden who was thought to have been killed in the attack but no real proof or confirmation of that was offered. The main objective of the Khorasan group is to carry out attacks on the west and they've established a safe-haven in Syria. The White House claims the Khorasan group has been plotting to attack the U.S. homeland and that this attack was imminent as it was anticipated to occur within weeks. Ibrahim al-Asiri is a non-metallic bomb maker who has been working with the Khorasan group and presents a particularly serious threat to the U.S. homeland. The air strikes over Syria were performed at night when the command and control targets were empty. It's clear that the President doesn't want to kill any terrorists but thinks knocking out windows and taking out empty buildings is good enough. We're told by the White House that more strikes are forthcoming and that we're just seeing the beginnings of a sustained air campaign over the region.

September 24, 2014

The President addressed the nation and the rest of the world as he spoke before the U.N. General Assembly today on the rise of ISIS in Iraq and Syria, Russian aggression in Ukraine, global warming and he couldn't resist taking time to slam Israel. He called ISIS a cancer of violent extremism. President Obama refuses to call it Islamic extremism as he went on to say, "The United States will never be at war with Islam," and "Muslims are part of the fabric of our country." He said terrorists have perverted one of the world's great religions as he continued to defend Islam. As he attempted to rally his international audience he said, "Collectively, we must take concrete steps to fight extremist ideology," and that "ISIL must be degraded and ultimately destroyed." He said, "It's time for the world, especially in Muslim communities, to reject the ideology of the terrorists." When he said, the U.S. believes "right makes might," not the reverse, it wasn't surprising coming from him but at a time when "might" is the only thing Muslim terrorist's respect, it's time to flex our muscles to turn the tide of this war and eventually take them out to a man.

President Obama said, "We must think globally and act cooperatively" as he went on to refer to global warming as the greatest threat to the world. He slammed Israel when he said, "Israeli's have abandoned the hard work of peace" and "Innocent Palestinian's have been bombed" as he insisted that there must be 2 States in Israel. It was an unrealistic and ideological speech based on abstract and ethereal notions. He rarely touched on reality as he stressed multilateralism as the solution. This President believes in the U.N. and international cooperation but opposes American strength. President Obama's idealism clashes with reality as he attempts to force abstract progressive thinking on the rest of us. He didn't address the ISIS threat until he was 18 minutes into a 38-minute speech as his perverted priorities were on display for the world. When he said, "No external power can change the hearts and minds of these terrorists," he basically contradicted everything else he said because he was vaguely predicting failure.

As the President was laying out his idealistic perception of the world at the U.N., the 4th ISIS beheading took place as French travel guide, Ervay Gordell, was killed in retaliation for French air strikes on ISIS targets in Iraq. The timing of ISIS beheadings has been very inconvenient for the President whether it be a golf game on Martha's Vineyard or an ideological speech at the U.N., these beheadings have come at times that don't coincide well with the Presidents rhetoric of the day. As Ervay Gordell's head was still rolling on the ground the President was praising Islamic scholar Shaykh Abdullah bin Bayyah in his speech at the United Nations. Bayyah served as Vice-President of the International Union of Muslim Scholars until 2014 while Yusuf al-Qaradawi was President of this organization. These Islamic scholars serve as apologists for Islam speaking out on the peaceful attributes of Muslims but they are wolves in sheep's clothing who belong to the Muslim Brotherhood and have been accused of extremism for denouncing Jews for their "corruption" and describing Adolf Hitler as having put Jews in their place.

The President's speech progressed downhill as he launched into a list of America's flaws that was reminiscent of his apology tour during his first term. He couldn't resist bringing up the justified fatal shooting of Michael Brown by a police officer in Ferguson, MO. as he attempted to make the point that we have racial tensions of our own in America. He said, "A young man was killed and a community divided," as he was attempting to gin up his political base to get them to the polls in November but his comments were divisive and fell flat.

Nation of Cowards

September 25, 2014

Attorney General Eric Holder resigned today after serving 6 years. His reign as the nation's top cop was the 4th longest in U.S. history. Holder has been extremely divisive and always put politics ahead of the law. He was a huge gay rights advocate. His time as Attorney General is littered with corrupt and controversial actions that include the "Fast and Furious" cover up, Benghazi cover up, I.R.S. targeting of conservatives cover up, and the 2012 "Contempt of Congress" charge. Holder is a racist who often spoke of "racial animus" in the country and his Feb. 2009 **"Nation of Cowards"** comment on racism in America was a low point of his career. He actually traveled to Ferguson, MO. to fan the flames of hostility toward Police officers there after a young black man, Michael Brown, was shot and killed by a white Ferguson, MO. police officer after Brown who was 6'4" 240 lbs. made an unsuccessful attempt to grab the officer's gun while still in his squad car and then once the officer got out of his car, Brown charged him so the officer had to shoot his extremely large attacker. Several witnesses on the scene confirmed the officers account of the incident. The irony of a U.S. Attorney General speaking out against law enforcement is inescapable. Holder also signed off on NSA spying on Fox News journalist James Rosen and his family. Al Sharpton is Holder's closest confidant and Sharpton is now consulting with the White House on Holder's replacement.

Workplace Violence

The first domestic beheading of an American by a Muslim terrorist occurred today in Moore, Oklahoma. Alton Nolen, 30, was the Muslim who beheaded Colleen Hufford, 54, who worked as a receptionist at Vaughn Foods in Moore, Oklahoma. Nolen was radicalized while in prison and was yelling "Allah Akbar" while he stabbed and then beheaded Colleen Hufford and then stabbed Traci Johnson, 43, but was shot by Mark Vaughn (COO of Vaughn Foods) before he could behead Johnson. The shot sufficiently incapacitated Nolen until Police arrived and arrested him. Nolen wasn't seriously injured by the shooting so he will stand trial for the vicious murder and beheading of Colleen Hufford. Mark Vaughn is a reserve county deputy in addition to his responsibilities as COO of Vaughn Foods.

It should come as no surprise that the Obama administration has classified this horrific act of terror as **"workplace violence".** Heaven forbid we offend some Muslims by calling it what it is which was clearly Islamic Jihad and an act of Islamic terrorism. It really has more to do with the record because the Obama administration doesn't want a documented act of domestic Islamic terrorism recorded on their watch when in fact this is the 2nd act of domestic Islamic terrorism on their watch. Maj. Nidal Hassan, who murdered 13 people and injured many others during a shooting rampage at Ft. Hood while yelling "Allah hu Akbar", was the first to commit an act of domestic Islamic terrorism since Obama took office as President. These murders were also classified as workplace violence. Fox News recently reported that Hassan just penned a 6-page letter to Pope Francis which praised those who fight for almighty Allah. Does that sound like a man who merely committed workplace violence when he brutally murdered 13 people and injured several others while yelling "Allah hu Akbar"? The American people are smarter than that but the Obama administration has no problem conveying the message that we're all too stupid to recognize the truth. The Obama administration lost the trust of the American people a long time ago and this will be reflected on November 4th when Republicans take control of the Senate and maintain their majority in the House.

60 Minutes

September 28, 2014

In an interview on "**60 minutes**" tonight hosted by Steve Kroft, the President tried to downplay the air campaign in Iraq and Syria as a counterterrorism effort but when asked if he was saying this is not really a war he responded, "This is not America against ISIL. This is America leading the international community to assist a country with whom we have a security partnership with." When asked how ISIS acquired control of so much territory and if this came as a complete surprise to him, he responded, "Well I think, the head of our intelligence community, Jim Clapper, has acknowledged that I think they underestimated what had been taking place in Syria." Notice the wording where he says "they" instead of "we." Now that Clapper is already under the bus, Kroft asks if it's true that Clapper said we overestimated the ability and the will of our allies, the Iraqi Army, to fight. Obama answers, "That's true. That's absolutely true." As the President attempts to lay complete blame on James Clapper, we learn that the President only attended 42% of his intelligence briefings. The rest were given to him on paper to read but in such a case he can't ask questions of his intelligence officials and no one knows if the President even bothered to read the reports he received. If President Obama had bothered to take the time to attend his intelligence briefings he may have recognized the impending danger and could have acted earlier rather than later and his unfair use of James Clapper as a scapegoat wouldn't have been necessary.

The President went on to make the point that the situation in Iraq and Syria is not only a military problem, it's also a political problem. He said, "If we make the mistake of simply sending U.S. troops back in, we can maintain peace for a while. But unless there is a change in how, not just Iraq, but countries like Syria and some of the other countries in the region, think about what political accommodation means. Think about what tolerance means." When Kroft countered, and asked if he thought we can teach them that, the President responded and said it's a generational challenge that's not going to happen overnight. Once again, the Presidents ideology clashes with reality and he either can't process that or simply refuses to. If he thinks we can teach tolerance to Islamist countries, he's in for a very rude awakening.

Secret Service

September 30, 2014

Omar Gonzales, 42, who served in Iraq and suffers from PTSD, jumped the fence at the White House on 9/19 at 7:20PM and ran unimpeded to an unlocked door on the North Portico, made it all the way through a foyer, past a staircase leading, half a flight up, to the residence and finally made it deep into the east room before finally being wrestled to the ground by secret service agents at the doorway to the Green Room which is closer to the South Portico. Gonzales had a knife on him but could easily have been armed with something much more lethal. He had eight hundred rounds of ammunition in his car plus 2 hatchets and a machete. Fortunately, the Obama's weren't home at the time. This is an unprecedented incursion at the White House that never should have occurred. I could see the guy possibly making it over the fence and starting to run towards the front door but he should have been shot by secret service agents from the roof or caught by dogs that should have been released or even just tackled on the lawn by secret service agents before he ever made it near the front door and why was the front door unlocked and the alarm turned off? We later learned that the head usher at the White House ordered the front door alarm to be shut off because it was noisy and annoying when it was activated.

A few days after the White House incursion, it came out that on 9/16 when the President visited the CDC in Atlanta, secret service agents allowed an armed felon to ride on an elevator with the President. The armed felon was a security contractor at the CDC which is questionable to begin with but he was fired by officials at the CDC shortly after the incident. Secret Service director, Julia Pierson, appeared before the House Oversight Committee today and admitted that mistakes were made. While being questioned, she tried to downplay the Atlanta incident but basically failed in that endeavor. Pierson didn't perform well at the hearing and she resigned the next day. It's troubling that incompetence is so pervasive with this administration. It begins at the top with President Obama himself and abounds throughout the rest of his administration. Competence doesn't appear to be a priority with this President. The priority is politics!

Chapter 21

Illegal Subsidies

October 1, 2014

An Oklahoma federal judge ruled today that Obama Care subsidies are illegal because subsidies are contingent on each State having an Obama Care "Exchange" and 34 States never set up Obama Care Exchanges which are clearly called for in the law. **Illegal subsidies** could be the nail in the coffin of Obama Care! Insurance companies are predicting a 43% increase in premiums if subsidies are removed due to law suits and this new ruling by the federal court. Since subsidies are the life blood of Obama Care and the only thing that makes health insurance premiums remotely affordable, the death spiral will begin if they are removed. Walmart has already canceled employer provided health insurance for 30,000-part time employees and have raised premiums for all full-time workers so many Americans are already experiencing the negative results of Obama Care but this is just the tip of the iceberg.

Shock and Yawn

October 4, 2014

Obama's limited campaign in Iraq and Syria against ISIS is being referred to by U.S. military strategic planners as **"Shock and Yawn."** Marine General John Allen, who heads up the coalition of countries who've banded together to fight ISIS in Iraq and Syria, spoke from Baghdad yesterday and said we must stop using the word "destroy" and only use the word "degrade" when describing the mission against ISIS. Every day that goes by confirms the concerns of Obama critics who have accused him of doing the bare minimum in Iraq and Syria while attempting to show Americans that he's taking effective action when in fact he's just buying time to do as little as possible for the next 2 years until he can get out of office.

Former Secretary of Defense Leon Panetta has written a new book, "Worthy Fights," and is very critical of the President over numerous missteps he made while Panetta was Defense Secretary. Panetta confirms that President Obama could have obtained a Status of Forces agreement with Iraq that could have prevented the rise of ISIS and he also confirms the fact that the President insisted on a complete withdrawal for political reasons.

British aid worker Allan Henning was beheaded by ISIS yesterday making this the 5th high profile beheading by ISIS. After 5 high profile beheadings by ISIS, the media blew past this one as if it's just another common occurrence that happens every day. The sad fact is that these ISIS beheadings have become frequent and at this point no one will be surprised by the next one.

The last 3 have been British and French citizens so the next American may at least raise some eyebrows.

October 7, 2014

A large contingent of ISIS terrorists are focused on the town of Kobani, Syria near the Turkey/Syria border. Kobani is a town of about 60,000 Kurds so once again the Kurdish people are facing a very tough fight just as they have in northern Iraq and once again they are outgunned but have mounted a very tough defense. ISIS terrorists have penetrated the city limits and are blending in with civilians to evade U.S. air strikes which is a very effective and even expected strategy.

October 8, 2014

Operation "Inherent Resolve" or as U.S. military strategists call it, **"Shock and Yawn"** has so far been little more than a glorified light show of politically driven air strikes. As a Democrat President, you know you've hit rock bottom when Jimmy Carter begins speaking out criticizing your inaction on national security issues. Carter spoke up today and strongly criticized the President on his handling of the ISIS threat. Carter said President Obama should have acted much earlier in Iraq and Syria and that he basically allowed the rise of ISIS to develop and expand to become a serious threat to U.S. national security.

October 12, 2014

National Security Advisor, Susan Rice, appeared on "Meet the Press" and said that U.S. ground troops would offer no benefit in Iraq and Syria and she went on to confirm what we've heard repeatedly from the President that there will be no U.S. boots on the ground in Iraq or Syria. It's amazing that this administration even allows Susan Rice to appear on a Sunday morning talk shows given her track record in that setting. This statement wouldn't have been very controversial because it is what we've heard many times from the President but later in the day Chairman of the Joint Chiefs, Martin Dempsey, appeared on another Sunday talk show and said to achieve success against ISIS, ground troops will be necessary soon. There's no question as to who has more credibility in this contradiction. After only 600 coalition air strikes over Iraq and Syria against ISIS over 2 months, the huge Anbar Province in Iraq is on the verge of falling to ISIS so it's clear that we're not doing enough because ISIS continues to gain ground.

Ebola Mania

October 15, 2014

After over a week of increasing fear over the possible spread of Ebola in the United States, CDC Director, Dr. Tom Frieden, admitted today that the CDC hasn't been aggressive enough in managing Ebola and containing the virus. Now that we've seen the death of Thomas Eric Duncan on 10/8 who was a citizen of Liberia and entered the U.S. after lying on his questionnaire about exposure to the virus when traveling to the United States and set in motion a trace of his contacts in the U.S., Americans are questioning the handling of this crisis. The fact that 4500 people have died so far in West Africa with a death rate of 70% should be sufficient to begin taking extreme measures to protect Americans. The heightened screenings at JFK, Newark, Atlanta, O'Hare, and Dulles are considered a joke by concerned Americans most of whom favor a travel ban for people from Liberia, Guinea, and Sierra Leone in West Africa. Texas Health Presbyterian hospital in Dallas, Texas has been the scene of a series of missteps after 2 of their nurses who helped treat Thomas Eric Duncan contracted the virus. It became apparent that the CDC had lost confidence in this hospitals ability to treat Ebola patients when Nina Pham, the first nurse to contract the virus, was flown to the National Institutes of Health in Bethesda, Maryland and Amber Vinson, the second nurse who contracted the virus, was flown to Emery University Hospital in Atlanta. The fact that Thomas Eric Duncan was sent home with antibiotics from the emergency room of Texas Health Presbyterian after showing up there the first time while he had displayed definite symptoms of the virus, should be sufficient to conclude this hospital was ill prepared to deal with Ebola. He even told nurses in the emergency room that he had recently traveled to the U.S. from Liberia. 77 people who were in contact with Thomas Eric Duncan before he was admitted to the hospital are being monitored in Dallas.

The stock market had the worst day in 3 years today! The Dow dropped 460 points earlier in the day but rallied enough to close 173 points down. Airline and Hotel stocks took the biggest hits due to the fear the people will stop traveling because of Ebola fears.

CDC Director, Dr. Tom Frieden, appeared on "The Kelly File" tonight and proclaimed that he won't advocate a travel ban or even a 21-day quarantine to prevent people arriving from Liberia, Sierra Leone, and Guinea from spreading Ebola in the United States. To begin, Dr. Frieden does not set policy so this is coming directly from the White House. This is political correctness on steroids and it's dangerous for all Americans! This reckless arrogance from the White House isn't surprising but must be addressed by Congress. Congress isn't officially in session due to the upcoming mid-term elections but it's time for a special session to act to protect Americans because the President obviously wouldn't mind thinning out the population. I'm surprised he hasn't considered the fact that he could lose some illegal aliens who he sees as future Democrat voters. There must be a scheme to isolate infections to Republicans. I understand this sounds extreme but I don't put anything past this President. What reason could possibly exist for President Obama to be so reckless with the very real possibility of an Ebola outbreak in America?

Amber Vinson flew to Cleveland from Dallas on 10/10 to work on wedding arrangements and then flew back to Dallas from Cleveland on Frontier airlines on 10/13, 1 day before she began experiencing definite Ebola symptoms. Amber called the CDC before she boarded the flight from Cleveland to Dallas and they cleared her to fly. The CEO of Frontier Airlines made a televised appearance from the airplane Vinson flew in after it had been meticulously cleaned 4 times. He sat in the seat that Amber sat in to prove it would be safe to fly Frontier Airlines. The domino effects of this gaff by the CDC goes on and on.

October 16, 2014

A House Oversight and Investigations Committee hearing chaired by Tim Murphy (R-PA) was held today to question CDC Director Tom Frieden. When asked about waste disposal for Ebola patients in the U.S., Frieden said he wasn't sure. When asked about the CDC's green light for Amber Vinson to board the flight from Cleveland to Dallas he said her temperature was 99.5 and the CDC protocol calls for a threshold of 100.4 before someone should be prevented from flying commercially. The CDC is trusting Amber Vinson on her temperature so CDC protocols need to be reassessed. When asked about a travel ban for individuals traveling from Ebola stricken countries in W. Africa to the U.S., Frieden said the President feels a travel ban would create "increased avoidance" which is an awfully vague position.

October 17, 2014

The President named Ron Klain to be the U.S. Ebola Czar. If this President knew how to lead he wouldn't need a Czar but since he apparently does need one, the role of the Ebola Czar should be to keep the American people informed and to give them a feeling of security. Ron Klain should be at the bottom of the list of perspective Czar's which would fall somewhere on page 42 of the list. Ron Klain is a political hack with no medical training whatsoever. He served as Chief of Staff for Biden and served in a political role in the Clinton administration. Klain is a political intellectual with a law practice in D.C. He knows absolutely nothing about infectious disease. This role screams for a diplomat and Klain knows nothing of diplomacy. Time will tell just how effective this guy could possibly be.

October 21, 2014

Ron Klain has been on the job as Ebola Czar for 4 days now and we haven't heard a peep out of him. He's been totally missing in action. White House Press Secretary Josh Earnest said Ron

Klain starts tomorrow. Funny how the potential spread of Ebola in the U.S. didn't take 4 days off so why on earth would the so-called U.S. Ebola Czar take 4 days off? Fox News White House Correspondent Ed Henry asked Earnest why there was even any speculation over Klain's competence amid a flurry of such speculation over the last 4 days. Earnest, as he typically does, dodged the question which of course further heightens concern. Reagan's quote, "government is the problem," surfaced in even the main stream media recently which certainly confirms a high level of frustration with the government's response to the possible spread of Ebola in America.

October 24, 2014

Dr. Craig Spencer, who spent 1 month in Guinea treating Ebola patients with "Doctors without Borders," flew home from W. Africa to New York on 10/17. He had determined to self-monitor for Ebola symptoms by taking his temperature twice daily and staying alert for any other symptoms because the CDC hadn't established any other guidelines at that point. He later said he had begun to feel sluggish on Tuesday 10/21 but apparently didn't see that as a red flag so he went out on the town Wednesday night 10/22. He rode the A and L subway lines, went to a bowling alley in Williamsburg, Brooklyn, also went to a restaurant and rode home in an Uber cab. The next morning on Thursday 10/23 he reported having a 100.3 fever. He was rushed to Bellevue Hospital Center and placed in the isolation unit. The CDC later boasted about how efficiently the 1st responders had handled transporting Dr. Spencer from his apartment to the hospital but conveniently left out the fact that their loose guidelines had put an incredibly large number of New Yorkers at risk due to Dr. Spencer's movements the night before only 12 hours prior to displaying symptoms.

Our federal government has put all Americans in danger. Ebola warnings began back on 12/6/2013 in W. Africa. Every relevant country facing this danger has instituted a travel ban for people traveling from Guinea, Liberia and Sierra Leone except the United States. On 7/28/2014, State Department spokesperson Jen Psaki said, "We're monitoring and taking every precaution" yet Thomas Eric Duncan entered the U.S. by traveling to Brussels, Belgium first and then catching a flight to JFK and then on to DFW. He was diagnosed with Ebola on 9/28/2014 after a series of precautionary failures by Texas Health Presbyterian Hospital in Dallas, Texas. If this is representative of our government's efforts to "monitor and take every precaution," I'm not impressed.

October 26, 2014

The Governors of New York, New Jersey and Illinois have established mandatory quarantines for anyone arriving from Sierra Leone, Guinea, and Liberia. New York and Illinois are the bluest of blue States so it's interesting that Gov. Cuomo and Gov. Quinn have taken this action. The

White House quickly issued a warning to these Governors that mandatory quarantines will have "unintended consequences." It's not surprising that we're not seeing any leadership from the White House but threatening Governors who have the good sense to lead and make tough decisions is outrageous. These Governors are doing their job to protect the citizens of their respective States unlike the White House who not only doesn't care but is intent upon bringing harm to the American people in the name of political correctness. Many political pundits are accusing President Obama of an attempt to thin out the herd (population) in America. I don't think I'm ready to go there yet so I'll reserve judgment on that score for a later date but if any proof of this accusation surfaces, it's easily the most heinous act by a U.S. President in history. The White House Ebola Czar, Ron Klain, has become a national joke! Saturday Night Live has even jumped on the band wagon with a skit that slams Obama and Ron Klain over their handling of the Ebola crisis and they went after the President over numerous additional issues.

October 28, 2014

Fox News correspondent, Adam Housley, has uncovered State Department documents that were cleared by the highest levels of the State Department and reveal a plan to bring foreign nationals to the United States for Ebola treatment. The cost to do this would be staggering and the dangers associated with such an action aren't worth the risk. It's against the law to grant a VISA to a person with an infectious disease but the President does have broad authority to authorize VISA's for non-citizen's so if Obama decides to move forward with this controversial action he'll most likely experience an even bigger drop in his approval rating in the polls to the lowest level in history. **Ebola mania** is in full swing and the President should be calming nerves as opposed to heightening fears but when he thinks he's right he'll forge ahead and stay the course of his destructive agenda. Once control of the Senate is decided he'll move forward with the most destructive part of his agenda and won't be at all concerned with the consequences. A recent Washington Post/ABC poll reflects that 68% of Americans believe the country is on the wrong track and a recent poll of registered voters revealed that 83% of Americans are either extremely or very concerned about the future of our country, so a significant majority of the American people aren't very happy with our federal government, Democrat or Republican.

Chapter 22

De'tente

November 1, 2014

Deputy National Security Advisor, Ben Rhodes, made a statement today saying a deal with Iran on their nuclear program will be the most significant effort by the White House in President Obama's second term. He went as far as to say that they're working on strategies to do an end run around Congress on the deal. Rhodes said, "This is healthcare for us, just to put it in context." If the White House makes a bad deal with Iran without including Congress in the process, it could go down in history as the most destructive illegal Executive action ever issued. If Iran becomes a nuclear power based on a deal with the United States, it would launch a nuclear arms race in the Middle East. Turkey and Saudi Arabia would most likely be the first to respond with their own nuclear programs. Israel and Pakistan already have nuclear weapons. The Middle East could literally go up in smoke and put the whole world into a downhill slide that could lead to the end of mankind on earth. **De'tente** can be a good thing with a country that can be trusted but clearly Iran is not a nation that can be trusted. If anything, Iran can be trusted to use nuclear weapons once they become a nuclear power.

Election Day

November 4, 2014

With the majority in the Senate hanging in the balance, the mid-term Congressional and Gubernatorial elections today represent a hard-fought battle between Democrats and Republicans in many States with much at stake. The battle was particularly serious in swing States like North Carolina, Arkansas, Louisiana, Alaska, Kentucky, Colorado, West Virginia, Kansas, South Dakota, Georgia, and Iowa. Records were set for money spent on these campaigns such as over $100 million spent on the Senate race in North Carolina between incumbent Democrat Kay Hagan and Republican challenger Thom Tillis. The results were great for Republicans. As a matter of fact, it's been called a Republican wave victory with Republicans picking up 8 seats in the Senate giving them a 53-seat total for the majority. Louisiana is still in the hunt with a run-off election set for December 7, so since Republicans appear to have the edge there, they should wind up picking up a total of 9 seats for a 54-seat majority. Republican Governors made out very well too in hard fought races with big wins in Wisconsin, Michigan, Massachusetts, Florida, Illinois and Georgia. The Republican landslide continued when they picked up seats in the House increasing their majority there to 242 Republican seats compared to 174 Democrat seats. The exit polls revealed voter's true feelings when asked what issues they see as most pressing. The economy came in at 45%, Health Care at 25%, Immigration reform at 14% and Foreign Policy at 13%.

A Republican majority in both chambers of Congress will make life difficult for the President but he is expected to plow ahead with numerous illegal Executive actions designed to sidestep Congress. He's already eluded to controversial actions on immigration reform and climate control. The Senate under Harry Reid's leadership was not a deliberative body based on Reid's stonewalling tactics that led to gridlock, but under presumptive majority leader Mitch McConnell, the Senate will in fact return to a respected deliberative body.

November 5, 2014

The President addressed the nation today to speak about the results of the election. He advised the nation that he will meet with Republican and Democrat leaders at the White House in 2 days to discuss their agendas for the next 2 years. He went on to outline his own personal agenda which consists of the following:

1. Do more on early childhood education
2. Work together with Congress to close tax loopholes
3. Request funding for Doctors and Troops to fight Ebola in West Africa
4. Congressional approval for dollars to fight ISIS in Iraq and Syria
5. Immigration reform
6. Climate change
7. Affordable College education

He went on to say the people want him to get some things done and to help Congress get some things done but the emphasis was on unilateral action which should come as no surprise. He reminded the American people that they have 5 weeks to pass a budget for the balance of the fiscal year. When he uses the word budget he really means another continuing resolution because he has a big-time aversion to budgets. He likes the fiscal cliff scenarios that occur each time a continuing resolution expires because upon each of these occasions it sets the stage for House Republicans to defund undesirable and illegal executive actions or portions of recent problematic legislation such as portions of Obama Care. We've seen that this kind of action by House Republicans can result in a government shut-down which should be blamed on Senate Democrats and the President who block action taken by the House but the main stream media insures that the blame will fall on House Republicans. The President loves these political fights because he knows the main stream media will protect him along with Senate Democrats.

When the President opened the floor to questions from the press he was immediately asked about the possibility of executive action on immigration. The President reminded the press that he's consistently said he'd rather see Congress act on a comprehensive immigration bill but that he feels obliged to act alone if Congress doesn't do anything. He went on to say that he will act alone by the end of the year if Congress doesn't. When he speaks about Congress passing legislation on comprehensive immigration reform he's referring to the bill passed by the Senate which the House didn't take up. It's not as if he would consider anything else because he's been highly critical of the House for not acting on it. The President said he held off for a year to give John Boehner time to pass bi-partisan legislation on immigration and went on to say I believe my executive action should be a spur to get something done legislatively.

When asked if he thought he could work with the new Republican majority in Congress he said I'll need to see if I can work with them on areas of agreement and went on to say there are lines I'm going to draw on health care. He said he won't sign a bill that would repeal or undermine the structure of the law. He said he'll look at their list of improvements but won't allow the individual mandate to be changed. He went on to say that he won't read anything into the election and that he'll do what he thinks is right. He also said he heard those who didn't vote which is a ludicrous statement but it's his way of manipulating the results of the election. He said, "I'm going to try some different things to get our message across." He said, "I have a unique responsibility to make this town work." I've learned that President Obama's statements require interpretation based on his deceptive ways. It requires comparing his actions to his rhetoric. This President has a history of going it alone. His narcissistic personality won't allow him to work with Congress so when he says he'll work with Congress in the future you can take it to the bank that he won't. When he uses terminology like, "wherever we can find common ground", the omission of the word compromise is very telling. The fact that 387 bills were passed in the House over the course of the last 2 years that never saw the light of day in the Senate reinforces my assertion that the President has no interest in working with Congress. Harry Reid doesn't operate in a vacuum. He acts at the behest of the President. When the President says, he won't read anything into the election it's a bit more literal because in this instance he's saying he will ignore the results of the election and the voice of the American people. He doesn't care what the American people think. He thinks we all need to be led around on a leash and must be told what's best for us. When he says, he'll try some different things to get his message across, that should raise red flags and is certainly cause for serious concern. "Different things" coming from this President can't be good. The bottom line is that this President will push his policies through whether the American people like it or not. There's an arrogant stubbornness in his demeanor and he's hell bent on moving forward with his destructive agenda.

Grubered

November 10, 2014

Revealing videos of MIT health economist, Jonathan Gruber, who was the key architect of Obama Care, were just found and released by Fox News. Mr. Gruber made a series of talks at major Universities speaking on the crafting of Obama Care with great candor and exposing some very eye opening revelations on the philosophy behind the construction of this law. Gruber's arrogance was in rare form as he espoused the importance of the "lack of transparency" by the Obama administration and "the stupidity of the American voter" that enabled the law to pass. He spoke about "the lack of economic understanding of the American voter." Gruber goes on to openly reveal that Obama Care is full of taxes. Gruber said, "We knew it was a tax. We crafted a bill with tortured language to confuse the American people and to get it passed." Gruber was also caught on tape admitting that States who don't set up exchanges will not receive the "tax credits" needed to pass along to the consumer in the form of subsidies. With the Supreme Court set to hear the case in March 2015 on subsidies in the States who didn't set up exchanges and expected to hand down a ruling in June 2015, the timing of Gruber's admission on tax credits for those States was not good for proponents of the law. Fox News found and released 6 videos of Gruber talking down to the American people. The main stream media completely ignored the story.

To add insult to injury, Gruber was paid millions for his role in crafting Obama Care. The National Institute of Health paid him $2 million, The Department of Justice paid him $1.7 million and the Federal government paid him $400 thousand. The States of Minnesota, Wisconsin, West Virginia and Vermont paid him $1.6 million so Gruber received a grand total of $5.7 million for his role as the chief architect of Obama Care. The President and Nancy Pelosi denied even knowing Jonathan Gruber but those lies were quickly shot down. The President called Gruber "some advisor who never worked on our staff." Technically he wasn't on the Presidents staff but Gruber himself spoke of several oval office meetings with the President. He signed into the White House 19 times in 2009 so he was clearly advising the White House on Obama Care. Nancy Pelosi denied knowing Gruber but Fox News aired clips of Pelosi speaking highly of Gruber from the floor of the House on 11/13/2009. Harry Reid was caught on tape touting Gruber as being the most brilliant health economist back on 12/1/2009.
The American people got **"Grubered"** as his arrogant insults stung them to the core. The Obama administration got **"Grubered"** too as they were left flailing in their weak attempts to deflect and deny. More importantly though, this revelation of truth about Obama Care was needed to provide greater understanding of the strategies behind this socialistic law that was

crammed down the throats of the American people exclusively by Democrats in Congress and by the President himself.

Executive Amnesty

November 20, 2014

The President took to the airwaves this evening in a prime-time address to announce his executive action on immigration or more accurately his **executive amnesty** to end deportations for 5 million illegal aliens. Cable news networks were the only media outlets who would broadcast the Presidents prime time address. Apparently, the major networks didn't want to disrupt their lucrative regular prime time programing. The President began his 15-minute speech with more bellyaching about those pesky House Republicans who wouldn't take up the Senate bill on comprehensive immigration reform so he set the stage from a defensive posture. He then plowed ahead with more defensive bluster saying, "I know the politics of this issue are tough," and "Congress shouldn't shut down government because of this," and went in for the kill with, "Are we a nation who rips families apart?" He then went on to outline details of the executive action he would take announcing that deportations would halt for 5 million, in his words, "undocumented workers." With the knowledge that many have called his action "amnesty" he said, "Amnesty is the immigration system we have today," implying that deportations for the large numbers of people who came here illegally is such a long drawn out process that most are basically here to stay anyway albeit in the shadows. He went on to further justify his illegal action by citing executive orders issued by Bush 41 and Reagan that halted deportations for relatively small numbers of illegal aliens who have children who were born here in America. He failed to mention the low numbers involved in these orders and more importantly the fact that these executive orders were issued working in concert with Congress as they were complimenting legislation passed by Congress and were designed to enhance implementation of Congressional legislation. President Obama's action is that of a lone maverick as it has nothing to do with any legislation passed by Congress.

The President is also justifying his action when he refers to it as "prosecutorial discretion" when in fact his action is an abuse of "prosecutorial discretion." The President has created a Constitutional crisis with his extreme overreach. His action represents a complete undermining of the law. It sets a dangerous precedent that if Congress takes too long to pass legislation the President favors then the President can change the law, dictate law and unilaterally issue law. It's a legitimate function of Congress to refrain from passing legislation because they are acting based on the will of the people by not passing legislation the people don't want. The Presidents illegal action for 5 million illegal aliens provides cover for the creation of an industry of fraudulent documents that will surely be created for the other 7 million illegal aliens who are here so very few of these people will ultimately be deported. This is all about the creation of Democrat voters. The President would have us believe he's acting out of compassion when his only real concern is for the advancement of the liberal agenda.

At one point in his speech the President invoked scripture with a very loose paraphrase of Exodus 22:21 but didn't bother to share with us that he was paraphrasing. He said, "We shall not oppress the stranger for we know the heart of the stranger; we were once strangers too." I looked at every bible translation I could find online of Exodus 22:21 and the Presidents paraphrase turned out to be very loose indeed. The actual passage in the NIV is, "Do not mistreat an alien or oppress him, for you were aliens in Egypt." When the President says, "we know the heart of the stranger," his loose paraphrase reads more into the passage than is there. I believe he should have taken greater care to accurately quote scripture but his speech writers were probably more concerned with inserting words that worked for their purpose. The Obama administration should place more emphasis on our sovereignty as opposed to defending illegal aliens who illegally entered our country with no respect for our laws. Closet Muslims like Barak Obama shouldn't invoke the word of God to advance a political agenda.

November 21, 2014

The President signed his executive action today in Las Vegas, Nevada. Interestingly, this action was not executed as an executive order but was issued as executive memoranda. Most people don't realize that the President has issued 195 executive orders and 198 executive memoranda during his 6 years in office. With a total of 393 executive actions at this point in his Presidency, he's way ahead of any of his predecessors so the cover of executive memoranda enables him to say he's only issued 195 executive orders and conveniently leave the number of executive memoranda out of the equation. The cost for President Obama's amnesty for 5 million illegal aliens will cost $40 billion a year for a total cost of $2 trillion. This number includes the social security benefits these people will receive and they won't even be paying any taxes to help defray this cost because they earn so little that they will receive the earned income tax credit which will give them a tax refund each year. Another costly consequence of this action will be the loss of jobs for American citizens. The 5 million illegal aliens who will receive amnesty won't be eligible for Obama Care therefore employers won't be responsible for providing health insurance for them and employers will avoid having to pay the $3000. annual penalty for not providing health insurance for this group of people. This considerable savings will be too great to resist so millions of American citizens will suffer because they will be the people who won't be hired.

Record High Debt

December 2, 2014

The National debt now exceeds $18 trillion and represents a 70% increase since President Obama took office. Taxpayers pay $9 billion a week in interest. This **record high debt** is an economic train wreck that negatively impacts the global economy and is unsustainable. The President has openly admitted that he's not concerned about it. He once said he doesn't care to reduce the debt just for the sake of reducing the debt, whatever that means. The only thing this President is concerned with is spending and growing the size of big government. Make no mistake, the U.S. government is wildly out of control and many establishment Republicans share in the blame because they too are addicted to spending.

Chapter 23

Je Suis Charlie

January 11, 2015

As the front row of 44 Heads of State inched their way forward followed by 1.5 million marchers, the glaring absence of President Obama was inexplicable. Today's anti-terror rally hosted by French President Francois Hollande in Paris was in response to the vicious murder of 12 journalists at the offices of French magazine "Charlie Hebdo" in Paris on Wed. 1/7 by 2 Islamic terrorists who entered the Charlie Hebdo office and began firing automatic weapons at targeted journalists while shouting Allah Akbar and wound up shooting at police on the street as they made their escape while identifying themselves as Al Qaeda Yemen aka AQAP. The attack was meant to avenge the prophet Muhammad for disparaging cartoon depictions of Muhammad in the satirical French magazine, "Charlie Hebdo." The perpetrators of this attack, brothers Said and Cherif Kouachi, were found and killed 2 days later after they had taken control of a print shop in an industrial area of Paris. Later the same day a dramatic hostage standoff and shootout at a kosher grocery in Paris occurred as Amedy Coulibaly held 19 people hostage until he was shot and killed but not until he had shot and killed a Paris policewoman and 4 Jewish hostages. The pair of dramatic raids that took place on Friday 1/9 and the attack on the Charlie Hebdo offices on Wed. 1/7 left 17 dead in the wake of these Islamic terrorist attacks.

The Obama administration initially said the attacks were senseless acts of violence but later changed that depiction to acts of terror but as in the past, this administration refuses to use the label, "Islamic terrorism" or "Islamic Jihad." The Presidents insistence that the war on terror is over and Al Qaeda is in decline poses a serious threat to U.S. national security. The Presidents "head in the sand" approach to Islamic terrorism is troubling and dangerous. He sees terrorist actions like the attacks in Paris as an inconvenience to his domestic agenda of free college tuition, amnesty for illegals, climate change regulations and complete implementation of Obama Care among other initiatives he has planned here at home. The Presidents only foreign policy concern is the dangerous prospect of a nuclear deal with Iran which could prove to be catastrophic if it comes to pass.

When he chose to pass on attending the anti-terror rally in Paris he made a huge mistake. If he had at least sent Vice-President Biden or even Secretary of State John Kerry, the criticism wouldn't have been so intense but not sending a single high ranking member of the U.S. government to Paris for the march was a big missed opportunity by the Obama administration. Attorney General Eric Holder was in Paris for meetings but didn't go anywhere near the rally. As the world witnessed French President Francois Hollande, German Chancellor Angela Merkel, U.K. Prime Minister David Cameron, Israeli Prime Minister Benjamin Netanyahu along with the King and Queen of Jordon as they marched arm in arm on the streets of Paris joined by 1.5 million marchers who displayed signs that read, **"Je Suis Charlie"** (I am Charlie), the glaring absence of President Obama was chilling. White House Press Secretary Josh Earnest attempted to deflect criticism by saying U.S. military actions in Iraq, Syria and Afghanistan is a stronger response than marching in a rally but that just opened the door to further criticism that U.S. air strikes in Syria and Iraq are so few and far between that we're doing nothing more than slowing the terrorists down to some ineffectual extent. The Paris attacks also opened the door for renewed criticism of President Obama's actions to close the detainment facility at Guantanamo Bay because 81 of the remaining 127 Guantanamo detainees are Yemeni terrorists who would surely rejoin the fight once released. With the recent rise of Al Qaeda Yemen spurred on by the Islamic State in Syria and Iraq, we're witnessing alarming attacks like those that just occurred in Paris. The last thing we need to do is fuel the fire of Jihad by releasing Yemeni terrorists from Guantanamo.

Defiant and Delusional

January 20, 2015

After the President addressed the nation on the State of the Union tonight it became clear that he's come out of the closet as he delivered an address that finally revealed his far left political stance on the issues. His extreme liberal views were on full display tonight presumably because he has no more elections to deal with so why not take the gloves off and tell it like it is or more accurately, as it is in his own mind. The **defiant** nature of his address was highlighted when he said he has no more campaigns to run and before he could continue with his planned remarks, Republicans in the audience began to applaud which was met with a strong retort as the President quickly reminded his detractors, "I know, cuz I won both of 'em." The President won that round and his defiant demeanor continued throughout his address. The **delusional** nature of his address began early and never let up as he stated, "The shadow of crisis has past, and the State of the Union is strong." The President's depiction of the economy which he described as being incredibly strong was so far removed from reality that viewers at home must have been wondering what country he was talking about. After touting an economy that he described as "good news" and saying that "middle class economics works," he went on to contradict those assertions when he dove into the overall theme of his address which centered on what he calls "income equality" which really means income redistribution but that would be too revealing. If the economy were really that great there would be no justification for liberals to sound the trumpet of income redistribution but they conveniently ignore such sound reasoning.

The President reminded us that "10 million uninsured Americans finally gained the benefit of health insurance" but failed to mention that Obama Care was passed based on 16.4% (Gallup results) of Americans lacking health insurance in 2010, the year Obama Care was signed into law. In the first half of 2011 the percentage of uninsured ticked up to 16.8% but by the end of 1st quarter 2014 the percentage only dropped to 15.9% but by 1st quarter 2015 Gallup reports 11.9% of Americans lacked health insurance reflecting a net gain of 4.5% of Americans who gained health insurance during the 5 years since Obama Care was signed into law. I'm not impressed. After a complete overhaul of Americas health care system by the government which represents 1/6th of America's economy, to only experience a net gain of 4.5% is pitiful. The President also failed to mention the fact that of the 10 million who gained insurance, which is a questionable number at best, 6 million receive government subsidies and most of the balance qualified to sign up for Medicaid which they don't pay for and is substandard coverage at best. Americans who earn $50 grand a year or more are the people who are paying for the government subsidies and Medicaid expansion because they are paying higher health insurance premiums and higher taxes. This policy of robbing Peter to pay Paul is called income redistribution which is at the heart of Obama Care.

At this point in his address the President launched into a series of liberal issues to play to his base because for him this speech is all about politics as opposed to the actual State of the Union. He spoke of affordable high quality child care, paid sick leave, paid maternity leave, equal pay for women, free college tuition, health care, raising the minimum wage, a free and open internet, and finally the need to strengthen unions. After talking about all this free stuff, it became apparent that the President was delivering a populist message that liberals live for. The far left liberal Senator Elizabeth Warren spent so much time on her feet engaged in applause that she was probably worn out by the end of the speech. I've never witnessed a more stone faced group of Republicans during a State of the Union and surprisingly they were joined by many centrist Democrats all of whom must have been wondering how the President plans to pay for all this free stuff. The answer to that question came next when the President presented his proposal to raise taxes on the rich and pass that revenue on to the middle class which he must believe to be the group earning under $20 grand a year because they are the only ones who will take advantage of all this free stuff as they take their hand-outs and settle into the Presidents socialistic vision of a nanny state.

The President spoke of loopholes of inequality in the tax code and said we must stop rewarding companies who invest their profits abroad. Conservatives would like to simplify the tax code but that isn't what the President is talking about and regarding companies moving their profits overseas, if America didn't have the highest corporate tax rate in the world American companies would keep their profits here at home. We shouldn't be punishing the job creators but the President thinks government can create jobs which is delusional. The President doesn't even bother to distinguish between full time and part time employment and he doesn't focus on wages. Obama Care has created huge growth in part time employment and overall wages are extremely low. The President spoke about 800,000 new jobs but failed to mention that most of them are low wage part time jobs and he claimed to want job creating industries in America but his actions reflect the opposite as his regulation nation continues to choke the life out of Americas free enterprise system.

The President spoke of the bankrupt ideology of violent extremism but does anyone even know what violent extremism is? By failing to specifically define the enemy the President is basically tying one arm behind the back of our military as he refuses to effectively address the serious threat of Islamic Jihad. America's military could take out the Islamic State in Syria and Iraq and now Afghanistan if we were to go in with the full force that we are capable of but the President refuses to effectively address the chaos in the Middle East. He spoke of a chance to prevent a nuclear Iran but vowed to veto any new legislation that imposes tougher sanctions on Iran. He then took a sharp left turn and said, "No challenge poses a greater threat to future generations than climate change." This statement is so delusional I'm not sure where to begin. His delusional thought process continued as he spoke of "values on human dignity" which was a jab at enhanced interrogation and then went on to warn against "offensive stereotypes of Muslims" which was a poke in the eye of Charlie Hebdo in Paris and reflective of his defense of Islam which he surely embraces based on his actions. He then plowed ahead as he promised to close the detention facility at Guantanamo Bay as he said, "I will not relent in my determination to shut it down."

The President continued to reveal his far left political stance as he spoke of women's rights, immigration reform, gay marriage and voting rights. He said, "Gay marriage has become a story of freedom" and said we must "come together to make voting easier for every American" and went on to emphasize what he calls the need to reform Americas criminal justice system so it reflects and serves all of us as he fanned the flames of racial prejudice. The President spoke of the need for an infrastructure plan but failed to offer any details like a plan to pay for it. Another revealing aspect of the President's address was what he didn't talk about. For the first time since 2002, Al Qaeda was not mentioned in the State of the Union and the President conveniently ignored foreign policy aside from briefly talking about Cuba policy and a nuclear deal with Iran both of which are extremely problematic.

While Democrats have worked overtime to paint Republicans as the party of "no" the President did a great job of painting himself as the President of "no" when he promised 4 veto's if Republicans pass legislation on the following:

1. Any legislation that makes any changes to the President's illegal executive action providing amnesty to 5 million illegal aliens.

2. Any legislation that makes any changes to Obama Care.
3. Any legislation that makes changes to the Dodd-Frank Wall Street reform and Consumer Protection Act.
4. Any legislation that places new sanctions on Iran.

He's already made 5 veto promises but failed to mention his promise to veto any legislation passed to green light completion of the Keystone XL pipeline. By focusing exclusively on his own personal agenda as opposed to a bipartisan agenda, the President effectively ignored the will of the American people who resoundingly rejected the President's policies when they gave control of Congress to Republicans last November. The President rapped things up when he said his only agenda is to do what's best for America and that he will seek to work with Republicans to make this country strong. This statement requires interpretation because he's really saying it's his way or the highway and Republicans can take a hike. The President began by saying, "Tonight we turn the page" hoping Americans would assume that the content of page 2 is good but as he went on to detail the frightening aspects of page 2 and beyond, he raised the hopes of the far left and dashed the hopes of the rest of us.

Freshman Senator Joni Ernst of Iowa delivered the Republican response. She opened by saying she wouldn't respond to the President's address but that she would speak about the Republican agenda instead. She spoke of stagnant wages and lost jobs along with failed policies like Obama Care. She astutely defined the Keystone XL pipeline as a bipartisan infrastructure project as she played to the Presidents infrastructure proposal. She said we must repeal and replace Obama Care and spoke of the Presidents stale proposals. She addressed Washington dysfunction but had little time to effectively go into many details which is typical for the response to a Presidential State of the Union address. Senator Ernst's main objective was to humanize Republican's and she did a good job with the time she had to work with. The response to a State of the Union address is a challenging platform due to the time constraints and the lack of a live audience which begs the question, why not change the format? I suppose that's a question for another day.

Tax and Spend Budget

February 2, 2015

The Presidents $4 trillion FY 2016 budget goes to Congress today. He calls it "Middle Class Economics" because I suppose he thinks that sounds good but couldn't be further from reality coming from the President who has done more harm to the middle class than any previous President in history. Middle class Americans are working 2 to 3-part time jobs to survive because Obama Care has slashed full time employment and wages for part time jobs leave a lot to be desired. The Presidents $4 trillion budget calls for a 7% annual budget increase and will leave us with a $474 billion projected budget deficit for FY 2016. His budget calls for $478 billion in public works projects and $320 billion in new taxes. It increases funding for the IRS by 18% when IRS funding should be cut but since the IRS is the enforcement arm of Obama Care, the President wants to feed the beast. This budget ends sequestration which is the indiscriminate across the board spending cuts of discretionary spending that went into effect on 3/1/2013. Most Republicans want to end sequestration too because all politicians are addicted to spending. The only harm caused by sequestration that anyone can point to are the extreme cuts to defense so why wouldn't Congress pass legislation to end the defense cuts associated with sequestration and leave the rest of the cuts in place because sequestration cuts are the only reason our government has managed to reduce the annual budget deficit which the President loves to take credit for but no one seems to remember that President Obama warned of dire consequences right before these cuts went into effect. Fortunately, the sky didn't fall as predicted. The only good thing in the President's budget is $561 billion for defense which is desperately needed. When President Obama presents a budget, its common knowledge in Washington that it won't go anywhere. This one, more so than any previous Obama budget, is dead on arrival in Congress which should come as no surprise to the President. The President's **tax and spend budget** for 2016 is nothing more than a political tool that he'll exploit to advance his liberal agenda.

Government Handouts for Illegal Aliens

February 4, 2015

We recently learned that the 5 million illegal aliens who were pardoned by the President through his recent illegal executive action will receive retroactive tax refunds for the last 3 years if they did in fact file a tax return for those years. As it turns out, the federal government has been issuing taxpayer ID numbers to illegals for years which enabled them to file a return. Now that these illegal aliens are receiving social security numbers, they become eligible for the "earned income tax credit" and the "additional child tax credit" so since their income is generally quite low, they will receive a refund from the IRS based on these tax credits and since the refunds are retroactive going back 3 years, this will cost law abiding American taxpayers billions! It's outrageous that 5 million illegal aliens are being paid by the federal government for the years they lived and worked here illegally. They expressed their disrespect for our laws by coming here illegally in the first place, so why wouldn't we expect them to continue breaking our laws in the future? Americans welcome immigration but we are a sovereign nation with laws that must be obeyed so immigrants who would like to move here and live here must follow the process that is currently in place. Immigrants must take their place in line and pay the necessary fees so that they reflect the kind of respect for our laws that must be displayed to live here. When immigrants **earn** the right to live here they will develop a greater appreciation for the privilege of living in the United States of America.

Burned Alive

ISIS terrorists in Syria just released a sophisticated 22-minute video that climaxed with the brutal murder of a Jordanian pilot who had been held captive by ISIS for a few months. Lt. Muath al-Kaseasbeh, who was a well-known and highly respected fighter pilot in Jordon, was shot down over Syria and taken captive by ISIS. The highly-produced video was released on 2/3/15 but we later learned that Lt. al-Kaseasbeh was murdered on 1/3/15. During the 1 month time frame between the actual murder and release of the video, ISIS terrorists attempted to use the already dead Jordanian pilot as a bargaining chip to set up a trade for a female ISIS suicide bomber held by Jordan after her bomb failed to explode but whose husband's bomb did explode during a very destructive attack in Jordon. When ISIS failed to provide proof of life for Jordan's fighter pilot, Jordon backed off negotiations that never should have begun in the first place.

The shocking video which ISIS effectively uses for recruitment ultimately showed Lt. al-Kaseasbeh wearing an orange jumpsuit and standing in a cage with bars all the way around and on top. The Jordanian pilot appeared to have been soaked in a liquid as he awaited his brutal demise. The scene that unfolded next was one of the most barbaric scenes anyone in the modern world could imagine. A masked ISIS terrorist was shown with a long torch that he used to light the fuse of flammable material that led into the cage where Lt. al-Kaseasbeh helplessly looked on. As the flames followed the fuse towards the cage, viewers of the video witnessed the horror of what would transpire next. The flames quickly entered the cage as the victim's pants caught fire first and worked their way up to completely engulf the Jordanian pilot in flames. Screams could be heard as he tried to shield his face to no avail and then dropped to his knees as he **burned alive**. This cruel new practice of burning infidels shocked Muslims around the world as well as everyone else. Apparently, beheadings can be condoned by Islam but burning the infidel is where most Muslims draw the line. I believe ISIS terrorists determined that beheadings had become too routine and had therefore lost a certain amount of shock value hence the escalation to burning the infidel. As we've seen, Muslims are viewed as infidels as well as the rest of us when they don't support or participate in Jihad and Sharia Law.

President Obama's response was predictably insufficient. President Obama said, "[The killing] will redouble the vigilance and determination on the part of a global coalition to make sure that they are degraded and ultimately defeated. It also just indicates the degree to which, whatever ideology they're operating off of, it's bankrupt." He went on to say, "It's just one more indication of the viciousness and barbarity of this organization." Organization??? The Boy

Scouts are an organization! ISIS is an army of Islamic terrorists who have successfully formed an Islamic State or Caliphate in an expanse of land throughout Syria and Iraq the size of the UK. They've established their own banking system, currency, military and other forms of infrastructure as they brutally enforce Sharia law in the land they now control. President Obama is a closet Muslim who will defend Islam at all costs. His convoluted statements on every attack by radical Islam can only be viewed as defense of Islam. He flatly refuses to use the label, "Islamic terrorism" or "Islamic Jihad" and not only for himself but he has had every reference to radical Islam removed from every official document of the U.S. government including FBI training manuals and many other official government materials. His entire Cabinet and staff are forbidden to use the only definitive label for this huge threat to our national security. Their tongue-tied attempts at spin as they avoid the only reasonable label for this serious threat would be funny if they weren't so very sad and weak.

Extreme Ignorance

February 5, 2015

In the aftermath of the brutal burning of Jordanian fighter pilot Lt. al-Kaseasbeh, King Abdullah of Jordan is calling for help from the entire world. King Abdullah is effectively taking on the leadership role in the fight against radical Islam that should have been established by President Obama. King Abdullah vowed that Jordan will fight ISIS with everything they've got until they run out of fuel and bullets while the confused, wandering and directionless non-strategy of the U.S. White House shouts to the world that America has resorted to isolationism out of the perverted notion that if we're nice to the terrorists, they will in turn be nice to us which is such a naïve and ignorant thought process that it's embarrassing for the American people.

The U.N. committee on Human Rights issued a recent report that should cause all of us to lose sleep. The report details horrendous acts committed by ISIS terrorists in the name of Sharia law such as taking 10 to 12-year old girls into captivity forcing them into marriage with ISIS savages who rape these poor defenseless girls repeatedly. They are burying young Christian boys alive! They are crucifying, beheading and stoning children and adults as they enforce their cruel and evil Sharia law. While these acts have shocked the rest of the world, President Obama calmly explains it away with rambling and incoherent dissertations such as his remarks today during the National Prayer breakfast in Washington. The President had the nerve to say, "Unless we get on our high horse and think this is unique to some other place, remember that during the Crusades and the Inquisition people committed terrible deeds in the name of Christ and our home country, slavery and Jim Crow all too often was justified in the name of Christ." Of all the places to make such inflammatory remarks, the National Prayer breakfast has to be the worst of choices. Our President compared modern day Islamist terrorism to medieval Catholicism of

900 years ago with such broad strokes that he managed to seriously offend the whole of Christianity. It was one of the most thoughtless and mean spirited remarks I've ever heard. It's reflective of this President's **extreme ignorance**.

An Inconvenient Truth

February 10, 2015

In a recent interview with Vox.com, the President characterized the vicious murder of 4 Jews in a kosher market located in a Jewish neighborhood of Paris on 1/9/15, as random shootings of folks. President Obama's refusal to admit that the Islamic terrorists were targeting Jews is indicative of his politically correct practice of avoiding the obvious so he can maintain a position of neutrality as he subtly defends Islam. In the interview the President said, "It is entirely appropriate for the American people to be deeply concerned when you've got a bunch of violent, vicious zealots who behead people or randomly shoot a bunch of folks in a deli in Paris." He went on to say, "It is right and legitimate for us to be vigilant and aggressive in trying to deal with that, the same way a big city mayor has got to cut the crime rate down if he wants that city to thrive." The Presidents need to downplay the war on terror by comparing it to big city crime and his refusal to admit that Islamic terrorists were strategically targeting Jews in a kosher deli located in a Jewish neighborhood of Paris confirms the fact that ideology drives everything President Obama says and does. Reality is **an inconvenient truth** for this President. The Presidents refusal to define the enemy and to define the target of their aggression is inhibiting our ability to successfully fight the war on terror.

State Department spokeswoman Jen Psaki struggled during a press conference as she searched for words to replace the obvious words she was surely instructed to avoid at all costs when asked why the Obama administration refused to clearly define the events of 1/9/15 at the kosher deli in Paris. White House Press Secretary Josh Earnest was pressed hard by Jonathan Carl of ABC and Ed Henry of Fox News on this issue and he had to perform some verbal gymnastics as he clearly struggled in his lame attempt to speak in general terms. This certainly isn't the first time we've witnessed this kind of deception by the Obama administration and it most assuredly won't be the last.

Genocide

February 16, 2015

The Iran backed Shiite Houthi have successfully overthrown Yemen's government and taken control of the capital city of Sana'a and much of the countries northern territory. They now have their eyes set on a key oil producing province to the east of the capital. Sunni tribes in

Marib province are preparing to defend their land and warn of a civil war if the Shiite Houthi attempt an offensive to take Marib. While Yemen unravels Durna, Libya has become the next ISIS stronghold as Islamic terrorists advance their Jihad and move to gain more territory which is a key objective of these savages. Libya's government is unstable and the region has become a hotbed of Islamic terrorism. The fact that the U.S. has closed our embassies in both Yemen and Libya speaks volumes to the instability that exists in these countries. It's no wonder that Islamic terrorists are having a field day in Syria, Iraq, Yemen and Libya as weak defensive efforts by the U.S. backed coalition flounder because the good guys don't even have a strategy in place to successfully defeat ISIS and the Obama administration can't or won't effectively define who the enemy is.

ISIS terrorists have seized this opportunity to gain more territory and expand their reign of terror as they taunt U.S. led coalition forces and others in the region with beheadings and burnings of infidels whether they be moderate Muslims, Christians, Jews or anyone else who doesn't believe as they do. ISIS just released another highly-produced video of one of the most heinous acts they've committed to date. The video which was shot on a beach in Libya bore the title, "Taking the fight to the land of the cross" and begins with 21 Egyptian Coptic Christians lined up in their orange jumpsuits on their knees with a black robed ISIS terrorist standing behind each one. As the background music plays each ISIS terrorist pulls a long sword from its sheath at their waist and the swords are held up and seen gleaming in the sun. Screams of the Christian's are highlighted in the video as these ISIS savages decapitate all 21 victims as the camera rolls. It's become apparent that these mass executions represent the beginning of **genocide** by Islamic terrorists who are determined to establish an international Islamic State. ISIS vows to conquer Rome in the video apparently because Rome is symbolic to Christianity and it could also represent a move to garner support from Libyan's, many of whom hate Italy. ISIS has also formed a partnership with Ansar al-Sharia, an Islamist militia group in Libya who advocate implementing strict Sharia law across Libya so their initiative to expand the Islamic State throughout Libya is well under way.

The genocidal nature of this mass execution of 21 Christians is unmistakable as there appears to be no end in sight to the brutal beheadings and burnings of innocent civilians by ISIS. History is repeating itself as the atrocities committed by Islamic terrorists today are virtually the same as the beginnings of genocide by the Nazi's who set out to exterminate the Jewish population. Islamic terrorists today are setting out to exterminate Jews and Christians first because Christianity and Judaism throughout the Middle East predates Islam. Christianity has existed for over 2000 years but Islam has only been around for about 1400 years. When the one true God, the God of the Bible, made his covenant with Abraham's son Isaac by Sarah as opposed to his son Ishmael by Hagar, the nation of Israel became God's chosen and Ishmael's descendants formed the Arab world (Genesis 17:15-22) but Islam wasn't formed by the prophet Muhammad until about 622 AD. ISIS is unique though because they are initially fixated on Shia and other sects of Islam in the Middle East who may not share the same kind of enthusiasm that ISIS terrorists have for Islamic Jihad. ISIS terrorists believe they must establish a Caliphate that strictly enforces Sharia law so Muslims who may hold moderate beliefs must be eliminated immediately but their desire to eliminate Christians and Jews is fierce and is very high on their list of priorities.

Egypt's President Abdel Fattah el-Sisi launched air strikes on ISIS targets in Libya in response to the beheadings of 21 Egyptian Coptic Christians who were working in Libya at the time of their capture and ultimate demise. The Pope immediately denounced the mass beheadings of Coptic Christians in Libya without watering down his statement with politically correct rhetoric unlike President Obama who could only refer to the 21 Coptic Christians as "Egyptian citizens" in his statement as he once again struggled to defend Islam.

Fantasy World

February 19, 2015

The 3 day "White House Summit to counter violent extremism" concluded today as the President addressed the nation to explain why community organizers from 60 countries converged on the White House to engage in rhetorical gymnastics which the Islamic terrorists surely find to be quite amusing. The Presidents defense of Islam has now advanced to entertaining the terrorists with his vision of community organizing in the Middle East. I'm sure the terrorists are laughing so hard they can barely hold their AK-47's steady.

The President believes people in the Middle East have several "legitimate grievances" that need to be addressed. He spoke of "economic grievances" and "political grievances" and went on to say, "Political, civic and religious leaders must lead the way in their communities," and that, "We must lift up voices of tolerance and peace." The President contends "the notion that the west is at war with Islam is an ugly lie" and went on to say, "I refuse the notion that groups like ISIL represent Islam." The President believes we must address the grievances that terrorists exploit and that we must break the cycle of sectarian violence so he gathers a bunch of community organizers at the White House to discuss human rights, moral equivalence and job creation throughout the Middle East.

Clearly the Presidents **fantasy world** of ideological rhetoric willfully disregards the true enemy which realistic people know to be Islamic Jihad. He's willing to lecture us on the Crusades of medieval times but won't acknowledge the current threat of Islamic Jihad. As time goes on it's become increasingly apparent that Barak Hussein Obama is in fact a Muslim and its common knowledge that his Senior Advisor, Valerie Jarret is a Muslim who was born in Shiraz, Iran.

Collectively these two are acting as Islamists inside the White House and the destruction they've inflicted upon America is devastating. Once they conclude the bad nuclear deal with Iran they will have put the final nail in the coffin of America's demise, not to mention that of Israel too.

This President wants Americans to believe that all we need to do is get young people a job and then they won't turn to terrorism. This simplistic approach is nothing more than misdirection to distract Americans from the truth of the formidable enemy that we do in fact face which is the rapidly advancing juggernaut of Islamic Jihad. This President needs to wrap his head around the fact that the true enemy will not allow all this community building in the first place and that we must clearly identify and completely eradicate the enemy first before any community building can take place but President Obama's Islamic faith has blinded him to the truth. Make no mistake, this President hates America and will continue to chip away at the foundations of our democracy and our freedoms as his Communist beliefs and Islamic beliefs wreak havoc within our government and the lives of patriotic Americans.

Chapter 24

Road to Disaster

Israeli Prime Minister Benjamin Netanyahu addressed a joint session of Congress today and goes down in history along with Winston Churchill as the only foreign Heads of State to address a joint session of the United States Congress a total of 3 times. This was a huge blow to President Obama's ego because Speaker Boehner invited Prime Minister Netanyahu to speak before a joint session of Congress without consulting anyone at the White House in advance. It only took a modicum of common sense for Speaker Boehner to know that President Obama would not approve of Prime Minister Netanyahu's message that a bad nuclear deal with Iran threatens Israel's very existence and represents a very serious national security threat to the United States. Speaker Boehner's astute intuition turned out to be as predicted. Our narcissistic President was indeed livid. Criticism from the White House came fast and furious as they warned of the dire consequences of, in their words, this breach of protocol. The fact is that the legislative branch is a co-equal branch of government along with the executive branch and the judicial branch so Congress doesn't need the Presidents blessing to extend an invitation to a foreign Head of State. If our government was functioning as designed by our founding fathers, Congress and the President wouldn't be at odds with one another but President Obama ignored that dynamic with his dictatorial style of governing.

The Prime Minister began by thanking members of Congress and the President for their years of support for Israel and said he was deeply humbled to address the most important legislative body in the world for the third time. He reminded his audience that the alliance between Israel and the United States has always been above politics and must always remain above politics. He said he felt a profound obligation to speak to Congress about Iran's quest for nuclear weapons as he highlighted the reason for his address. He spoke of a courageous Jewish woman, Queen Esther, who exposed the plot of Persian Viceroy Haman to destroy the Jewish people 2500 years ago and gave the Jewish people the right to defend themselves. Haman's plot was foiled and the Jewish people were saved. The Prime Minister went on to speak of another Persian potentate, Iran's Supreme Leader Ayatollah Khamenei, who now "spews the oldest hatred, the hatred of anti-Semitism with the newest technology. He tweets that Israel must be annihilated." He spoke of 6 million Jews murdered by the Nazi's and the 60 million people who died fighting World War II and compared that piece of history to the great threat posed by Iran today not only to Israel but to peace worldwide. He reminded us that Iran was taken over by religious zealots in 1979 who imposed a dark and brutal dictatorship on the Iranian people. He said, "America's founding document promises life, liberty and the pursuit of happiness. Iran's founding document pledges death, tyranny and the pursuit of Jihad. And as States are collapsing across the Middle East, Iran is marching into the void to do just that." He went on to detail the extent to which Iran has extended its tentacles throughout Arab countries in the Middle East. He said, "In the Middle East, Iran now dominates four Arab capitals, Baghdad, Damascus, Beirut and Sana'a. And if Iran's aggression is left unchecked, more will surely follow. So, at a time when many hope Iran will join the community of nations, Iran is busy gobbling up the nations."

The Prime Minister explained that, "Iran and ISIS are competing for the crown of militant Islam. One calls itself the Islamic Republic. The other calls itself Islamic State. Both want to impose a militant Islamic empire first on the region and then on the entire world. They just disagree among themselves who will be the leader of that empire. So, when it comes to Iran and ISIS, the enemy of your enemy is your enemy. The difference is that ISIS is armed with butcher knives, captured weapons and YouTube, whereas Iran could soon be armed with intercontinental ballistic missiles and nuclear bombs. We must always remember - - I'll say it one more time - - the greatest dangers facing our world is the marriage of militant Islam with nuclear weapons. To defeat ISIS and let Iran get nuclear weapons would be to win the battle, but lose the war. We can't let that happen." He went on to speak about two major concessions that we know would be a part of any deal with Iran. He said, "The first major concession would leave Iran with a vast nuclear infrastructure, providing it with a short break-out time to the bomb," and the second major concession is the 10-year sunset clause that lifts all restrictions on Iran's nuclear program after a decade. He spoke about the verification process for restrictions in the deal and the role of international inspectors who merely document violations but lack the ability to stop them. He spoke of the UN's nuclear watchdog agency, the IAEA (International Atomic Energy Agency), who caught Iran operating secret nuclear facilities on two occasions, facilities inspectors didn't even know existed. The Prime Minister said, "Iran has proven time and again that it cannot be trusted." He reminded his audience that Iran's Supreme Leader openly says "Iran plans to have 190,000 centrifuges, not 6000 or even the 19,000 Iran has today, but 10 times that - - 190,000 centrifuges enriching uranium." He said, "My longtime friend, John Kerry, Secretary of State, confirmed last week that Iran could legitimately possess that massive centrifuge capacity when the deal expires."

The Prime Minister summed up the two major concessions when he said, "So you see, my friends, this deal has two major concessions: one, leaving Iran with a vast nuclear program and two, lifting the restrictions on that program in about a decade. That's why this deal is so bad. It doesn't block Iran's path to the bomb; it paves Iran's path to the bomb." The Prime Minister made the case that lifting sanctions would provide plenty of cash for Iran to fund more terrorism. Iran is still at the top of the State Departments "State Sponsors of Terrorism" list which President Obama conveniently fails to mention when speaking of a deal. Prime Minister

Netanyahu asked the questions, "Would Iran fund less terrorism when it has mountains of cash with which to fund more terrorism?" and "Why should Iran's radical regime change for the better when it can enjoy the best of both worlds: aggression abroad, prosperity at home?" He outlined the nuclear arms race that would ensue throughout the Middle East if Iran becomes a weaponized nuclear power. He said, "A deal that's supposed to prevent nuclear proliferation would instead spark a nuclear arms race in the most dangerous part of the planet." He reminded us that the alternative to this bad deal isn't war as some would attempt to have us believe but that the alternative is a better deal. He said, "Iran's nuclear program can be rolled back well beyond the current proposal by insisting on a better deal and keeping up the pressure on a very vulnerable regime, especially given the recent collapse in the price of oil." He went on to emphasize our need for a better deal which could alleviate the need to go to war. He said, "Ladies and Gentlemen, history has placed us at a fateful crossroads. We must now choose between two paths. One path leads to a bad deal that will at best curtail Iran's nuclear ambitions for a while, but it will inexorably lead to a nuclear armed Iran whose unbridled aggression will inevitably lead to war. The second path, however difficult, could lead to a much better deal that would prevent a nuclear-armed Iran, a nuclearized Middle East and the horrific consequences of both to all of humanity."

He wrapped up by speaking of the firm resolve of the Jewish people to defend themselves. He said, "We are no longer scattered among the nations, powerless to defend ourselves. We restored our sovereignty in our ancient home. And the soldiers who defend our home have boundless courage. For the first time in 100 generations, we, the Jewish people, can defend ourselves. This is why - - this is why, as a prime minister of Israel, I can promise you one more thing: Even if Israel has to stand alone, Israel will stand. But I know Israel does not stand alone. I know that America stands with Israel. I know that you stand with Israel." He closed when he referenced Moses leading the Jewish people out of slavery in Egypt to the gates of the Promised Land. "And before the people entered the land of Israel, Moses gave us a message that has steeled our resolve for thousands of years. I leave you with this message today, (speaking in Hebrew), "Be strong and resolute, neither fear nor dread them." "My friends, may Israel and America always stand together, strong and resolute. May we neither fear nor dread the challenges ahead. May we face the future with confidence, strength and hope."

Prime Minister Netanyahu exemplified the stature and strength of a true leader capable of leading all who would embrace his vision of a strong alliance between Israel, America and our key allies in the Middle East who are committed to stand strong against the threat of Islamic Jihad. His vision of strength stands in stark contrast to President Obama's policy of appeasement. Radical Islam respects strength but goes in for the kill when they smell weakness. President Obama wreaks of weakness! His scent of weakness has emboldened the enemy. President Obama's incompetence and inability to lead has forced Prime Minister Netanyahu to step in and fill the leadership void left in the wake of President Obama's practice of leading from behind. Prime Minister Netanyahu is willing and capable to lead but the Arab countries in the Middle East have never followed an Israeli leader so it's unlikely that they would begin now. They do recognize and respect Netanyahu's strength so a strong Israeli leader is not without merit but it's unrealistic that Arab countries would follow Israel.

The United States Congress must stand strong, arm in arm with our allies in the Middle East. The Obama administration will fight Congress every step of the way but we must not relent in our resolve to stand strong as we face the threat of Islamic Jihad. Our weak American President refuses to lead so the U.S. President is no longer the default leader of the free world. Our key allies in the Middle East know they can't trust President Obama. They know he would take them down the **road to destruction** that he's hell-bent to follow. The Obama administration is the only entity who's already conceded to a nuclear armed Iran and most assuredly the only one who thinks it's a good idea. Prime Minister Benjamin Netanyahu has done a great job of sounding the alarm and raising awareness around the world that a nuclear armed Iran cannot be allowed under any circumstances. We can only hope and pray that his voice is heard loud and clear here at home and throughout the rest of the world.

Formal Charges

March 25, 2015

Sgt. Bowe Bergdahl was formally charged by the U.S. Army today on charges of desertion and misbehavior while with the enemy. Sgt. Bergdahl had deserted his post in far eastern Afghanistan on 6/30/2009 and found his way to the Haqqani network of the Taliban where he was captured and held captive for 5 years. (refer to Chapter 17 "Deal with the Devil" for details) Sgt. Berdahl was formally charged with 1 count of a high-level grade of desertion which includes avoidance of hazardous duty and 1 count of misbehavior while with the enemy. U.S Army forces command made the announcement today from Fort Bragg in North Carolina. An article 32 preliminary hearing will come next which is like a civilian grand jury. A general or special Court Marshall could come next. The article 99 charge of misbehavior while with the enemy is by far the more serious charge. Sgt. Bergdahl could easily spend the rest of his shameful life in prison but the death penalty is also on the table and he could lose $300,000. in back pay. Sgt. Bergdahl's platoon mounted a search to find him which continued for the 5 years he was held captive and resulted in the deaths of 6 brave Americans. President Obama traded 5 Taliban commanders who had been detained at Guantanamo for the return of Sgt. Bergdahl. Once Sgt. Bergdahl had been returned, National Security Advisor Susan Rice made the claim that he had served with honor and distinction. Now that Sgt. Bergdahl has been formally charged our President is looking like the fool that he is although I'm sure he will find a way to spin this development in such a way as to justify his actions. I believe most Americans understand how one-sided this trade was in favor of the Taliban and how foolish our President was to make the trade.

Historic Understanding

April 2, 2015

After 15 months of negotiations, the President and Secretary of State John Kerry announced the framework of a prospective deal with Iran on their nuclear program today. The President addressed the nation from the rose garden and Secretary Kerry spoke from Switzerland where negotiations were held. The President called it an **historic understanding.** This understanding is indeed historic but that doesn't necessarily indicate that it's good. The deadline for finalization of this deal is the end of June. If a deal based on the framework announced today is agreed to, it will be a very bad deal, but the President's remarks today basically announced great success. Anytime this President announces success I've learned to prepare for the worst. Red flags went up here at home and throughout the Middle East when Iranian Foreign Minister Zarif, who was in Switzerland at the time, spoke to the people of Iran and the rest of the world and announced a different understanding of the parameters of this prospective deal than what we were told here at home. We were told the heavy water facility at Arak would be dismantled but Zarif told Iranian's this facility would undergo modernization. The Arak facility is capable of producing weapons grade plutonium which we were told would end but that doesn't square with Zarif's announcement of modernization at that facility. We were told that Iran's uranium stockpile would be "neutralized" which is extremely vague but Zarif said Iran would be allowed to keep their stockpile of heavily enriched uranium. We were told that Iran would be allowed to enrich uranium in only one facility at Natanz to an enrichment level of 3.67% for 15 years (weapons grade is about 90%) at which time they would be free to complete their quest for nuclear weapons. Zarif simply announced that Iran would be allowed to continue uranium enrichment. We were told that Iran's formally secret underground facility at Fordo will stay open but that no uranium enrichment would be allowed there. Zarif simply announced that the Fordo facility will continue to operate. The Fordo facility is 3000 feet underground below a mountain and was constructed and operated in complete secrecy until an Iranian whistleblower revealed the existence of the facility. If an Iranian hadn't revealed the existence of this facility, we never would have known about it because U.N. inspectors failed to learn of it. This framework allows Iran to continue operating 6100 of their 19,000 centrifuges but none of them must be dismantled. This framework doesn't call for any dismantlement but President Obama had previously announced dismantlement as the goal of any potential deal with Iran. We were told that all sanctions will be lifted once Iran has implemented all aspects of the deal but Zarif told Iranians that sanctions would be immediately lifted upon signing of the deal.

Verification is the most important aspect of any potential deal but we learned there would be no unannounced inspections which contradicts President Obama's promise of "unprecedented verification." Apparently, an appointment must be made by U.N. inspectors before any inspection can take place which allows ample time for Iran to move things around and hide anything that doesn't meet the parameters of the deal. We were told of snap back sanctions if Iran is found to be noncompliant but the wording "snap back" is an oversimplification because much coordination is required with all countries involved to re-implement sanctions. We're negotiating from a position of weakness because we aren't using the economic leverage that we could be using. At this point we really don't have sufficient details on the verification process but we do know that Iran has blocked inspection attempts in the past so why wouldn't they maintain the same uncooperative posture that they're known for now. Iran is getting everything they want in the framework of this potential deal and all we're getting is vague promises from a country we know can't be trusted. If this framework winds up being finalized, we will be making Iran a richer country and as the worst offender of State sponsored terrorism in the world Iran will have more money than ever to more effectively fund their evil proxies throughout the Middle East. Iran's Supreme Leader Ayatollah Khamenei hasn't approved anything yet so Iran could still walk away from this framework. President Obama hasn't mentioned anything about seeking Congressional approval because he has no such plans. It's totally unacceptable for any deal to be made without Congressional approval. The American people must have a voice in this.

Retired Lt. General Michael Flynn formerly with the Defense Intel Agency said the Obama administration is acting out of "willful ignorance" which is a very astute observation. It will be up to the U.N. Security Council to enforce any potential deal which is a dubious proposition at best so why would we have any interest at all in such a weak framework? President Obama wants this deal so he can say he established peace with Iran through diplomacy. His narcissistic mind tells him this will be great for his legacy but such a deal would kick the can down the road for the next President to deal with which would be a much more difficult proposition at that time as opposed to effectively dealing with this issue now. Our President tells us we only have 2 choices. He says we either make this deal with Iran now or go to war which is a tactic he is using to scare the American people. The 3rd and best choice the President hasn't either thought of or is willfully ignoring is to take immediate steps to re-establish the strong sanctions that were lifted when Iran agreed to come to the negotiating table in the first place. With the price of oil at about $42. a barrel right now, Iran could be brought to their knees with stronger sanctions. Most of the Iranian population is quite young so they have their whole lives ahead of them. They would most likely exert extreme pressure on their government to provide relief from the crippling sanctions. Our Presidents extreme naivete on foreign affairs has come at a high cost to the American people and to Israel. I believe he will unilaterally make a bad deal in the end so if Congress fails to stop him we will be forced to live with a bad deal or worse yet, not live at all.

High Stakes Brinksmanship

April 20, 2015

While the Iranian backed Shiite Houthi's control Sana'a, Yemen along with all northern Yemen, AQAP, Al Qaeda Arabian Peninsula, has just taken control of the southern port city of Aden, Yemen. AQAP has been disruptive in Yemen for some time but the Shiite Houthi's have grown stronger and are supported by Iran so they pose the greatest threat even though AQAP is still a major concern. AQAP is Sunni and the Houthi's are Shiite so they have always been at odds with one another and work to marginalize each other at every turn. Saudi Arabia which borders Yemen to the north has been conducting air strikes over Yemen targeting Shiite Houthi's who have taken control of northern Yemen. Obviously, the instability in Yemen poses a threat to Saudi Arabia so they are flexing some muscle to disrupt the efforts of Shiite Houthi's there. When the United States learned of a 9-ship convoy of Iranian vessels steaming toward the port city of Aden, Yemen, the USS Theodore Roosevelt (aircraft carrier) was moved from the Persian Gulf to the Gulf of Aden below Yemen along with the USS Normandy (guided missile cruiser) and 8 additional U.S. warships plus 3 supply ships. The Iranian convoy consists of 7 cargo ships and 2 frigates and is believed to be transporting weapons and supplies to the Shiite Houthi's in Yemen. The major concern over the weapons cache on the Iranian vessels is that several missiles are believed to be on board that the U.S. and our Middle East allies wouldn't want to be delivered to the Shiite Houthi's in Yemen.

April 21, 2015

The White House and the State Department insist the U.S. ships are in the Gulf of Aden to monitor ship lanes and not to intercept any Iranian vessels. The Pentagon called it routine re-positioning. State Department spokesperson Marie Harf said, "This discreet movement of U.S. assets is for discreet purposes." There's nothing discreet about a 100,000-ton nuclear powered aircraft carrier with 5000 troops and 78 aircraft on board being flanked by a guided missile cruiser plus 8 additional warships and 3 supply ships. With a total of 8000 troops on board the 12 U.S. ships, this imposing show of force is representative of some very **high stakes brinksmanship**.

Saudi Arabia abruptly announced they would cease air strikes over Yemen today and say they've achieved their goals but are moving on to new actions. Much speculation began to surface accusing the White House of exerting pressure on the Saudi's to end their air strikes over Yemen in appeasement to Iran while nuclear talks are still underway due to Iran's proxy of Shiite Houthi's in Yemen. The appearance of support for an Iranian proxy in Yemen by the Obama administration risks offending our Sunni Arab allies in the Middle East and why would we remain at the negotiating table with Iran when they're supplying money, weapons and supplies to the Shiite Houthi's in Yemen? It's preposterous that politics is governing our national security.

April 22, 2015

Saudi Arabia resumed airstrikes over Yemen today after taking a 24-hour break even though they announced they would cease these strikes yesterday. Once the bombing resumed the Iranian convoy of 9 ships that were headed for Aden, Yemen reversed course overnight and appear to be headed back to their home port. I believe the Iranians feared that Saudi Arabia would bomb their ships once they reached Aden, Yemen and that this fear was a bigger motivating factor than the U.S. warships positioned in the Gulf of Aden because they believe Saudi Arabia has the backbone to act while Iran wasn't really concerned about the U.S. bluff given Obama's reputation of weakness and appeasement. I suppose the desired result was reached but what if Iran had called the U.S. bluff and continued to the port city of Aden, Yemen. It's an interesting question to consider but the actual outcome surely has the White House wiping their brow in relief after dodging a bullet that could have been quite explosive.

Slap in the Face

May 11, 2015

The President is holding the Gulf Nations Summit at Camp David this coming weekend and 4 of the 6 heads of state who were invited declined to attend. Most notably, King Salaman bin Abdulaziz Al Saud of Saudi Arabia will not attend the summit but King Hamad bin Isa Al Khalifah of Bahrain, Sultan Qaboos bin Said Al Said of Oman and Prime Minister Muhammed bin Rashid Al Maktoum of UAE will not be making the trip either. These leaders will be sending their foreign ministers but their decision to stay home sends a strong message to the White House that they don't like the bad nuclear deal with Iran that President Obama is attempting to make. This snub is more like a **slap in the face** directed at President Obama to give him a wake-up call while he continues negotiations with Iran that will pave the way for them to become a nuclear power and sets the stage for intense nuclear proliferation throughout the Middle East. Saudi King Salaman is also upset about the instability in Yemen due to Iran's proxies, the Shiite Houthi's, who have overthrown the government in Sana'a and are wreaking havoc throughout Yemen so once again the spotlight is directed at Iran who happens to be the world's largest State sponsor of terrorism. President Obama's weakness and incompetence have cost him the respect and trust of world leaders everywhere but most notably in the Middle East. When our most important allies have lost trust in the American President, our status as the world's super power is diminished to a very great extent which should give all of us reason for serious concern.

Obama Care Fraud

May 14, 2015

A Senate investigative committee recently revealed that 11 of their 12 investigators were easily able to beat the system and obtain Obama Care tax credits by using false social security numbers and declaring false income levels. These investigators reported that there was no effort on the part of HHS to verify the false information they submitted. They discovered 2.6 million inconsistencies at HHS on Obama Care enrollees so HHS has paid out billions based on false information. The fraud that is currently taking place was predicted some time ago by many who could easily detect the likelihood of the fraud that would and did occur. Now American taxpayers are paying the price for the existence of inefficient government bureaucracies like HHS who is attempting to manage $1/6^{th}$ of our economy which was scooped up by the U.S. Government when they took control of our entire health care system without a single Republican vote in Congress.

Delta Force

May 15, 2015

President Obama authorized a raid on the home of ISIS Minister of finance, Abu Sayyaf, near the Al-Amr oil field in eastern Syria. The U.S. Army **Delta Force** based out of Fort Bragg, North Carolina conducted the strategic raid in Syria. They arrived in 2 Blackhawks and an Osprey and managed to kill 32 ISIS fighters plus Abu Sayyaf himself in the firefight that ensued. Sayyaf used women and children as human shields none of whom were ultimately harmed. In the end, it came down to hand to hand fighting but the elite Delta Force proved to be too powerful for ISIS fighters. Abu Sayyaf was a senior commander for ISIS and managed their finances plus he was head of ISIS oil and gas operations. He was responsible for coordinating the sale of their oil on the black market. Sayyaf's wife, Umm Sayyaf, was captured and held for interrogation. She was head of ISIS human trafficking operations which supports their slavery practice. A Yazidi woman was freed from her role as the Sayyaf's slave and she's agreed to cooperate fully to provide any intelligence that she may be positioned offer. Most importantly, Sayyaf's laptop computers, cell phones and numerous documents were recovered and should prove to be an invaluable source of intelligence on ISIS operations. Abu Sayyaf was a close associate of ISIS leader Abu Bakr al-Baghdadi so there's a strong possibility we may gain important intelligence that could lead to al-Baghdadi's ultimate capture or demise.

Losing

May 18, 2015

The recent successful Delta Force raid in Syria has now been overshadowed by the fall of Ramadi, Iraq to ISIS. Ramadi is the capital of Anbar Province and is located only 70 miles west of Baghdad. Ramadi is a key city in the region and to add insult to injury the U.S. sacrificed a lot of blood and treasure when we took Ramadi the first time in 2006 during the surge when over 1000 American soldiers made the ultimate sacrifice of their lives so to watch it fall after that incredible sacrifice is especially painful particularly for the families and friends of those Americans who died there. Once again, the Iraqi's, who were trained by the U.S. military, abandoned their posts and ran as soon as the fighting began even though their numbers were far greater than that of ISIS. They dropped their weapons on the spot and abandoned their vehicles all of which were supplied by the United States. U.S. made Tanks, Humvees, rocket propelled grenades, and other weaponry fell into the hands of ISIS due to the weakness and fearful nature of the Iraqi security force. They've shown us repeatedly that they're not up for the fight. The Pentagon merely downplayed the fall of Ramadi as they called it a setback and announced they have no plans to change their strategy of limited air strikes. We are **losing** in Iraq and our feckless President has no will to do anything about it!

Iraq's President, Faud Masum, has authorized the use of Iranian backed Shiite Militias in their attempt to retake Ramadi. This weakens Iraq's Prime Minister, Haider al-Abadi even though he is Shiite and it exacerbates sectarian strife between Sunni's and Shia's in Iraq. If the Iran nuke deal is ultimately agreed to, Iran would receive a signing bonus of $50 billion plus major relief from the sanctions that would be lifted. This huge windfall for Iran would provide large sums of money that Iran would give to its proxies like Hezbollah, Hamas, Shia Militias throughout the Middle East and Assad in Syria who is also Shiite. This could set up the ultimate Sunni / Shia faceoff as ISIS is Sunni. The expanding sectarian conflict is a predictable outcome of President Obama's failure to establish a status of forces agreement with Iraq to leave a residual force of 10 to 20 thousand U.S troops in Iraq to guard the gains that were made. The rise of ISIS and further growth of Al Qaeda can be directly attributed to this failure of the Obama administration. ISIS has now taken and occupy Fallujah, Mosul, and now Ramadi in addition to large swaths of land in Iraq and Syria while their expansion to Libya is in full swing. The Obama administration orchestrated the removal of Muammar Gaddafi from power in Libya which resulted in a power vacuum that ISIS and other terrorist groups have successfully exploited. Hillary Clinton was Secretary of State when Gaddafi was ousted from power in Libya and played a major role in that effort. Secretary of State John Kerry and White House Press Secretary Josh Earnest are downplaying the grim situation on the ground in Ramadi. John Kerry is delusional and Josh Earnest is the voice of President Obama who too is delusional.

Ramadi was a city of 500,000 but now over 100,000 have fled from Ramadi in April alone and thousands more are currently attempting to get out but as ISIS goes door to door slaughtering infidels it's become increasingly difficult to get out of the city. ISIS also considers other Muslims to be infidels if they're deemed to be apostate. 500 bodies of those slaughtered by ISIS were seen lining the streets of Ramadi. Another 34,000 did manage to flee Ramadi in just 4 days since 5/14.

ISIS moved into Ramadi undetected under the cover of a sand storm. Their strategy proved to be extremely effective because U.S. drones could not detect them so they moved in unimpeded and in short order ISIS suicide bombers driving 27 U.S. military armored personnel vehicles detonated powerful bombs that each of these vehicles had been armed with, each one every bit as powerful as the bomb that decimated the Alfred P. Murrah Federal building in Oklahoma City. The sheer shock and awe from these powerful bomb blasts filled the Iraqi fighting force with fear and sent them running for their lives. As is the case with much of the U.S. weaponry and military vehicles ISIS now utilizes, they were acquired when Iraqi troops fled from previous ISIS offensives and simply picked up by ISIS soldiers as they moved in.

The Obama administration ascribes to the rationalization that Muslims throughout the Middle East behave the way they do because of their grievances and if only we were to address those grievances they would surely change and the violence would end. This extremely naïve assertion ignores the fact that their Islamic ideology is the impetus behind their evil actions.

May 21, 2015

Palmyra, Syria just fell to ISIS. ISIS now controls over half of Syria in addition to their gains in Iraq. Palmyra is in central Syria and is home to ancient treasures that ISIS will surely destroy as they attempt to erase history. The historical Roman ruins and other ancient artifacts in Palmyra, all of which are over 2000 years old, are in serious jeopardy of extinction. ISIS gained control of an air base there and the cities prison which is filled with hundreds of ISIS supporters who will be set free to join the fight with ISIS. Assad's army in Syria which was formally known as a strong fighting force did the same thing that Iraqis in Ramadi, Iraq did when faced with fighting ISIS; they ran. Retreat seems to be the favored option when ISIS approaches in both Iraq and Syria.

President Obama was in Connecticut yesterday and during a speech at a university there he once again declared climate change aka global warming as the greatest national security threat we are faced with today. Really!!! He also said, "We are not **losing**" against ISIS and called the fall of Ramadi, Iraq a "tactical setback" while ISIS now controls the entire Euphrates river valley that leads into Baghdad. The Presidents delusional declarations defy logic and conventional wisdom in the face of much more pressing issues such as the rapid momentum established by

ISIS throughout the Middle East as they advance their goal of a global Caliphate that spells death to the infidel and make no mistake, we are all infidels in their eyes. President Obama has disillusioned our allies and emboldened our enemies in his blind quest to keep his head firmly buried in the sand.

Chapter 25

Shut Down

May 26, 2015

The 5th U.S. Circuit Court of Appeals in New Orleans ruled today to uphold the injunction that has temporarily **shut down** the Presidents illegal executive action granting amnesty to 5 million illegal aliens who broke our laws when they illegally entered our country. The court denied the White House request for a stay on the injunction. The Obama administration has now filed an appeal to the Supreme Court on this case. Deportations will not be halted now as this case either lands in the Supreme Court or continues to be litigated in the lower federal court. This is a victory for the 26 States who filed the lawsuit claiming the President had overstepped his constitutional authority. Texas led the way on this lawsuit so this makes things especially painful for the President because he can't stand Texas. Judge Jerry E. Smith who was appointed by Ronald Reagan and Judge Jennifer Walker Elrod who was appointed by George W. Bush ruled to uphold the injunction but Judge Stephen A. Higginson, an Obama appointee, dissented.

G7 Summit

June 8, 2015

President Obama held a press conference today upon conclusion of the **G7 Summit** in Krun, Germany. The President spoke prior to taking questions from the press to detail the issues that were dealt with during the summit. Climate change and Russian aggression in Ukraine were 2 major topics of discussion but Iran nuclear negotiations, threats posed by ISIS, Cyberespionage and the economic crisis in Greece were also discussed. Many needs were identified but no specific actions were arrived at to meet the needs that were agreed upon. The only actual accomplishment was to raise more questions with no actual solutions. The President nevertheless was quite upbeat as he shifted and opened the floor to questions from the press. The press was more concerned with court rulings here at home with a focus on the looming Supreme Court ruling on King vs. Burwell and the recent ruling by the 5th U.S. Circuit Court of Appeals on the Presidents illegal executive action on immigration. They did also ask about the U.S. strategy or lack of one to defeat ISIS in the Middle East.

The President attacked the court ruling on immigration and said it must be repealed. He said Congress needs to act on a comprehensive immigration plan but in the interim the President promised to work on all fronts to fix the broken immigration system. It never occurs to him that he could work with Congress as a coequal branch of government to reach a consensus or compromise solution but given his dictatorial style, that is not an option for this President.

Regarding the pending Supreme Court ruling on King vs. Burwell which will decide if States who failed to set up a State Exchange will be eligible to receive subsidies through the Federal Exchange, he said we must assume that SCOTUS will do the right thing and uphold the federal subsidies for individuals in States with no State Exchange. He did go on to say that this case never should have been taken up by the Supreme Court and that it was due to a contorted reading of the statute and a twisted interpretation of 4 words which simply isn't true. The statute is crystal clear in its wording that specifically says only State Exchanges can issue subsidies. Jonathan Gruber who was the main architect of Obama Care confirmed that the statute was written in such a way as to force States to establish State Exchanges. Obviously, the Obama administration miscalculated because 34 States did not establish a State Exchange hence the dilemma and the possibility of an Obama Care death spiral if the Supreme Court rules against Federal subsidies for States with no State Exchange. The President went on to insist that the horrors of Obama Care have not come to pass and that it's working very well and doesn't need fixin (he did say fixin). The President must have missed the recent announcement by the major health insurance companies that premiums will increase by a margin of 20% to 43% for 2016. Blue Cross Blue Shield of North Carolina announced a 26% increase while increases of 20% in Texas, 30% in New Jersey and a whopping 43% in South Dakota were announced. We now know the Presidents promises on Obama Care were never trustworthy because he had previously assured us that rates would go down by $2500. annually for the average American family. Not only have premiums not gone down as promised but they've gone through the roof with catastrophic increases.

When asked about his strategy to deal with ISIS in Iraq and Syria plus other regions in the Middle East, the President announced that no complete strategy exists yet. He said, "When a finalized plan is presented to me by the Pentagon, I will share it with the American people." The Pentagon responded recently to the claim by the President that they had failed to develop a strategy to defeat ISIS because this criticism had already come up and they assured the press that several strategies had been submitted to the White House and all were rejected. The President went on to say that we need "a train and assist posture." He went on and on about the need for more training of Iraqi security forces and that Iraq needs more recruits. He maintained that we've made significant progress in many areas but had to concede that the fall of Ramadi in the Anbar Province was a setback. He never discusses going after ISIS in Syria. ISIS maintains their command and control center in Raqqa, Syria so this should be a primary target but this President refuses to attack ISIS in Syria. The President did speak of the need to stem the flow of foreign fighters entering Syria at the Turkey/Syria border and said we need to monitor that border carefully but simply watching the huge influx of outsiders who enter Syria at the Turkey/Syria border to join ISIS won't help. It should have been abundantly clear that the growth of ISIS from 2000 to 30,000 members in one year was a very good indication of their rapid expansion. ISIS may have as many as 60,000 to 70,000 members but arriving at an estimate of their numbers is very difficult so I believe the 30,000 number is a very conservative estimate that may be quite low. When the President spoke of the need for a political agenda of inclusion between the various sects in Iraq he confirmed his delusional condition. Sunni's, Shiite's and Kurds in Iraq have been at odds with one another for centuries and have never shown any signs of inclusion that would lead to peaceful coexistence. Also, the new government in Baghdad is led by Prime Minister Abadi who is Shiite and therefore loyal to Iran and opposed to working with Sunni and Kurd factions. The 3 sects in Iraq have always fought with one another and always will but President Obama can't or won't accept that fact. His unrealistic ideology is once again preventing him from accepting and dealing with reality. Albert Einstein said, the definition of insanity is "doing the same thing over and over again expecting a different result," so based on that definition it becomes painfully clear that our President does indeed fit that criteria. We're training Iraqi security forces repeatedly because our President believes we can arrive at a different result but so far, we get the same results every time which is that Iraqis can be counted on to cut and run when ISIS attacks while leaving their American supplied weaponry and vehicles for ISIS to intercept.

Preservation Order

June 25, 2015

In the continuing effort to recover missing e-mails from the former head of the tax-exempt division of the IRS, Lois Lerner, the House Oversight and Government Reform Committee held another hearing today to learn the status of recovery efforts by the IRS. Prior to taking the 5th during an earlier House hearing in 2013, Lerner claimed her laptop computer experienced a local hard drive failure. We then learned that her computer had been shredded to destroy all evidence so in August of 2013 a House subpoena with an attached "**preservation order**" was issued to the IRS attempting to recover the backup servers. In today's hearing, we heard from Treasury Deputy IG Timothy Camus who testified that 422 backup tapes containing 24 to 25 thousand Lois Lerner e-mails were erased on 3/4/2014, 8 months after the House subpoena and preservation order had been issued. Camus went on to say that interviews, sworn statements and a review of the employees' e-mails turned up no evidence that they were trying to destroy evidence. House Oversight Committee chairman, Jason Chaffetz, said "It just defies any sense of logic" and that "It gets to the point where it truly gets to be unbelievable. Somebody has to be held accountable."

Rep. Thomas Massie, R-KY., asked Camus if incompetence was to blame for the tapes being erased. Camus said, "One could come to that conclusion." I agree with Jason Chaffetz that it defies logic and is unbelievable. Lois Lerner should be held accountable but it appears we're nowhere near to achieving that goal. The Obama administration is the most corrupt and least transparent administration we've witnessed to date. It's incredible to me that this administration has evaded accountability on so many fronts. It seems they are Teflon because nothing sticks.

Judicial Activism

The Supreme Court upheld Obama Care subsidies issued by the Federal exchange to people who live in one of the 34 States that failed to establish a State exchange with a 6-3 ruling on King v Burwell that was announced today. Chief Justice John Roberts wrote the majority opinion and solidified his role in saving Obama Care twice now with highly questionable justification. At the heart of the controversy is the phrase "established by the State" which appears 7 times in the law. Chief Justice Roberts said the phrase is ambiguous and concluded that "State" in this instance represents the federal government. This is **judicial activism** at its worst. "State" in this instance clearly represents the 50 States of the United States because it's used in context with State exchanges but Chief Justice Roberts and the other 5 Justices who ruled to uphold Obama Care subsidies issued by the federal exchange reached the conclusion that "the intent of the law was to improve health care, not destroy it." The bizarre and odd contortions these 6 Justices had to perform to reach that conclusion is indeed difficult to accept. Chief Justice Roberts wrote in his opinion that its "untenable in light of the entire statute" and that "We must take care not to undo the intent of the statute" while maintaining that the full context of the law upholds the subsidies. The most bizarre twist is that the chief architect of Obama Care, Jonathan Gruber, had previously stated that the wording "established by the State" was intentionally written like that as motivation to push States to establish State exchanges so we already knew factually what the intent of that wording was but 6 Supreme Court Justices chose to blind themselves to that reality because it wasn't part of the official record. It's been said that justice is blind but in this instance ignoring the facts does not look like justice to me.

Justice Antonin Scalia wrote a blistering and compelling 21-page dissent. On page 2 of his dissent he wrote, Words no longer have meaning if an exchange not established by a State is "established by the State." It is hard to come up with a clearer way to limit tax credits to State exchanges than to use the words "established by the State." And it is hard to come up with a reason to include the words "by the State" other than the purpose of limiting credits to State exchanges... Under all the usual rules of interpretation, in short, the Government should lose this case.

Later in his dissent he wrote, it was the job of Congress to fix the law, not the court's (page 19, 20). Rather than rewriting the law under the pretense of interpreting it, the court should have left it to Congress to decide what to do about the Act's limitation of tax credits to State exchanges... The Court's insistence on making a choice that should be made by Congress both aggrandizes judicial power and encourages congressional lassitude.

On page 20, 21 he writes, Today's opinion changes the usual rules of statutory interpretation for the sake of the Affordable Care Act... Having transformed two major parts of the law, the Court today has turned its attention to a third. The Act that Congress passed makes tax credits available only to an "Exchange established by the State." This Court, however, concludes that this limitation would prevent the rest of the Act from working as well as hoped. So, it rewrites the law to make tax credits available everywhere. We should start calling this law SCOTUScare.

Perhaps the Patient Protection and Affordable Care Act will attain the enduring status of the Social Security Act or the Taft-Hartley Act; perhaps not. But this Court's two decisions on the Act will surely be remembered through the years. The somersaults of statutory interpretation they have performed ("penalty" means tax, "further [Medicaid] payments to the State" means only incremental Medicaid payments to the State, "established by the State" means not established by the State) will be cited by litigants endlessly, to the confusion of honest jurisprudence. And the cases will publish forever the discouraging truth that the Supreme Court of the United States favors some laws over others, and is prepared to do whatever it takes to uphold and assist its favorites. I dissent.

I believe by changing the meaning of words the Supreme Court has set a dangerous precedent as all future rulings will be questionable. The Supreme Court has always been marginally political but at this point they've become highly politicized. Clearly Chief Justice Roberts is determined to uphold Obama Care even if it takes the Court down a path to rewrite the law.

Legislating from the Bench

June 26, 2015

One day after the Supreme Court announced their ruling on King v. Burwell upholding Obama Care subsidies in all 50 States, they announced their ruling on Obergefell v. Hodges which made same-sex marriage legal in all 50 States. These 2 rulings are 2 of the most impactful rulings of the last 50 years. Not since the ruling on Roe v. Wade in 1973 that legalized abortion and the 1963 ruling that took prayer out of public schools have we seen such sweeping rulings but now that same-sex marriage has been found to be constitutional, our country's traditional family values fall under further attack and Americas moral decline has descended to its lowest point in our short history. This ruling is another example of judicial activism and a prime example of **legislating from the bench** as the Court rewrites law with no rational constitutional basis. The constitution is silent on marriage! The 5 liberal justices pointed to the 14th amendment as their justification for this ruling but the 14th amendment was passed while Lincoln was President and was intended to provide equal rights for African Americans who were trapped in slavery and makes no mention of marriage. Abraham Lincoln and our founding fathers of the previous century are turning over in their graves. These devout Christian men would never have approved of same-sex marriage! The 14th amendment assures equal protection under the law to all citizens. Citizens are assured "due process" which prevents citizens from being illegally deprived of life, liberty or property. The 14th amendment was ratified in 1868 when the topic of same-sex marriage was the furthest thing from anyone's mind so this Court's decision to read marriage into the 14th amendment represents a move to usurp the role of Congress. Congress empowers the judiciary but in this case the judiciary acted alone.

This ruling was 5 – 4 with Chief Justice Roberts, Justice Scalia, Justice Alito and Justice Thomas dissenting. Justice Kennedy wrote the majority opinion. States will now be required to issue marriage licenses in all 50 States and all States must recognize same-sex marriages that were performed in another State. Same-sex marriage is now considered to be a fundamental right. The 4 dissenters say the court shouldn't possess the power to change the thousands year old definition of marriage. Congress is the only branch of government that has power to initiate such a change by passing legislation and then the court could only give that new legislation an up or down decision if a case should reach them. The Court does not have the power to initiate such a radical change to the definition of marriage but in this case, they did it anyway. I fear the future litigation this ruling will ignite on religious freedoms will further complicate this miscarriage of justice. The people should retain the power to define marriage through their representation in Congress. Justice Scalia's dissent was especially scathing as he compared the Court's ruling to a Nazi takeover of the States. He said the Court has eviscerated the Constitution. The fact is that the States were making significant progress working through the issue of same-sex marriage on their own. 36 States had already legalized same-sex marriage even though federal courts forced 11 of those States to do so. If the Supreme Court had justly deferred to the States through a less radical decision, the States would have continued working through this issue and could have reached resolutions on their own without the intrusion of the U.S. Supreme Court. This issue goes to the heart of States rights but the Supreme Court has now restricted those rights. This decision sets up a slippery slope that could descend into the erosion of our religious freedoms and threatens the solidity of the 1st amendment. I seriously don't understand why this has become such a huge issue because the National Health Interview Survey (NHIS) found that only 1.6% of Americans identify as gay or lesbian. Such a small percentage of gay and lesbian people in America shouldn't be cause for this much attention and reflects how insignificant their numbers are most likely due their extreme departure from normal sexual relations.

President Obama celebrated this ruling with a victory lap in the Rose Garden and he had the White House lit up in rainbow colors to honor gay people in America. The White House is the people's house and President Obama is merely a temporary guest there so he seriously offended all bible believing Christians in America when he had no legitimate right to do so. This represents one more divisive act to disrupt harmonious relations among the American people. As a Christian I love all gay people and see them as sinners in need of a savior just like all the rest of us but same-sex marriage is completely out of the will of God which can be verified in the bible therefore it's something I cannot recognize as being legitimate in the eyes of God.

This ruling doesn't change anything for true evangelical Christians who look to a much higher authority for the definition of marriage and consider God's word, the Bible, to be the final authority on the matter. The Supreme Court cannot change the hearts and minds of true believers in Christ who respect God's word. God's word cannot be changed and it stands for all time. Genesis 2:21-24 is the key scripture that defines marriage as being between 1 man and 1 woman with 21-23 laying the foundation and 24 solidifying it. Both Mark 10:6-9 and Matthew 19:4-6 support Genesis 2:21-24 so God saw fit for emphasis to define marriage as being between 1 man and 1 woman in both the Old Testament and the New Testament. The New Testament passages are red letter passages so they represent the exact words of Jesus. Other passages such as Leviticus 18:22, Leviticus 20:13 in the Old Testament and Romans 1:26-27 in the New Testament condemn homosexuality and lesbianism calling it detestable and a perversion, therefore these passages support Genesis 2:21-24, Mark 10:6-9 and Matthew 19:4-6. Gay people are sinners in need of a savior just like all the rest of us so I'm not condemning or judging gay people. Their sin is no different from adultery or any other sin but when it comes to marriage, God's sacred institution must be respected. Gay Christians and even some other more liberal Christians ignore these passages and pretend they don't exist or are outdated which is ludicrous. Bible believing Christians accept the Bible as God's word and acknowledge that God's word is absolute truth that cannot be redefined and stands for all time.

Repressive Totalitarian Regime

July 1, 2015

President Obama announced today that the United States will re-open the U.S. Embassy in Cuba that was closed 54 years ago, in 1961. In addition, he said Cuba will be allowed to open an Embassy in the United States. The President expressed his desire for Congress to lift the trade embargo we imposed upon Cuba but didn't take questions from the press once he'd finished his comments. This sends a very bad signal to our legitimate allies around the world. The Castro's in Cuba operate a **repressive totalitarian regime.** They've imprisoned many Cubans as political prisoners because they criticized the regime. The Cuban people are basically prisoners in their own country. They live in extreme poverty and the regime goes to great lengths to limit opportunity because people who live in poverty are easier to control. Cubans who work at the beach resorts aren't paid a salary and must rely on tips as their only source of income.

If the U.S. were to open channels of trade with Cuba we would only be propping up the regime itself because the people would be deprived of taking advantage of trade opportunities. Open trade with Cuba would create hard currency reserves for the Cuban regime and would not help the Cuban people at all. The regime supports drug trafficking in Columbia and Venezuela and makes a lot of money from those relationships. The regime also manages an anti-American campaign. The biggest problem is Cuba's ties to Iran through their relationship with Venezuela because Hezbollah maintains a strong presence in Venezuela and Hezbollah is an Iranian proxy. We would indirectly be supporting Hezbollah if trade channels were to be opened with Cuba and we'd be indirectly supporting drug trafficking operations in Columbia and Venezuela.

Congress must authorize the $6.5 million needed to refurbish the old and run down Embassy in Cuba and the Senate must approve the Presidents appointment for a U.S. Ambassador in Cuba. I pray our Republican majority in Congress will have the guts to do the right thing by blocking the finances needed to refurbish the Embassy in Cuba and to block the appointment of a U.S. Ambassador to Cuba.

Stunning Historic Mistake

July 14, 2015

The P5+1 agreed to a nuclear deal with Iran today that paves the way for Iran to have nuclear weapons and Intercontinental Ballistic Missiles capable of transporting a nuclear bomb from Iran to the United States. The P5 consists of the United States, Russia, China, France and the United Kingdom. The +1 is Germany. Iran will have nuclear bombs within 10 to 15 years and ICBM's within 8 years but could have both much sooner by cheating on the deal which they are notorious for. Iran has been evading inspections by the IAEA (International Atomic Energy Agency) for years and has an underground nuclear facility at Fordo which is 3000 feet underground beneath a mountain. The Fordo facility operated secretly for years until an Iranian whistleblower revealed the existence of this secret underground facility so if not for this Iranian who clued us in on this site, we never would have known about it because the IAEA failed to discover it on their own. Everything Israeli Prime Minister Benjamin Netanyahu warned us about (which is detailed in the previous chapter of this book) came to fruition in this deal as we now know the content of the final deal. The biggest problem with this deal is the sanctions relief that Iran will receive because Iran was going to get a nuclear bomb and ICBM's anyway so why would we pave the way for Iran to become a nuclear power and reward them with hundreds of billions of dollars in sanctions relief that they will surely use to fund terrorism around the world when we could have continued to crush their economy by imposing even harsher sanctions on top of the existing ones. The debilitating sanctions are the motivation that brought Iran to the negotiating table in the first place because their economy has been severely damaged by the sanctions. President Obama argued that the other P5+1 countries agreed to impose sanctions initially based on negotiations with Iran to cut a deal on Iran's nuclear program. He contends that upon the conclusion of negotiations with a deal in place, the other P5+1 countries were set to lift their sanctions immediately with no regard for anything the U.S. Congress may do. In addition, the arms embargo on Iran wouldn't have been lifted without this deal but now they will be able to buy conventional weapons from Russia in 5 years and ICBM's in 8 years. The arms embargo should never have been part of this deal but negotiators for the P5+1 capitulated and agreed to it. Israeli Prime Minister Benjamin Netanyahu called this deal a **stunning historic mistake**. We are legitimizing Iran's nuclear aspirations with this 159-page deal. This is a dark day for America and Israel.

The P5+1 relented on every original objective they had identified at the beginning of negotiations. The key goal was to perform anytime anywhere inspections of both covert sites and declared sites to effectively verify compliance with the terms of the deal. The final deal allows Iran to have up to 24 days from the time an inspection request is made to decide if access will be allowed at covert sites and the wording in the deal says inspectors can "press" to inspect covert sites but the covert sites are the sites where all the nefarious nuclear activity is taking place so these sites should be under intense scrutiny. The inspections process calls for an arbitration committee made up of Iran and the P5+1 which will convene within 2 weeks of an inspection request and then have another 11 days for a total of 24 days before a decision is made on access to inspect covert sites like the underground site at Fordo or the military site at Parchin. The fact that the arbitration committee has the option to deny access at covert sites is very troubling and the process the committee will establish to arrive at that decision is unclear so we don't know if it's based on majority rule or if only one country like Iran themselves could rule to deny access to covert sites which Iran has already done with the IAEA. Monitoring equipment will be set up in Iran's declared sites but of course their covert sites will not be outfitted with monitoring equipment. The deal does call for the elimination of 2/3rd's of Iran's centrifuges and Iran is required to reduce their stockpile of enriched uranium by 98% over 15 years. I believe Iran will just move their enriched uranium out of the country most likely to Russia and then retrieve it at the end of the 15 years when they're completely free to produce as many nuclear bombs as they like. Iran will be free to continue research and development on advanced centrifuges throughout the 15 years the deal is in place so upon conclusion of this 15-year deal, Iran will have advanced centrifuges in short order.

Nuclear proliferation is already underway in the Middle East with Saudi Arabia, Jordon and Egypt, all of whom have made deals with Russia for Russian oversight of nuclear reactors for development of nuclear weapons. All our Sunni allies in the Middle East are very concerned about Iran as a nuclear power. President Obama called the nuclear deal with Iran a "dramatic breakthrough" and Hillary Clinton has voiced her support for the deal while Iranian President Rouhani was in the streets of Tehran with large numbers of Iranian citizens who were chanting death to Israel and death to America while burning U.S. and Israeli flags. Why would we make such a bad deal with a country determined to destroy America and Israel? The deal preserves Iran's nuclear infrastructure and provides a $150 billion windfall of frozen assets within 6 months for Iran to more effectively fund terrorism around the world. Iran will be free to begin selling oil to Western Europe and even China once the sanctions are lifted so this will further fill their coffers with more money to fund terrorism. Iran will use these new-found funds to more effectively support Hezbollah in Lebanon, Hamas in Gaza, Shiite Houthi's in Yemen and President Bashar al-Assad in Syria. Hezbollah and Hamas are camped out on Israel's northern and western borders so their new-found wealth becomes a huge threat to Israel. The Shiite Houthi's recently overthrew the government in Yemen and pose a threat to our ally, Saudi Arabia. President Assad in Syria has destabilized Syria and thrown that country into such turmoil that it enabled ISIS to grow there and to this day maintains their base of operations in Raqqa, Syria.

Once the flood gates open for trade with Iran the sanctions regime will be highly reluctant to re-impose sanctions because it would be too costly to once again shut down trade with Iran. The Obama administration is using the terminology "snap back" sanctions and would have us believe that sanctions could be snapped back in place at the drop of a hat if Iran is caught cheating but nothing could be further from the truth. This deal reeks of capitulation and appeasement on the part of the P5+1. Iran is holding 4 Americans hostage in Iran and their release didn't even come up in negotiations. Christian Pastor Saeed Abedini, Jason Rezaian and Amir Hekmati are Americans languishing in Iranian prisons while enduring torture and deplorable conditions. Robert Levinson is a former FBI agent who disappeared in Iran in 2007 and is thought to be held hostage in Iran but we don't know definitively about his status. It's shameful that we would agree to a nuclear deal with Iran and make no attempt to obtain the release of these 4 Americans as a stipulation of the deal. President Obama explained that if we had brought up the 4 American hostages as part of the nuclear deal, Iran would have countered with additional concessions but given the fact that Iran threw in the lifting of the arms embargo to the deal at the 11th hour why didn't we counter at that point with the release of the 4 American hostages? The P5+1 relented on the arms embargo while nothing was done to obtain the release of the 4 Americans Iran is holding hostage. President Obama and Secretary of State John Kerry are the worst negotiators on the planet.

Congress has 60 days to review the deal and can then pass legislation blocking the deal but President Obama has already vowed to veto this legislation if it makes it to the oval office so Congress must obtain a 2/3rd's super majority in both chambers of Congress to override a

Presidential veto. The President has an ace in the hole with the U.N. if he can't veto legislation that blocks the deal. He's asked the U.N. Security Council to pass a resolution that would allow Russia, China and the other P5+1 countries to lift their sanctions immediately. This would take the teeth out of any legislation the U.S. Congress may be able to pass that would block the nuclear deal with Iran. It's a roll of the dice either way because no deal would have been a risk and the bad deal that was made is an even bigger risk but we'll never know the outcome of walking away from negotiations with no deal along with ratcheting up sanctions. The sad fact is that President Obama has succeeded in cramming this bad deal down Americans throats just as he did with Obama Care and every other failed initiative this administration has supported. The President has prioritized legacy over logic and has once again succeeded in dividing Americans while this terrible deal plays out for years to come. Iran doesn't even recognize a deal with infidels as being legitimate or binding so since we are the great Satan and infidels to Iran they will not comply with the terms of this deal. To Iran the nuclear deal is just words on paper that are meaningless. May God help us all!

July 15, 2015

The President held a press conference today to defend the Iran nuclear deal with the press. His narcissism was on full display as the President filibustered his way through the press conference and only called on 7 journalists during a 70-minute press conference. Finally, when journalists weren't firing off the exact questions he was looking for, he turned the press conference into a soliloquy as he pulled out his notes and began covering point by point exactly what he wanted to say. He chastised Major Garret with CBS when he asked why the President was content to leave 4 Americans in Iranian prisons instead of including their release in the nuclear deal. The President called the question nonsense and told Major Garret he should be ashamed for asking it. Sounds like that question wasn't part of the Presidents talking points.

July 20, 2015

The 15 member U.N. Security Council passed a resolution this morning that approves the Iran nuclear deal. The resolution passed with a unanimous affirmative vote. The Iran nuclear deal has now become binding international law and member nations who participated in the sanctions regime are now free to lift their sanctions. President Obama did an end run around Congress to get this resolution so once again our imperial President has ignored our nation's political process and acted as a dictator. The American people had no say in this decision because Congress hasn't even had time to digest this complex 159-page deal much less the opportunity to pass legislation that could have blocked the deal. Meanwhile Iran continues to shout death to America and death to Israel and has already vowed their continued support of Hezbollah in Lebanon, Shiite Houthi's in Yemen, Hamas in Gaza, Assad in Syria, plus Iranian allies in Palestine and Bahrain.

Hard Sell

August 5, 2015

President Obama addressed the nation today from American University in Washington D.C. and delivered one of the most dishonest speeches he's ever made. Dishonesty is a very common trait of this President so he's very comfortable lying through his teeth. He did set a new low on this front today as he made numerous statements that had nothing to do with the truth. He's doing the same kind of **hard sell** on the Iran nuke deal as he did on Obama Care when he told bold lies like, "If you like your Doctor you can keep your Doctor...period!" and "If you like your health insurance plan you can keep your plan...period!" Both lies were confirmed to be lies when everyone lost their Doctors and when everyone had to switch to an Obama Care approved health insurance plan or pay a tax penalty that increases with every passing year. The Obama Care lies went on and on from there and we've all witnessed the disaster that is Obama Care with rising health insurance premiums, deductibles and co-pays and the fact that more people became uninsured than those who gained the benefit of health insurance which for the most part were low income people who acquired Medicaid for the first time. If the nuclear deal with Iran proves to be as bad as our experience with Obama Care, we are in for a world of hurt.

President Obama claimed to have been a stalwart supporter of Israel throughout his Presidency. I bet Israeli Prime Minister Benjamin Netanyahu fell out of his chair on that whopper. He said inspections can take place at undeclared sites within 24 hours but he was either confused or just flat out lied because it takes 24 days just to get a final decision by the arbitration committee to determine if an inspection will be allowed. The President said inspections of Iran's nuclear facilities will continue after 15 years but the problem with this deceptive statement is that inspections can be denied at undeclared sites from day one and the deal allows Iran to enrich uranium, fire up their heavy water reactors for plutonium and construct advanced centrifuges that are only used for nuclear weaponry at the end of 15 years but I fully expect them to cheat based on their track record and most likely will have a nuclear bomb with ICBM's much sooner.

Throughout much of his 55-minute speech the President returned to his first term apology tour style and apologized profusely for America's foreign policy prior to his Presidency. The apologies went on and on clearly reflecting his disdain for American exceptionalism and American strength. He doesn't realize what a joke these apologies are to most every head of State in the world. He's merely channeling his weakness and it's so obvious to everyone else but he nevertheless plows ahead with more and more apologies for the (in his eyes) big bad United States of America. The President also took this opportunity to do some enthusiastic and insulting Republican bashing especially when he linked hardliners in Iran who chant death to

America to the GOP implicating that Republicans share a common cause with Iranian hardliners due to their opposition to the Iran nuke deal because in his mind Republicans are bringing death to America by opposing the Iran nuke deal. President Obama is the one bringing death to America with the Iran nuke deal itself. The President never once even mentioned Islamic jihad but then of course he's never referred to Islamic jihad. He didn't even bring up extremists (his cleaned-up word) whatever that is and didn't say anything about terrorism. If the Iran nuke deal works out as well as Obama Care, his 1st term $800 billion economic stimulus and the complete withdrawal from Iraq leaving no residual force that resulted in the rise of ISIS, we are in big trouble. Things haven't gone well in Libya, Yemen, Iraq and Syria or even here at home so why would anyone believe the Iran nuke deal will work out any better.

Deal Breaker

August 7, 2015

Iran's heavily sanctioned Revolutionary Guard Kuds Force Commander, Gen. Qassem Suleimani, defied a U.N. travel ban and traveled to Moscow on 7/24 to discuss weapons deals including the purchase of the S300 anti-aircraft missile defense system. While there he met with Putin and Russia's Defense Minister, Sergei Shoygu, to work through details of the arms deal. Gen. Suleimani was designated as a terrorist by the United States in 2005. Suleimani was responsible for the deaths of over 500 Americans in Iraq and he heads up Iran's secret nuclear program which of course enables Iran to cheat on the nuclear deal. On 7/29, only 2 days after Gen. Suleimani returned to Iran from Russia and before we learned he had traveled to Russia, Secretary of State John Kerry assured Congress that all international sanctions would remain in place on Suleimani which includes the travel ban. Once again Secretary Kerry's extreme naivete' has proven to be dangerous. Earlier today Iranian officials confirmed that Gen. Suleimani had indeed traveled to Russia last month to discuss arms purchases from Russia. Before the ink was even dry on the nuke deal, Iran has violated the deal so it's clear that Iran has no intent of abiding by the terms of the nuclear deal. This initial violation should be a **deal breaker** but I'm sure the Obama administration will let it slide and just try to sweep this revelation under the rug as if it never occurred.

Chapter 26

From Bad to Worse

August 19, 2015

The UN's nuclear watchdog, the IAEA, has made 2 side deals with Iran and we're beginning to learn some important details on one of the side deals. The IAEA, independent of the P5+1, has agreed to allow Iran to conduct their own inspections at undeclared military sites like Parchin. We know that Iran has used military sites like Parchin to conduct testing in their pursuit of the weaponized use of a nuclear bomb. Secretary of State John Kerry told Congress that they are not entitled to know details of the side deals but Secretary Kerry's possible knowledge regarding details of these deals remains unclear. His solid position is that we should just trust the IAEA which is absurd.

Fox News exclusively uncovered and disclosed some significant details on the side deals that were gleaned from an actual IAEA document they obtained. The IAEA is responding to military concerns on the part of Iran as they believe Iran is entitled to maintain a certain level of secrecy regarding their military operations. All photos, videos and environmental samples will be provided by Iran and Iran will be allowed to use their own monitoring equipment. No Iranian scientists will be required to make themselves available for interviews. At this point you could drive a Mac truck through the holes in the verification process of the Iran nuclear deal. Our knowledge of the Iran nuke deal before we learned of the side deals was sufficient to recognize this is a bad deal but now we've gone **from bad to worse.**

Russian Triad

September 11, 2015

Russian President Vladimir Putin has maintained strong relationships with Iranian President Hassan Rouhani and Syrian President Bashar al-Assad for some time but these long-standing alliances have morphed into an undeclared **triad** formed to prop up Assad in Syria. Assad is an Iranian proxy and as Shiites they are working together to shield Assad from the threat of the Sunni Islamic State in Syria but at this point Russia has entered the picture in Syria in support of Assad and Iran's interests in Syria. The Russian build up in Syria is centered near the port city of Latakia, Syria where Russia is constructing an air base and initially extending an existing runway at Latakia airport to accommodate Russian military transport planes which the U.S. has spotted on satellite photos. Russia has deployed 1500 troops near Latakia, Syria along with 2 tank landing ships loaded with Russian T-90 tanks, anti-aircraft missiles, 8 attack helicopters, 12 transport helicopters, 12 SU-24 attack aircraft, 12 SU-25 ground attack aircraft, 4 flanker fighter jets, armored personnel carriers and surveillance drones. This is the largest Russian foreign deployment since the breakup of the U.S.S.R. under Gorbachev's leadership.

President Obama's failure to effectively fight ISIS in Syria and Iraq has opened the door for Russia to step in and establish a foothold in Syria based on their strong relationship with the Assad regime. Another side effect of President Obama's feckless policies in the Middle East is that U.S. Middle Eastern allies like Saudi Arabia, Egypt, Kuwait, Oman and the UAE are hedging their bets and establishing relationships with Russia because they don't trust the United States to support them. President Obama has effectively forfeited America's status as the Worlds superpower and is allowing Russia to step in and fill the void which Putin is very happy to do. It gives Putin the opportunity to look like the good guy who had the guts to step in and take on ISIS and serves to take the focus away from Russia's takeover of Crimea and Russian aggression in Ukraine. Now that the refugee crisis is having such a profound negative effect on EU countries and other surrounding countries, they will all see Putin as the hero who stepped in to provide relief from the threat that ISIS poses and the landslide of side effects that has so negatively impacted the EU, Hungary, Turkey, and Austria. Putin may help the Assad regime fight ISIS but his primary motivation is to establish a Russian foothold in the Middle East. Putin is making radical changes to the geopolitical landscape in the Middle East all of which benefits Russia and reduces U.S. influence in the region.

Love and Mercy

September 24, 2015

Pope Francis arrived in Washington DC yesterday for the first time in his life as he embarks on an historic mission of **Love and Mercy** in the United States. President Obama received him at the White House and they met privately together while he was there. Today Pope Francis became the first Pope to speak to a joint session of Congress in the House chamber. Later this afternoon the Pope will travel to New York City where he will address the General Assembly at the U.N. in the morning and will visit the 9/11 memorial and museum at ground zero in lower Manhattan adjacent to 1 World Trade Center in the afternoon. Pope Francis will make several additional stops along the way in New York City and will hold Mass in several locations while he's there. The Pope will travel on to Philadelphia on Saturday 9/26 for the final stop on his visit to America. So far on this trip he has touched the lives of Americans in a very special way.

I was somewhat apprehensive in advance of his arrival to America due to statements the Pope has made on Capitalism, immigration, income inequality and the environment which I first believed to be political commentaries but came to understand through the power of the Holy Spirit that his thoughts on these challenges we face around the world today are based on biblical principles and have no political intent. I believe the Holy Father is misunderstood on these topics and that his comments have been unfairly characterized as being political when in fact they have been largely misinterpreted. I've come to understand that when the Pope is challenging us on Capitalism he isn't roundly condemning Capitalism but his intent is to caution us about the love of money which is totally biblical. When he speaks to income inequality he isn't endorsing government handouts but is reminding us that no one should be deprived the dignity of a job because dignity is something everyone should have access to. When he speaks to immigration he isn't advocating for illegal immigration but is reminding us that everyone can, through the grace of God, make meaningful and productive contributions to society and that all of us are descendants of foreigners or were foreigners before we were afforded to right to live in the land of the free and the home of the brave. When he speaks to the environment I believe he is reminding us that we all bear the responsibility of good stewardship for God's provision of the earth we live in. Good stewardship is also totally biblical and as Pope Francis points out, good stewardship applies not only to the earth itself but to the whole of creation including mankind which expands his admonitions on the environment to include respect and love for one another. His admonition on this issue becomes as simple as the golden rule itself in its call to treat others as we would have them treat us in addition to a respect for the earth we live in with a similar sentiment to treat the environment as we would like the environment to provide comfort and beauty for us. Liberal politicians attempt to twist the Pope's message on the issues of Capitalism, immigration, income inequality and the environment to fit their political agenda but their misguided intent is designed to serve their own selfish interests while the Pope calls us to serve the common good. The Pope also spoke to the sanctity of life and to the God ordained institution of marriage between one man and one woman so he proves to be an equal opportunity vessel of truth as he admonishes both liberals and conservatives. Unfortunately, liberals conveniently overlook the Pope's message on abortion and same sex marriage because it's in opposition to their ideology.

I believe the Pope's overall message is one of Love, Mercy, Forgiveness and Giving, but above all else, Love. I believe his intent is to shed **light** on these challenges and to suggest that all of us should approach these challenges with a frame of mind centered in Christ! This is a very different message from the one liberal politicized people attempt to convey. The Pope hasn't offered any specific political solutions or policy recommendations to address these challenges but offers a message centered in **Love and Mercy** that we must all take and work through with the help of the Holy Spirit which can be enhanced through a deep and intimate love relationship with Christ! The Pope's visit prompted me to seek wisdom and understanding from God so it is my prayer that all Americans will be inclined in a similar manner to draw closer to Christ and that such an inclination would be heightened by the Pope's visit to America.

As a non-denominational Bible believing Christian I insist that everything must be able to be reconciled through God's word and I have found that this Pope's message is completely consistent with the truth of God's word and that when his message is viewed through the lens of the Bible, the Holy Spirit will provide understanding which could lead to meaningful spiritual growth. Now that I've been provided a closer look at Pope Francis, I see nothing but love emanating from him. The Pope's role is to comfort the afflicted and to afflict the comfortable. He pricks our collective conscience and takes us out of our comfort zone to lead us on a path of spiritual growth and a deeper reliance on Christ as we confront the challenges we face in the world today.

Russian Demarche

October 1, 2015

A Russian 3 Star General entered the U.S. Embassy in Baghdad, Iraq yesterday and delivered a **demarche** or written diplomatic appeal to an American defense staffer one hour prior to Russia conducting air strikes on moderate Syrian rebels of the Free Syrian Army over Hama, Syria in the Homs province which is in western Syria far from ISIS controlled areas in eastern Syria. The demarche warned the United States to immediately pull all military personnel and warplanes out of Syria. Russia conducted additional air strikes over Talbiseh, Syria today which is also in Homs province again targeting moderate Syrian rebels who are of course Bashar al-Assad's enemies. Russia falsely claims their air strikes over Syria are only targeting ISIS sites. The Syrian rebels under attack were trained by the C.I.A. so the United States has a vested interest in these foreign fighters and should be taking steps to protect them but has failed to do so. Secretary of State John Kerry delivered a statement from the U.N. yesterday and delivered the message that the United States will not withdraw from Syria and that we will continue air strikes on ISIS targets in Syria along with U.S. coalition allies. Later in the day Secretary Kerry appeared with Russian Foreign Minister Sergey Lavrov at the U.N. to confirm the Russian activity in Syria. Secretary Kerry appeared to be weak and confused while Minister Lavrov was decisive and strong. Shortly after this message was delivered Secretary of Defense Ash Carter held a press conference at the Pentagon and basically announced no consequences for Russian air strikes over Syria. Secretary Carter's muddled and weak statements on this issue should come as no surprise given the Obama administrations feckless foreign policies.

The Russian air strikes over Syria are humiliating for the United States and represent Russian contempt for the United States so it's difficult to reconcile Secretary Carter's weak comments. In addition, Russia's air strikes on Homs province occurred only one day after President Obama's 90-minute meeting at the U.N. with Vladimir Putin which was portrayed to be productive on reaching an understanding between the 2 leaders on Russia's military presence in western Syria. This just adds insult to injury for the United States because Putin cleverly makes President Obama look naïve and deceived which was surely by design. President Obama should have been better prepared for this type of Russian deception which they are known for because they frequently say one thing and do another but President Obama's practice of leading from behind once again left him caught off guard.

The United States has also learned that Iranian Kuds force troops are now in Syria to fight the moderate Syrian rebels of the Free Syrian Army on the ground but they will also serve as spotters on the ground to help coordinate targeting for Russian air strikes. The only response from the Obama administration has been to hold deconfliction talks with Moscow in an attempt at airspace coordination over Syria to avoid unintended engagement in the air. A video teleconference call took place today between the Pentagon and Moscow to facilitate deconfliction talks. Turkey, France and the United States have all been conducting air strikes on ISIS targets in Syria so the entry of Russian aircraft into Syrian airspace presents a crucial need to coordinate the use of that airspace. Deconfliction talks are welcomed by Russia because it serves as deflection from Russia's military incursion in Syria and represents U.S. acceptance of Russia's efforts to prop up the Assad regime in Syria. ISIS may eventually become a target of Russian air strikes but not until Russia effectively takes out the moderate Syrian rebels who oppose Assad. The Obama administration should have established a no fly zone a long time ago over certain areas of Syria to create safe zones for moderate Syrian rebels but no such effort has been made. Russian military leaders in Moscow are surely breaking out the vodka and caviar in celebration.

October 2, 2015

Russia made it clear today that they are very serious about their mission in Syria which is designed to prop up the Assad regime. Russian planes carried out 18 new air strikes over Idlib and Aleppo provinces plus strikes again over the city of Hama, Syria. ISIS does maintain a presence in Aleppo province but moderate Syrian rebels also have a presence there. There are no ISIS militants in Idlib province or in the city of Hama in Homs province so the Russian air strikes are targeting moderate Syrian rebels for the most part. It appears that Russia's strategy is to take out all opposition to the Assad regime in Syria beginning with the moderate Syrian rebels of the Free Syrian Army and then ISIS after that but by taking out the moderate rebels first, Russia can make the case that the Assad regime should be supported to take out ISIS.

Deafening Silence

October 1, 2015

Israeli Prime Minister Benjamin Netanyahu addressed the General Assembly at the U.N. today and delivered an eloquent but powerful 46-minute message. The speech was Netanyahu's wake up call for a complacent world. He scolded the entire general assembly over anti-Israel bashing and reminded them that Israel is civilizations front line to fight barbarism in the Middle East. He spoke to the reality of Israel's fight for its very existence and reminded them that best intentions don't prevent the worst outcomes. He spoke of Iran's global terror network and said the U.N. must make sure Iranian violations aren't swept under the Persian rug and that all nations must work together to destroy Iran's global terror network. He boldly vowed that Israel will not remain passive on genocidal dangers and will speak out against it. He reminded the world that the Jewish people know the consequences of remaining silent when he said, "Throughout our history the Jewish people have learned the heavy price of silence." He went on to criticize members of the general assembly when he said, "The response from this body, the response from nearly every one of the governments represented here has been absolutely nothing. Utter silence! **Deafening silence!**" After this he paused for 45 seconds and directed a steely gaze upon members of the body which was incredibly powerful as it emphasized this point and most likely created either discomfort or anger among his audience. He went on to say, "If Iran's rulers were working to destroy your countries, perhaps you'd be less enthusiastic about the deal."

Prime Minister Netanyahu vowed that, "Israel will not allow Iran to break in, sneak in or walk into the nuclear weapons club." Also in response to threats from Iran of Death to Israel he said, "Your plan to destroy Israel will fail. Israel will not permit any force on earth to threaten its future." Then directing his criticism back onto the general assembly members, he said, "When it comes to the annual bashing of Israel at the United Nations, its déjà vu all over again. Enough! When will the United Nations finally check its anti-Israel fanaticism at the door?" To emphasize this point he said, "Yet last year this assembly adopted 20 resolutions against Israel and just 1 resolution about the savage slaughter in Syria. Talk about injustice! Talk about disproportionality! Twenty! Count them. One against Syria!"

It was incredibly refreshing to hear the truth from a true leader which is something we've been deprived of in the United States for almost 7 years now. We can only hope and pray we survive for one more year when, God willing, the United States will once again receive the benefit of true leadership. At this point in the lead up to the 2016 Presidential election, Democrats have failed to offer up a true leader but there are several Republicans in the field who could provide the critically needed trait of true leadership.

Prime Minister Netanyahu must walk a tight rope to navigate U.S. relations while dealing with reality simultaneously. It was incredible to see an empty desk where Samantha Powers, U.S. Ambassador to the U.N., normally sits while Netanyahu addressed the General Assembly. This was obviously a deliberate insult by the Obama administration which possesses such unbelievable disdain for Israel.

Search for the Truth

October 22, 2015

The House Select Committee on Benghazi chaired by Congressman Trey Gowdy held a televised hearing today to question Hillary Clinton in their **search for the truth** on the failures of the State Department to provide adequate security for American diplomats serving in Benghazi, Libya and their failure to mount a U.S. military response and rescue effort once our diplomatic mission there came under attack on 9/11/2012. The simplest and least expensive solution would have been to just temporarily bring our people in Benghazi home considering the anniversary of 9/11 which is exactly what the British and the Red Cross did in Benghazi! Hillary Clinton was Secretary of State at the time so she has a lot to answer for since the terrorist attack on our diplomatic mission in Benghazi happened on her watch. The Obama administration mounted a cover up after the attack which continues to provide an effective smokescreen designed to hide the truth from the American people because the Nov. 2012 election was only 2 months away and President Obama's reelection mantra that "GM is alive, Osama bin Laden is dead and Al Qaeda is on the run" wouldn't ring true if the American people knew that an Al Qaeda inspired terrorist attack took place on our diplomatic mission and C.I.A. annex in Benghazi. The Arab Spring was supposed to represent a decline in Islamic terrorism and the ouster of Gaddafi in Libya was supposed to be good news so with the election on the horizon President Obama didn't want the truth to be known. They were also concerned with offending the fledgling new Libyan government that replaced Gaddafi because they didn't want to steal any thunder from them.

In addition to the security deficiencies and the failure to mount a rescue effort in Benghazi, the Obama administration doesn't want the American people to know that the C.I.A. was involved in a gun running operation in Libya. The C.I.A., at the behest of Secretary Clinton's State Department, maintained a post in Benghazi to facilitate the collection of arms left behind by Gaddafi after his ouster to sell the weaponry to Qatar who would in turn send the weapons to Syrian rebels and they were also selling weaponry including Mortar to Libyan rebels. It's important to note that the Obama administration utilizes the label "rebels" as a ruse as it's nothing more than a cleaned-up word for Islamist terrorists. Given the complexities of the various sects throughout the Middle East, they are frequently at odds with one another. For instance, of the various Sunni terrorist sects in Syria many are indeed fighting against the al-Assad regime in southern Syria but others are supporting ISIS in the north since they too are Sunni. The Shia terrorist sects in Syria support the al-Assad regime for the most part and are fighting against ISIS but of course both Bashar al-Assad, given his association with not only Iran but also Russia, and ISIS are all bad guys.

Ahmed Abu Khatallah, a terrorist aligned with the Ansar al-Sharia militia group in Libya, is suspected of orchestrating and carrying out the attack on the U.S. Diplomatic Compound and the C.I.A. annex in Benghazi. The attack was a strategically planned professional hit. The Islamist terrorists who carried out the attack were highly trained and capable of expert mortar targeting. Three mortars fired from half a mile away made a direct hit on the C.I.A. annex which killed Navy Seals Glen Doherty and Tyrone Woods during the second wave of the attack and to pour salt in the wound, they were using 120 mm Mortar purchased from the Clinton State Department facilitated by CIA contractors so Hillary Clinton provided the weaponry that killed Woods and Doherty. Ambassador Christopher Stevens and Communications Specialist Sean Smith were killed at the Diplomatic Compound in Benghazi during the first wave of the attack. Based on these revelations, the assertion by the Obama administration that the attack was a protest in response to a You Tube video that escalated out of control has been exposed as a lie to cover up the truth. A spontaneous protest wouldn't consist of heavily armed and highly trained Islamist terrorists capable of executing a devastating attack that killed 4 Americans.

During the hearing on Capitol Hill today Congressman Jim Jordan (R-OH) presented a copy of an e-mail that then Secretary of State Hillary Clinton sent to her daughter Chelsea about 3 or 4 hours after the attack in Benghazi which clearly stated the attack was "not a protest" and that it was an Al Qaeda like terrorist attack that took place. Congressman Jordan also presented the transcript of a phone conversation between Hillary Clinton and the Prime Minister of Egypt that took place the day after the attack which confirmed that the attack was not an out of control protest in response to a You Tube video and that it was in fact an Al Qaeda like terrorist attack. These communiques don't line up with the video story which Hillary Clinton maintained 4 days after the attack when she told Gold Star families of the victims that she would find the producer of the video and throw him in jail. Susan Rice who was serving as the U.S. Ambassador to the UN at the time of the attack took to the airwaves days after the attack and appeared on 5 Sunday morning talk shows to advance the video cover up story. Now that we know then Secretary of State Hillary Clinton confirmed the attack was "not a protest" in response to a You Tube video the very day after the attack, it clearly discredits the video story that was maintained by the Obama administration for months after the attack. After 8 years of "Liar in Chief" Barak Obama, America doesn't need another "Liar in Chief" in Hillary Clinton who is currently campaigning to become the Democrat nominee for the 2016 Presidential election.

The House Select Committee on Benghazi is made up of 7 Republicans and 5 Democrats. Elijah Cummings (D-MD) is the ranking Democrat on the committee and is an extremely partisan Democrat so he doesn't care about revealing the truth because it could harm Hillary's Presidential aspirations. Three of the remaining Democrats on the committee line up with Elijah Cummings but Tammy Duckworth (D-IL) who also serves as a Lt. Colonel in the Army National Guard appears to be genuinely interested in discovering the truth about the attack on our

Diplomatic Mission in Benghazi on 9/11/2012. Tammy was serving in Iraq when her UH-60 Black Hawk helicopter was hit by a rocket propelled grenade on 11/12/2004 and she lost both legs in the attack so the fact that 2 Navy Seals were killed in the Benghazi attack apparently doesn't sit well with her. All 7 Republicans on the committee are committed to revealing the truth. This committee conducts most of their hearings behind closed doors and would have held the Hillary Clinton hearing behind closed doors but Hillary requested that her hearing be televised. Their work is not done yet as they still need to question several other pertinent people including Gen. David Petraeus and former Secretary of Defense Robert Gates.

Democrats were praising Hillary for her performance during the hearing because she managed to remain calm and collected for the most part throughout the long day. She did lose her patience at one point when she angrily declared, "what difference, at this point, does it make!" The FBI was surely watching this hearing with great interest because they are conducting a criminal investigation on Hillary Clinton to investigate her use of an unsecure private e-mail server for all e-mail correspondence while serving as Secretary of State which was highly irresponsible and against rules established by the Obama administration. The results of the FBI investigation could be very damaging to Hillary Clinton's campaign in her bid to occupy the oval office in 2017 but the Obama administration may attempt to obstruct the FBI investigation because the results could be damaging to President Obama as well as Hillary Clinton so there's no guarantee we'll ever get to the truth regarding Hillary's role in the Benghazi cover up and her use of an unsecure private e-mail server. Both the House Select Committee on Benghazi and the FBI investigation will be a cloud hanging over Hillary Clinton's Presidential campaign for some time and only time will tell if the truth ever comes out or not.

Game Changer

November 13, 2015

The world changed overnight after ISIS terrorists committed the worst attack on French soil since World War II. France is America's oldest ally. France gifted the "Statue of Liberty" to America. America grieves with the French people over these horrendous attacks. The attacks in Paris overnight were highly coordinated multipronged attacks that left 129 dead and 352 injured, 100 of which are in critical condition. There were 6 coordinated attacks around the city with ISIS terrorists using Kaleshnikov AK-47 assault rifles, explosive vests utilized by suicide bombers and Grenades. It was a low-tech assault that was nevertheless devastating due to the highly-coordinated planning. These attacks were highly premeditated and required a sophisticated support structure. The terrorists utilized passports form Egypt, France and Syria to enter France. One gunman was a French radical who posed as a Syrian refugee. French President Francois Hollande has declared a "state of emergency" in France for the first time since 2005 and closed French borders. Basically, the State has taken complete control of the country. Subway systems have been shut down along with the air space over Paris and the State can enter any home at any time without a warrant. The Eiffel Tower and the Louvre were closed. This is the first time since 1944 that Paris has been essentially shut down with a mandatory curfew in place. He also declared the terrorist attacks to be an "act of war." After the most devastating attack on Paris since World War II, 1500 French troops have been deployed in Paris. France is at the highest security level in their history. In a televised interview, earlier in the day before the attacks broke out in Paris, President Obama declared that ISIS has been contained in Iraq and that yes, they move in and out of Syria but that they haven't moved beyond the region so he implied that beyond Iraq and Syria ISIS really doesn't pose a threat. I bet he'd like to have a do over on that one! ISIS Jihadists recently placed a bomb on a Russian commercial flight that took off from Sharm al-Sheik airport in Egypt and then blew up over the Sinai desert killing all 219 Russians on board, then they perpetrated a deadly suicide bombing in Beirut, Lebanon and now we're dealing with the Paris attacks. All those locations are beyond Iraq or Syria. President Obama is feckless and has his head stuck in the Arabian sands.

The deadliest attack occurred at Bataclan concert hall where a sold-out crowd of young fans were enjoying the "Eagles of Death Metal," a band from California. The promoter and marketing director for the band perished in the attack. Victims were literally shot one by one while the terrorists yelled "Allah Akbar" and declared "this is for Syria." One of the terrorists was quoted as having said, "What are you doing in Syria, you're going to pay now." Security was light at the concert hall due to the limited notoriety of the band. It only took 4 terrorists to inflict such devastation on so many. Five additional attacks took place at various locations around Paris. At 9:20PM Paris time, a suicide bomber detonated an explosive vest she was wearing outside the Soccer stadium in Paris. At 9:25PM an attack occurred in the 10th district of Paris when gunmen in rented vehicles opened fire on patrons of Sidewalk Bistros that left 15 dead. One American perished in the Bistro attack. 23-year old Nohemi Gonzalez who was participating in an International exchange program in Paris was shot and killed while innocently sitting at a sidewalk Bistro. Nohemi was a student at Cal State Long Beach and was spending a semester studying in Paris. This vibrant young life was snuffed out in an instant by barbaric ISIS Jihadists. At 9:30PM a second suicide bomber detonated his explosive vest outside the Soccer stadium. At 9:36PM a car bomb in a black Fiat that was registered in Belgium exploded in another Paris Restaurant district killing 19. At 9:42 4 gunmen opened fire at the Bataclan concert hall killing 89 in the deadliest attack. At 9:53 a 3rd suicide bomber detonated his explosive vest outside the Soccer stadium. The Soccer stadium suicide bombers attempted to enter the stadium to facilitate more destruction but thankfully failed to do so. These terrorists wore no masks or hoods while perpetrating their evil terrorist acts. 4 of the attackers were killed by authorities and 3 more died at their own hand when they blew themselves up. It only took 7 men and 1 woman to carry out these attacks. 1 is still at large. The professionalism of the terrorists is very disturbing. This was the most sophisticated terrorist attack on Western soil since 9/11/2001. No chatter was picked up prior to the attack most likely due to the encryption apps now being utilized by the terrorists. This one was totally missed by every counter-terrorism operation that exists around the world.

Stunning

November 16, 2015

Stunning new developments coming out of Turkey and France this morning. President Obama held a press conference from the G20 summit in Antalya, Turkey while President Hollande addressed his parliament from the Congress of France in Versailles, France. President Obama announced no change to the current failed strategy of containment in Syria and Iraq and no change to our current rules of engagement which are way too restrictive on our military. He doubled down on the critical need to sooner rather than later allow 10,000 Syrian refugees to enter the United States and implied the need to take in more after that. The vetting process is virtually impossible because there is no data base in Syria that would provide the necessary baseline and intelligence to work from. America does possess ownership revolving around actions we've taken in Syria and Iraq and we do have a humanitarian responsibility to the refugees but if we can't properly vet these people then we are opening ourselves up to significantly increased threats of attacks on our soil. President Obama called the Paris attacks "a setback" and spoke vaguely about stepping up counter terrorism initiatives. He is not providing the necessary leadership needed to sufficiently motivate our allies to strengthen their efforts. He made no admission of the serious missteps his administration has made. He didn't address the fact that we've been unable to break encryption technology utilized by ISIS called "Telegram" which has been so critical to the success they're having. Play Station 4 gives them another communication platform because it utilizes Pier systems for communication. This pier to pier communication can't be detected by law enforcement. They have the capability to go dark which leaves us in the dark! He didn't address the 900 open FBI investigations underway at home which FBI director, James Comey, warned about just prior to the Paris attacks because these open investigations represent 900 loose ends in the United States. When President Obama was pressed by the media for a stronger response he became agitated and animated. This is a clear sign of his narcissism. His demeanor was such that he was clearly upset as if to say, how dare you question me! ISIS released a new 11 minute video this morning that warned of eminent attacks in Washington DC and new attacks across Europe soon. We are in a stalemate with ISIS as they prepare to strike on U.S. soil but President Obama sees no need to do anything different! We are fighting Islamic ideology so we can't afford to view this challenge through a traditional western lens that is based in past conventional warfare. We're involved in a global war on terrorism. The Obama administration is back stepping when they should be escalating the efforts of the United States!

In contrast to President Obama's feckless response, French President Francois Hollande delivered a truly strong address to his parliament. He announced specific and dramatic escalations to their counterterrorism efforts and called the Paris attacks an "act of war." He addressed the pain of the French people which President Obama failed to do. France mounted powerful new air strikes overnight over Syria in a significantly increased effort to combat ISIS. French air strikes last night focused on ISIS sites at their base of operations in Raqqa, Syria. The United States averages 7 ineffectual air strikes a day compared to hundreds daily during the Iraq war. 3 out of 4 of these sorties return to their base with their ordnance remaining on board the plane due to the rigorous rules of engagement.

President Hollande strongly suggested to his parliament that they pass legislation for a 3-month extension to the French state of emergency currently in place. He spoke to the additional funding it will take to accomplish his goals. He acknowledged that the threat of ISIS can be extinguished and promised a "pitiless" response from France. He displayed true leadership! Today President Hollande has the full support of the French people. No previous French President has ever come out swinging and displaying a more hawkish response than the President of the United States to the threats that both countries face. This historic development is **stunning** and precedent setting.

November 17, 2015

The investigation into these attacks by France and their allies including the United States has yielded some valuable intelligence in their pursuit to identify the perpetrators of the Paris attacks. They've learned that Abdelhamid Abaaoud, a tactical ISIS commander, was the mastermind of the Paris attacks on the ground and have discovered an apartment in Brussels, Belgium where Abaaoud and 2 additional terrorists were staying and where they planned the Paris attacks. This was a self-contained ISIS terrorist cell and Abaaoud was responsible for maintaining the cell structure of this cell.

November 18, 2015

An overnight raid was conducted at a Paris suburban apartment in Saint-Denis where authorities believed 28-year old Abdelhamid Abaaoud was hiding out. A serious firefight erupted and once the smoke cleared from the 5000 rounds fired into that apartment and a bomb explosion that rocked the building when a female terrorist in the apartment blew herself up, authorities discovered that Abaaoud was indeed there and was killed in the raid. Authorities learned that an attack on the Paris business district was being planned there. So far 60 arrests have been made in over 400 raids that have been conducted by authorities in Paris. They've confiscated 75 weapons including a rocket propelled grenade launcher.

November 19, 2015

Nine raids conducted in Brussels, Belgium overnight yielded the detention of 9 suspects believed to be associated with the Paris attacks. Authorities have learned that Abdelhamid Abaaoud was moving freely between Belgium, France and Syria. Europe has open borders so no passport is required to travel between countries in Europe but Abaaoud's ability to move freely in and out of Syria is quite disturbing. Authorities have also learned the identity of the 8th terrorist who is still at large after the Paris attacks. His name is Salah Abdeslam and as it turns out there was a 9th participant named Mohamed Abrini who was the driver of a 2nd Black Fiat used in the Bistro attack. Authorities are still in pursuit of these 2 terrorists.

November 20, 2015

An Al Qaeda affiliated group conducted attacks this morning at the Radisson Blu hotel in Bamako, Mali. Mali is a French speaking former French colony in West Africa. 27 people died in this attack including 1 U.S. citizen. The terrorists held 124 people as hostages in the hotel for several hours but released all of them that afternoon but not until 27 had been killed previously. When Al Qaeda is witness to the kind of success ISIS just experienced in Paris, they see their relevance in decline so they go on the offensive to save face and maintain their relevance as a powerful terrorist network as they engage in Jihad Olympics that create multiple attacks by competing terrorist networks in quick succession of one another.

Chapter 27

Islamic Jihad in America

December 3, 2015

Islamic Jihad raised its ugly head today in San Bernardino, CA. when a married couple viciously attacked innocent American's who had gathered for a Christmas office party. Syed Farook and his wife Tashfeen Malik stormed into the office party wearing tactical gear and immediately opened fire on the unarmed people there with AR-15 semi-automatic long rifles. They quickly murdered 14 people and seriously injured 21 others. The Muslim duo made it in and out in short order but nevertheless left 14 dead in the wake of their evil Islamic terrorist attack. The attack took place at the San Bernardino Inland Regional Center where employees of the county were celebrating their Christmas office party. Syed Farook had been employed by the county for several years as a health inspector who inspected restaurants for cleanliness standards, hence his knowledge of the office Christmas party. A few hours after the attack authorities responded to a report of a black SUV that fit the description of the vehicle used to escape the scene of the pairs evil rampage. Once authorities caught up with the black SUV a firefight ensued and a short time later the terrorists lay dead in the rented vehicle.

A raid on the couple's home in Redlands, CA. yielded a cache of weapons that was quite alarming. The home was a virtual bomb factory where FBI agents discovered 12 pipe bombs, remote control cars used as detonation devices, thousands of rounds of ammunition, several guns and a few go-pro cameras. The detonation devices and pipe bombs were signature Al Qaeda in terms of their makeup. The FBI confiscated computers and 2 phones all of which the couple had attempted to destroy. The phones were found in a dumpster behind the home. FBI forensic experts are presently working to recover data from the computers and phones. 2 handguns had been legally purchased by Syed but the rifles were obtained through an illegal straw purchase by a longtime friend of Farook's. The rifles were semi-automatic but had been altered with a mechanism that converts the weapon to fully automatic mode. This mechanism failed to function properly during the attack otherwise the carnage could have been even worse. FBI agents estimated the cost of the weaponry discovered in the home to be about $30,000. which would have been prohibitively expensive for a couple living on Syed's county salary.

Syed Farook was a U.S. citizen born in Chicago to Pakistani parents. He was raised in southern California. Syed Farook met Tashfeen Malik on-line and then traveled to her home in Pakistan where they met in person for the first time. Tashfeen Malik has been tied to a radical Mosque in Pakistan. Malik was raised in Pakistan but her parents had moved to Saudi Arabia where she would visit them frequently. Sunni Wahhabi's known for Islamic terrorist activities direct operations throughout the Middle East from their base in Saudi Arabia. Farook and Malik traveled to Mecca in Saudi Arabia where they became engaged to be married and then Tashfeen Malik successfully traveled to the U.S. legally on a K-1 fiancee Visa in July of 2014. The couple married in Riverside, CA. a month later. They had an infant daughter of 6 months who Tashfeen dropped off with Syed's parents before their murderous rampage. Only radical ideology would motivate a mother to abandon her baby to commit Jihad. Farook attended Mosque every day first in Riverside and later at a San Bernardino Mosque after he moved to the home in Redlands, CA. FBI agents quickly discovered that Tashfeen Malik had pledged allegiance to ISIS on a Facebook page shortly before the attack was carried out.

The blood was barely dry at the scene and few details had been released when President Obama issued a statement calling for much stronger gun control measures. California has some of the strongest gun control laws in the country which failed to prevent this violent act of Islamic Jihad. The President said, "We're going to have to, I think, search ourselves as a society to make sure that we can take basic steps that would make it harder... for individuals to get access to weapons." He also said, "We do not yet know why this terrible event occurred," and eluded to workplace violence but of course this was only minutes after the first reports were issued through the media. He later had to adjust his messaging and only went as far as calling it violent extremism. Shortly after President Obama issued his initial statements, Presidential candidate Hillary Clinton expressed similar sentiments during a campaign speech when she made impassioned pleas for tighter gun control measures. The President's misguided response displays his complete disregard for the evils of Islamic Jihad that threaten our very way of life in America! Tighter gun control measures don't even come close to addressing the serious threat America is facing today. There are almost 300 million guns in the hands of Americans today. The Jihadists already have their weapons. They're only waiting for their opportunity to murder more innocent Americans!

December 4, 2015

An overnight raid on the Riverside, CA. home of Enrique Marquez, a longstanding friend of Syed Farook, was executed last night. Authorities believe that Marquez purchased the rifles used by Farook and Malik in their recent attack. This is of course an illegal straw purchase. Marquez allegedly purchased the rifles 3 years ago. Marquez and Farook were childhood friends and at that time even lived next door to one another in Riverside, CA. prior to Farook's move to Redlands, CA. FBI agents didn't disclose their findings in the Marquez home.

Authorities did reveal today that Tashfeen Malik had been communicating with an ISIS recruiter named Mohamed Hassan who was formerly living in the U.S. but has since left the country. FBI agents are conducting a search to find Hassan.

December 6, 2015

President Obama addressed the nation from the White House this evening supposedly to alleviate fears of **Islamic Jihad in America**. He failed miserably! It had been announced through the media that this would be an oval office address but the American people saw him standing in a confined space with a couple of flags behind him that could have been in the basement of the White House. The President got off to a pretty-good start sounding strong and determined during the first 7 minutes but we didn't hear anything new. He then took a very sharp left turn and went downhill from there as he launched into a tirade on gun control. He also scolded Republicans in Congress criticizing them for not accomplishing anything but of course the President and Senate minority leader Harry Reid have successfully blocked any productive legislation Republicans attempt to pass. The President failed to offer any substantive solutions as he focused on politics. He accused Americans of launching a war on Islam but no one has ever even suggested such a thing. He spoke of "tiny fractions of radicals" which is delusional. No one really knows how many Muslims embrace radical forms of Islam but it's obviously a whole lot more than a tiny fraction. He admonished Americans to reject any criticism of Islam. He spoke of one nation, one people with common ideals stressing we're all equal but coming from the most divisive President in our history his message fell flat. His tone and messaging was very defensive overall. He didn't offer any change to his existing strategy which can barely be defined as a strategy. If Americans had established any expectation of a strong response from President Obama, they were left very disappointed.

Showmanship

January 5, 2016

President Obama held a political pep rally to torch the Constitution at the White House today. The President is once again unilaterally writing law with a new executive action on gun control. The President's announcement on new gun control measures was quite dramatic as he wiped away tears at key moments. Where was this emotion after the Paris terrorist attacks or the San Bernardino terrorist attack? Today's emotion was pure **showmanship**. President Obama never displays emotion over Islamic Jihad but his demeanor changes dramatically when addressing tragic shootings by mentally ill people. Apparently lives lost at the hands of the Sandy Hook shooter, the Aurora, CO. theater shooter, the Charleston, SC. Church shooter among others are the only lost lives deserving of emotion but lives lost at the hands of Islamic Jihadists aren't worth shedding a tear over. The President was surrounded by family members of shooting victims associated with killings by mentally ill people but no family members of victims who died due to Islamic Jihad were present today.

The gun control measures in this executive action would have done nothing to prevent any of the mass shootings that have occurred in the past and would only place a hardship on law abiding American gun owners. This executive action goes far beyond the President's authority because the new licensing requirements in this action were proposed and rejected by Congress 3 times. Once Congress exhausts their ability to change the law in a specific way it becomes a dead issue. The President can't follow up with executive action that contradicts the will of the people as expressed through the efforts of Congress. The President is usurping the role of Congress as he unilaterally writes law which is completely unconstitutional. He has created a new crime and new law with this executive action. There are also serious concerns over the mental health provisions in this executive action because they pave the way for government abuse of sane law abiding gun owners who could arbitrarily be declared to be incompetent to own a gun. This is an assault on the 2nd amendment, the separation of powers and the Constitution itself. I expect this executive action on gun control will be blocked in federal court just as the Presidents illegal executive action on immigration was blocked by the 5th U.S. Circuit Court of Appeals in New Orleans, LA.

Disconnected

January 12, 2016

President Obama delivered his final State of the Union address this evening from the House chamber of the Capital. He delivered an ideological legacy speech that was very political and **disconnected** from reality! There were two things to be thankful for though as this was the shortest of the 8 SOTU addresses he's delivered and it's the last one we'll ever have to sit through. The President had the nerve to call for unity in the country when he's been the most divisive President in the history of our great nation. He made one truthful statement when he said "this is a time of extraordinary change" but he failed to acknowledge that all this change has been destructive and has only angered most Americans and left them with nothing more than the hope that one day we can right the ship before it sinks. The President was critical of what he called "the unwarranted pessimism" that exists in the country. He was completely unleashed as he lectured the American people while embellishing his legacy. His true legacy is one of destruction that has left America a much weaker nation than we were before he took office. We're $19 trillion in debt, the workforce participation rate is only at about 60%, the economy has only seen stagnant 1% to 2% annual growth, we're more vulnerable than ever to Islamic terrorist attacks and the nation is more divided than ever. Of course, the President didn't mention any of these realities in his address because he has a serious aversion to reality.

This was an address with plenty of smoke and mirrors as the President set up one strawman after another to take our eyes off the shiny ball in the middle of it all. The big picture of that shiny ball we're not supposed to see is one of all the problems and challenges we now face that were effectively swept under the rug and left to grow and fester during President Obama's 2 terms. We're faced with a serious amount of debt, high unemployment, low wages, a serious deficiency of full time employment, and the threat of Islamic Jihad as the Middle East spirals out of control. Iran chose the day of the President's SOTU address to apprehend 10 U.S. sailors in the Persian Gulf who ventured into Iranian waters while traveling from Kuwait to Bahrain on 2 U.S. Naval Riverine vessels. Iran shot a video of these sailors stripped of their weapons and shown on their knees with their hands clasp behind their heads in their vessel. This video is intended to show Americans in surrender to Iran representing Iran with the upper hand over America. Of course, Iran showed the video to the world because the weakness and naivete' of the Obama administration gives Iran the ability to humiliate America with complete impunity. The President made no mention of this event during his SOTU address but did make the claim of avoiding war with Iran due to the nuclear deal that was spearheaded by his administration.

The President spoke of many accomplishments when he made questionable claims of economic recovery, health care reform, strength on terrorism, same sex marriage, veterans who are well cared for and renewed relations with Cuba. He took credit for cheap gas and took credit for stamping out the Ebola epidemic. He spoke of the need for immigration reform and the need to focus on inequality. He attacked capitalism and spoke of recklessness on Wall Street. He warned of the dangers of global warming. He went on to lecture us over Muslim criticism as he launched into a lengthy defense of Islam. He said ISIS doesn't present a significant threat to the U.S. and vowed to shut down the detention facility at Guantanamo Bay in Cuba. He lectured Americans over what he called a lack of civility and this coming from the most divisive President in history. He made several veiled swipes at Republicans and was critical of a lack of cooperation in Washington. One of the most eyebrow raising statements was when he said, "Our brand of Democracy is hard" which implies that our Democracy doesn't work and should be replaced. This was a speech of lofty rhetoric and was more of a "State of Denial" address than that of the State of the Union.

Focus on Islam

February 4, 2016

President Obama spoke at the National Prayer Breakfast today after making an appearance at the Islamic Center of Baltimore yesterday. It's no surprise that he would be promoting Islam yesterday while speaking at a Mosque but today he continued with a strong **focus on Islam** at the National Prayer breakfast. The President's choice to make an appearance at the Islamic Center of Baltimore raised some eyebrows. Of all the Mosque's he could have chosen, this one is known to be one of the most radical Mosque's in America with a history of having officials connected to Islamic terrorism. This Mosque engages in gender apartheid and calls homosexual's mental deviants. The FBI prepared a file on this Mosque for the President which confirmed their affiliation with the Muslim Brotherhood and the Islamic Society of America another Muslim Brotherhood affiliate. Both support suicide bombers and profess hatred of Israel. This Baltimore Mosque had ties to Imam Anwar al-Awlaki who was the 1st U.S. citizen to be taken out in a drone strike in Yemen on 9/30/11. He was a senior recruiter for Al Qaeda and planned terrorist operations for Al Qaeda.

At the Islamic Center of Baltimore yesterday, the President spoke of distorted impressions of Islam and Muslim persecution. I've never heard this President speak of the highly prevalent Christian persecution by Muslims. He said political rhetoric fuels threats against Muslims while speaking from a Mosque that represents political Islam and when his visit there was clearly being used as a political prop. At the National Prayer breakfast, the President spoke a lot about fear and based on the context of his remarks it was a clear veiled reference to Americans resistance to allowing large numbers of un-vetted Muslim refugees from Syria to indiscriminately enter our country. The President was talking down to these Americans as though they have no real understanding of Islam. President Obama frequently displays this contempt for Americans while talking down to the people as though they're too stupid to formulate their own opinions based on their own personal convictions.

The Empty Seat

February 13, 2016

Supreme Court Justice Antonin Scalia died today while on a quail hunting trip in the Big Bend region of Presidio County in Texas. He is survived by his wife Moreen Scalia. After Justice Scalia failed to show up for breakfast this morning he was found unresponsive in his room. It was announced that his death was the result of a heart attack but no autopsy was performed and conspiracy theories abound that question the cause of death. In the absence of an autopsy we'll never really know the actual cause of death with any real certainty. Justice Scalia was 79 years old upon his death. Justice Scalia was a man of faith who led the conservative wing of the Supreme Court and was a fierce defender of the Constitution. He was an originalist who believed that we should all view the Constitution through the lens of the framers. Liberals see the Constitution as being living, breathing and malleable because they believe it's outdated and they possess a strong desire to radically change it to advance their liberal agenda. Liberals have attacked Americans freedom of speech, freedom of religion, our right to privacy and our right to bear arms while espousing political correctness which is more about silencing their opposition.

Justice Scalia was born in Trenton, New Jersey and was raised in Queens, New York. He was a devout Catholic, an avid hunter and an opera lover. He was incredibly likeable and was known as "Nino" by his closest friends and colleagues. He was a prolific joke teller but was also a highly intellectual jurist. He maintained strong relationships with all his colleagues on the bench. He was best friends with liberal Justice Ginsberg and her husband who share his love of opera. He was also close to liberal Justice Kagan who frequently accompanied him on trips to the shooting range for target practice and even joined him on some hunting trips. Justice Scalia was a luminous figure who was unpretentious, gregarious, loved good food, good wine and a good cigar. He was a strict Constitutionalist, was highly original and was the most eloquent Justice on the Supreme Court. He wrote colorful opinions that will be widely read by law students and others for years to come.

Justice Scalia's untimely death sets the stage for an epic battle in the Senate between Republicans and Democrats regarding the confirmation process of President Obama's replacement nominee. Battle lines have also been drawn between Senate Republicans and the White House. President Obama announced that he will nominate a successor in due time. Senate majority leader Mitch McConnell issued a statement confirming the need to delay confirmation of the President's nominee until 2017 when the next President takes office to give the American people a voice on Justice Scalia's replacement as we go through the election process this year. The Senate has every Constitutional right to refuse confirming any Obama nomination to the Supreme Court because article 2 of the Constitution requires an "advise and consent" role by the Senate as they go through the confirmation process. Senate Democrats wasted no time in leveling obstructionist charges at Senate Republicans.

The empty seat left vacant by Justice Scalia's death has aroused great concern. Obviously, a delay to fill Justice Scalia's vacant seat will create an 8 seat Supreme Court for a year. There is precedent for having an 8 seat Supreme Court for an extended timeframe so it is something that has been effectively dealt with before. Great concern exists over several landmark cases that have already been taken up by the Supreme Court. Looming decisions on immigration action, abortion restrictions, EPA carbon emissions regulations, affirmative action and religious freedoms hang in the balance. The Supreme Court under the leadership of Chief Justice John Roberts has the option to hold cases over until next year or in the instance of 4-4 decisions, they can kick those cases back to the lower federal court that ruled on these cases prior to appeal in which case the original decision by the lower federal court would stand. Democrats are understandably anxious to fill Justice Scalia's vacant seat with a 5th liberal Justice which would stack the deck in favor of liberal decisions by the Supreme Court. If this were to occur, 5-4 decisions would abound that favor liberal initiatives and the conservative wing of the Supreme Court would be rendered virtually powerless to advance any conservative initiatives. The Supreme Court shouldn't be so politically charged but the fact is that this Supreme Court in recent times has been highly politicized with a tendency to legislate from the bench. Republicans are hopeful that the American electorate will elect a Republican President to take over in 2017 who would then nominate a more appropriate replacement to fill Justice Scalia's vacant seat. Battle lines have been drawn as the fight rages on to fill the crucial 9th seat on the Supreme Court.

Totalitarian Ideology

March 10, 2016

Attorney General Loretta Lynch appeared before the Senate Judiciary Committee today and as the hearing progressed she was questioned about possible legal action against climate change deniers in the energy industry. ExxonMobile appears to be the primary target of this outrageous accusation. Lynch said, "We have referred it to the FBI to consider if it meets the criteria we could take action on." This constitutes a serious threat coming from the Obama administration. Climate change isn't settled science as it's still very much in question. Those who believe climate change represents a serious threat to our future like to assert that 97% of scientists agree that climate change is real, man-made and dangerous but the Wall Street Journal recently revealed that this assertion comes from a handful of surveys and abstract exercises in various locals so it's a very weak assertion to cling to.

Lynch confirmed that if action is taken it could come in the form of a civil racketeering prosecution aka a RICO (racketeer influenced and corrupt organization) civil case with the full force of the U.S. government behind it. This possible legal action could be compared to the civil case brought by the Clinton administration that alleged fraud by the tobacco industry. It represents one more attempt by the Obama administration to regulate every aspect of public life and it's also about redistributing wealth. It gives us insight into the **totalitarian ideology** of the Obama administration. It's designed to silence the opposition. The threat alone coming from the DOJ could cause energy companies to think twice about expressing their beliefs. This is an attack on the 1st amendment and is only the beginning of a systematic stripping of our freedoms by liberal Democrats.

Charade

March 21, 2016

President Obama became the first U.S. President to visit Cuba since, 1928 today. The President met with Cuban Communist dictator, Raul Castro today as he attempts to normalize U.S. relations with the Communist country. He's paving the way for American companies to do business in Cuba bringing trade, tourism and even internet access to Cuba. The Castro regime benefits in numerous ways and the United States gets nothing aside from an ability to do a limited amount of business there with little hope for decent profits due to Cuba's strict control over business done there. Raul Castro took advantage of photo ops with our President while standing before a huge mural of the Argentinian Marxist revolutionary, Che Guevara who has been highly revered by the Castro regime in Cuba.

President Obama appeared with the Communist dictator during a press conference after they had met privately together. While the U.S. President touted his efforts to normalize relations with Cuba and the benefits he believes will be positive for both countries, Castro took shots at the United States. The Communist dictator had agreed to answer one question from the press and wound up fielding two but he appeared to be confused as if he was struggling with the English translation. His confused appearance was most likely by design because it enabled him to dodge both questions but he did take the opportunity to criticize America on issues surrounding race relations, health care, poverty, education and human rights all of which are prevalent issues in Cuba but Castro's criticism was purely directed at the United States. When Castro was asked about political prisoners being held in Cuba he asked for a list of names as a dodge but he did deny having any political prisoners in Cuba which we know to be a lie because there are hundreds in Cuban prisons. President Obama said he welcomes Castro's comments. The President's trip to Cuba was a **charade** that only served to embarrass the American people.

New Normal

March 22, 2016

Islamist Jihad strikes again today in Brussels, Belgium with homicide bombings at Brussels Zaventem Airport and the Maelbeek Metro Station killing 35 people including 4 Americans who were at the airport and seriously injuring 230 others including 9 Americans. Two bombs were detonated by homicide bombers at the airport in ticket counter locations where many people were waiting in line to check in for their flight. One bomb was detonated at the metro station about an hour after the explosions at the airport. ISIS claimed responsibility for the attacks. ISIS terrorists have been moving back and forth between Syria and Belgium with ease so it makes sense that ISIS would be involved. The airport in Brussels closed after the attacks and the rest of the city was placed on lockdown. The Sint-Jans-Molenbeek district in Brussels is known as a hotbed of terrorist activity so the Jihadists who committed these terrorist attacks were most likely operating out of this area and authorities began searching homes there shortly after the attacks.

President Obama was still in Cuba when he learned of the terrorist attacks in Brussels. The President was scheduled to address Cuba's Communist leaders today so he devoted all of 51 seconds at the beginning of his talk to address the terrorist attacks in Brussels before moving on to his planned remarks. Later in the day President Obama attended a baseball game in Cuba as Raul Castro's guest where they were spotted on camera doing the wave with the other fans there. The optics of our President laughing and doing the wave with Castro shortly after a devastating terrorist attack on a NATO nation couldn't have been worse. Based on the treaty, an attack on a NATO nation is an attack on all NATO nations so an attack on Belgium equates to an attack on the U.S.

March 23, 2016

President Obama traveled from Cuba to Buenos Aires, Argentina this morning to meet with Communist leaders there. He displayed more concern for climate change than ISIS during his visit there. During a talk to a group of young people in Buenos Aires President Obama spoke to them about differences between capitalism and socialism when he remarked, "For your generation you should be practical and just choose from what works," as if one is no better or worse than the other. He attended a State dinner in Buenos Aires where he was seen on camera doing the tango with a beautiful Argentinian woman. Once again, the optics of our President doing the tango with a hot young Argentinian woman shortly after a terrorist attack on a NATO nation were not good. It appears that President Obama is beginning to treat terrorist attacks around the world as the **new normal** which is more than a little disconcerting.

Debt Dilemma

May 2, 2016

Puerto Rico is $7.2 billion in debt. They have bond payments due today that total $470 million which they are unable to pay so Puerto Rico is now in default on their debt. Socialism in Puerto Rico has led to 46% of their population living below the poverty level. The government in Puerto Rico has followed an unsustainable socialistic path for some time so finding themselves in default on their debt today should come as no surprise but as reality sets in on their self-inflicted economic problem, solutions are in short supply. Of course, they will look to the U.S. federal government to bail them out but the precedent a bail out would establish is the bigger problem. Illinois, Michigan and California are so deep in debt that they too are on the verge of default so if the precedent is set that the U.S. federal government will be there to save the day based on a Puerto Rico bail out, we will find ourselves on a path that will lead to default on our nation's $19 trillion in debt which is not an option. We've seen the result of socialism in Europe and South America and its not pretty. Greece was the first domino to fall but Venezuela and Spain aren't far behind. Socialism is an economic time bomb that should be avoided at all costs but the utopian ideology of socialism is too great an attraction for the short sighted. For the time being Puerto Rico's economic future hangs in the balance as we witness yet one more failed State due to Socialism.

Bathroom Insanity

May 9, 2016

Liberals in America have opened a new can of worms with their insistence that transgender people should be able to use the public bathroom, locker room or shower based on the gender they identify with. The latest statistics on the size of the transgender population in America reveals that only 0.3% of the U.S. population identifies as being transgender. Why would we be so concerned with the public bathroom issues of such a small group of people? I could understand efforts to provide psychological help for these confused individuals but simply insisting that they should be allowed to use the public bathroom based on the gender they supposedly identify with is **bathroom insanity**. Sexual perverts will surely exploit this insane initiative. Why wouldn't liberals be concerned with the safety of young girls using public bathroom facilities who will be preyed upon by male perverts who were permitted to use public women's bathrooms, locker rooms and showers because they were wearing a dress or simply because they claim to identify as female when they are in fact a biological male?

The North Carolina legislature recently passed a bill that was signed into law by Governor Pat McCrory which dictates that individuals must use the public bathroom based on the gender that is on their birth certificate. This launched an earthquake of protests via social media from the liberal left. It should be noted that this bill only applies to public restrooms, locker rooms and showers in public schools, government buildings and highway rest stops. Privately owned businesses are not affected by this legislation. This legislation was in response to a new Charlotte, NC. city ordinance that allowed for transgender individuals to use public bathrooms based on the gender they identify with as opposed to the gender on their birth certificate. North Carolina became the target of highly charged rhetoric coming out of the White House which condemned their action calling it discriminatory. The Obama administration contends that the North Carolina law is discriminatory to transgender individuals in the same way that Jim Crow laws of the 1950's and 60's were discriminatory to black people based on the Civil Rights Act of 1964. Governor McCrory preempted legal action by the federal government by filing suit against the DOJ this morning asking the federal courts to clarify federal law on this issue. Governor McCrory said, "The Obama administration is bypassing Congress by attempting to rewrite the law and set restroom policies for public and private employers across the country, not just North Carolina. This is now a national issue that applies to every state and it needs to be resolved at the federal level."

Attorney General Loretta Lynch responded about 2 hours after Governor McCrory announced the North Carolina law suit against the DOJ when she announced a federal civil rights counter suit filed against North Carolina this morning charging that North Carolina House Bill 2 violates federal law and that it represents state sponsored discrimination. AG Lynch made it clear that the federal government retains the right to withhold billions in federal funding for education and housing that would normally be provided to North Carolina. Many states across the country will surely follow North Carolina's lead as they too file suit against the federal government demanding clarification of federal law on this issue. This litigation should eventually make it to the Supreme Court for final resolution.

May 10, 2016

The White House issued a decree today on the transgender bathroom issue. This wouldn't even be an issue if the White House hadn't made it an issue. This decree which was signed by the DOJ and the Education department issues guidelines that dictate schools must allow individuals to use the bathroom, locker room or shower based on the gender they identify with. The White House decree was sent to every school district in the country and although it isn't law it does threaten to withhold federal education funds from schools who are not in compliance with the decree. The Obama administration bases their position on the manufactured transgender bathroom issue on the Civil Rights Act of 1964 which speaks to gender based discrimination but the words transgender or gender identity cannot be found in the Civil Rights Act of 1964. This law clearly refers to discrimination that targets women and blacks and not mentally ill men who think they're a woman in a man's body.

Massacre

June 12, 2016

The deadliest mass shooting in U.S. history and worst terrorist attack on U.S. soil since 9/11 occurred early this morning at Pulse nightclub in Orlando, Florida. Pulse is the premier gay nightclub in Orlando. It was near last call at about 2:00AM Sunday morning when 29-year old Omar Mateen entered the nightclub and opened fire. This was the beginning of a 3-hour siege as Mateen fired rounds into the crowd from a 223 caliber AR-15 semi-automatic long rifle. Club patrons initially thought the gunfire was part of the music but quickly learned of their horrific plight. There were 320 innocent people inside the club who were just there to relax and enjoy a Saturday night out with friends when an evil Jihadist turned a night of innocent fun into their worst nightmare. The terrorist called 911 at about 2:30AM but initially hung up before speaking to the 911 operator, then he called again and told the 911 operator that he pledged alliance to ISIS and to their leader, Abu Bakr al-Baghdadi, and he also referenced the Tsarnaev brothers (perpetrators of the Boston Marathon bombings) in praise of their evil act. He went on to describe himself as an Islamic soldier of the Caliphate. He falsely claimed he was wearing a suicide vest and that there was a truck outside loaded with explosives that he would detonate if Police entered the nightclub. He also threatened to put suicide vests on 4 of the dead victims.

He condemned U.S. bombings of ISIS in Syria and Iraq and said there would be more attacks in the next few days. The 911 operator attempted to call him back after this call but he didn't answer.

He was yelling Allahu Akbar (Praise Allah) while killing his victims. At one point while many already lay dead the terrorist isolated 30 people and held them hostage for the next 3 hours while he made Facebook posts along with 16 phone calls including the 911 call and sent a text to his wife, Noor Salman. A police hostage negotiator was speaking with Mateen off and on during this time. A few of the Police officers slipped in to remove some of the wounded victims before a swat team entered the club by ramming holes in a rear wall at about 5:00AM then entered and engaged the terrorist in gunfire taking his life and saving the 30 hostages. The terrorist was yelling out his allegiance to ISIS right before police killed him. When the carnage ended at 5:14AM, 49 innocent people lay dead in the nightclub and another 53 people were taken to the hospital with serious injuries. ISIS claimed responsibility for this attack and called Omar Mateen a soldier of the Caliphate. In the end the terrorist lay dead with his spirit already in hell where he will rot for all eternity!

The next day a few of the survivors said they had seen the terrorist in the nightclub having a drink at about 1:00AM so he had obviously been casing the club as he formulated his evil plan prior to the act. He had learned that the only rear exit was locked shut so he knew the only possible exit point was through the front entrance where he stationed himself during the **massacre**. His victims could only escape to one of the bathrooms but he eventually entered the bathrooms where he killed many of his trapped victims. Victims in the bathrooms had been calling and texting family and friends to inform them of their plight and to say their last goodbyes before they were brutally murdered in cold blood.

Omar Mateen was a U.S. citizen who was born in New York to parents who had immigrated to America from Afghanistan in the early 1980's. He lived in Ft. Pierce, Florida. His father, Seddique Mateen, had previously expressed support for the Taliban. His ex-wife, Sitora Yusufiy, told authorities that Omar was unstable, that he beat her frequently and that her parents had to come and rescue her from him. He was currently married to Noor Zahi Salman and they have a 3-year old son. Authorities learned that Salman had driven Mateen to Pulse nightclub for surveillance purposes and had also driven him to Disney world to surveil the amusement park as he was planning an attack there. She also took him to buy ammunition. She admitted to authorities that she knew of Omar's plan to attack Pulse nightclub. A federal grand jury has been convened to consider over 100 counts of murder and attempted murder against Salman. The charge of conspiracy to commit mass murder could lead to the death penalty for Salman. Salman told authorities that Omar was either bi-sexual or gay and authorities also learned that Omar had used a gay dating app and that he had been a patron of Pulse nightclub for over 3 years. He was clearly struggling with demons who tormented him from within. Omar had worked as a security guard for G4S solutions since September of 2007 and was a licensed gun owner. G4S solutions is a large security agency and ironically is a major contractor for the Department of Homeland Security. G4S had done a security screen on Mateen in 2007 and again in 2013 and they advised that no red flags were detected. Mateen purchased the firearms used during the massacre at an Orlando gun store about 1 week prior to the attack. He passed the background check and purchased the AR-15 long gun along with a semi-automatic 9 mm hand gun.

The FBI had opened an investigation on Mateen in May of 2013 that lasted 10 months after Mateen had tormented co-workers with threats of Jihad and then 3 months after the 1st investigation concluded the FBI opened a 2nd investigation in relation to Mateen's relationship with Moner Abu Salah who attended the same eastern Florida Mosque as Mateen. Salah had traveled to Syria where he was associated with the Syrian based al-Nusra front which is an extension of Al Qaeda. Salah was in Syria when he blew himself up in a suicide bombing in July of 2014. The FBI had learned that Mateen followed the web site for Anwar al-Awlaki (a senior recruiter for Al Qaeda) where he followed al-Awlaki videos and ISIS propaganda that surely contributed to his radicalization. The FBI knew that Mateen had traveled to Saudi Arabia in 2011 and again in 2012 and that he had expressed his desire to become a martyr for Islam. Both FBI investigations were eventually closed as inconclusive. Sadly, it appears that political correctness is influencing the FBI, preventing them from taking appropriate actions. The Obama administration is so sensitive to political correctness that they can't effectively govern. This failure of leadership is very frustrating to many Americans but unfortunately there are just as many who are oblivious to the failures of the Obama administration.

The President addressed the nation this afternoon and made no mention of Islamic Jihad but did at least identify the attack as terrorism. He moaned about the ease of obtaining a firearm and emphasized hate as the motivation for the killings. The President and other liberals like to isolate hate as motivation in lieu of telling the truth about Islamic Jihad. This gives them a talking point on hate and provides cover for their omission of truth about Islamic Jihad. These liberals want Islam to become the dominate religion in America because this will further divide the American people along lines of race and religion. Liberals like the President understand that a divided populace will be easier to control than a unified populace. Their focus on hate as a singular motivation intentionally ignores the fact that hate is central to Jihad and Jihad is exclusive to Islam. They don't want the people to make that connection even though it's painfully obvious.

June 13, 2016

The President addressed the nation again today from the White House with a heavy focus on gun control. He dropped yesterday's reference to terrorism and replaced that with extremism whatever that is. Sometimes I eat too much ice cream which could be characterized as extremism so the term clearly lacks specificity. The President does describe extremism as a perversion of Islam which begs the question, where do Muslims stand on excessive ice cream consumption? Obviously I jest but the point is that labels like extremism are broad and vague as opposed to Islamic Jihad which leaves no question as to the meaning. The President said we don't yet know the motivations of Omar Mateen but we do know that his singular motivation is Islamic Jihad. Kill the infidel! Islam considers homosexuals to be the worst kind of infidel so it makes perfect sense that Mateen would target Pulse nightclub in Orlando. Islamic Sharia law dictates torture and death for homosexuals which occurs every day in Saudi Arabia. They frequently throw homosexuals off tall buildings to kill them. How can the President declare such strong support for the LGBT community while simultaneously displaying strong support for Islam when Islam is a sworn enemy of the LGBT community?

The President's focus on gun control suggests that it would solve the problem. If terrorists have difficulty obtaining a firearm, they will just use explosives for a high kill count. Omar Mateen could have easily walked into Pulse nightclub wearing a suicide vest and would have killed just as many if not more. President Obama complained about easy access to firearms and complained that we're lax on assault weapons. He said, "We make it very easy for individuals who are troubled, who are disturbed, who want to engage in violent acts to get very powerful weapons very quickly." The Presidents shameful use of misdirection to dishonestly shape public opinion is dangerous. His motivation is to advance a political agenda of gun control with no regard for our constitutional right to protect ourselves from the dangers that exist in today's world like Islamic Jihad and even the very real possibility of government tyranny which is what our founding fathers had in mind when they passed the 2nd amendment.

June 14, 2016

The President addressed the nation again today from the Treasury department, once again with the focus on gun control. This was more of an angry lecture than a speech. The Presidents anger was so apparent that veins were popping out of his neck. His anger was directed at his critics on gun control with the presumptive Republican nominee for President, Donald Trump as the main target although the President didn't call him out by name. Obviously, his anger should have been directed at the terrorist but we didn't see this. The Presidents misplaced anger reflects his failed leadership. He's more concerned with his political enemies here at home than he is with our true enemy which is Islamic Jihad.

The President began by attempting to make the point that no outside source directed Omar Mateen. This couldn't be further from the truth because Mateen was directed to commit his evil act by Anwar al-Awlaki videos, ISIS calls for Jihad in America, his association with Moner Abu Salah and the Mosque that both Mateen and Salah attended. He was also influenced by his father and wife. President Obama spoke of a war of words and said that rhetoric condemning Islamic Jihad will incite the terrorists to commit more and more attacks. He called AR-15's "weapons of war" which launched a new talking point for Democrats who favor new gun control legislation. The President expressed empathy for Islam but not for American citizens who now live in fear of Islamic Jihad. He failed to reassure the American people that their government will protect them from this evil force that threatens our very way of life. He offered no hope of an end to the violence of Islamic Jihad. It's sad that we have a President who isn't proud to be an American, who has no pride in our country and is so committed to the formation of a global society that he's lost sight of America's potential to be the shining light on a hill that the rest of the world looks to for inspiration and hope for a better life.

Rising Global Threats

June 15, 2016

CIA director, John Brennan, appeared before the Senate Intelligence Committee today and delivered a sobering message on the rise of ISIS and other threats we face today. He said he's never seen a time when our country has faced so many threats on the global stage. He warned of the rapid growth of ISIS in Libya and Egypt as he described their Sinai branch in Egypt as the most active foreign branch and the Libya branch as their most developed foreign branch with 5000 to 8000 fighters there. He spoke of the extensive and sophisticated use of social media by ISIS with Twitter, Telegram and Tumbler being utilized as their favored propaganda mechanisms. He noted that ISIS has successfully infiltrated refugee streams with their fighters and warned of the dangers associated with this Trojan Horse tactic.

Director Brennan reminded us of the critical need to step up cybersecurity to combat destructive new malware and of nuclear proliferation predominately in the Middle East due to the Iran nuke deal. In addition to all these concerns in the Middle East we have China's provocative actions in the South China Sea, North Korea's nuclear activity and Russia's association with Iran along with their close relationship with Assad in Syria. 51 State Department officials spoke out recently calling for air strikes on Assad's military assets in Syria while condemning Obama administration failures in Syria beginning with the Presidents failure to act after setting a red line on chemical weapon use by Assad in Syria. This was a huge embarrassment for Secretary Kerry and President Obama. Director Brennan emphasized our need to adapt and innovate as we face the daunting challenges of the volatile and complex world we live in. These revelations coming from the director of the CIA don't line up with talking points coming out of the White House designed to downplay the threats we face as cover for their inaction. Director Brennan's courageous move to speak out with the truth on the multiple threats we face today should be applauded by the American people because he won't receive any praise from the White House.

Chapter 28

Tragic Failure of Leadership

June 23, 2016

The Supreme Court issued a ruling today on the Presidents illegal executive action on immigration that would have essentially provided amnesty for 4 million illegal aliens currently living in the United States. The State of Texas brought the original law suit and they were joined by 25 additional States. The Supreme Court decision was 4-4 so the original decision by the 5th Circuit Court of Appeals in New Orleans will stand which ruled that the President's action was beyond his power to issue so deportations will continue for those who are here illegally. President Obama is not a happy camper. He addressed the nation from the White House today to complain about the outcome of the case. He said it was "heartbreaking for undocumented immigrants" (illegal aliens) and complained that Congress hasn't acted to pass comprehensive immigration reform legislation. The President went on to promise that immigration reform will get done eventually. It should be noted that if Justice Scalia were still alive the Supreme Court decision would have been a 5-4 ruling in favor of shutting down the Presidents executive action on immigration and that would have been the end of it. It should also be noted that if the Presidents nominee to the Supreme Court (Merrick Garland) had been confirmed by the Senate to replace Justice Scalia, the decision would surely have been 5-4 upholding the Presidents executive action on immigration. As it is this case could wind up back in the Supreme Court next year once the 9th seat is filled.

June 28, 2016

The House select committee on Benghazi issued their findings today in an 800-page report that documents every known detail surrounding the before, during and after of the terrorist attack on our diplomatic mission and CIA annex in Benghazi, Libya on 9/11/12. The committee conducted over 100 witness interviews over a 2-year timeframe and the investigation cost about $7 million. Their findings are highly incriminating for the State Department. The President had refused to answer questions from this House committee but appears to be in the clear because we learned that Secretary of Defense Leon Panetta and the President did order a rescue mission that was never launched so accountability rests with the State Department.

We learned that over 600 requests for security had been made prior to the attack by our team at the diplomatic mission in Benghazi and that not only were all requests denied but the paltry existing security at the mission was reduced prior to the attack. It turns out the State Departments reason for denying adequate security was that guards with machine guns out front would not be esthetically pleasing. This embarrassing excuse is just cover for their politically correct concern over offending Libyan officials with an American show of force. A White House meeting took place at 7:30PM EST on 9/11/12 that lasted about 2 hours to discuss possible response scenarios with concerns over the Libyan government reaction at the forefront of their discussions. This is when White House officials hatched the false narrative of a You Tube video as motivation for the attack which we all now know was an outright lie. They also agreed that Libyan officials must agree to any deployment of U.S. assets in response to the attack. This concern over our diplomatic disposition with Libyan officials and the political backdrop in America with the Presidential election coming up in 56 days, caused State Department officials certainly including Secretary of State Hillary Clinton to risk the lives of our diplomats in Benghazi by refusing adequate security and failing to mount a rescue mission. Their gamble cost the lives of Ambassador Christopher Stevens, Communication Specialist Sean Smith and Navy Seals Glen Doherty and Tyrone Woods. These brave Americans were sent into a failed State that had become a terrorist safe-haven and were left there to die on the anniversary of 9/11 with inadequate security and no hope of rescue. The House select committee found that not a single asset had even been pointed in the direction of Benghazi to rescue our people there at the time Ty Woods and Glen Doherty were killed which took place 8 hours after the attack began. We had a team in Croatia that could have made it in time to save Ty Woods and Glen Doherty but they were told to stand down. We also had a FAST team (Fleet Antiterrorism Security Team) who sat on a plane for 3 hours in Rota, Spain while changing in and out of their uniforms 4 times due to diplomatic sensitivities surrounding their appearance as State Department personnel hashed out concerns that prevented the departure of this team. Rep. Mike Pompeo (R-KS) who served on the House committee said, "We expect our government to make every effort to save the lives of Americans who serve in harm's way. That did not happen in Benghazi. Politics were put ahead of the lives of Americans, and while the administration had made excuses and blamed the challenges posed by time and distance, the truth is that they did not try." The simplest and least expensive solution would have been to temporarily bring our people home considering the anniversary of 9/11 which is exactly what the British and the Red Cross did.

The fact is that the administration knew immediately that this was a terrorist attack. Rep. Jim Jordan (R-OH) said, "Obama administration officials, including the Secretary of State, learned almost in real time that the attack in Benghazi was a terrorist attack. Rather than tell the American people the truth, the administration told one story privately and a different story for the American people." The President's National Security Advisor, Susan Rice, appeared on 5 Sunday morning talk shows and blatantly lied to the American people when she blamed the terrorist attack on our diplomatic mission in Benghazi on a You Tube video. Rep. Peter Roskam (R-IL) spoke to this when he said, "In the days and weeks after the attacks, the White House worked to pin all the blame for their misleading and incorrect statements on officials within the intelligence community, but in reality, political operatives like Ben Rhodes and David Plouffe were spinning the false narrative and prepping Susan Rice for her interviews." This shameful chapter in our country's history, thanks to then Secretary of State Hillary Clinton, must be embedded in the minds of all Americans so that the bravery of those Americans who served and died in Benghazi and the cowardice of Hillary Clinton and those who conspired with her to leave our good people in Benghazi to die and then lied about it to the American people will never be forgotten.

Transgender Soldiers

June 30, 2016

Secretary of Defense Ash Carter addressed the nation today to announce an end to the ban on transgender individuals to serve in the U.S. military. Secretary Carter said that transgender individuals may now serve openly in the military with no fear of condemnation. We learned that there are already over 2500 transgender individuals presently serving in the military and another 1500 in the reserves. These transgender individuals may now officially change their gender identity with no fear of discharge. Secretary Carter assured us that leadership studied all data available to them on this issue and that they consulted several outside experts and medical professionals in their decision-making process. He said a guidebook will be issued to leadership on transgender treatment in the military. He advised that transgender individuals in the military will receive health insurance with transgender coverage and transgender related care. This vague advisement raises even more questions. What exactly does transgender related care consist of? Are we talking about sex change operations at the expense of the American taxpayer? Do we really need mentally challenged individuals serving in our military? This is just one more example of damage done by the liberal progressive movement espoused by the Obama administration. This creates more division in America by the most divisive administration we have ever experienced.

Ramadan Killing Spree

July 4, 2016

Islam's holy month of Ramadan has been a very active month of terrorism this year with Jihadists mounting a killing spree in numerous locations. It began with the deadly attack at Pulse nightclub in Orlando, Florida on 6/12. On 6/28 an attack on the airport in Istanbul, Turkey that left 44 dead and 239 injured came next. The attack on the airport in Istanbul was a highly-coordinated attack consisting of 3 suicide bombers who strategically blew themselves up in both the international terminal and domestic terminal of the airport. This devastating attack took place near the entrances outside the secure areas in the airport where of course there are still plenty of people to target. We learned that the 3 suicide bombers consisted of a Chechen

Russian, one from Uzbekistan and the other from Kyrgyzstan, both former Russian States. ISIS claimed responsibility for this attack so these Russians were associated with ISIS.

The next attack occurred on 7/1 in Dhaka, Bangladesh where 7 Jihadists armed with explosives and assault weapons stormed a restaurant popular with tourists and held about 30 people as hostages for several hours. In the end, 24 lay dead 22 of which were among the hostages, 2 were police officers and 3 of the hostages killed were American students. 24 police officers were injured during the siege. ISIS claimed responsibility for this terrorist attack while Al Qaeda also claimed the operation could be theirs. ISIS does maintain a branch in Bangladesh and there is also an Al Qaeda affiliate group there. These terrorist groups are in competition for supremacy in Bangladesh which is a country of 146 million Muslim citizens.

Finally, one day before the end of Ramadan 2016, a truck bombing in Baghdad, Iraq left over 200 dead and 170 seriously injured. This suicide bombing took place in a Shia district of Baghdad where many Christians reside and where a feast marking the end of Ramadan was taking place. The truck was filled with explosives so the devastation was extensive. ISIS was responsible for every attack we witnessed during the Islamic holy month of Ramadan this year. The Obama administration non-strategy of "degrade and destroy" obviously isn't working! ISIS is growing and winning while we are losing due to President Obama's dangerous rules of engagement and his determination to run the clock out on his time in office to pass this devastating problem on to the next administration in 2017.

Extremely Careless

July 5, 2016

Five days after Bill Clinton met privately with Attorney General Loretta Lynch for 30 minutes on her private jet which was parked on the tarmac of the airport in Phoenix next to Bill Clinton's private jet, FBI director James Comey announced the completion of the FBI investigation into Hillary Clinton's use of a private unsecure e-mail server while she served as Secretary of State for the Obama administration throughout his 1st term. It should be noted that the Clinton/Lynch meeting was discovered by a local reporter who happened to get a tip that he followed through on so the only reason we know about it is that they got caught. This highly suspect meeting represents a conflict of interest and prosecutorial misconduct on the part of AG Lynch. Just the appearance of impropriety is against legal ethical standards. Of course, both Clinton and Lynch denied any wrongdoing saying they just talked about Bill's grandkids and golf. How in the world do a former President and the sitting Attorney General who doesn't play golf and doesn't have any grandkids talk about golf and grandkids for 30 minutes?

Director Comey began his remarks with a scathing report of Secretary Clinton's negligence to properly protect her classified communications while serving as Secretary of State. He went on to advise us that she used several different unclassified and unsecure personal servers and several devices which conflicts with Clinton's lie that she only used 1 device for convenience. He said they discovered 110 e-mails that were marked classified when they were sent and that 8 of them were top secret also in conflict with Clintons lie that she never sent or received any e-mails marked as classified. Director Comey advised that they discovered thousands of deleted and unrecoverable e-mails so we can only imagine the damage done by these highly questionable deleted e-mails. We learned that Secretary Clinton used her personal e-mail outside the U.S. near very dangerous and sophisticated adversaries who could easily penetrate her unsecure servers that Director Comey described as being more porous than g-mail. After laying out this very disturbing set of circumstances condemning Clinton's use of unsecure private e-mail servers, Director Comey took a sharp left turn as he advised that although Clinton's mishandling of classified communications was **extremely careless**, there is no case for criminal charges, no intentional misconduct and that "no reasonable prosecutor should bring this forward." He said the stakes are too high to indict and then fail to convict in court. It appears that "lack of criminal intent" is at the center of Director Comey's failure to recommend indictment even though the federal statute states that gross negligence does not require criminal intent. There is no difference between gross negligence and extremely careless as they are one in the same.

It's been commonly alleged that there is one set of rules for the Clinton's and another entirely different set of rules for the rest of us. Hillary Clinton's negligent use of private unsecure e-mail servers is just one more example of this and now that it's been made known that Hillary Clinton will not be held accountable for her dangerous actions we can only conclude that the Clintons are above the law.

Bastille Day

July 14, 2016

Islamic Jihad on the French Riviera sounds like something out of an action movie but today it became reality in Nice, France. As the French and many visiting tourists celebrated Bastille Day on the French Riviera, Mohamed Bouhlel was making last minute preparations to commit the unthinkable. A huge crowd enjoying the celebratory atmosphere along the Promenade of Angels in Nice had just been treated to an impressive fireworks' display to top off a beautiful day of celebrations. As the crowd was only just beginning to disperse to sidewalk cafes and other nightlife venues in Nice, Mohamed Bouhlel drove a very large rental truck up to a blockade set up to prevent vehicles from entering the fireworks viewing area and convinced police that he was there to deliver ice cream to the crowd. When police there made the regrettable decision to clear the way for the truck, Bouhlel floored it and began systematically mowing people down as he gained speed while shouting "Allah Hu Akbar." Those who were in the middle of the crowd found themselves helpless to move out of the way as the speeding truck picked them off in short order. Bouhlel was also shooting people in the process. When the carnage ended 84 people lay dead and another 200 were injured. Police ran Bouhlel down once he had exited the truck and shot him while on the run. Bouhlel died on the spot.

Mohamed Bouhlel was 31 years old and was a French citizen from Tunisia. He worked as a delivery driver and was known by police as a petty criminal. Authorities later learned that he had been radicalized only recently but he was obviously an enthusiastic Jihadist who managed to inflict terror, death and great destruction upon the good people in Nice.

Secret Cash Ransom

August 2, 2016

On January 17, 2016 Iran released 4 Americans they had held hostage for years. It was a day when many Americans were giving thanks for answered prayer as Jason Rezaian, Saeed Abedini, Amir Hekmati and Nosratollah Khosravi-Roodsari were released from an Iranian prison and returned to America. At the time, it had been explained that their release was a good will gesture on the part of Iran after the nuke deal had been finalized. Around the same time, Americans were apprised of a $1.7 billion payment to be made to Iran to settle a long-standing arms deal that was never executed due to the ouster of the Shah of Iran in 1979. The original arms deal resulted in a $400 million payment by Iran that was held in a U.S. based trust fund to support military equipment purchases by Iran from the United States. When the Shah was ousted in 1979, the U.S. froze the trust fund and a claim was filed at The Hague on the disputed debt.

On August 2, 2016, we learned that a cash payment of $400 million was made to Iran simultaneous with the departure of the hostages for their return trip home. Congress hadn't been informed of this cash payment when it was made back in January so this was news to them too. Pastor Saeed Abedini explained that he and the other 3 Americans boarded a plane in Tehran on the evening of 1/16/2016 to be flown home and were told they would take off in 20 minutes but much later they were informed that they wouldn't be taking off until the other plane arrives. Several hours later, early the next morning, an unmarked cargo plane landed in Tehran and an Iranian video showed pallets of cash being offloaded from the cargo plane. Once the $400 million in untraceable Swiss Francs and Euros was unloaded, the plane containing the hostages took off to take them home to the United States. How could this clandestine cash payment paid in untraceable unmarked bills be anything but a secret ransom payment for the return of the hostages? We would never have known about this secret cash payment if it hadn't been for the Iranian video that surfaced.

Spin by the Obama administration came fast as they scrambled to discredit any notion that the $400 million in Swiss Francs and Euros paid to Iran was a secret ransom payment. State Department spokesman, John Kirby explained that the timing of the $400 million cash payment was a mere coincidence but on 8/18 his story changed dramatically when he admitted that the cash payment was held up until it was confirmed that the hostages had been released and were in the air. He refused to call it ransom as he struggled with the absurdity of the spin but admitted the cash was used as "leverage" as if there's any difference. It becomes obvious that the spin doctors have reached the end of their rope when the spin consists of nothing more than mere semantics. White House Press Secretary, Josh Earnest said Iran would use the money to prop up their currency and to build needed infrastructure. Anyone who believes this nonsense is extremely naive. As the largest State sponsor of terrorism, the untraceable cash surely went to fund Islamic Jihad. President Obama said, "We do not pay ransom for hostages" and explained that the payment was made in cash because "We don't have a banking relationship with Iran." He said the payment was not a secret and that the only new information was that it was a cash payment. The fact that this payment was made in cash is a very significant new development. The President downplayed that by noting that the payment had to be in foreign currency due to U.S. sanctions that still exist but he failed to address the fact that we weren't informed back in January that the amount was $400 million and that it was paid in cash. These are big pieces of the puzzle that should have been revealed initially for the sake of transparency but transparency isn't exactly a priority for this administration.

The first question that arose in my mind was why wouldn't we tell Iran we can't pay the $1.7 billion now because of sanctions that prevent us from doing so. We could have just assured Iran that payment would be made by wire transfer once sanctions are lifted when Iran meets the necessary criteria to have sanctions lifted. We weren't under any obligation to make a cash payment. U.S. policy has always been that we don't pay ransom for hostages so the hostages should have been dealt with another way. The State Department still officially considers Iran to be the largest State sponsor of terrorism in the world so the likelihood that the $400 million in untraceable cash went straight to Hezbollah in Lebanon, Hamas in Gaza, Shia militia's in Syria, Shiite Houthi's in Yemen and other bad actors in the region associated with Iran can't be ignored. Essentially, the United States is indirectly funding terrorism in the Middle East.

First, we trade 5 high level Taliban Commanders who had been detained at Gitmo for one American deserter and now we make a secret cash ransom payment to Iran for the return of 4 Americans they were holding hostage. There's a very good reason why our policy has always been to never pay ransom to our adversaries because it only gives them incentive to take more hostages which is exactly what happened this time. Iran has captured 3 more Americans in Iran since the $400 million cash ransom payment was made. Siamak Namazi, Baquer Namazi and Reza Shahini, all of whom have dual citizenship with the U.S. and Iran, are now being held hostage in an Iranian prison.

No banking relationship with Iran?

August 24, 2016

Today we learned that 2 days after the U.S. paid $400 million in foreign cash to Iran as ransom to release 4 Americans they were holding hostage, the U.S. paid Iran $1.3 billion to cover the interest on the $400 million that had been held in a U.S. based trust fund since 1979 resulting from a weapons deal with the Shah. We had previously been informed that a total of $1.7 billion would be paid to Iran so the total amount wasn't in question but the transactional nature of the $1.3 billion interest payment is very much in question today. The State Department reported that the U.S. paid Iran in 13 separate $100 million wire transfer transactions on the same day which was only 2 days after an unmarked cargo plane delivered $400 million in Swiss Francs and Euros to Tehran in the middle of the night for the release of 4 Americans. Prior to this new revelation of a $1.3 billion interest payment made by wire transfer to Iran, President Obama told us that we had to pay the $400 million to Iran in cash because we don't have a banking relationship with Iran due to U.S. sanctions on Iran. If this were true, how did the U.S. pay Iran $1.3 billion by wire transfer 2 days after the $400 million cash payment was made? Clearly the President blatantly lied to the American people when he claimed the only way money can change hands between the U.S. and Iran is in cash because of U.S. sanctions on Iran. President Obama has been so consistently dishonest with the American people that this lie is just one more on top of countless others but the greater sin here is the fact that Congress was kept in the dark and was never notified of these payments to Iran so these actions by the Obama administration are unconstitutional and obviously very dishonest.

Cash is King

September 7, 2016

James Rosen with Fox News had been investigating the $1.3 billion paid to Iran to cover interest on the $400 million that had been held in a U.S. based trust fund to support military equipment purchases by Iran going back to 1979, and Rosen discovered that the $1.3 billion was actually paid in 3 separate cash payments and not 13 separate payments of $100 million each by wire transfer which was recorded as a Treasury Dept. "Judgement fund" payment on 1/19/16 so we're also dealing with falsification of records. The Treasury department maintains a "Judgement fund" for such payments but federal code specifies that Judgement fund payments can only be made by wire transfer so a huge cash payment made from the Judgement fund would be illegal but when did such minor details deter the Obama administration. We now know that a total of $1.7 billion in untraceable cash has been paid to Iran by the United States which will surely be used by Iran to fund terrorism around the world. Brilliant!!! Give the largest State sponsor of terrorism in the world $1.7 billion in untraceable cash. Instead of fighting Islamic Jihad around the world, we're indirectly funding it.

September 8, 2016

The executive director of the Foundation for Defense of Democracies, Mark Dubowitz, submitted written testimony to the House Financial Services Committee today in which he claimed, "If there was no mechanism through the formal financial system to send Iran the $1.7 billion in settlement money, the $11.9 billion in [Joint Plan of Action] sanctions relief funds from its oil escrow accounts, and the $20 billion from Iran's total liquid, unencumbered assets following the implementation of the [Iran Nuke deal], Iran received as much as $33.6 billion in cash." Dubowitz called the $33.6 billion, "the worst-case scenario," adding that it also could have been paid "in gold and other precious metals." Dubowitz related that further details are shrouded in mystery.

September 17, 2016

Now that we know that all of the various funds previously described here were paid in cash, it began to appear as though President Obama was being honest with us with regard to our inability to pay Iran by wire transfer due to sanctions but according to a Treasury Department spokesman today, the U.S. actually wired money to Iran twice in 14 months which contradicts President Obama's claim that since we don't have a banking relationship with Iran we can't wire money to them because of sanctions. During July 2015, the same month that the Iran nuclear deal was announced, $848,000. was wired to Iran to settle a claim over architectural drawings and fossils that are now housed in the Tehran Museum of Contemporary Art and Iran's Ministry of Environment, respectively. All nuclear related sanctions were still in place when this wire transfer was made. Then, in April 2016, the U.S. wired $9 million to remove 32 metric tons of its heavy water which is used to produce plutonium for nuclear weapons. Sanctions were still in place for Iran's support of terrorism and for human rights violations when this $9 million was wired to Iran.

It appears Iran simply demanded cash for the $1.7 billion and upwards of $33.6 billion in cash and precious metals that was paid to Iran and that the Obama administration simply conceded to their demand. It only takes a modicum of common sense to deduce that Iran demanded cash because this is the only mechanism they can utilize to forward that money to the various terrorist organizations Iran supports in the Middle East. Why would the Obama administration cave to Iran's demand for cash when it is indeed possible for the U.S. to send funds to Iran via wire transfer? This smells to high heaven and the Obama administration should be held accountable for their irresponsible actions but apparently, accountability is just too much to ask of this administration! This means that the United States is indirectly funding terrorist organizations in the Middle East to the tune of billions of dollars.

Questionable Priorities

President Obama recently approved a 10 year $38 billion "Memorandum of Understanding" military aid package for Israel. Israel will receive $3.8 billion annually for 10 years, up from $3.1 billion for the previous 10-year deal with Israel which expires in 2018. Israel loses its ability to spend a portion of the funds on Israeli military products as opposed to the previous deal. This stipulation will be phased out gradually until all funds are required to be spent with American military industries. Israel also had to concede any ability to ask for or receive any additional funds from any new legislation Congress may pass to increase the amount. Congress had nothing to do with this $38 billion military aid package and several Republican Senators in addition to Speaker Ryan and many Republicans in the House expressed dissatisfaction with the terms of the deal as they believe it places too many limitations on Israel's ability to allocate these funds based on their own assessment of how to do so. They also feel the amount should have been much more based on the recent Iran nuclear deal because Iran is now flush with cash due to the nuclear deal and cash ransom paid for the release of U.S. hostages, so as the largest State sponsor of terrorism in the world (official U.S. State Department designation) they will utilize much of their windfall to more effectively fund terrorist organizations in the Middle East which threatens Israel's national security. Now that Iran will be a weaponized nuclear power with ICBM's within 10 years if not sooner based on cheating on the deal which they're notorious for, they too are a threat to Israel's national security. Congress must still approve the funds for this agreement annually which is nothing more than a formality because they can't make changes.

The deal was concluded after months of negotiations and Israeli Prime Minister Benjamin Netanyahu and other officials in Jerusalem had considered waiting to finalize the deal until the next U.S. President is in place in order to possibly secure a much better deal but President Obama was anxious to finalize the agreement before the end of his term because he wanted to bolster his legacy and to deflect criticism that he had been insufficiently supportive of Israel so the pressure was intense on the U.S. side. This new agreement, for the first time, includes funding for Israel's Iron Dome missile defense system ($5 billion of the $38 billion total) as opposed to separate Congressional approval for missile defense on an annual basis. This stipulation is a double-edged sword because Congress may or may not have approved more on an annual basis for missile defense based on current events in the Middle East. Compared to

$150 billion pledged to Iran as a result of the weak nuclear deal, the $1.7 billion in cash paid to Iran to supposedly to settle the 1979 arms deal when everything points to hostage ransom, the $11.9 billion in cash for sanctions relief which never should have been paid and $20 billion in cash to cover Iranian unencumbered assets which is extremely vague ($183.6 billion total to Iran), the paltry $38 billion in military aid pledged to Israel over 10 years represents the highly **questionable priorities** of the Obama administration. Of course, military aid isn't the only area where we support Israel but this dollar for dollar comparison is apples to apples because Iran will use all their funds to strengthen military concerns including nuclear so Israel's military aid package designed to strengthen their defense must work to offset Iran's military advances therefore I believe we should have offered more support in this critical area. We must also remember that supporting Israel is beneficial for America because Israel is our only true ally in the Middle East and because we partner with them in research and development of innovative new initiatives like Cyber warfare defenses which is a defense category that Israel has made extraordinary advances in. Israel is light years ahead of everyone in this critical new area of defense.

AIPAC (American Israel Public Affairs Committee) expressed strong approval for the updated military aid package and they certainly deserve credit for holding Congress and the Obama administration's feet to the fire to maintain their strong support for Israel. This organization works tirelessly in support of Israel and they do indeed perform a very important role in Washington DC and around the rest of the country in their strong support for the nation of Israel!

Jihadist strikes NYC and New Jersey

September 17 through September 22, 2016

On a beautiful September Saturday evening (9/17) in the Chelsea neighborhood of Manhattan, Islamic Jihad strikes as a pressure cooker bomb explodes in a dumpster near 23rd and 6th Ave. injuring 29 people. A few hours later an unexploded pressure cooker bomb was located by authorities just 2 blocks away. Earlier Saturday morning, a pipe bomb exploded at the beach in Seaside Heights, NJ. along the path of a Semper Fi 5K Charity Run just prior to the beginning of the run. This Marine charity run was planned to begin earlier in which case many Marines could have been killed or injured but thankfully the run was delayed. Sunday night authorities located a backpack containing 5 explosive devices under an overpass in Elizabeth, NJ. which was subsequently exploded by authorities. The FBI was working with local law enforcement throughout events following the initial explosion in Chelsea. Monday morning 9/19 authorities had identified 28-year-old Ahmad Khan Rahami as the bomber from 12 fingerprints found on the unexploded pressure cooker bomb found in Chelsea. The FBI issued an alert that went off on virtually everyone's smart phones in the surrounding area early Monday morning which showed a recent photo of Rahami, identifying him as the bomber. Later Monday afternoon a tavern owner in Linden, NJ. who had seen the alert discovered a man fitting Rahami's description sleeping in the doorway of his tavern so he contacted the police who arrived on the scene to discover the man was indeed Rahami. When they engaged him from across the street knowing he was dangerous and probably armed, he began firing his hand gun at them and when police returned fire a brief exchange of bullets resulted in 2 wounded police officers and a badly wounded Rahami who was then taken into custody and taken to the hospital in Newark to tend to his wounds.

Ahmad Khan Rahami was born in Afghanistan near Kandahar. This region is basically headquarters for the Taliban. His wife, Asia, was also born in Afghanistan as confirmed by Pakistan's foreign office because it was originally reported she was born in Pakistan. He is a naturalized U.S. citizen and lives with his family in Elizabeth, NJ. in an apartment above their fried chicken restaurant. Locals in the area said the family fried chicken joint is a favorite Muslim hangout that frequently stays open all night and that police said they've received several complaints from locals due to the late-night activity. Turns out Rahami is no stranger to the FBI. They began investigating him in 2014 after his father called the FBI to report a violent incident that occurred in their home. Rahami had stabbed his brother in the leg and attacked his mother too. The FBI interviewed him and then released him from their custody. He was charged with aggravated assault and illegal weapons possession by local authorities after the domestic incident and spent 3 months in jail but a grand jury failed to indict so he was subsequently released.

Rahami began buying explosive materials on e-bay on June 20, 2016 and was registered with e-bay using the last name Rahimi. On July 12, this e-bay user (Rahimi) bought an electric igniter for a fireworks system, then on July 31 the user bought a circuit board which authorities said could be used in explosive devices. On August 10, the user bought what authorities believe to be citric acid. The FBI described citric acid as a precursor for improvised explosives. Rahami's mother traveled to Turkey in August 2016 and his wife, Asia, traveled to the United Arab Emirates with their child in June 2016 which is interesting in terms of the timeframe. Asia leaves town at approximately the same time her husband began buying explosive materials on e-bay which doesn't appear to be coincidental. Asia returned to New Jersey on 9/21 at the request of the FBI so I'm sure they interviewed her as soon as they could get to her. Ahmad made 3 separate trips to Afghanistan and Pakistan prior to the bombing, 2 of which we have some details on. Ahmad traveled to Kandahar, Afghanistan in 2011 and again in 2013. A very important detail about these trips is that he spent most of his time in Quetta, Pakistan which is known as a Jihadi hotbed and that's not to say that Kandahar isn't, but Quetta is the wild wild east so to speak, basically a no man's land for regular law abiding Pakistani citizens. Quetta is not very far from Kandahar and the Afghanistan/Pakistan border is quite porous so travel between these 2 centers of Taliban activity is easy. He spent 3 months in Quetta in May 2011 and then again from April 2013 until March 2014. When he returned to New Jersey, family members and friends said he had changed dramatically as he had begun wearing traditional Muslim garb and espoused Jihadi activity for the first time in his life. Rahami studied both al-Qaeda and ISIS material on the internet so he wasn't necessarily only associated with the Taliban. As long it was Islamic Jihadi material he was all in.

The FBI discovered Rahami's journal in the family apartment. It contained a treasure trove of Jihadi material. We learned he was a follower of Anwar al-Awlaki, a senior al-Qaeda recruiter who was taken out by a U.S. drone strike in Yemen. He praised bin Laden and held Nidal Hassan, the Ft. Hood Jihadist, in high regard. Of greatest significance, Rahami wrote about Abu Mohammad al-Adnani, the official spokesman and senior leader of ISIS who is described as chief of its external operations and 2nd in line only to the big dog himself, Abu Bakr al-Baghdadi. ISIS announced in late August 2016 that al-Adnani had been killed near Aleppo, Syria but confirmation is quite difficult so there really is no absolute certainty of his death. Rahami referred to him as Brother Adnani in his journal and mused over whether to strike now or not and Rahami also made an entry in the journal that confirms Adnani's admonishment of Jihadi's to stay home and strike unbelievers in their own backyard. Now comes the real zinger which is that the FBI left out any reference to al-Adnani being included in Rahami's journal in their report which weakened the indictment against the very much alive Rahami. First the Obama administration attempts to make us believe al-Qaeda is decimated and on the run which couldn't be further from the truth and now they're trying to whitewash Rahami's association with ISIS to downplay the ability of ISIS to inspire Jihadi's to attack at home instead of traveling to Syria to join the Jihad there. They did the same thing with Omar Mateen, the Orlando Jihadi, who killed 49 people and seriously injured 53 more at Pulse nightclub.

General Assembly Swan Song

September 20, 2016

President Obama addressed the U.N General Assembly for the last time as POTUS today. He delivered an ideological message void of reality. He spoke of "global integration" while ignoring the great divide between democracies of the world and less developed 3rd world dictatorships as he overlooked the major challenges we face in today's world like the rise of ISIS, the great geopolitical threat posed by Russia, China's provocative actions in the South China Sea, the collapse of Venezuela's economy, and the nuclear threat posed by North Korea and Iran just to name a few. These issues are apparently not worth mentioning before an international body of diplomats. Rather, he spoke as if he's President of a dream world of utopian ideals. He intimated that either we have increased global integration or we have war as if those are the only choices. He said, "In Europe and the U.S. you see people wrestle with concerns about immigration and changing demographics and suggestions somehow that people who look different are corrupting the character of our countries." This slanted statement has nothing to do with reality. The American people and the people of Europe understand the benefits of legal immigration which creates a diverse society but with a common productive purpose. President Obama is attempting to shove illegal immigration and refugees who can't be vetted down our collective throats which is not only dangerous; it's very expensive because illegal aliens, by the very nature of their disrespect for our laws, are unwilling to make a productive contribution to our society and therefore become a drag on economic growth as well as refugees who refuse to assimilate to our society. Many people in Europe were at one time largely open to taking in illegal immigrants along with immigrants taken in legally but couldn't be properly vetted, as is the case with the Syrian refugees who have been infiltrated by terrorists based on CIA Director Brennan's assessment, and they learned the hard way when this turned out to be an unmitigated disaster they had jumped into head first without looking at their landing place. The Obama administration is making the same mistake even after witnessing the disaster in Europe but our Republican-controlled Congress is thankfully slowing things down to at least a somewhat limited extent so we aren't experiencing the negative consequences all at once as has been the case in Europe. The Somali refugees in Minnesota refuse to assimilate to our culture which is extremely problematic and now we are beginning to take in large numbers of Syrian refugees who the Obama administration is quietly just allowing in without even informing our Congress, so in this instance the American people aren't even given a choice.

As the President progressed on this theme he said, "We must reject any forms of fundamentalism or racism or a belief in ethnic superiority that makes our traditional identities irreconcilable with modernity. Instead we need to embrace the tolerance that results from respect of all human beings." This as if we're a bunch of unruly school kids! The sort of tolerance he's referring to is to allow refugees to enter our country willy-nilly with no ability to vet them and to maintain our open borders to allow illegal immigrants to just cross the Rio Grande not only to stay and take advantage of our unrestrained welfare system but to come and go freely between the U.S. and Mexico so they can take their plunder back home and support their extended families in Mexico and beyond. It's true that there are many in their ranks who come with the desire to work for a living but this creates a backdoor underground of people who are off the grid as they're paid in cash because they don't have social security numbers. This results in lower wages for law abiding U.S. citizens who too desire to work but also desire a fair wage which really shouldn't be too much to ask for. The President took a jab at the Republican nominee for President, Donald Trump, who wants to build a wall on our southern border with a clever plan to make Mexico pay for it. President Obama said, "The world is too small for us to simply be able to build a wall and prevent it from affecting our own societies," as if this extremely vague statement held any real meaning and no, he didn't elaborate sufficiently to fill in the blanks. He gave no consideration to the prospect of a positive affect regarding the restoration of our sovereignty as a nation of laws instead of a lawless society with open borders.

Some of the Presidents statements in this speech were just way over the top. When he said, "The end of the cold war ended the shadow of nuclear Armageddon" I almost fell out of my chair. He didn't stop there though as he said, "We've taken away terrorist safe havens, strengthened the non-proliferation regime, resolved the Iranian nuclear issue through diplomacy." Regarding the terrorist safe havens, ISIS not only has a very large safe-haven in and around Raqqa, Syria, they've established a Caliphate there with a very sophisticated infrastructure. They still control Mosul, Iraq and they move freely between northern Syria and northern Iraq. The Taliban is alive and well in Afghanistan and Pakistan as well as Al-Qaeda. Hezbollah in Lebanon and Hamas in Gaza are thriving with no active threat to their well-being and the list goes on. The non-proliferation regime is a joke! Participating nations merely put up a good front for the sake of appearances. The nuclear issue with Iran isn't remotely settled. The IAEA is the biggest joke of all. They aren't even allowed to enter Iran's military facilities like Parchin. Now that we have this weak nuclear deal with Iran, nuclear proliferation will surely escalate dramatically in the Middle East. There's little direct evidence of this at this point but as the nations in fairly close-proximity to Iran keep a close eye on Iran and determine if they cheat on the nuclear deal, I believe we'll see a sharp uptick in nuclear proliferation in the Middle East as Iran makes significant advances in this area whether they cheat or not. They've already test launched long range missiles in violation of the deal. Iran's nuclear infrastructure remains, so in 10 years they could ramp up their nuclear program in short order as the deal allows. We must also consider North Korea as they've been testing long range missiles and recently exploded an extremely powerful nuclear bomb underground which caused a low-level earthquake. Pakistan is a wild card who deserves close scrutiny as their advancing relationship with Russia is not only raising eyebrows, it's extremely dangerous particularly when we examine Russia's close relationship with Syria.

The President continued with extremely vague statements that are still just hanging out there. When he said, "We need to close the gap between rich and poor nations" and "We need to make the global economy work for all people and not just those at the top," I was left puzzled and no, he didn't follow up with sufficient details to support these vague statements. These statements that appear to be about an equality driven global marketplace hint at income re-distribution and even serious concessions expected of wealthier nations to prop up nations that just aren't innovative and capable of creating wealth. When he said, "the world is more prosperous and less violent than ever before," he created a contradiction to the focus on rich and poor nations. How could the entire world be more prosperous when many nations in the world, of which there are too many to name, are struggling economically? Venezuela ring a bell! Asserting that the world is less violent than ever before is so far removed from reality that I don't even know where to begin. Another contradiction was when he claimed, "unions have been undermined and manufacturing jobs have disappeared." This statement isolates unions as victims and as the only cause of the loss of manufacturing jobs due to alleged unfair treatment. NAFTA and the looming prospect of TPP are virtually the exclusive cause of the loss of American manufacturing jobs so the undermined union theory just doesn't hold water. Our President believes that strong unions are the only vehicle by which manufacturing jobs are supported but this ignores the extreme corruption at the top with union leaders who line their pockets with overly inflated salaries and bonuses that rob workers of hard earned union dues when that money should represent an investment to support fair wages and to serve workers interests. Unions need to be brought into the 21st century with vastly different structure with an eye to balance designed to create a fair environment for both workers and employers. This would require a willingness on the part of union leaders to accept significant change which would be like asking them to donate half of their inflated salaries to charity!

When the President claimed we've "established a framework to protect our planet from the ravages of climate change," it was just so over the top that it couldn't be taken seriously. It's not so much that we've established a framework to protect our planet so much as his reference to the ravages of climate change of which there is absolutely no proof. Liberal environmentalists would most assuredly challenge my assertion of no proof but this ignores the lack of veracity of their so-called proof. When the pockets of a handful of scientists are lined with extremely large sums of money by the likes of George Soros and Al Gore, many scientists would have no problem claiming the earth is flat after all, so this doesn't exactly offer sufficient support for their claim! This speech was a feel-good speech of broad strokes that missed the mark of any legitimate analysis of today's world but the President appeared to enjoy giving it and his audience at the U.N. was in large part very happy with it based on their enthusiastic response at the end.

Clarity and Strength

September 22, 2016

The Prime Minister of Israel, Benjamin Netanyahu, addressed the U.N. General Assembly today. What a contrast between a true leader who speaks the truth with **clarity and strength**, Prime Minister Netanyahu, and the President of the United States. Of course, President Obama played to a full house 2 days prior and Prime Minister Netanyahu, who this body in large part considers to be the devil in a suit, appeared before small numbers in a largely empty hall with a noticeably absent Secretary of State, John Kerry. Hmmm... Do you suppose that may have something to do with the fact that President Obama is a globalist and Prime Minister Netanyahu who understands the importance of Israel's sovereignty and who speaks to the interests of Israel as his priority while going on to chastise Israel's adversaries, of whom there are many, may not meet with the approval of Arabs and globalists who are determined to possess the Temple Mount and even the whole of Jerusalem? That said, I must quickly go on to acknowledge that Prime Minister Netanyahu expressed thanks to President Obama for the United States partnership with Israel which is so incredibly important to Israel's very existence as Israel is literally surrounded by adversaries who would just as soon wipe Israel off the map as opposed to seeking their friendship.

Prime Minister Netanyahu reminded the General Assembly that last year they filed 20 resolutions against Israel and only 3 against the rest of the world. This is so wrong on so many different levels. He went on to speak about UNESCO, the U.N. body that is responsible for preserving world heritage, and noted that UNESCO has recently denied the connection between the Jewish people and the Temple Mount in Jerusalem! This is obviously because the Temple Mount is the most cherished religious site in the world, even surpassing Mecca in Saudi Arabia for Muslims. For Jews and Christians, the desecration of the Temple Mount by a Mosque having been built there is a very difficult pill to swallow given the fact that it was the site of the original Jewish Temple which had been destroyed once and rebuilt later only to be destroyed again and is considered the most holy site for the Jewish people to honor and worship the one true God, the God of Abraham, Isaac and Jacob. Christians fully understand the Temple Mounts historical and religious significance as the most holy site historically but also the site of prophesied future events revolving around the end times as prophesied in the Bible when the Jewish Temple is rebuilt for the 3rd time. Preparations have been underway to rebuild the Jewish Temple for many years so that when the time comes they'll be prepared to do it in short order. This controversy will swirl until future events pave the way for the Jewish people to rebuild the Jewish Temple.

Given UNESCO's outrageous condemnation of Israel and the U.N.'s escalating overall disdain for Israel, Prime Minister Netanyahu said that the U.N. has gone from "a moral force to a moral farce." This was the scathing zinger of the Prime Ministers speech. He went on to note that more and more nations now see Israel as a potent power as Israel enjoys relations with 160 countries who now have strong ties to Israel. More specifically, he went on to share that Israel leads the world in re-cycling waste water. This critical innovation is so ground breaking that it could revolutionize our ability to provide this most important resource of drinking water. On cyber security, Israel is light years ahead of everyone! Israel represents one tenth of 1% of the world's population yet they're the world's foremost authority on this critically needed new technology. Israel is 200 times above its weight in cyber security. Presently, Israel is involved in

20% of the world's cyber security but that percentage could easily increase dramatically in the future. He pointed out that since Israel's deepest relationship in the world is with the United States of America, certainly much more so than any other, that the U.S. is poised to be the primary beneficiary of this critical new technology. Regarding the Iran nuclear deal, the Prime Minister said, "Israel will not allow the terrorist regime in Iran to develop nuclear weapons, not now, not in a decade, not ever!"

Chapter 29

Immunity

Hillary Clinton's bid to become President of the United States should be very much in question due to her corrupt practices going back to 2009 when she was sworn in as Secretary of State under the Obama administration's 1st term and had a private unsecure e-mail server set up in the basement of her Chappaqua, NY. home. While she served as Secretary of State for 4 years it appears she sold access to the State Department (quid pro quo aka pay for play), which can be extremely productive and lucrative for foreign diplomats, as she traveled the globe meeting with said diplomats of the highest level. I can only say it appears so because there is clearly one set of rules for the Clinton's and another entirely different set of rules for the rest of us so proof becomes nothing more than a mere inconvenience for the Clinton's even when it's incredibly compelling. An investigation into her corrupt practices was initiated early in 2016 by the FBI and when results were presented, the evidence of corruption at the highest levels was so damning that the American people could only surmise that she would at the very least be indicted for said corruption but no such indictment would be forthcoming. Bill played a major role in this corruption while he traveled around the world throughout the same 4-year timeframe as he accepted huge sums of money from foreign entities just to speak to the members of these various entities. As Bill crisscrossed the globe on high dollar speaking engagements it was like a planned follow up to Hillary's State Department trips as Bill collected up to $500,000. per speaking engagement. Hillary hit the lucrative speaking circuit too once she wrapped up her time as Secretary of State so beginning in 2013, she was out there too raking it in from the likes of Goldman Sachs and other big time Wall Street brokerage firms. To this day, Hillary refuses to release the transcripts of her speeches to Goldman Sachs. Must have said something the little people (little people to her) may not appreciate.

Based on Hillary's account, the Clinton's were not only dead broke when they left the White House in 2000 but that they had some serious mortgage debt so to hear it from Hillary it sounded dire. Well they muddled through somehow to go on to enjoy a net worth today of well over $100 million, some reports have it at more like$250 million. The Clinton's do of course enjoy the privilege of Bill's lifetime pay since he was POTUS and Hillary's having been a U.S. Senator which is only about $600,000. annually between the two. 600 grand a year is nothing more than walking around money for the Clintons. Their main source of income is the highly lucrative speaking circuit described in the previous paragraph. The Clinton's lived high buying a mansion in Georgetown DC in addition to the Chappaqua, NY. mansion and traveled of course staying in 5 star hotels at great cost, with all the travel expense being picked up by the Clinton foundation. Nice!

In a late Friday afternoon document dump today designed to slip this past as many as possible, we learned that 5 high level Clinton staffers including her legal team received **immunity** from prosecution for any possible role regarding her unsecure private e-mail server that she used exclusively for official U.S. government business when she was Secretary of State. Clinton legal team members, Cheryl Mills, Clinton's long standing attorney who served as her Chief of Staff at State and Heather Samuelson also on the legal team along with Paul Combetta who worked for Platte River (the company that managed Clinton's unsecure server) and also known to be the man who utilized bleach bit, the most intense server scrubbing method known to today's technology, to scrub the Clinton server to hide 30,000 + deleted e-mails that may have shown up otherwise, plus John Bentel and Brian Pagliano, also with Platte River and the man who set up the private server in the Clinton's basement, who had previously received prosecutorial immunity for his testimony to the FBI and testimony before Congress in which case he took the 5th. Pagliano received additional protections under this new immunity deal which protects all 5.

September 28, 2016

FBI director, James Comey, appeared today before the House Judiciary Committee to answer questions surrounding prosecutorial immunity that was given to 5 members of Secretary Clinton's high level staff members. The atmosphere was extremely tense and even downright ugly as House members grilled the FBI director attempting to understand why on earth the FBI would recommend, and the DOJ issue immunity to Clinton staff members who were involved in a cover up operation of the most extreme corrupt nature. Of great importance is that the FBI's role is to investigate, end of story, period! In this instance the FBI conspired with the DOJ to play a role in the decision-making process to decide if immunity would be issued. This level of corruption makes Nixon's indiscretion's look like child's play. Director Comey gave vague, deceptive and sadly insufficient responses to his query. He grew angry at one point when Congressman Trey Gowdy (R-SC), who has known Director Comey personally for many years due to his previous work as a prosecutor in South Carolina, told the Director that this was not the FBI he once knew. Director Comey fired back with an aggressive defense of his FBI agents who had worked on this case. This was the only good thing the Director had to offer today because this is not at all the fault of any FBI agent. As a matter of fact, we've heard rumblings of the extreme frustration of the agents who worked on the case and even many others who were every bit as much troubled with their Directors weak position as he caved to pressure that surely came from the very highest levels of our government and yes, I'm pointing to President Obama. No one will ever obtain proof of this but all it takes is to follow the trail and utilize some common sense. This deal stinks to high heaven. No grand jury was called and no subpoenas were issued by the DOJ hence the obvious trail to the White House. What an incredibly obvious situation where the DOJ at AG Lynch's behest intentionally dropped the ball and I wonder who above her may have had something to do with this incredible travesty of justice! Could it have been POTUS? Let's see, oh yes, he's the only one who could have played a role at the top here. Does anyone really believe that AG Lynch did this unilaterally? I don't think so. Director Comey testified regarding Hillary's unsecure private e-mail server, that without knowing more, we can't call it a crime because there's insufficient intent. Really!!! This is beyond the pale as intent is written all over Clinton's unsecure private e-mail server and subsequent cover up actions.

Flash back to December 2014 and the cover up begins when Hillary Clinton advised Cheryl Mills to delete everything they hadn't already turned over to the State Department so this is where the deletion of 30,000 + e-mails began. Based on instructions from Hillary Clinton, Cheryl Mills immediately calls Platte River Networks and orders them to delete everything left on the server. Fast forward to March 2, 2015 when the New York Times publishes an article disclosing the fact that Hillary Clinton was using a secret private e-mail server. When the Chairman of the House Select Committee on Benghazi, Congressman Trey Gowdy (R-SC), learns of the NYT article revealing the secret server he issued a letter on March 2nd to the U.S. District Attorney for Washington DC who in turn orders the preservation of any e-mails on the private server. The next day on the 3rd a preservation order letter from the House Select Committee on Benghazi with a demand that nothing should be destroyed and that all e-mails must be preserved went to Hillary Clinton. Then on March 4th an official subpoena went to Hillary Clinton demanding the preservation of any e-mails on her private server. At this point, Cheryl Mills sent a communique to Platte River Networks in mid-March as a heads-up that a preservation subpoena had been issued to Secretary Clinton for any e-mails on the private server, this with the knowledge that she had already ordered Platte River to destroy everything back in December 2014. The communique was just a written formality as far as Mills was concerned at the time but when Platte River received this new information, Brian Pagliano with Platte River came to the realization that there were still 30,000 + e-mails on the server that he hadn't yet deleted. At this point Pagliano freezes up and just does nothing based on knowledge of the official subpoena. Next, a conference call takes place on March 25th between David Kendall, a Clinton attorney, Cheryl Mills, Hillary Clinton and Platte River as a follow up to confirm that everything had in fact been deleted and this was when Pagliano confessed that there were still 30,000 + e-mails on the server. Then on March 27th David Kendall sent a letter to Congressman Gowdy advising him there was nothing left to preserve. Of course, Platte River had been admonished by the Clinton team during the March 25th conference call and ordered to get rid of the e-mails that remained so on March 31st Paul Combetta uses bleach-bit to scrub everything including the back-ups destroying the entire e-mail archive permanently. Finally, on this particular timeline, on June 10th Brian Pagliano cut an immunity deal with the FBI and agreed to appear before the House Select Committee on Benghazi to testify so a subpoena was issued to Pagliano to testify and provide documents before said committee and a date was set for September 10th, 2015. Prior to the hearing date Pagliano's attorneys wrote a letter to Congressman Gowdy advising him that Pagliano would plead the 5th at the September 10th hearing given the FBI investigation. By now Brian Pagliano had already received requests to appear before Senate Committee's too. Brian Pagliano did show up for the September 10th House hearing and did indeed plead the 5th and that was it for some time.

Moving back now to the September 28th, 2016 House Judiciary Committee Hearing, Director Comey described the immunity for 5 high level Clinton subordinates as being productive immunity as if issuing immunity in the first place wouldn't obstruct any ability to conduct a productive investigation because the only people who could take you further down the rabbit hole are the people who gained immunity and then clammed up. Brian Pagliano recently ignored a subpoena to appear before Congress to provide testimony and just simply failed to show up, this coming from a cocky young man thumbing his nose at the U.S. Congress whose incredibly important oversight role here is being thwarted. He surely would have taken the 5th anyway but that just heightens his incredible show of disrespect for Congress. Is this the kind of productive immunity Director Comey was referring to? I don't know about you but I'm having a little trouble with the productive aspect of the Director's reasoning not to mention the fact that the other 4 are clammed up tighter than a vice clamp tightened on a piece of wood. Director Comey was previously within prosecutorial discretion as a defense for his personal actions but now that these immunity deals have been issued by the DOJ, that goes out the window.

When the Director was questioned specifically about Cheryl Mills and Heather Samuelson's immunity deal and its purpose he said they had to grant immunity to get their laptops. It's important to note here that when the Director was asked if they found classified documents on Mill's laptop, he responded that yes there was so since it's a felony to keep classified documents in an unsecure location, Mill's should have been prosecuted but since she gained immunity this can't happen. I suppose it becomes easier to rationalize on this since Hillary Clinton did the same thing with impunity and no indictment was leveled on her so what's one more. Congressman Jason Chaffetz (R-UT) asked the Director if they couldn't have just subpoenaed Mill's and Samuelson's laptops and he responded going that route would have taken too long. What's the rush! Is the Obama administration attempting to obstruct justice by speeding things up to realize a wrap before this year's November election? One can only surmise this must be the case because there is no other reasonable motive. Congressman Chaffetz later said the DOJ is handing out immunity like candy! Director Comey testified they were only giving out immunity to low lying fruit. I beg to differ because Cheryl Mills is anything but low lying fruit! When the FBI went to Hillary Clinton's Georgetown mansion to interview her as part of their dishonest investigation, Cheryl Mills accompanied Clinton as her legal representation, this after Mills had been granted immunity. When the Director was asked if it's usual to allow a witness in a subsequent prosecution, a target of the investigation, to be present in the room when the FBI interviews the primary target of the investigation, the Director simply replied that he knows of no precedent. When a witness to a criminal act is allowed to represent Secretary Clinton after having been questioned by the FBI and subsequently given immunity even though she was a target of the investigation, the Director's response that he knows of no precedent for such a scenario is sadly insufficient!

Finally, when the Director of the FBI was asked when or if the FBI will further investigate Cheryl Mills and Heather Samuelson, the Director said he can't confirm if the FBI has even taken up an investigation at this point. When pressed further as to when this might occur he responded he couldn't say and that the FBI doesn't confirm or deny investigations. This highly evasive answer further feeds into the extreme frustration members of Congress and the American people are experiencing over the cryptic nature of the FBI's investigation of Secretary Clinton. Now clearly Mills and Samuelson can't be prosecuted on anything relating to Clinton's unsecure private e-mail server but through the process of further investigation into their activities in association with Secretary Clinton who knows what else there could be that hasn't seen the light of day yet. If Secretary Clinton is elected as our next President on November 8th she will be in the clear from anything further that may surface because the President elect cannot be prosecuted for anything beginning 90 days prior to inauguration which occurs on January 19, 2017, less than 90 days from November 8th.

JASTA

September 28, 2016

Congress passed **JASTA** a few days ago, Justice for American Survivors of Terrorist Acts, by an overwhelming majority. The President has already telegraphed that he will veto it. Support for the bill was bi-partisan and it passed easily possibly because many members of Congress are up for re-lection and don't want to be the guy or gal who refused to support 9/11 survivors. The bill which was very carefully crafted only to go after the guilty, opens the door for any survivor of a terrorist act foreign or domestic, whether it be due to a family member who perished as the result of a terrorist act or even having survived one themselves with injuries, to file suit against the foreign entity that was the cause of the terrorist act. The rub is that any foreign entity can do the same to us, for instance if they deem a drone strike by the U.S. to be an act of terror, they can file suit against the U.S. government. The legal ramifications are endless! This is a New York City attorney's greatest dream come true because they stand to make a fortune on these types of suits alone as all suits originating in the United States will originate in Federal Court in lower Manhattan. Foreign entities who file suit against a U.S. entity will begin their process in their home country and court. Here's where it gets complicated because let's say we're talking about a law suit that originated in the United States against a foreign entity, the defendant in that foreign country must be compelled to show up in court in Manhattan and vice versa. Now we'll just need to wait for a precedent to be established on if The Hague, the international criminal court located in the Netherlands in the capital city of the province of South Holland, could enter the fray to coordinate between the various foreign entities in some sort of oversight capacity. For instance, they were apparently prepared to do so regarding $400 million paid to the U.S. and subsequently held in trust to facilitate arms deals with Iran going back to 1979 just before the Shah of Iran was ousted from power. President Obama asserted that if we hadn't paid Iran back with interest on this money that The Hague would have stepped in to facilitate the legal process between the United States and Iran. Since we did indeed pay Iran back with interest and in cash no less, all in Swiss francs and Euros, we'll never know for sure.

One of the most interesting aspects of this legislation is that it allows for and insists on discovery! Saudi Arabia, a Muslim nation that's been shrouded in mystery, will be compelled to offer evidence relevant to any given case as well as any other foreign country or entity and again vice versa. Royalty and other high level government officials in Saudi Arabia are incensed by this because given Sharia Law and other atrocities that are commonly practiced by Saudi Arabia including the export of Wahhabism, the most violent radical form of Islam, there are many dark secrets that could be uncovered and would subsequently taint Saudi Arabia's reputation as just another Muslim country with a whole lot of oil. Of course, a spotlight is now on 9/11 survivors who will most assuredly begin filing law suits against the Muslim government of Saudi Arabia for their role in possibly facilitating the 9/11 attacks in NYC, Washington DC and just outside Philadelphia. 15 of the 19 perpetrators of the 9/11 attacks were from Saudi Arabia and Wikileaks has exposed many other old secrets regarding terrorism originating in Saudi Arabia!

One very interesting aspect of this new law is Section 5. Section 5 has a provision that makes it possible for the U.S. Secretary of State to request a "stay" for up to 6 months if and only if the sitting Secretary of State shows up in person to make this request. This is a card the Secretary would throw in the event of projected dangerous blow back by a foreign government who deems a law suit to be so incriminating and revealing that possible retribution could have a negative impact on national security. Now, negotiations to reach a settlement would be expected during the 6-month stay but if a settlement isn't reached, the Secretary of State may once again show up in person to request another 6-month stay and this could go on ad infinitum to keep a law suit just hanging out there. The Judge must of course approve any given request by the Secretary of State for a stay but put yourself in the Judge's shoes and ask yourself if you would deny a stay requested by the sitting Secretary of State? I suppose given criteria that reveals possible abuse of approved stays already granted could be sufficient to deny a request but it would take solid evidence of abuse.

Dire projections are already being floated regarding possible blow back coming specifically from Saudi Arabia. Saudi Arabia owns a substantial amount of U.S. debt which they could begin to sell off to the highest bidder so the concern here is that the U.S. becomes a debtor nation to a much less desirable nation. They could also begin refusing to buy future debt creating one less ally the U.S. can sell debt to, which may not be such a bad thing. Already in response to the passage of this bill, Saudi Arabia began manipulating the price of oil causing it shoot up. The previous standard of tort protection as the result of sovereign immunity for terrorist acts goes out the window with this new law but it's important to note that this is only in relationship to acts of terrorism.

History in the Making

A couple of days after Congress overwhelmingly passed JASTA, the President vetoed it as promised. Surprise, Surprise! Congress had promised a veto override and knew they had the votes for it and override it they did! Today, by an overwhelming majority, Congress for the 1st time since the President took office in 2009, handed the President a veto override on a major piece of legislation, JASTA. **History in the making!** These things don't happen often because it takes a 2/3rd majority in both the House and the Senate to successfully override a Presidential veto. The House passed this measure by a vote of 348 to 77 with 1 recorded abstention and the vote in the Senate was 97 to 1 with 2 non-votes. Senate minority leader, Senator Harry Reid (D-NV), was the sole no vote and coming from him this too is no surprise because he retires at the end of the year so why not throw President Obama a bone on his way out. Let the games begin! Law suits will begin to fly and I sincerely hope that at least some of the 9/11 survivors will receive justice for the terrible injustice that rained down on their loved ones on 9/11/2001. Since there's no precedent for this, no one knows how things will play out but play out they will so we should all pay careful attention to the fallout of this new law now that it has overcome a Presidential veto. We could see some very good things happen for American survivors of terrorist acts and we could also see some very negative consequences from this new law. Now that things are in motion, we'll just need to wait and see.

The Plot Thickens

October 3, 2016

Earthshattering new information on the immunity deal the FBI negotiated with Cheryl Mills and Heather Samuelson surfaced today. As it turns out, the FBI promised to destroy both Mills and Samuelson's laptops once they had looked at them to close the deal to get them. The FBI did of course get both laptops, looked at them, discovered classified information on both and proceeded to destroy both laptops. Based on the law, which is just a minor inconvenience for the Clintons but is precedent setting for the FBI, it's illegal to destroy any device that had classified information on it because it automatically by law becomes property of the U.S. government at that point. This is just incredible! The FBI at the highest levels made a conscious decision to break the law, attempt to keep it under wraps, and destroyed both Mills and Samuelson's laptops after they found classified information on both! When Director Comey testified in front of the House Judiciary Committee and gave sworn testimony that the FBI did indeed find classified information on Mills laptop, he proved that when he instructed FBI agents to destroy both laptops in violation of the law he knew exactly what he was doing. Blatantly breaking the law!!! Not only that, this proves he committed perjury by omission in front of a Congressional Committee! Just a minor detail, no biggie! Director Comey intentionally breaks the law by destroying U.S. government property! Now I'm sure he would argue that they had to destroy the laptops because that was a stipulation of the immunity deal they made with Mills and Samuelson so how could the FBI make such a deal with full knowledge that they would likely end up destroying the property of the U.S. government? Director Comey's omission regarding destruction of U.S. government property now becomes easier to understand but it also places emphasis on his uncertainty regarding the legality of his actions! There's no way all this happened in a vacuum! AG Lynch had to be coordinating with Valerie Jarrett, Senior White House advisor to the President, and even the President himself by taking FBI documents to the White House to keep the President apprised of unfolding revelations.

The bottom line is that everyone's collective butts are covered every which way because AG Lynch and the President conspired to establish an unshakable defense even if that meant in the worst-case scenario that Presidential pardons would be needed whether they come from President Obama before he leaves office which would most assuredly be their preference or by Hillary Clinton herself if she were to become our next President. Hillary Clinton and her 5 subordinates along with Director Comey and any of his subordinates who would need protection under the law are covered. Of course, if Hillary were to lose the election, the timeframe for pardons would be moved up at all costs so President Obama could commit the evil deed before it's too late which would most likely be the case anyway! Why take any chances and better to just get it all wrapped up before January 19th, 2017 so everybody will be happy except of course the American people who got screwed! Nixon is turning in his grave!

Chapter 30

Transition

November 14, 2016

Post-election drama is in full swing with daily protests by disgruntled young people on College campuses and in major cities where Clinton had a lot of support. Chants of "not my President" rang out while they marched down the streets carrying placards that describe their disgust. Organized operations like "moveon.org" and "black lives matter" are fueling the fire with paid protesters funded by the likes of George Soros who has operatives in the field to handle the logistics. Many of the protests turned violent with Trump protesters destroying local property and even beating up Trump voters when they were identified. Several were ganged up on and beaten for simply wearing a "make America great again" ball cap. Portland, OR. was the scene of the worst violence where night after night protesters destroyed cars setting some on fire and busted out windows in local business. Protesters in several major cities blocked traffic on Interstate highways and other major roadways. As arrests were made authorities learned that many were professional protesters who had flown in from other parts of the country. It's troubling that so many young people today don't know how to deal with disappointment or adversity. The scenes we're witnessing of young people who look so depressed you'd think their smart phones have been taken away are widespread. The questionable practice of handing out participation trophies to every team member win or lose is proving to be highly detrimental because kids aren't learning how to deal with the inevitable occasional loss or failure that we all experience in life. College campuses are providing safe places where students can retreat to wallow in self-pity. Some even have puppies they can hug and crying sessions are held for the crybabies. This madness needs to end but faculty and staff are encouraging it so the lunatics are running the asylum! There appears to be no end to the protests anytime soon as they are consistently held daily with large numbers of participants who display lots of enthusiasm albeit quite negative. I would think they will surely lose momentum sometime soon as their normal social lives are surely being interrupted. President Obama should speak out against the violent protests but he's been silent on the issue.

President elect Trump appeared on "60 minutes" last night with his family. CBS correspondent Lesley Stahl hosted this edition which lasted the full hour. Stahl did her best to trip him up hoping to catch him unprepared or to get a response that wasn't presidential but her efforts were to no avail. President elect Trump was totally prepared with concise answers that made good sense and provided nothing that would stir up controversy. His demeanor was presidential with a reassuring sense of command as Stahl gradually became aware, much to her chagrin, that this is a serious man with a populist agenda that the viewing audience was surely impressed with. Lesley went on to address the family hoping to find a conflict between President elect Trump and the family business. It was easy to detect that Stahl's disappointment had reached a climax when Eric, Ivanka and Donald Jr. reassured her that they would be staying in New York City to run the business while their father runs the country. They of course went on to express their utmost confidence in their father as leader of the free world. Trump was very much in command of this important appearance before the American people he was elected to govern and had a reassuring presence that I think eased a lot of tension over his temperament that was under constant attack by the main stream media throughout the campaign. The main stream media has engaged in a great deal of fearmongering since Trump won the election. Their frustration over Clinton's loss has thrown them into a tailspin. The media's dishonesty was exposed during the campaign with their heavily biased reporting as well as the credibility of the pollsters which has been shattered by their inaccuracy. At this point the media is struggling to find their way and they aren't making progress. They're focused on criticizing the President elect and the people who elected him aren't receptive to their obvious anger. Fox News is the only televised outlet with a balanced and honest approach at this point. The people elected their next President and the people choose news outlets they trust. With so few trustworthy news outlets today it doesn't take long to decide which one to follow.

President Obama held a press conference at the White House today to address questions about domestic issues prior to making his last trip overseas as POTUS. White House Press Secretary Josh Ernest had provided the President with a list of reporters to call on so this was a choreographed press conference with nothing but softballs for the President. As expected there were several questions about President elect Trump. It was apparent from the outset that this pool of reporters hold a pessimistic outlook about our incoming President. Questions revolved around his temperament, ability to govern with the implication that he's unfit, qualifications, lack of experience, concerns coming from leaders abroad, harsh words directed at Trump by President Obama during the campaign and changes to policy regarding the ACA, the Paris climate agreement and the Iran nuke deal. All fair questions but all were posed with a negative disposition. The President was somewhat conciliatory and measured in his responses overall and refrained from the type of harsh rhetoric he had used during the campaign. He was of course defensive of his policies and he offered a great deal of advice for President elect Trump all of which was in support of his policies. In his opening statement, he said his administration is leaving things in good shape and that they had stabilized the global economy. I find it interesting that President Obama's focus is on the global economy and not our own economy here at home which given it's dismal 1% GDP growth is probably the reason why he'd rather not talk about it. His assertion that he's leaving things in good shape is of course not at all the case. This press conference was as much about consoling the press and Democrats overall so the President was compelled to explain the challenges and importance of a cohesive transition of power and even reminded everyone that elections have consequences which was a phrase he formerly used to backhand his opposition with. He said the office has a way of waking a man up and advised to judge him after a couple of years. The President did express concerns about trade as his vision of globalization conflicts with Trump's vision of America first and placed emphasis on his grave concern that the President elect would attempt to dismantle the ACA while selling us all one more time on how great he believes it is. On Trump's temperament, the President cautioned that whatever you bring to the office will be magnified and expressed some elements won't serve him well unless he recognizes and corrects. The Iran nuke deal and the Paris climate agreement are two more of President Obama's awful deals targeted to be dismantled by Trump that the President attempted to vigorously defend. He said that after a year, Iran had abided by the nuke deal which is a totally false statement and he continued with additional weak assertions. President Obama wasn't even asked about the Paris climate deal but he went there anyway. He detailed a litany of talking points he considers to be good about the climate deal to once again try to convince us that it's needed all of which the press eagerly devoured. It's clear that President Obama will continue to defend his failed policies as he comes to terms with a President elect who move the country in a very different direction.

November 15, 2016

The President has embarked on his final overseas trip making his first stop in Athens, Greece. He appeared today with Greek President Pavlopoulos and chose to begin his criticism of President elect Trump on foreign soil. His remarks were in part defensive comments on his policies and the rest was his somewhat subtle yet harsh criticism directed at President elect Trump. Coming from the most divisive President in U.S. history, President Obama warned that President elect Trump would create "a rise in a crude sort of nationalism or ethnic identity" in America "built around an us vs. them" scenario. He went on to predict a culture clash when he said, "some will seek comfort in culturalism or tribe or sect." The Presidents prediction of divisions in our society that already exist is divisive in and of itself. He creating unwarranted fears that will put many Americans on the defensive before our President elect even has a chance to bring people together. The underlying message President Obama is sending is that illegal aliens won't be given the same opportunities as American citizens which he sees as an injustice. At least he's making an accurate accusation because illegal aliens will finally be held accountable for disrespecting our laws by coming and staying in America illegally. President Obama overlooks the fact that it's unfair to those who respect the process and get in line as they follow the law to earn the right to become a U.S. citizen and misses the point that Americans have been negatively impacted by the great influx of illegal immigrants who create fewer jobs and lower wages for American citizens. The President went on to make false claims that he had raised wages and invested in infrastructure and continued with a general defense of his policies with no specifics.

November 20, 2016

President Obama traveled from Greece to Germany and spent a couple of uneventful days with Chancellor Angela Merkel. They held a joint press conference and the President answered several questions about his loss to President elect Trump so we heard many excuses which I'm sure was a painful experience for the President. Challenges in Syria came up and the President offered that we must continue to push for a political transition and settlement with a cessation of indiscriminate bombing and a focus on humanitarian efforts. He went on to add that we must pressure Assad for a lasting peace through the people all of which sounds quite noble with good intentions yet all totally unrealistic. A question came up about the continuing protests by young liberals back home and the President responded that, "I wouldn't advise them to be silent." Not exactly the response that many who had hoped for a de-escalating statement to potentially bring an end to the violent protests had in mind.

The President traveled from Germany to Lima, Peru for the Asia Pacific Summit where President Obama's focus was on globalization. He held a press conference today and in his opening statement he spoke of global environmental standards and global supply chains while attempting to convince us that everyone benefits from trade agreements like the Trans Pacific Partnership. He failed to address the extreme trade deficit that America is subjected to under such an agreement as he focused on U.S. exports with no mention of the excess imports to America from other countries. He reaffirmed America's commitment to the TPP knowing full well that President elect Trump has no intention of participating. He did state that not participating would undermine America's ability to benefit so I suppose that was his way of messaging doubt to his audience who knew full well that Trump isn't inclined to participate. Questions from the press revolved around concerns about President elect Trump and the questionable condition of the Democrat party. Once again, the questions about a Trump White House projected doom and gloom. The President was diplomatic on questions about Trump this time but did caution about possible pitfalls and was full of excuses for the diminished state of the Democrat party. When asked if he would withhold public criticism of Trump while he serves as POTUS as Bush did for him, the President said, "I'll speak out if there are core questions about our values and ideals." That certainly leaves the door open to a great deal of public criticism given the extreme ideological differences these two possess. It's clear now that President elect Trump will need to deal with a hostile press and predecessor during his time in office which I'm sure he's anticipated so his twitter account will be quite active as well as his utilization of You Tube videos to bypass the dishonest press as he goes directly to the American people with his unique style of messaging.

Saving Face Tour

December 6, 2016

President Obama made the first in a series of farewell speeches today as he prepares to embark on what I like to call his **saving face tour** around the country. He's been motivated by President elect Trump's fast pace start by saving 800 jobs when he recently convinced Carrier to keep a plant in Indiana instead of moving to Mexico and convinced a Japanese banking company to invest $50 billion here in America creating over 50,000 jobs. Trump hasn't even been inaugurated yet and his proactive efforts have yielded positive results as he creates and saves American jobs. Today's speech at MacDill AFB where CENTCOM, U.S. Central Command, is located was all about propping up his failures in the Middle East as successful endeavors. He began by stating that Al Qaeda is a "shadow of its former self" which couldn't be further from reality. Al Qaeda and its affiliates like the al-Nusra Front in Syria and Lebanon are stronger than ever with a substantial Al Qaeda presence in Afghanistan and beyond. The President claimed Afghanistan is secure and able to protect itself with the help of 10,000 American troops. He did admit the situation there is still tough due to the Taliban presence but claimed we've made a significant difference and that America is safer for it. The truth is Afghanistan is a powder keg that still presents a major challenge. The President went on to speak about ISIS as though great progress had been made in our fight against them in Iraq and Syria. He once again used the excuse that the supposed inability to establish a new status of forces agreement with Iraq was the reason for the complete and abrupt troop pullout in 2010 that led to the rise of ISIS and paved the way for them to take Mosul along with the rest of northern Iraq as they established a Caliphate in northern Syria and Iraq based in Raqqa, Syria. A new status of forces agreement could have easily been established because the U.S. had successfully ousted Saddam Hussein and paved the way for Prime Minister Maliki to head up the new government there so after everything we did for Iraq President Obama could have demanded a new status of forces agreement and Maliki would have relented. President Obama said when Iraq reached out for help we took the fight to ISIS with the Iraqi security force backed up by our equipment and troops which has grown to 5000 at present. He claimed the Iraqi government is committed to unity while the divide between the Shiite led government in Baghdad and the Sunni's and Kurds in Iraq is greater than ever. The President said that as the fight for Mosul is underway, ISIS is being squeezed in Raqqa, Syria but failed to mention that the fight for Mosul is extremely slow going and will rage on longer than anyone can even imagine. He said there has been a shift in how we fight the terrorists as we utilize a network of partners and claimed we've cut the flow of foreign fighters to ISIS in half and cut ISIS propaganda in half. The network of partners the President referred to only consists of the Iraqi security force along with the Kurdish Peshmerga with outdated weaponry and our 5000 troops in Iraq so it isn't this vast coalition he eluded to so we have a long way to go in the fight against ISIS. The fact is that we have 15,000 troops in

Afghanistan and Iraq hampered by unreasonable rules of engagement with no end to the fight foreseen any time soon so there isn't much to brag about.

The President went on to say we must keep the terrorist threat in perspective and that they are just thugs and murderers and not a new world order. He said they don't pose an existential threat to our nation and that we can't follow a path of overreach. He claimed we must save resources and lives while we maintain the wisdom to hold to our values and the rule of law because the terrorists want to change who we are. He proclaimed we can't be driven by fear and that we can get these terrorists and stay true to who we are. As if that useless stream of rhetoric weren't sufficient he went on to say we must fight terrorists in such a way that we don't create more terrorists which opened the door to segue to the need to do away with the detainment facility at Guantanamo Bay in Cuba. We were reminded that he cut the detainee population there from 242 to 59 at present and said that fear won't allow us to transfer the remaining 59 to U.S prisons. He admonished that Gitmo will be judged harshly by history. The fact is that many of the terrorists who were released from Gitmo have returned to the fight and fanned the flames of terrorism with renewed vigor as seasoned fighters and strong recruiters.

The Iran nuclear deal came up as the President said we must draw upon the strength of our diplomacy. He claimed we've secured nuclear materials and chemical weapons around the globe with diplomacy. He couldn't have picked a worse example of the successful use of diplomacy. The Iran nuclear deal is a terrible deal that paves the way for Iran to become a weaponized nuclear power in 15 years or sooner if they cheat which they've already done with excess heavy water reserves and test firing ICBM's in violation of the deal. He went on to assert we must help refugees in search for a better life and that we can't stigmatize good Muslims as he warned against discrimination with religious tests. He said we're a nation of hope not fear and a nation of civil rights as he added right makes might and not the other way around. His righteous discourse failed to note that refugee streams have in fact been infiltrated by terrorists which was the case with the terrorists who were responsible for the deadly mass shootings at the Bataclan theater and sidewalk cafes in Paris not long ago. It was President Obama's failure that led to the rise of ISIS and his failure to effectively fight ISIS that caused the refugee problem in Syria. 6 million Syrians have been driven from their homes with many winding up in Aleppo, Syria creating a huge mass of humanity crammed into confined spaces with unimaginable living conditions. Initially many made their way across the nearby border into Turkey and large numbers were then able to make their way to Germany and France which has been problematic for these European countries. These displaced Syrians don't even qualify as refugees because they weren't free in the first place. They can't be properly vetted because there's no database in Syria with records on them so they're an undefined lot with very limited options. If this speech was any indication of the rest of his farewell tour we're in for a load of empty rhetoric that sounds good to his liberal base. His omissions are the key to the lack of truth and substance so it's necessary to fill in the gaps to acquire a complete picture of reality.

Slaughter

December 15, 2016

Russian and Syrian fighter jets are bombing Aleppo, Syria killing large numbers of civilians as they finish off the rebel opposition fighters who tried and failed to take out the Assad regime. Syrian ground forces and Iranian Shia Militias are also working their way through Aleppo between bombing runs as they **slaughter** civilians and rebel opposition fighters. There have been reports of soldiers indiscriminately shooting women and children in the streets. There is so much death and destruction in and around Aleppo that many are calling it genocide. Rebels have pulled out of eastern Aleppo after a 4-year occupation and some of the remaining civilians are finally able to evacuate during a brief cease fire. Aleppo was once the largest city in Syria and now it sits in shambles after a relentless bombing campaign by Russia and the Assad regime. White House Press Secretary Josh Earnest condemned the actions of the Assad regime aided by Russia and Iranian Shia Militias. The hypocrisy of the Obama administration is obvious to anyone who's been paying attention because they did nothing in Syria when a difference could have been made. It's too late now but back in 2013 we could have shut down ISIS when there were only 20,000 fighters in Syria and Iraq and stopped the Assad regime in their tracks after they crossed President Obama's red line and used chemical weapons on civilians. Assad was sending a message to the rebel opposition that there are consequences for their rebellion. Russia hadn't intervened in Syria yet and may not have if we had acted when we could have made a difference without starting another war. When President Obama made the red line threat he said Assad's days are numbered and since that time 1749 days have passed.

Bashar al-Assad is a proxy of Iran and President Obama was too concerned with possibly jeopardizing the Iran nuclear deal so he chose to refrain from acting in Syria for fear he would anger Iran. We should have heard directly from President Obama on the massacre that's taking place in Aleppo but he would probably rather not place emphasis on one of his biggest failures. Secretary of State John Kerry made a statement today from the State Department and said we've provided $6 million to assist in humanitarian aid for evacuees from Aleppo. He said we've engaged in talks to end the violence but efforts have been thwarted by the Assad regime in their effort to take back Aleppo and the rest of northern Syria. He spoke at length about the need for a diplomatic process to achieve peace but bemoaned Assad's reluctance to engage in peace talks with the opposition. 500,000 Syrians have been slaughtered over the last 5 years and there's no end in sight to Assad's relentless actions to finish off the rebel opposition. The deep sectarian nature of this conflict offers little hope for peace and the rebel opposition to the

Assad regime isn't strong enough to hold out much longer against superior forces of the Assad regime, Russia and Iranian Shia Militias. We've witnessed the displacement of 11 million people, the destabilization of Turkey, Lebanon and Jordon, the ascendancy of Iran in the region, the emergence of Russia as a global power, diminishment of the American position in the world, the refugee crisis in Europe, the resurgence of fascism in Europe and a new threat to national security in America. President Obama and Secretary Kerry's failure to lead back in 2013 when a difference could have been made will go down in history as one of his biggest failures.

Sour Grapes

December 16, 2016

Democrats continue to live in denial over Trump's victory in the general election. They just can't accept him as our next President. They're living their worst nightmare because they know their liberal agenda is toast. Some D list Hollywood celebrities led by Martin Sheen formed a group called "Unite for America" and produced a television commercial that speaks to Republican electors of the electoral college imploring them to ignore their mandate to cast their vote for President elect Trump and to vote for someone else on December 19th. Greg Gutfeld with Fox News diagnosed these crazed liberals as having THD, Trump Hysteria Disorder. Michelle Obama's THD was on full display in an interview with Oprah Winfrey yesterday when said proclaimed, "Now we're feelin' what not havin' hope feels like." Coming from the First Lady of the United States this doesn't reflect the kind of gracious attitude one would expect to facilitate a peaceful transition of power. The apple cart has been upset and the end of the status quo within the Washington DC establishment is within sight. The days of Washington DC elites placing their socialistic will over the will of hard working middle class Americans has come to an end. President elect Trump's policy of "America first" doesn't fit the liberal agenda of globalization in which America is just another nation among nations, no better or stronger, just one of many nations. In a fit a rage, Democrats including President Obama are actively engaged in obstructing a peaceful transition of power. They've latched onto a narrative that President elect Trump engaged in a conspiracy with Russia to interfere with the outcome of the election by hacking the DNC, Hillary's private unsecure server and John Podesta's personal e-mail account. They have no proof of their allegations. Their allegations are based in pure speculation and wreak of a political motive.

White House Press Secretary Josh Earnest who speaks for the President insists that Trump was aware of malicious cyber activity by the Russians and even contends that it's factual when there is no definitive proof. The CIA and FBI were in a contentious position on this until today when FBI Director Comey caved to pressure and said he now agrees with the CIA, DNI and NSA that Russia was involved in the hacking. Leadership of every intelligence agency has refused to appear before the House or Senate intelligence committees behind closed doors to brief them on their findings so I find their refusal to be a strong sign that they do not possess definitive proof of Russia's involvement and that their motive is purely political. WikiLeaks founder, Julian Assange, issued a statement that he did not receive anything from Russia and Craig Murry, UK Ambassador to Uzbekistan confirmed that an insider with the DNC leaked the e-mails to WikiLeaks. President Obama can't accept the outcome of the election so he must find something to blame it on and Russia fits the narrative he's established. Russia makes for a convenient scapegoat to justify why Hillary Clinton lost an election that a decent candidate could have won for the Democrats. She was a terrible candidate who has the likeability of a root canal. She failed to present an uplifting message to the American people and did nothing but attack Trump. Hillary won the popular vote by about 3 million votes so if the Russians really did have such a profound effect on the election she would have lost the popular vote by a wide margin. She lost the electoral vote which is the only vote that counts because she didn't resonate with hard-working middle class Americans in the fly over States who had suffered to such a great extent under the Obama administration and who knew they would get more of the same from Clinton. She was more concerned with transgender bathrooms than our failing economy. Democrats are so out of touch with so many Americans that I'm surprised Hillary hasn't received a participation trophy yet! The **sour grapes** displayed by President Obama and Hillary Clinton won't help Democrats rebuild a party in shambles that has lost touch with working class Americans.

Jihad in Berlin

December 19, 2016

An Islamic Jihadist drove a 25-ton truck through a pedestrian blockade and then into a crowd of people at a Christmas Market in Berlin today. There are 16 Christmas markets in Berlin and they're a cultural tradition that attract many tourists and locals throughout the Christmas season. The popular Christmas Market at Breitscheidplatz across from Kaiser Wilhelm Memorial Church on the Kurfuerstendamm was the scene of this terrorist attack that left 12 people dead and 48 injured with 18 seriously injured, 2 of which are Americans. The terrorist driver of the truck ran away from the scene immediately after the truck stopped and he escaped capture. He remains at large as a wide scale search is under way. German authorities learned the driver had applied for asylum in Germany because his asylum papers were found in the truck. He had been arrested in 2015 carrying false Italian identity papers after spending 4 years in an Italian prison for torching a refugee camp after arriving in Italy via boat from Tunisia and was a known radical Islamist whose Muslim Imam and roommate in Germany were also known to be radical Islamists affiliated with ISIS. He was scheduled for deportation earlier this year but the paperwork in Tunisia that was needed to complete the process was missing. The Tunisian terrorist had hijacked the truck and killed the Polish driver who was left in the passenger seat of the truck having been shot and stabbed several times. The truck was hijacked shortly before the attack and an autopsy revealed the Polish man had been stabbed first then put up a strong fight but was subsequently shot and killed right before the truck slammed into the crowd. ISIS claimed responsibility for this attack praising the terrorist as an ISIS soldier. The goal of ISIS with this attack is the polarization of German society and they've been quite successful. Chancellor Merkel has established a welcome culture in Germany having taken in almost 1 million refugees predominately from Syria and now after numerous violent incidents including the mass sexual assault of over 1000 women by Islamist men on New Year's Eve 2016 in Cologne, the German people have lost patience with the huge influx of Muslim refugees who can't be properly vetted. There have been 11 major Islamist terrorist attacks in Europe this year alone so the rising anxiety of people throughout Europe is understandable and especially so due to open borders throughout European countries. The numerous red flags relating to the perpetrator of this attack that were missed by German authorities have left the German people extremely frustrated with the dangers that have been brought upon them.

December 21, 2016

German authorities have learned more about the perpetrator of the terrorist attack on the Christmas Market at Breitscheidplatz in Berlin. His name is Anis Amri and he's 23 years old. He was an asylum seeker and had been denied asylum but managed to avoid deportation due to missing paperwork in Tunisia. He had 6 aliases, a fraudulent Italian passport and was known to have been in contact with Abu Walah, Germany's ISIS recruiter. He was known to visit online terrorist bombing sites and had a criminal record in Tunisia and Italy. He was on a no-fly list in the U.S. plus a terror watch list and was under covert terror surveillance until September this year and then authorities lost track of him. There's a reward for his capture the equivalent of $100,000. U.S.

December 23, 2016

The Islamist terrorist who committed the truck attack in Berlin was shot and killed early this morning in Milan, Italy. Anis Amri had taken a train from Berlin through France and into Italy where he exited the train in Milan. Milan police noticed Amri wandering around the train station at 3:00AM and when they approached him and asked for ID he reached in his bag, pulled a gun and shot one of the officers then another officer shot and killed him. They didn't know who they were dealing with until he was dead, ran his DNA with his photo and learned he was the most wanted man in Europe for the Berlin terrorist attack. The Italian officer who was shot is recovering in the hospital. ISIS released a video of Amri today in which he pledged allegiance to ISIS. It's difficult to reconcile the fact that he had so many various encounters with authorities in Italy and Germany having been on a terrorist watch list as a known radical Islamist and under surveillance before he committed the deadly attack in Berlin. There were more red flags than you'd find in Beijing yet he evaded surveillance in Germany and 12 innocent people celebrating Christmas in Berlin lost their lives.

Betrayal

President Obama just committed the equivalent of flipping a middle finger at the Nation of Israel on the eve of Hanukkah. The President refused a U.S. veto of a UN Security Council Resolution today that condemns Israel and places Israel in violation of international law. The U.S. abstention from the vote and refusal to veto the resolution enabled the resolution to pass today in an unprecedented shameful action of the United States of America against the sovereign nation of Israel. UN Security Council Resolution 2334 condemns Israel for establishing Jewish settlements on Jewish land and prohibits Jews from praying at the western wall in addition to placing the Temple Mount and eastern Jerusalem under PA control. This new resolution essentially repeals UN resolution 242 which passed after the 1967 war and established the basis for peace but intentionally left borders in the Sinai, Golan Heights and the old city of Jerusalem a little vague and subject to future negotiations as an incentive for peace. UN resolution 242 established the concept of land for peace which is now rendered useless because resolution 2334 abolishes any possibility of a land for peace deal so it essentially cements permanent conflict. The absurd new resolution is the anti-Semitic action of the 5 permanent members of the UN Security Council, any of whom could have unilaterally vetoed this resolution. China, France, Russia, UK and the U.S. bear responsibility for allowing this resolution to pass along with Venezuela, New Zealand and Senegal who co-sponsored the resolution plus all 14 countries of the UN Security Council who voted in favor of the resolution. The greatest weight of responsibility rests upon the United States though because Israel's Ambassador to the U.S., Ron Dermer, said he has iron clad proof that the United States was the sole country who coordinated and crafted this resolution at the UN. Prime Minister Netanyahu and Israel's International spokesman, David Keys, have confirmed Israel's possession of proof that it was a U.S. operation all the way and that President Obama personally masterminded the vote. The Obama administration has issued a statement that denies having set this resolution in motion but Israel has promised to present their proof that the U.S. spearheaded the resolution to the Trump administration after inauguration. The Obama administration is notorious for deceptive actions on major agenda items so this represents one more dishonest move by President Obama which solidifies his practice of "Destruction by Deceit."

This stunning anti-Semitic resolution represents a radical shift in U.S. policy with Israel. It's an insult to Israel and an insult to anyone who cherishes freedom. The resolution supports the

Palestinian Authority which is a terrorist organization founded by the father of modern terrorism, Yasser Arafat. The PA pays monthly support to Arab families of suicide bombers who kill Jews in Israel and they give substantial financial support to Hamas in Gaza which is an affiliate of the Muslim Brotherhood. Under the Obama administration, the U.S. has been giving financial aid to the PA so President Obama is supporting a terrorist organization that commits terrorist acts against Israel, our most important ally in the Middle East while stabbing Israel in the back. This **betrayal** of Israel is also a betrayal of American Christians and Jews. A bipartisan backlash has begun with members of Congress on both sides of the aisle speaking out against the President's unprecedented decision to create a dangerous problem for Israel and threaten a peaceful transition of power here at home. The UN has lost all credibility as an international force for good. This resolution kills any chance there may have been for a 2 State solution for peace in Israel because it removes the only bargaining chip Israel had which is land. There has never been a true opportunity for peace though because a lasting peace will never exist between the PA and Israel due to the extreme hate Arab Islamists of the PA and Hamas in Gaza harbor for Israel. President elect Trump issued a statement that the U.S. role at the UN will change upon his inauguration on January 20th. His pick for U.S. Ambassador to Israel is David Friedman, an Orthodox Jewish bankruptcy attorney from Long Island, NY. who wisely opposes a 2 State solution. The Trump administration will end any financial support for the PA and will stand firmly with the sovereign nation of Israel in resolute opposition to UN resolution 2334. President elect Trump may also move the U.S. Embassy from Tel Aviv to Jerusalem as a statement of solidarity with Israel and will surely use economic leverage with the UN by pulling U.S. funding which amounts to 22% of the UN's operating costs. The resolution will most likely stand though because it would be necessary for Russia and China to agree to repeal it, so given their strong support in favor of the resolution there's no chance of repeal. Prime Minister Netanyahu stated Israel will continue settlement activities and will reassess ties with the UN. Only time will tell what the future holds for the contentious relationship between Israel and the PA in addition to the U.S. and Israeli relationship with the UN.

December 28, 2016

Secretary of State John Kerry delivered an extremely anti-Semitic speech today. He rambled on for 73 minutes with a repetitive message condemning Israel for establishing settlements on Jewish land they legally possess. His tirade condemned Israeli settlement activity 42 times and belabored the need for a 2 State solution that will never come to pass because the Arabs in Israel have only one objective which is to possess all the land. The Islamist terrorists of the PA along with the rest of the Arab world throughout the Middle East won't be satisfied until Israel no longer exists. The only event that will bring peace to Israel is Christ's return. President Obama along with Valerie Jarrett, WH Senior Advisor, Susan Rice, National Security Advisor and Ben Rhodes, Deputy National Security Advisor have conspired to attack Israel at the end of the

President's term in a radical shift of U.S. policy toward Israel that will only last 29 days. Their actions stem from petulance and failure as they take out their frustration on Israel and plot to sabotage President elect Trump, making it much more difficult for him to mitigate the damage done. The Obama administration is using East Jerusalem as a bargaining chip to force Israel to concede to their demands of a 2 State solution that will never bring peace. Secretary Kerry childishly said Israel must decide if their attacks on the Obama administration are worth losing east Jerusalem. He maintains that Arab leaders throughout the Middle East will normalize relations with Israel if they agree to a 2 State solution. The deceptive assertions of the Obama administration are the only defense for their indefensible actions. They think they can lie to the American people with impunity but they aren't fooling anyone. The left supports their lies and conservatives see right through their lies.

Secretary Kerry summed up his attack on Israel with what he called principles that Israel must adhere to. He made 6 demands of Israel without asking anything of the Arab Islamist terrorists of the PA who don't even want peace. He began with a demand of Israel to provide what he called secure internationally recognized borders based on 1967 lines that would include land swaps. This demand is so vague it could never be resolved. Demand number 2 was for two clearly defined States. Demand 3 was acknowledgment of the so-called Palestinian refugees and an offer of compensation for their suffering. Demand 4 was that Jerusalem would be the shared Capitol of the 2 States. Demand 5 was to end what he called Israeli military occupation in so-called Palestinian territory. Demand 6 was to end all conflict with a resolution to all outstanding claims of the so-called Palestinians. Secretary Kerry ended his tirade with a demand of Israel to demonstrate they're serious about making peace. He declared the U.S. sees peace slipping away. The idealistic vision of the Obama administration is delusional and terroristic in nature. Their utter disdain for Israel is apparent as they clearly don't want to recognize Israel's right to exist. They're no better or different than the Islamist terrorists who surround Israel.

Prime Minister Netanyahu delivered a message later in the day in response to Secretary Kerry's speech. He expressed his extreme disappointment with the speech and noted how unbalanced it was with its slant favoring the Islamist terrorists of the PA while blaming Israel for no peace. He called out the insane provision in the UN resolution that calls the western wall occupied Palestinian territory and expressed his hope there will be no more damage done to Israel from the UN. He pointed out that it was by President Obama's direction that, "the U.S. organized, advanced and brought this resolution to the UN," which the Obama administration denies but PM Netanyahu said he will present proof of his assertion to President elect Trump after his inauguration. He said, "the U.S. should stop this game, this charade," and went on to remind us that, "Israel is a sovereign nation that is the master of its own fate." He noted that Palestinian children are not being educated for peace and that the PA has said they should never accept a

Jewish State. He said, "this conflict is about Israel's very right to exist," and that "the PA's refusal to recognize an Israeli State is the core of this conflict." He reminded us that Israel gave back 90% of the Sinai Peninsula and pulled their settlements from Gaza to give it to the Palestinians then got rockets rained down upon them by Hamas in response to Israel's sacrifice in the name of establishing peace. In addition, the Islamist terrorists of the PA pays a monthly salary to families of suicide bombers who kill Jews so why would Israel give up more land in the name of peace when the so-called Palestinians consistently reject peace. He said, "the U.S. has become an arbitrator for the Palestinians," and proclaimed that, "Israel will not go back to 1967 lines." Judea and Samaria, also known as the West Bank is legally possessed by Israel. Military occupations are clearly permitted under international law following an aggressive attack by a neighboring State. Jordon attacked Israel in the 1967 6-day war and Israel prevailed so the West Bank is occupied Israeli land under international law. Israel was attacked by superior forces with superior armaments and prevailed in the 1948 war, the 6-day war of 1967 and the Yom Kippur war of 1973 so the UN Security Council has no legitimate grounds for stepping in to designate Israeli land as occupied Palestinian territory.

Israel has made hundreds of overtures for peace and the response from the so-called Palestinians has always been more terrorist attacks on Israel. The irrational action of the Obama administration is a shameful insult to the only civilized Democracy in the Middle East who is never the aggressor but is under constant attack by the Islamist terrorists who surround them. President Obama intentionally targeted Israel's Capitol, Jerusalem and designated east Jerusalem as occupied Palestinian territory and Jerusalem isn't even mentioned in the Quran. Mecca and Medina are the holy sites of Islam and Jerusalem is the Holy city of the one true God, the God of Abraham, Isaac and Jacob. It's bad enough that the Temple Mount has been desecrated by a Mosque but now to deny Jews their God given right to pray at the western wall is disgraceful. President elect Trump, who has expressed his strong support for Israel, is respecting the fact that America has but one President at a time so he hasn't been able speak out with specifics yet but once he's inaugurated he will take strong action to rectify to damage done by the Obama administration. The roadblocks President Obama is setting up designed to box President elect Trump in will present a challenge but they can be overcome so it will be refreshing to the American people and to Israel to have a President who respects and appreciates Israel, our key ally in the Middle East.

Land Grab

December 29, 2016

The radical environmental agenda of the Obama administration was in full swing today as our President executed a huge federal **land grab** in Utah and Nevada. The Antiquities Act of 1906 was established to protect small parcels of land as historical sites but President Obama took advantage of it today with environmental interests in mind in addition to strengthening big government control over land in the United States. Most politicians and citizens in Utah vehemently oppose the President's action to seize 1.35 million acres of land in Utah known as "Bears Ears" which he just designated as a national monument. "Bears Ears" is a pair of buttes in southeastern Utah, San Juan county, at 8700 ft. elevation and with a little imagination the buttes resemble a pair of bears ears. Governor Gary Herbert, Senator Orrin Hatch and Congressman Jason Chaffetz of Utah have all expressed serious opposition to President Obama's action to designate 1.35 million acres surrounding "Bears Ears" as a national monument because it's such a large parcel of land that is prime real estate for private development of ranches and fossil fuel production. Utah Attorney General, Sean Reyes, has vowed to sue the federal government over this seizure calling it an "egregious overreach" by President Obama. The President utilized the Antiquities Act in this seizure because he believes it will be more difficult for President elect Trump to retract his action but there are differing views on that at this point. It's easy to see that a strong case can be made that 1.35 million acres of land doesn't qualify as a small parcel of land to be set aside as an historical site. The President also seized "Gold Butte" in Nevada which is a 30,000-acre parcel of land to be designated as a national monument. This one isn't quite as controversial because Nevada's economy revolves around the casino business and this is of course a much smaller piece of land than the huge land grab in Utah. President elect Trump now has one more executive action that represents big government overreach to deal with after inauguration.

Cold War De Ja Vu

The Obama administration has insisted that Russia hacked the DNC plus Clinton's campaign manager, John Podesta's personal e-mail account then sent the e-mails to Wiki Leaks so they could release them for public consumption therefore indirectly interfering with the U.S. Presidential election since the content of the e-mails revealed corrupt practices by the Clinton campaign and Hillary personally. Their flawed reasoning is that Russia favored Trump for President and tipped the scales in his favor for Russia's benefit. Democrat talking points that have been repeated ad infinitum by Democrat pundits is that 17 U.S. intelligence agencies confirm that Russia was responsible for the hacking. This assertion lacks credibility though because the FBI and CIA have refused to brief members of the House and Senate Intelligence Committees behind closed doors. It's understandable that the information is classified so it can't go out to the media but why can't Congressional members of the Intelligence Committees be briefed behind closed doors? Those of us who are skeptical would be willing to take the word of Congressional intelligence experts that Russia was in fact the perpetrator of the hacking but the fact that the Obama administration insists on keeping them in the dark raises red flags big time.

The FBI and DHS released a 13-page report on Russian hacking of the DNC and John Podesta called "Grizzly Steppe" – Russian Malicious Cyber Activity. The generic report is flawed, confusing and a leap of logic that really makes a more compelling case for 3rd party hackers as the perpetrators. The 3098-word report only has 398 words of actual analysis that is void of evidence. This wreaks of a political motive to place blame on Russia due to the undesirable outcome of the election for Democrats. The Obama administration along with Clinton have no credibility because they've proven to be dishonest on a consistent basis. It's also curious that while Wiki Leaks was releasing the e-mails for weeks before the election there was no mention of any suspicion that Russia was attempting to influence the outcome of the election. It was only after Clinton lost that suddenly 17 intelligence agencies serving under the Obama administration agree that Russia hacked the DNC and Podesta. Also after all the years of known hacking by China of U.S. government entities and American companies there was never such a huge outcry. In each instance, there would be a brief complaint due to the theft of intellectual property or government information by China then it would just blow over in short order. Now that Democrats need a new scapegoat for Hillary's loss, we've heard the constant drumbeat of Russian hacking for over a month now. First it was FBI Director James Comey's announcement that the FBI had reopened their investigation into Clinton's private unsecure e-mail server. Then it was the Alt Right which consists of about 250 nut jobs. Next it was election fraud in Michigan, Wisconsin and Pennsylvania so a recount effort was launched which yielded more votes for Trump in the end. Fake news on social media even came up as an excuse. It was also the Electoral College because Hillary won the popular vote by 3 million votes and this excuse persists to this day. Finally, it had to be those pesky Russians who hacked the DNC and John Podesta and they seem to be very happy with this one because they're milking it for everything they can. It hasn't occurred to Democrats that they picked a flawed candidate who ran a terrible campaign with no positive message. Clinton had the singular focus of attacking Trump which couldn't match Trump's brilliant marketing approach built around branding with unforgettable short positive messages like "build the wall," "drain the swamp," "best jobs President ever," "defeat and destroy ISIS," strengthen our military," "take care of veterans" and everyone's favorite, "make America great again." Trump also branded his opponents during the primary by calling Ted Cruz – "Lyin' Ted," Jeb Bush – "Low energy," Marco Rubio – "Little Marco" and our favorite throughout the campaigns with Hillary Clinton as "Crooked Hillary."

President Obama just announced 9 new sanctions on Russia and the expulsion of 35 Russian diplomats from the U.S. and the closure of 2 luxury Russian compounds, 1 in Maryland and 1 in Long Island, New York, where high level Russian dignitaries stay when they visit the United States. It's also been widely reported that these Russian compounds are really used for intelligence gathering by Russian spies. The President's actions haven't quite satisfied excuse seekers who see this as nothing more than a slap on the wrist for alleged Russian hacking that presumably cost Hillary the election. The Russian Foreign Ministry sent out a tweet that said it was **cold war de ja vu** and pictured a baby duck with LAME stamped over the duck to emphasize President Obama's lame duck status. Vladimir Putin announced that Russia will not expel any U.S. diplomats or retaliate in any way even though they would be justified and that they will just wait to see what the new administration chooses to do after inauguration. In reply to Putin's announcement, President elect Trump tweeted that it was a good move by Russia and that he always knew Putin was very smart. Putin's next chess move was to snub President Obama in his annual statement to foreign leaders when he made no mention of the U.S. President. Trump and Putin will be formidable adversaries for one another. Putin has run circles around President Obama but now he'll face a true leader with strong negotiating skills. They're sizing each other up at this point but once Trump is inaugurated the high stakes games will begin.

Chapter 31

Caught off Guard

January 6, 2017

As passengers were gathering at the baggage claim at the airport in Ft. Lauderdale, Florida ready to collect their bags to head out on a cruise, Esteban Santiago pulled his gun from his pants waist and began shooting unsuspecting people in the head. His shooting spree lasted for about 3 minutes as he emptied a magazine, reloaded another and emptied it. Airport police quickly responded, spotted the shooter, commanded him to drop his gun and get down which he did and they were able to apprehend him as he surrendered. In no more than 3 minutes the unthinkable occurred and as travelers who had hit the floor got up in stunned shock, they witnessed those who had become targets laying in pools of blood with 5 dead and 6 more seriously injured. At this point airport authorities went into damage control mode as they locked down the airport and commanded everyone in the immediate area of the shooting to get back down as they took defensive measures in the event of another possible shooter. Once word spread throughout the airport everyone there had become terrorized at the prospect of another shooter. A short time later someone heard a loud noise in the parking garage, then someone else heard something loud in a different terminal and in no time authorities had directed travelers to stairwells taking them to the airport tarmac and people were seen running away from the terminal on the tarmac as airport police stormed the parking garage and terminal 1 in search of another possible shooter. Terrorized travelers throughout the airport didn't know what to expect next as authorities worked to get the situation under control which they were finally able to do without further incident. It took several hours to clear the airport while everything shut down and no traffic was allowed in or out of the airport.

Esteban Santiago had boarded a flight in Anchorage, AK. after properly checking his unloaded gun in and checked his bag with the gun, then flew to Minneapolis and then on to Ft. Lauderdale on a one-way ticket. When he arrived in Ft. Lauderdale he claimed his bag, went to the nearest restroom where he entered a stall, loaded his gun and then emerged into the baggage claim area with an extra clip and began shooting. With Santiago in custody the investigation began and we learned some very alarming things about Santiago that raised many questions as to why he was permitted to fly with a gun today which led to disastrous results. He had served in the Puerto Rican National Guard and then the Alaskan Army National Guard. He served a year in Iraq and returned to Anchorage where he eventually received an honorable discharge for poor performance. He had been under psychiatric care for PTSD and had been diagnosed with psychosis. He had been arrested once on domestic violence charges and had other brushes with the law. On one occasion, he went to the FBI office in Anchorage where he told agents he had voices in his head that commanded him to view ISIS videos. An investigation was initiated and the FBI took his gun but later returned the gun to Santiago without placing him on a no-fly list. The FBI had found a picture of Santiago wearing an Islamist style scarf wrapped around his neck and shoulders while holding up one finger in a Jihadist style symbol. With all these red flags, Santiago successfully boarded a one-way flight to Ft. Lauderdale with a checked gun with the intent to commit the unthinkable and has subsequently admitted to his premeditated intent. How could the FBI have dropped the ball being **caught off guard** on this one given all the signals that revealed a mentally disturbed man with Jihadist propaganda swirling in his head from viewing many ISIS recruitment videos? He clearly possessed the mental aptitude to calmly and properly check his gun after purchasing a one-way ticket to travel to Minneapolis then on to Ft. Lauderdale with the intent to commit Jihad which he successfully executed leaving 5 innocent people dead and 6 more injured. His psychosis opened a window in his mind that accepted the entry of Islamist Jihadist propaganda that fueled his heinous act. Questions abound that ask how this occurred given the numerous red flags known to authorities. Santiago will be tried in a court of law before a jury of his piers so only time will tell the outcome of his fate but the fate of his victims and their families has been set in stone and will haunt the survivors for years to come.

Farewell

January, 11 2017

President Obama gave his farewell speech last night in Chicago. He addressed a raucous crowd of liberals who were eating it up. The President didn't disappoint his adoring crowd with his Picasso like depiction of his time as POTUS. The President began with a blank canvas of the nation in distress he inherited and filled it with amazing accomplishments that had his fans cheering every step of the way. He boasted of 20 million people who had gained affordable health care when the truth is 12 million acquired substandard health care with Medicaid that most States have refused to sufficiently fund based on the fiscal hardship forced upon them and 8 million more low income Americans who received taxpayer funded subsidies for worthless health insurance with an average of $6000. deductible. He boasted of fast paced job creation when the truth is Americans who were satisfactorily working in full time positions with good pay found themselves working 2 to 3 part-time jobs with low wages. He boasted of outstanding economic growth when the truth is our economy has been limping along at 1.5% average GDP growth. He boasted of preventing Iran from becoming a nuclear power when the truth is he paved the way for Iran to become a weaponized nuclear power with ICBM's within 10 years if not earlier if they cheat which they've already done with no consequences. He boasted of significant advances in combating climate change when the truth is the President bypassed Congress and issued executive orders placing unnecessary oppressive regulations on the coal industry, oil production and a wide range of companies and corporations that has hampered economic growth with increased energy costs and caused many hard-working Americans to lose a good job due to excessive concern over unsettled science. He boasted that race relations have improved when the truth is he was the most divisive President in our history and has set race relations back by decades with his endorsement of the radical "black lives matter" movement that has endangered the lives of police officers across the land and even the death of many. This was a speech of soaring rhetoric as the President preached about rising income inequality, a rejection of fear, an emphasis on inclusion, the need to restore a sense of common purpose and a warning against hyper partisanship when he was the most hyper partisan fear mongering President ever whose sense of common purpose is a "his way or the highway" approach to every issue that has created divisions so wide that common ground as a nation is just a pipe dream.

Political Contradiction

January 17, 2017

President Obama just commuted a 35-year prison sentence for the traitor, Army Intelligence Analyst, Private Bradley Manning, who leaked over 750,000 highly sensitive classified documents that set off a Taliban killing spree in Afghanistan. The Taliban began killing anyone in Afghanistan with short dark hair who looked American based on information in the leaked documents about U.S. translators in the region and Afghan villagers thought to be assisting Americans were also killed. CIA Station Chiefs had to be pulled out of the region. Manning had copied dossier logs that described our military activities around the world. Classified documents leaked by Manning were found on Osama Bin Laden's computer after he was killed in Pakistan. Manning turned the classified documents over to Julian Assange who published them in WikiLeaks and became famous as he launched WikiLeaks as a major source of sensitive intelligence for public consumption. Manning's grave crime made him not only a traitor but also a political celebrity of the far left. His standing shot up further with the left when he announced he believed he is a woman in a man's body and changed his name to Chelsea. His transgender transformation makes his commutation popular with the left and serves as justification for the commutation because concern was high over his threat to commit suicide in prison. Manning has been behind bars for almost 7 years and now instead of serving the balance of 28 years he'll be released on May 17th. Under the Espionage Act this was a treasonous crime so Manning's crimes were punishable by death but prosecutors chose not to make it a capital offense. This commutation sets a dangerous precedent because it incentivizes leaking and it will have a negative effect on recruitment of intelligence agents. It's a slap in the face of every active duty military serviceperson and to the intelligence community at large. President Obama has issued more commutations than any President in U.S. history. He's issued 1715 commutations, 504 of which were originally life sentences, and he's issued 212 pardons. This compares to only 11 commutations and 189 pardons by George W. Bush 43.

The hypocrisy of the Obama administration and Democrats at large can't go unnoticed. They were so very exercised over WikiLeaks revelations of e-mails obtained by alleged Russian hacking of the DNC and John Podesta that they experienced an extended melt down and now WikiLeaks revelations of sensitive classified information obtained from Private Manning that led to the death American operatives in Afghanistan, the death of Afghan villagers who helped us, the rise of ISIS and accelerated the Arab Spring is no big deal because of politically correct sensitivity toward a guy who's confused about his gender. The President issues new sanctions on Russia and has 35 Russian diplomats kicked out of the country and Democrats bloviate for weeks about the evil Russians as if they've caused a crisis of monumental proportions when the e-mails had no effect on the election and resulted in nothing more than an embarrassment for a few corrupt Democrats. Democrats exploit WikiLeaks revelations that merely embarrassed them for political purposes to delegitimize our President elect but WikiLeaks revelations that result in death and destruction and launched WikiLeaks into the spotlight become a mere aside because they serve no political purpose other than making the perpetrator of the leaks a martyr because he decides he's a woman in a man's body. The President and Congressional Democrats find themselves in the middle of a **political contradiction** surrounding WikiLeaks with their politically convenient points of view so now we'll be forced to endure their political spin as they work their way forward to the next manufactured crisis. The inauguration of President elect Trump will surely lead to a continual state of crisis from their point of view so they'll be very busy for the next 4 to 8 years.

President Obama commuted the sentence of Oscar Lopez Rivera, a Puerto Rican nationalist who was arrested and tried for seditious conspiracy, use of force to commit robbery, interstate transportation of firearms and conspiracy to transport explosives with intent to destroy government property in 1977. In 1981 Lopez Rivera was convicted and sentenced to 55 years in federal prison and in 1988 he was sentenced to an additional 15 years for conspiring to escape from Leavenworth federal prison. He was one of the leaders of the FALN, Fuerzas Armadas de Liberacion Nacional, a far-left Puerto Rican clandestine paramilitary terrorist organization that was supported by the Castro regime. He is a hard core unrepentant terrorist who led the FALN in a communist plot to plant over 100 bombs in New York City in the 1970's plus several more bombs in Chicago for a total of 130 bombings based on records of the Fraternal Order of Police. This terrorist had 35 years left to serve in prison so he'll be out after serving only half that sentence. A dangerous terrorist like Lopez Rivera should never see the light of day but President Obama obviously believes it's acceptable to release him now. The commutations of Private Manning and Oscar Lopez Rivera will go down in history as 2 of the most shameful final official acts of our 44th President and serve to emphasize his disgraceful overall record on national security. The President poured salt on the wound by releasing 14 more hard core terrorists from Guantanamo Bay in his last days as President leaving 45 of the worst in the detainment facility in Cuba.

Destruction by Deceit

President Obama and his White House Senior Advisor, Valerie Jarrett, have both made statements in recent interviews that Barak Obama's presidency was scandal free. This completely dishonest statement can only be perceived as an attempt to throw a bogus statement out there with the intent to make it stick. Since this is so incredibly over the top let's take a trip down memory lane to review the numerous scandals associated with the Obama administration. Let's begin with the illegal "Fast and Furious" gun running operation that cost the loss of many lives including a U.S. Border Patrol agent and caused Attorney General Eric Holder to become the first U.S. Cabinet head in our history to be found in contempt of Congress. We'll move on to the terrorist attack on our Diplomatic Outpost and CIA annex in Benghazi and the subsequent cover up consisting of numerous blatant lies to the American people coming from Hillary Clinton who lied to the gold star families of the victims over their caskets, White House National Security Advisor, Susan Rice, who took to the airwaves of 5 Sunday morning talk shows to perpetrate the lie that the attack was the result of a "youtube" video and President Obama himself as he propagated this lie. The list goes on with IRS targeting of conservative groups to deny their legitimate requests for tax exempt status, the VA scandal with veterans literally dying while held up on weeks long waiting lists just for an appointment, the comedy of errors associated with Obama Care implementation including the exorbitant cost and security failures of the healthcare.gov website, DOJ snooping on journalists, NSA's violation of the 4th amendment by spying on the American people, the trade of 5 Taliban Commanders being held at Gitmo for Bowe Bergdahl who deserted his post in Afghanistan which cost the lives of 6 American soldiers who were forced to search for him, and Hillary Clinton's private unsecure e-mail server used while she served as Secretary of State. The Iran nuclear deal is a scandal because it was executed without Congress and we got nothing in return other than a very serious threat to national security not to mention the threat to Israel.

In an interview with Steve Croft on "60 minutes" the President said, "By almost every measure, the country is better off than when I came in." When he campaigned for Hillary Clinton he claimed his policies were on the ballot so given the outcome, the electorate conveyed their repudiation of his policies. The electorate knew Hillary was running to advance 4 to 8 more years of President Obama's policies when the American people were desperate for change. Most of the American people believe we're in need of a growing economy, stronger national security, better health care and less big government interference in their lives. The mood of the electorate is not one of believing we're better off after 8 years of President Obama's failed policies. The President also said, "I'm the best President I've ever been right now" which reveals he's oblivious to the fact that his legacy is one of a failed Presidency. His signature socialistic health care plan is on its way to being repealed and replaced. The newly sworn in 115th Congress has already passed legislation to strip funding from the ACA. Our sluggish economy that's presently experiencing 1.5% GDP growth hasn't made it above 2% GDP during his 8 years. He's the worst foreign policy President in our history. The Middle East is in shambles with civil war presently underway in Syria, Libya, Yemen and Iraq. The U.S. relationship with Israel has never been so strained as it is today. Iran is well on their way to becoming a weaponized nuclear power with ICBM's. China's provocative actions in the South China Sea presents a ticking time bomb now that they've created islands with the express purpose of a militarized presence designed to control trillions of dollars of interstate commerce that flows along sea lanes in the South China Sea. North Korea has made significant advances in their weaponized nuclear capabilities. Russia has become a greater geopolitical threat after their invasion and acquisition of Crimea and their advances in eastern Ukraine that even threaten the Baltic States.

Our most powerful adversaries have made threatening advances with impunity as they've taken advantage of a severely weakened United States under President Obama due to his inaction. Race relations are worse than they've been in decades. We're a severely divided nation with a hyper partisan political climate and a populous with a deep divide between coastal progressive liberals and conservatives in the heartland. This great divide is accentuated by the rise of social media as the people have multiple outlets to express their polarized views with Twitter and Facebook being the most prevalent. President elect Trump is faced with a huge challenge as he looks to unify the American people. One major problem is the fact that the definition of success is quite different for conservatives on the right and politically correct progressive liberals on the left. President elect Trump's agenda of America first, sensible fair trade, eliminating illegal immigration, strengthening our military and growing our weak economy with lower taxes and less big government regulation doesn't line up with the agenda of the left which advocates for globalization, free trade, open borders, intense government regulation to combat climate change, universal health care, welfare on steroids and big government control of virtually every aspect of our lives. In one sense our diversity can be viewed as a positive aspect of our society but a deep divide between two well defined highly polarized groups can create a tense environment that doesn't necessarily translate to strength as a nation. In 2017, unity is nothing more than a pipe dream. As always only time will tell what the future holds. One thing that's certain is that under an unconventional President in Donald J. Trump, it will make for a fascinating ride full of unprecedented events.